Troubled Minds

Arne S. Steinforth

Troubled Minds

On the Cultural Construction of Mental Disorder and Normality in Southern Malaŵi

PETER LANG
Frankfurt am Main · Berlin · Bern · Bruxelles · New York · Oxford · Wien

Bibliographic Information published by the Deutsche Nationalbibliothek
The Deutsche Nationalbibliothek lists this publication in the Deutsche Nationalbibliografie; detailed bibliographic data is available in the internet at <http://www.d-nb.de>.

Zugl.: Münster (Westfalen), Univ., Diss., 2008

Cover illustration:
The so-called Chilema or Crippled Trees, Malosa, Zomba District

D6
ISBN 978-3-631-58717-1

www.peterlang.de

To Christine

Acknowledgments

For the successful conduction of this study, I am indebted to a large number of persons and institutions for facilitating its realization in various ways. First of all, I would like to express my appreciation to the German Academic Exchange Service (Deutscher Akademischer Austauch Dienst DAAD, Bonn) and in particular to Helga Islam for kindly supporting my field research in Malaŵi by a one-year scholarship, thus laying the financial foundations for all subsequent endeavours. Most grateful mention shall further be made of the supervisors of my research at the Westfälische Wilhelms-Universität Münster – Annemarie Fiedermutz of the Institut für Ethnologie as well as the second reviewer Timm J. Filler (Institut für Anatomie) who provided additional support from a medical perspective. Both their effort was essential for the conceptualization, conduction, and evaluation of this study and is very much appreciated. Along with them, a number of professors in the abovementioned and other institutes have contributed significantly to the success of the research and the completion of this study. As their representatives, I express my thanks to Helene Basu, Andreas Hartmann, Franz Pera, Josephus D.M. Platenkamp, Reinhard Hildebrand, Barbara Meier, and Heinz Grotzfeld. For their invaluable help in the editing of this thesis, moreover, my gratitude goes to Nadine Beckmann and Christine Durant.

More thanks go to Florian Diederich and Elmar T. Peuker (and all at AG Complementary Medicine, Münster), as well as Angelika Wolf and Hansjörg Dilger (and everyone at AG Medical Anthropology, Berlin). For further scientific support, I gratefully mention Gabriele Alex (Heidelberg), Claude A. Boucher (Mua), Steve Chimombo (Zomba), Vera Kalitzkus (Witten/Herdecke), Marko Kerac (Blantyre), Sabine Klocke-Daffa (Tübingen), Sabine Luig (Berlin), Brian Morris (London), Alister Munthali (Zomba), Martin Ott (Lilongwe), Steven Paas (Zomba), Menno Welling (Limbe), and Susan Reynolds Whyte (Copenhagen).

In Malaŵi, a never-ending number of informants, friends, colleagues, and other kinds of amicable people deserve my gratitude. To begin with, I owe thanks to Joseph Chakanza, Felix Chingota, and Shareef Mohammad (Department of Theology and Religious Studies, Chancellor College, Zomba) for their care and warm-hearted support. Likewise, I give my deep appreciation to Klaus Fiedler (and everyone at Kachere Series, Zomba) for hospitality, advice, encouragement, computer facilities, the latest newspapers, and countless *nsima* lunch breaks. More thanks go to all those who assisted me in my endeavours to obtain and process field data. Among these, special credit should be given to L. Dennis Bisika, Maxwell Mponda, Francis Banda, and Doreen Sapanga for their invaluable research assistance. The latter, along with Amayi Thoko, also deserves thanks for interview tape transcriptions and translations, and I further thank Janet Kholowa for priceless language instructions. For his efforts to provide me with an operational vehicle, I gratefully mention Patrick Chilungwe (and everyone at Montfort Garage, Blantyre). As representatives of all those who kindly shared their thoughts, time, and *khonde* with me, I am obliged to Musa Chiwaula (FEDOMA, Blantyre), Steven Msowoya (MACOHA, Blantyre), and Miriam Namanja (PODCAM, Blantyre). Most especially, I wish to express my gratitude to Olive Goba and her family (Zomba) for her hospitality, inspiration, understanding, prayers, and care.

My love and very special thanks go to my extended family that provided me with every support imaginable. In addition to my parents Rotraut and Harm Steinforth, my brother Dirk, and Marion, I also wish to point out Sigurd Schoepke whose encouragement and broad-minded openness have always been both motivating and inspiring. My particular appreciation, love, and admiration goes to Toni Steinforth whose boundless support reaches out beyond the limits of her own physical existence – the ending of which, in February 2008, leaves an emptiness never to be remedied. I also wish to express my gratitude to the Durant part of the family, among whom I will point out Judy and Charles as well as Marc and David Durant, Joan Benton, and Elda Smith. Additionally, there are far too many friends in Canada, Germany, Malaŵi, and elsewhere who – maybe most of all – deserve being mentioned here. I beg their forgiveness as I, among all of them, single out Arne Clasing, Marc Mallett, Gunnar Rechenburg, and Frank Renner (along with their wonderful partners and kids) for years and years of organizational, emotional and medical support, long night discussions, the latest football scores, and their precious friendship. Further, I want to thank those friends in Malaŵi whose company and support made this field research a positive experience in yet one more way. Among all of these, I name Mairi MacDonald for her tireless efforts to connect the disconnected, as well as most gratefully remember the late John Woodcock for his incomparable ways of empowering the disempowered and making sports a matter of human equality. His passing in February 2006 is a great loss to many people in Africa and Europe alike, and I consider myself fortunate that I got to know him.

A final and most special thank you goes once again to Christine Durant who, ever after a sweaty February morning in Zomba's Fegs Distributors, kept me safe and sane throughout twelve months of field research in Malaŵi as well as through the maddening, endless process of final thesis formulation, oral examination, and thesis re-editing. Keeping my mind focused, my feet on the ground and my worries at bay, she contributed more to the success of this project and to my personal happiness than I could possibly put down in words. Just like my gratitude, love, and admiration.

To all of these and many more – *zikomo kwambiri.*

Arne S. Steinforth,
Münster, in March 2009.

Table of Contents

Appendices

Illustrations

Maps

Figures

I.

Introductory Considerations

According to recent estimates, an approximate 500 million persons worldwide are categorized as disabled. Arguably, these numbers are on the increase, independent from the economic wealth or the medical care system offered within a given country, and in every society the affected persons range among the socially disadvantaged (Barnes, Oliver & Barton 2002: 2). At the same time, the question that arises is whether people are actually born with a disability – or if, as a phenomenon, disability should rather be seen as a result of a complex process of classification on the basis of culturally defined normative representations (Stiker 1997: 158-160). Cultural processes of allocation establish a – frequently implicit – notion of the normal human condition, thus distinguishing the normal from the other, the deviant – or disabled. From any perspective, it is evidently crucial to recognize the importance of collective representations for the understanding of any cultural concept of disability as well as for the living conditions of the affected persons. And it is not helpful from the perspective of constructive social anthropology to consider cultural notions as mere impediments to the implementation of allegedly super-cultural, biomedical concepts of disability. Rather, it may be agreed that

> "The notion that cultural beliefs are only barriers to development is changing" (Devlieger 1995: 94).

Accordingly, the subject of this thesis is explicitly not disability as defined within a Western framework. Rather, it focuses on African – or, more particularly, Malaŵian – concepts of 'problems of the mind', most of which would be labelled as disabilities according to present Western systems of classification (WHO 2001a). As a monograph in medical anthropology, this study depicts and analyses the cultural representation of mental disorders in an African society on different levels, thus creating a multi-layered, holistic outlook on the phenomenon not only in its medical, but also in a more complex cultural framework that, to mention the obvious, also incorporates factors such as religious and social perception, or economic activity. By that, this thesis means to outline the cultural embeddedness of the phenomenon as such and point out its culturally determining conditions which should not only contribute to the ethnographic understanding of cultural fact and process, but which shall also provide basic tools to alter the prospects of persons living with mental disorders in Southern Malaŵi.

1. Theoretical Overview

It has been justly pointed out that social anthropology so far does not give appropriate attention to questions of disability (Klotz 2003: 1; Shakespeare 1994: 283). Nonetheless, disability issues have been recognized and addressed within anthropological discourse over a considerable length of time. But in spite of these early efforts to fully include disability in the wider field of anthropological research – as undertaken by scholars like Ruth Benedict (Benedict 1934)[1] – this whole complex still leads a rather shadowy existence as expressing itself in the lack of anthropological monographs. Most of the research conducted in the context of disability and culture therefore still acts on the misleading assumption of a universal applicability of biomedical notions, giving little consideration to the cultural specificity of the phenomenon.[2] Arguably, the marginalization this whole phenomenon experiences within social and cultural sciences may be seen as reflecting its neglect within Western societies (Sagner 2001: 175-176).

In itself, the definition of the term *disability* is the basis for an ongoing scientific discourse that still does not seem to be satisfactorily concluded. As a technical term, it is closely connected to international health standards that try to establish it as a universal term. In 2001, a revised edition of the ICIDH was issued, published as the *International Classification of Functioning, Disability and Health* (ICF, formerly referred to as ICIDH-2).[3] As a classificatory system, the ICF follows a concept of functional health, defining its aims as *(a)* providing a basis for a better understanding of health conditions, their outcomes and determinants; *(b)* establishing a terminological framework in order to enhance communication; *(c)* facilitate comparability; *(d)* introducing a systematic coding scheme. In all of this, the WHO asserts claims to interdisciplinary, international,

---

1 These sources will find more consideration in a later section of this chapter (see *Chapter I.1.c*).

2 Accordingly, Mike Oliver defines disability as independent from the body as such. On the contrary, he describes disability as "a consequence of the failure of social organisation to take account for the differing needs of disabled people and remove the barriers they encounter" (Oliver 1996: 42).

3 Up to the late 1970s, no official system of classification was internationally recognized with respect to disabilities. The 1980 *International Classification of Impairments, Disabilities and Handicaps* (ICIDH) provided by the World Health Organization defined disability in functional terms – and in distinction from the categories impairment and handicap (WHO 1980).

and intercultural applicability (WHO 2001b: 5). In credit for the new ICF system, some critics attest that

> "It is important to appreciate that disability is not an intrinsic or defining feature of a subset of human beings (and as such is not analogous to other human differences such as gender and race), but is a universal condition of humanity itself" (Üstün et al. 2001: 5).

This new concept classifies disability according to its manifestation on a physical, personal, or social level, giving consideration to its essentially relational character. It also recognizes the fact that so-called ADM disorders – i.e. alcohol, drug, and mental disorders – cause a degree of limitations due to which its burden on society far surpasses conditions such as HIV/Aids or cancer (Üstün et al. 2001: 4-5; WHO 2001b). While this re-definition of disability terminology as formulated in the ICF constitutes a major improvement to former ICIDH standards by creating more space to include the social determination of disability phenomena, its applicability is still debateable within an anthropological discourse. Convincingly, the universal practicality of the term disability is denied by many medical anthropologists, arguing that a disability is strictly culture-specific and therefore defined according to emic concepts of faultiness, abnormality, or deviation – which may, e.g., include young age, illegitimate birth, excessive freckles, or small buttocks – that by far exceed even the most generous of Western definitions (Whyte & Ingstad 1995: 5-7). Disability is not an ontological category – but may, at best, serve to describe a process of cultural allocation that would more clearly be addressed as either social stigmatization or activity limitation. The current study, at the same time, does not examine social deviation as a general phenomenon – and therefore, an altogether different term needs to be introduced. Accordingly, the present thesis will only apply the term disability with reference to data reproduced from other sources, i.e. from indirect – from published material – or direct quotes from Anglophone interviews. In all other cases, the term mental disorder will be used as a substitute for the sake of a closer depiction of cultural representations.

While it is important to investigate the living conditions of persons with disabilities in their social environment, it is, from an anthropological perspective, equally central to develop an understanding for the cultural construction of the condition as such. The current thesis applies emic notions as recorded in the Southern Region of Malaŵi which shall be complemented by etic observations. Therefore, the material compiled here represents both intentional and functional data in order to achieve a high degree of validity.[4]

---

4 This distinction has first been introduced by Wilhelm Emil Mühlmann who, in short, defines intentional data as reflecting emic cultural conceptualization, thus shedding light on a cultural

1(a) Theoretic Framework

Even within the framework of cosmopolitan biomedicine – such as reflecting and reflected by current European or North American contexts –, the term disability is subject to repeated definition and re-definition (Jenkins 1998b: 225). In the field of disability studies, questions concerning an adequate linguistic approach to the phenomenon of disability are under constant discussion. According to common legal definitions, disability is distinguished from other health disorders by two general criteria, representing *(a)* limitations in the physical and/or the intellectual capacities of a person on the one hand, and *(b)* as implying a prolonged duration of the condition.[5] The classificatory standards of the World Health Organization form the basis for this legal situation (WHO 2001a; ibid. 1980). While recent definitions of disability recognize its close interconnection with social conditions, it is still up to cultural specification to determine the social embodiment of disability in its cultural surrounding.

The present study is not a primarily theoretical discussion. It is an ethnographic study that presents and analyses the findings of anthropological field research conducted to examine mental disorder within its larger cultural framework. If a more theoretical approach would have been followed, different standards and methods would have been applied during the field research proper – such as limiting it to a small scale case study, addressing a less broadly defined set of emic categories, or taking a more etic perspective on the phenomenon as a whole. Nonetheless, a number of theoretical considerations as well as on the wider discussion need to be outlined, and this section subsumes the theoretical approach and assumptions underlying the present study. The basic question that requires clarification in this study lies in the conflict between two complementary theoretical concepts which address the cultural construction of deviance from opposing perspectives.

Tracing the Stigma

Western biomedical concepts imply a basic assumption which – according to an idealistic notion of a human state of normality defined by complete physical and

---

hierarchy of values. Functional data is, on the other hand, not meant to *understand* but to *explain* cultural phenomena, thus taking a clearly 'etic' and interpretative perspective towards them (Mühlmann 1938: 108-114).

5 According to common medical reference, limitations of perception, cerebration, conversion, learning as well as behaviour are pointed out. The minimum duration of disability is usually a critical element of legal disability definitions due to its significant role in labour legislation. German law, e.g., recognizes a condition that inhibits full participation in a given work process for six or more months as disability (see § 3 of German Schwerbehindertengesetz; Pschyrembel [ed.] 1994: 171).

mental well-being – identifies disease as a 'lack of health' in a person.[6] Correspondingly, bio-medically defined concepts of disability – and its terminological siblings *handicap* and *impairment* (WHO 1980) – operate from the same, *quasi* negativist perspective on the person, defining difference as a lack of certain attributes which are rooted in a non-explicit, culturally defined notion of normal human capacity (Fougeyrollas 1987: 54). In response to this realization, Erving Goffman introduced the category of stigma into sociological discussion. According to his understanding, three types of stigma may be distinguished – those based on *(a)* criteria of physical deviance, *(b)* criteria of deviations of personal character, and *(c)* criteria of group affiliation. In case of disabilities, he sees stigmatization as a social reaction on the affected person's failed attempt to receive acceptance as a 'normal' member of society. His theoretic approach describes disability – as well as other forms of divergence from the cultural norm – as social deviation which leads to immediate stigmatization on the basis of external, ontological factors, most likely resulting in social marginalization. In the eye of society, a person with a disability is thus reduced from a complete, normal person to an incomplete, contaminated existence (Goffman 1967).[7]

It has been argued that Erving Goffman defines stigma as an essentially static concept – while recent field data from Malaŵi supports the notion that stigma as a category is subject to situational modification as well as processes of change on a personal and larger cultural level (Braathen 2005: 13, 58). In consideration of this recent addition to the definition of stigma, one element of this study's objective is to investigate to which extent societies in Malaŵi classify and stigmatize persons with mental disorders according to the above-mentioned criteria of physique, behaviour, and – less prominently here – social group affiliation, thus evaluating the relevance of the stigma approach in a particular cultural context.

Locating Competence

It is, at the same time, only legitimate to assume that the global multitude of cultural models provide more than one possible perspective on mental difference. The deterministic approach that defines disability as a form of damage or

---

6 More exactly, it is seen as a dysfunction of vital processes leading to subjectively experienced or objectively identifiable alterations of a person's physical, intellectual, and/or mental condition (Greifeld 1995: 20; Pschyrembel [ed.] 1994: 824).

7 In cultural anthropology, Goffman's stigma thesis has been received and applied in a number of studies. Accordingly, Joyce Dreezens-Fuhrke contrasts traditional and modern ways of dealing with deviation in a Javanese setting while Deliane Burck accounts for the stigmatization of children labelled as mentally retarded in Zimbabwe (Dreezens-Fuhrke 1996; Burck 1989).

impairment imposed on a given person – who is then stigmatized due to ontological criteria – may constitute a fundamental cultural representation in European and North American societies, but it may not claim universal super-cultural validity.[8] Subsequently, Robert Edgerton applies the concept of competence as a complementary approach to the social construction of deviance (Edgerton 1993; ibid. 1967), and in recent studies, Richard Jenkins has expanded this notion, subsuming that

> "'Competence' is the capacity or potential for adequate functioning-in-context as a socialised human" (Jenkins 1998a: 1).

Taking a more contextual stance on the labelling of social difference, it may thus be argued that no singular model determining the perception of mental disorder can be identified across cultures. Otherness may not necessarily be stigmatized, and may be a question of cultural models of classification as well as of contextual negotiation in which way and to which degree stigma and/or competence are attributed to a person. The notion of competence thus contrasts the deterministic idea of *quasi*-universal stigmatization of difference with the more inclusive approach that cultures define competence – and, therefore, potential for integration and participation – on the basis of social functionality. Susan Reynolds Whyte supports this approach with respect to her East African data, and according to her,

> "The term competence refers to ability, skill or fitness. It encourages us to ask: for what? Competence and its inverse point towards tasks and actions, the application of abilities. Intellectual competence may be measurable by tests, but mental competence and its lack can only be studied in the context of human life (Whyte 1998b: 153).

Competence is therefore closely related to social networks – an observation that is backed up by evidence within a wider African context.[9] The socially stigmatizing effects of lacking competence are therefore perceived as the inability to perform culturally defined obligations in the social sphere, making incompetence a question of interpersonal relations rather than an essentialist category.[10] While a certain degree of difference or other-ness may thus be

---

8 As one explanatory approach, Henri-Jacques Stiker traces the origins of Western ideas of impairment back to the historical impact of World War One experience (Stiker 1997: 123).

9 Therefore, it has been assumed that, throughout sub-Saharan Africa, "Scattered, informal reports suggest that, while cases of neglect and abuse certainly do occur, other small-scale communities may have successfully integrated persons with mental retardation within the framework of their indigenous cultural practices" (Serpell, Mariga & Harvey 1993: 33).

10 Comparing North American to African societies, Patrick Devlieger therefore explains that, among the latter, "having a disability of any kind does not directly mean that incompetence is necessarily implied. It is in the way that disability is associated with either a lack of social

culturally recognized, stigmatization is not inevitably its social consequence. In an ideal scenario, this concept counteracts the stigmatization of persons with disabilities within their respective social environments on the basis of their productivity, their accomplishments for the communal well-being – thus compensating for their other-ness. Considering the notion of capacity as an axiomatic presumption ascribed to the person on a social and cultural basis, it represents a local variant which, therefore, gives leverage for further anthropological examination. Therefore, this study will also assess the degree and character of competence allocated to persons with mental disorders in Malaŵi, thus giving a full picture of the social factors determining the social positioning of the affected person.

Contextualizing Medicine

The conflicting models of a social allocation of stigma as opposed to competence are a central objective of the current study. Assuming that both mechanisms do occur on some level within the cultural contexts in question, the inquiry obviously aims to identify those emic criteria at the bottom of these cultural processes.

A number of more precise aspects are of central concern here. At first, it is elementary to locate the social positioning of the other (as defined in the context of this study). Here, it must be clarified *(a)* whether the phenomenon and the persons affected by it exist only on the margin of cultural life – or whether conditions such as disability are located not on the fringes but, as Patrick Devlieger suggests, within the creases of society (Devlieger 1999: 299). Although this distinction may appear negligible at first sight, it reveals a substantial difference upon closer analysis: it addresses not only the degree of cultural recognition and awareness of other-ness, but it also identifies if the respective persons are considered as on the outside of the social system – or just in between its classificatory categories. Moreover, the negotiation between stigma and competence also raises the question *(b)* how normality – in the sense of normal, i.e. non-pathological mental performance – is defined in cultural terms. In essence, it is this identification of an *ab-normal* condition that underlies processes of stigmatization, and it is the reflection of a person's 'normal' characteristics that allows society to attribute competence to him or her (Sagner 2001: 199). This question directly leads to the fundamental problem of *(c)* how the human condition of other-ness correlates with cultural notions of personhood. As the utmost consequence of marginalization, depersonalization as a potential

embeddedness, or a lack of overcoming the difficulties that are associated with impairment, that one can speak of incompetence" (Devlieger 1998: 60).

threat has been addressed before (Nicolaisen 1995: 38-55). The fundamentally relational character of personhood in Malaŵi (Morris 2000: 49) in contrast to the likewise relational character of African concepts of disability (Devlieger 1995: 104) suggests a direct relationship between personhood and normality – and the conceptual proximity of cultural concepts of deviance and non-personhood.

In a Western discourse, the apparently easy definition of medicine as the science dedicated to the restoration and maintenance of human health by diagnostic and therapeutic means masks more fundamental questions. While health disorders and their treatment are indisputably universal features of human culture, the intercultural application of the term medicine may conceal the more extensive semantic dimensions attributed to a single phenomenon which must, therefore, be considered as more than just medical. In Malaŵi, this terminological pitfall becomes apparent in contexts such as the role of *asing'anga* or traditional healers (see below). While their activities are generally identified as medicinal, closer observation – of activities such as magic services in the field of love, property protection, or professional success – reveals that either this is not their only field of professional expertise or that the Western notion of medicine requires some extension.

This issue is by no means trivial. In contrary, it has been argued that the medicalization of phenomena such as spirit possession reflects a biomedical bias disregarding its full ritual character (Olivier de Sardan 1994: 7-8). Thus, the reconciliatory rituals in the context of spirit vocation (see *Chapter IV.2.d*) may be interpreted as bearing more religious than therapeutic meaning – while conceding that both are, actually, closely intertwined. This reflects the more general problem of applying Western notions – such as medicine – in a non-Western context, hence blurring the semantic complexity of cultural phenomena in favour of primarily functional criteria. For the sake of this thesis, no alternative term for medicine will be introduced, and it will be applied to Malaŵian phenomena on the general basis of a Western understanding. It is, nonetheless, important to bear in mind that medicine in its local context cannot be fully separated from other spheres of society, and that the term medicine follows strictly analytical purposes, denoting a function that is, in most instances, not the only semantic level of a given phenomenon. Spirit rituals in Malaŵi, e.g., hence are vehicles of complex cultural meaning, parts of which may be interpreted in terms of the restoration of cosmological or social equilibrium while other aspects qualify as medical activities from a Western perspective. As a basic theoretic prerequisite, this thesis argues on the assumption that the application of purely biomedical terminology would be misleading in the description, analysis, and overall understanding of those Malaŵian health conditions under investigation here. Especially in the context of mental health issues – and in recognition of their large degree of autonomy from biomedical categorization –, this study regards Malaŵian concepts of mental disorder as culture-specific or, in other words, culture-bound – an argument that will later be substantiated by more circumstantial analysis of emic mental disorder categories.

Being introduced into medical anthropology by the Chinese psychiatrist Pow Meng Yap in the 1960s (Yap 1969; ibid. 1965), the concept of culture-bound syndromes supports the idea that many predominantly mental health disorders are to a high degree determined by cultural factors (Kleinman 1980: 163-166). While the categories presented in this study do not necessarily qualify as culture-bound syndromes according to more strict definitions,[11] numerous articles have already stressed the implicitness of the term as such – arguing that every disorder is specific for its cultural context, and that no syndrome is fully independent from cultural bonds (Lux 2003: 158; Hahn 1995). Therefore, this study will, in fairly liberal terms, adopt an explicitly culture-specific position towards Malaŵian notions of mental disorder in the sense of acknowledging the general cultural determination of conditions of distress (Carr & Vitaliano 1985: 244-266).

Identifying Levels of Disorder

In medical anthropology, a specific perspective on human suffering has been established in order to give more consideration to the personal experience as well as the complex social embedding of the phenomenon. Therefore, Arthur Kleinman distinguishes the categories of disease, illness, and sickness – denoting the condensed cultural knowledge of a given condition, the subjective experience of a person, and the social agreement between both, respectively. More precisely, he argues that

> "A key axiom in medical anthropology is the dichotomy between two aspects of sickness: disease and illness. Disease refers to a malfunctioning of biological and/or psychological processes, while the term illness refers to the psychosocial experience and meaning of perceived disease. Illness includes secondary personal and social responses to a primary malfunctioning (disease) in the individual's physiological or psychological status (or both). Illness involves processes of attention, perception, affective response, cognition, and valuation directed at the disease and its manifestations (i.e., symptoms, role impairment, etc.). [...] Viewed from this perspective, illness is the shaping of disease into behavior and experience" (Kleinman 1980: 72).

---

11 I.e. according to a number of closely defined forms or taxons. Here, classical models distinguish categories such as *(a)* the startle matching taxon, *(b)* the sleep paralysis taxon, *(c)* the genital retraction taxon, *(d)* the sudden mass assault taxon, *(e)* the running taxon, *(f)* the fight illness taxon, and *(g)* the cannibal compulsion taxon (Simons & Hughes [eds.] 1985).

Sickness, moreover, acts as a mediating category that reflects the understanding of a given health disorder within a given cultural context. Together, this distinction provides an elementary tool for specifying the social contextualization and meaning of health disorder. The relevance of this fundamental dichotomy cannot be overemphasized.

In the context of this study, all three levels are relevant. The personal 'ill'-experience will be reflected in numerous accounts of (former) persons with mental disorders; the disease category is represented in the troublesome relationship between emic nosological categories and biomedical pathology, and sickness resembles the broad cultural negotiation between the potential explanatory models belonging to different spheres of cultural discourse. In this line of argument, the objective of this study has a strong focus on the level of sickness – in terms of the cultural negotiation, interpretation, and construction of mental disorder. However, the present study does not base its approach on a strict differentiation of this terminological trilogy. In part, this reflects the idea that these categories are only distinct as long as a specific, structural difference can be discerned between the pseudo-objective notion of disease and the more culturally defined concept of sickness (Greifeld 1995: 17-18).[12] It may be argued that, on every level, the cultural conception of health disorder represents a social agreement, and data from a Malaŵian background also supports that no structural difference between the diagnoses provided by a biomedical health institution and the next door neighbour is culturally recognized. Therefore, while acknowledging the importance of this terminological distinction, this thesis generally addresses health disorders in terms of sickness, thus referring to categorization as recognized within the cultural context of Malaŵi – unless biomedical categories, i.e. diseases, are explicitly indicated.[13]

1(b) Question Formulation

It is not uncommon for an anthropological field research to produce unexpected results which, in turn, demand modifications, re-specification and/or amplifications in the research objective (Gregory & Altman 1989: 44). In case of the present study, the insights gained at an early point of the field research period required some redefinition which augmented the scope of the research significantly, and the research objective finally applied therefore reflects the cultural concepts identified in the field. Primary research outlines had meant to

---

12 Further critic evaluation of Kleinman's model of disease and illness is, e.g., provided by Thomas Lux (Lux 2003: 160-169).

13 Accordingly, the Chicheŵa expression *matenda* – or, more rarely, *nthenda* – is translated as sickness.

address Malaŵian notions of disability with a particular focus on those cases connected to mental limitations.

Field research in Malaŵi commenced in February 2004, and the Southern Region of the country was selected as the wider research setting. Here, preliminary field results – obtained in interviews with representatives of organizations for persons with disabilities, traditional healers, and other specialists from different districts and ethnic groups throughout the Southern Region – indicated early on that local classifications do not differentiate between what would in biomedical terms be regarded as disabilities and mental illness. The social conception of the phenomenon as such is locally interpreted and categorized in a particular terminological context, thus making it artificial and futile to forcefully introduce biomedical categories for the study of non-biomedical concepts.[14]

In recognition of these emic systems of categorization, a modification and extension of the initial research objective became necessary in order to fully reflect the Malaŵian cultural framework. By collecting data on local nosological categories applied with reference to primarily mental health disorders – i.e. those that were associated with human processes such as cognition, reasoning, behaviour, or social interaction –, it was possible to demarcate a reasonably consistent field of research which shall be addressed here under the generic, blanket term *mental disorder* which will be defined more thoroughly later on. The focus of research as presented here therefore includes not only more strictly defined cases of disability, but it deals with all forms of conditions which are locally recognized as affecting a person's mental capacities.

The process of defining a research objective which retains its validity even outside of a biomedical model was one of the first conceptual difficulties in the research presented here. For lack of a direct semantic equivalent for the concept of disability and in order to approximate the indigenous notions presented in Southern Malaŵi, research questions were therefore focusing on problems affecting a person's mind or brain – *mavuto okhudza nzeru kapena ubongo wa munthu* in Chicheŵa. The information obtained on this complex proves hard to subsume under a general term that makes sense within a Western context. As a fairly broad yet tangible surrogate term, the term *mental disorder* will be employed here. In the United Kingdom, a 2007 Mental Health Bill defines mental disorder as denoting 'any disorder or disability of the mind.'[15] While it

---

14 On the basis of rich intercultural evidence, Richard Jenkins likewise concludes that "The distinction between 'mental retardation' or 'learning difficulties' and 'mental health problems' or 'psychiatric illness', that is so familiar in Europe and North America, is another example of gross categorisation. It is not always locally applicable or sensible" (Jenkins 1998b: 224).

15 This bill represents an amendment to the Mental Health Act of 1983. The 1983 definition thus

may be argued that the term lacks a clear definition within the biomedical discourse, could be replied that this circumstance actually promotes its use in the interdisciplinary context of this study, along with the fact that it is, by and large, also not connected to strong implicit connotations. Its applicability may further be supported by its two components and their interpretation. In agreement with Susan Reynolds Whyte, the term 'mental' is favoured here over similar terms – such as cognitive, emotional, behavioural, or intellectual – in order to describe the health disorders investigated here, arguing that, while

> "Intellect is generally defined as the ability to reason, perceive or understand relations or differences [...], mental capacity refers to abilities of mind, a broader term that includes will, intention and feelings, as well as intellect" (Whyte 1998b: 153).

While thus apparently implying a differentiation of the research topic from other i.e. physical disorders, it should be emphasized that the definition of 'mental' as applied here follows a combination of emic and etic representations. It is, therefore, not a strictly analytic category meant to advocate a medicine based on a constructed body-mind-dualism; neither does it contradict Western endeavours addressing the psychosomatic and/or psychosocial character of diseases.

The selection of the term 'disorder' reflects a very basic rendition of the emic Malaŵian perception of the phenomenon as such – i.e. a human condition that is outside of the orderly or normal, a confusion or irregularity. As a term, *dis-order* therefore expresses a deep connection to concepts of the normal human person, appropriate social interaction, and cultural order which, as the following chapters will substantiate, underlies the ethnically and socially distinct levels of discourse in Southern Malaŵi. In the context of the present study, mental disorder shall therefore denote all forms of health disorders which lead to, or correspond with, impediments concerning the mental behavioural disposition of the person as acknowledged within the multifaceted cultural contexts of Southern Malaŵi, and mental disorder describes a condition that is perceived as pathological from an emic perspective, and which, by definition, is outside of the realm of the culturally accepted norm.

Due to the modifications in the research objective and further results obtained during the subsequent in-depth field research, a number of interconnected questions were formulated. While the overall research topic of this study – i.e. the cultural construction of mental disorder in Southern Malaŵi – is indicated by

---

replaced saw mental disorder as "mental illness, arrested or incomplete development of mind, psychopathic disorder and any other disorder or disability of mind" (Great Britain 1983: Section 1). It also provided closer specifications of some subcategories such as severe mental impairment, mental impairment, psychopathic disorder, and mental illness.

its title, this very general query can be broken down into a number of more specific questions. The first one would be *(1)* how mental disorder is culturally represented and incorporated. Not all cultural phenomena are expressed with the same density in a given society. The amount of references a cultural system makes to a phenomenon such as mental disorder – but also the exact contexts in which it is included – create a basic picture of its social contextualization and, in essence, its cultural construction. After that, further inquiries need to address *(2)* how the system of classification is structured. In order to develop a deeper understanding of the cultural conception of the phenomenon, it is a prerequisite to assess and semantically analyse the terminological arsenal applied to categorize mental disorder and present viable definitions for its various culturally recognized forms. By this, a basic ethnographic landscape of the various concepts of mental disorder in Malaŵi can be provided. At the same time, the results of this inquiry directly question *(3)* how this definition is reflected in cultural notions of normality and, more specifically, of normal mental competence. This aspect is crucially relevant in a number of respects. It localizes mental disorder within a wider framework of personhood, makes a connection to the context of age-related disorders, and it provides additional delimitation to the embodiment of minor cognitive problems such as learning impediments. By asserting an emic definition of normal competence, the differences perceived in states of mental disorder can be outlined more precisely, and the social criteria underlying mechanisms of allocation may be analysed.

The results of previous queries directly lead to the question of *(4)* what the causative factors recognized for mental disorder are. Here, cultural concepts such as magic and spirit possession – which by themselves constitute wide fields for anthropological research already – have to be considered within the limits of their connection to the greater context of mental disorder. Along with them, other models of explanation require further attention – such as divine intervention or a seemingly near-scientific notion of 'natural' causation. In order to clarify prevalence and cultural meaning of each of these categories, it is necessary to assess *(5)* what therapeutic services are locally available and how they are perceived. Closer knowledge of the various health services in the country are helpful to develop a bigger picture of the pluralistic medical framework in which the social phenomenon as such is embedded. On the basis of the data obtained in the context of this and the previous question, another vital issue needs developing, asking *(6)* how local notions of curability are defined and how they correspond with mental disorder. This question responds to the specific interconnection between cases which would, by biomedical standards, be addressed as disability and mental illness, respectively. The lack of differentiation leads to the question of specific cultural notions of curability. In the light of all this information obtained, it is finally crucial to investigate *(7)* how this cultural construction of mental disorder develops with regard to recent and future processes of transformation. This issue will give an outlook on the historical dimension of mental disorder in Malaŵi, at the same time providing a valid hypothesis on future developments. While any such prognosis is necessarily impaired by its speculative character, it may nonetheless be viable to formulate some theses that go beyond the present *status quo*.

1(c) Current State of Research

The current state of research on the cultural construction of mental disorder in Malaŵi is pieced together from a number of separate scholarly lines. First, the field of medical anthropology provides some important information on the overall research question, including issues of disability within its wider research objective. To a limited degree, studies on mental health and transcultural psychiatry are also of some interest here, giving consideration to the fact that disability and psychiatric phenomena are part of the same cultural discourse in Malaŵi. Finally and most particularly, social anthropology has produced a small but remarkable school of publications on the anthropology of disability itself. These studies can be seen as part of the wider, interdisciplinary field of disability studies which therefore merits particular attention. The data available from a specifically Malaŵian context will be described as well, restricting the outlook to contributions focussing on the explicitly medical question of this study.[16] While it is certainly impossible to give appropriate credit to all publications which are relevant in the line of the current research, the following evaluation will only point out a small selection of works referred to in the context of this study.

Over the last decades, the field of medical anthropology has received increasing scholarly attention that expresses itself in a large number of publications focussing on the culture of health and disease. For some time, early medical anthropology struggled to emancipate itself from the biomedical paradigm of interpreting health and disease. The works of Erwin Ackerknecht may be mentioned as early recognitions of foreign, non-Western medical systems as cultural configurations that must be analysed within their specific cultural context. Thus anticipating the emic/etic distinction of analytical perspective, he also questioned the universality of normality, describing 'normal'

---

16 In the area of more general ethnographic data, another number of authors should be acknowledged. As a particularly important researcher, J. Matthew Schoffeleers should be pointed out whose extensive work on the anthropology of religion in Malaŵi provides most vital data (Schoffeleers 1997; ibid. 1992; ibid. 1991; ibid. 1979; ibid. 1968a; ibid. 1968b; ibid. 1966; ibid. [ed.] 1979; ibid. & Roscoe 1985).

and 'pathological' not as absolute ontological categories but as cultural variants (Ackerknecht 1971).[17] In recent years, scholars such as Arthur Kleinman had a considerable impact on the current debate, giving new direction to medical anthropology.[18] Owing to his background in both psychiatry and medical anthropology, Kleinman has conducted significant research in a Chinese setting. In his work, he also focuses on culture-specific disorders (also known as culture-bound syndromes), reaching a better understanding of the phenomenon in both anthropology and medicine (Kleinman 1980). Later on, Arthur Kleinman and Byron Good edited an anthology on *Culture and Depression* which, even more so than Kleinman's 1980 monograph, transcends the borders between medical anthropology and transcultural psychiatry (see below).

With respect to medical anthropology in Malaŵi, a number of studies merit special attention. Over the years, Brian Morris has published invaluable material gained from extended field research conducted in different areas of the country. His extensive study on *Cheŵa Medical Botany* (Morris 1996) provides crucial anthropological data on Malaŵian medical models, and a number of other articles contribute immensely to the scholarly understanding of the anthropology of medicine (Morris 1989; ibid. 1986; ibid. 1985). Other contributors have likewise expanded the debate of medical anthropology in Malaŵi, and here, Joseph Chakanza must be pointed out for his significant research on religious healing (Chakanza 2000b; ibid. 1998).[19]

Some references tackle questions of mental health and transcultural psychiatry which, due to the particular structure of the research topic as redefined according to emic categorization, plays a part in the context of this study.[20] At the same time, questions of transcultural psychiatry constitute a late

---

17 Earlier contributors to the discussion on the character and perspective of anthropological research data have offered a distinction between 'intentional' and 'functional' data (Vajda 1964; Mühlmann 1938).

18 Likewise, Arthur Kleinman questions Ackerknecht's systematic approach, criticizing him for advancing "a misleading dichotomy between »primitive« and »modern« medicine [...]. Ackerknecht, who has had an enormous impact on studies in this field, viewed non-Western cultures from an ethnocentric perspective based on the organizational structure professional medicine had evolved in the West" (Kleinman 1980: 29).

19 Other anthropological studies follow special questions. Thus, Anne Drake explores Malaŵian categories of sickness and provides a deeper understanding of cultural models of causation, giving particular attention to phenomena such as *mdulo* (Drake 1976). This notion is later elaborated by Joseph DeGabriele (DeGabriele 1999) and will be explained below. Arnold Wendroff examines the techniques of traditional medicine with a special focus on healer-patient interaction (Wendroff 1985) while Jerome Msonthi focuses on the traditional institutionalization of traditional medicine in Malaŵi (Msonthi 1983a; ibid. 1983b; ibid. 1983c). Angelika Wolf, finally, addresses the cultural embodiment of HIV/Aids in a number of publications (Wolf 2004; ibid. 2003; ibid. 2000; ibid. 1996).

20 A lot of work has been done in a transcultural context, contributing valuable information to the

addition to the overall research question and will thus only be considered to a limited degree while the main focus of this thesis is on medical anthropology as well as its common ground with intercultural disability studies.

As one of the first scholars to question the prevalent psychiatric doctrine, Thomas Szasz supports a critical stance on the definition of mental difference. Questioning both the supremacy of psychiatry as such and expounding the problems of labelling a given condition as pathological, Szasz's works on the *Myth of Mental Illness* as well as the *Manufacture of Madness* have done a great deal to disenchant Western psychiatry and reveal the arbitrary – or rather, culture-specific – character of its models of categorization. In his view, the term mental illness signifies nothing else than culturally disapproved forms of behaviour (Szasz 1976; ibid. 1961). Michel Foucault reaches similar conclusions in *Madness and Civilization*, challenging the understanding of psychiatry as an exact medical science (Foucault 1989).[21] The works of Ari Kiev have contributed greatly to delineate transcultural psychiatry as an independent field of research. Following a number of previous publications in that field,[22] his fundamental work on *Transcultural Psychiatry* questioned cultural definitions of 'normal' and 'abnormal'. Stressing the importance of culture-bound syndromes (also known as culture specific-disorders), Kiev had a significant impact on psychiatry, anthropology, and other, related fields (Kiev 1972: 65-92).

Especially from the 1990s onwards, the interdisciplinary faculty of disability studies has produced a substantial amount of publications. While some authors argue strongly in terms of anthropological field data and intercultural comparison for the sake of a wider theoretical discussion, others take a more sociological approach, including public health, policy, or activist approaches for their argument. Up to the present day, anthologies are the richest source of data on the anthropology of disability. Distinguished scholars such as Benedicte

---

question as such. It should be stressed that the notion of inter-cultural comparison differs significantly from the approach applied here. In spite of the fact that Arthur Kleinman has contributed significantly to the branding of the "new cross-cultural psychiatry" (Kleinman 1977), it is nonetheless important to note the methodological differences. The present study explicitly follows an anthropological approach, i.e. locating, describing and analysing a phenomenon (mental disorder) in its all-encompassing cultural context – as opposed to contextualizing it in the broader international framework of comparative analysis. It is, therefore, a case study that aims to formulate results derived from and valid for a particular cultural framework rather than develop universalist theories on the cultural conception of mental disorder as a whole.

21 In this study, Michel Foucault takes a culture-historical attitude towards mental illness, examining its representation throughout from the European middle-ages onwards. Here, he reveals the highly controlling character of current psychiatric treatment, questioning its humanitarian as well as its scientific basis (Foucault 1989).

22 His classic study on *Magic, Faith and Healing* (1964) deserves special attention in this context. Here, Kiev examines the mechanisms of 'primitive' psychiatry, describing the interconnection psychiatric systems and the cultural contexts these models derive from.

Ingstad and Susan Reynolds Whyte merit highest attention for their anthropologically motivated compilations on *Disability and Culture* as well as their more recent anthology on *Disability in Local and Global Worlds* (Ingstad & Whyte [ed.] 2007; ibid. [eds.] 1995). Including rich field data from their own research in Botswana and Uganda and articles with other ethnographic foci, Ingstad and Whyte make a crucial contribution not only to the cultural semantics of disability but to its African conceptions in particular. Following a more sociological line of argument, an anthology by Colin Barnes and Geoff Mercer explores disability in the common ground between activism, medical sociology, and disability theory (Barnes & Mercer [eds.] 1996). Later, Barnes and Mercer publish another book in cooperation with Tom Shakespeare in 1999. In their study *Exploring Disability*, the authors give special attention to Goffman's notion of labelling and stigmatization (Goffman 1967) as well as the impact of factors such as the political recognition of disability or its embodiment in the media (Barnes, Mercer & Shakespeare 1999). A number of other anthologies similarly explore the cultural representation of disability.[23]

Edited by Richard Jenkins in 1998, *Questions of Competence* is another anthology that takes a more anthropological perspective on the phenomenon by including ethnographic data from a wide range of cultural contexts. Their collection elaborates on the notion of (in)competence as derived from Edgerton's 1967 classic, thus providing important contributions to the understanding of disability in its cultural setting (Jenkins [ed.] 1998). Also compiling ethnographic data on *Disability in Different Cultures*, Brigitte Holzer, Arthur Vreede and Gabriele Weigt provide valuable material to the anthropological discourse on disability. The collected articles address not only the cultural conceptualization of the phenomenon as such, but they also focus on cultural processes such as migration, knowledge transfer, self-help movements, and its theoretical implications on the intercultural study of disability (Holzer, Vreede & Weigt [eds.] 1999). A multitude of further contributions exist, some of which follow innovative approaches to the issue.[24]

---

23 Thus, Len Barton edits another compilation of articles which subsume current theoretical and methodological developments and give special consideration to the connections between disability and issues such as education, social embodiment, and cultural representation (Barton [ed.] 1996). In 1997, Lennard J. Davis edited a *Disability Studies Reader* which gives a wide overview over the field of disability studies by drawing together contributors from various academic fields such as biology, education, or fine arts. Commencing with a historical outlook on the phenomenon, the articles analyse disability with regard to its legal representation and social stigmatization, once again giving Goffman's stigma approach a critical appraisal. Further, questions of gender, education, and other cultural factors including literature are discussed in connection to disability (Davis [ed.] 1997).

24 A particularly interesting approach is followed by Jane Hubert whose anthology, edited in 2000, discusses disability as well as mental illness in a cultural as well as historical context (Hubert

As it has been emphasized fairly recently, the inclusion of questions of disability into the field of medical anthropology – as well as into other disciplines of cultural anthropology as a whole – still require some intensification (Sagner 2001: 175; Shakespeare 1994: 283). Up to the present, only a small number of more circumstantial monographs have been published, whereas the bigger part of the essential works in this field are available as articles in journals and anthologies. One of the earliest anthropological studies focussing on issues of disability is the 1934 article *Anthropology and the Abnormal* by Ruth Benedict who, comparing the social concept of epilepsy in North America and Siberia, points out the differences – and thus arbitrariness – of cultural interpretation. Normality and abnormality, she argues, is an allocation based on socially defined values and forms of behaviour (Benedict 1934: 71-73).[25]

It has been argued already that only a small number of anthropological monographs have been published with an explicit focus on issues of disability. Likewise, it has been emphasized that these are required in order to broaden the debate by providing more ethnographic substance to it. One of the earliest theses on the culture of disability was provided by John Gwaltney who examined 'the cultural accommodation to blindness and other disasters in a Mexican community' (Gwaltney 1970). Robert Murphy, later, gives a powerful insight into *The Different World of the Disabled* in Western societies (Murphy 2001).[26] In a specifically African context, the number of monographs discussing the interaction of disability and culture are still limited. On the basis of her field data from Eastern Zimbabwe, Deliane Burck published a monograph on the *Ideas and Practices concerning Disability and Rehabilitation* (Burck 1989). With reference to her studies in Indonesia, Joyce Dreezens-Fuhrke has provided material analysing disability in Javanese society according to its symbolic value (Dreezens-Fuhrke 1996).

[ed.] 2000). In an ambitious sociological study, Dieter Neubert and Günther Cloerkes interpret disability as a form of manifest otherness which results from the spontaneous identification of physical, mental, or behavioural deviance by the respective community. Likewise, they argue that this otherness is generally connected to negative connotations, conceding largely with Goffman's notion of stigma as a *quasi* inevitable allocation (Neubert & Cloerkes 2001).

25 In the same year, John Koty gives some consideration to questions of disability in the course of his comparative survey on the treatment of the old and sick within non-Western societies (Koty 1934). Some years later, Jane and Lucien Hanks investigate the social status of persons with disabilities on its cultural basis in a comparative study, concluding that categories such as normality and deviation are largely culturally defined concepts (Hanks & Hanks 1948).

26 Due to his own health condition occurring later on in his academic career, the late Robert F. Murphy (1924–1990 AD) acquired first-hand data on the social factors determining disability in the United States, considering his own life situation as "a kind of extended anthropological field trip" (Murphy 2001: xi).

With respect to Malaŵian conditions, only a very limited amount of publications are dedicated to questions of disability and/or mental illness. One of the few thorough ethnographic investigations in this field was provided by Karl Peltzer. From a methodological perspective, his extensive study on traditional psychosocial health care in Malaŵi may be characterized as taking a psychological approach (Peltzer 1987).[27] Apart from this, most of the few literary sources on mental disorder in this country argue from an education or a development perspective. In an unpublished manuscript handed in at Chancellor College in Zomba, Alastair and Wendy Ager investigate the needs of mentally retarded persons in the country, stressing the need for appropriate medical facilities and a change in medical paradigm (Ager & Ager 1989). It is a most fortunate coincidence that, just prior to the realization of this field research in Malaŵi, local disability agencies conducted a representative survey on activity limitations nationwide in cooperation with an independent European development research organization (Loeb & Eide [eds.] 2004). While providing important statistical data on the basis of a mainly quantitative methodology, their survey also gives a glimpse into the cultural realities within which disability is located. Additionally, Stine Hellum Braathen has contributed some important material in the context of the cultural representation of albinism, evaluating the character and process of social stigmatization (Braathen & Ingstad 2006; Braathen 2005).

All in all, the need for more concise anthropological accounts on the cultural conceptions of disability and mental illness – as subsumed here under the superordinate term *mental disorder* – is recognizable. This thesis represents a contribution that, hopefully, will encourage the discussion on issues of mental health in the complex framework of Malaŵian cultural traditions.

1(d) Methodology

The research was structured according to a number of research focuses. In the beginning, networks had to be re-established with Chancellor College and other scientific institutions. Parallel to that, research was conducted in some of the major archives in the country, including the National Library in Lilongwe, the National Archives, Chancellor College Library, and – some time later – the National Herbarium Library, all of which are located in Zomba. Furthermore, networks with significant organizations in the area needed to be created.

---

27 While giving thorough consideration to its cultural background, Peltzer examines mental disorder on the basis of a psychosocial paradigm, obtaining and evaluating field data according to a clearly defined structural model that has been criticized as a simplification of the actual cultural conditions (Morris 1996: 108-109).

Organizations – governmental and non-governmental – for persons with disabilities as well as mental health facilities were central, and the introductory interviews conducted here proved tremendously helpful to gain an insight into the cultural conditions from a public health perspective.[28] Within the mass of information obtained during this first phase of the research, particular emphasis was given to the terminology as applied in the different cultural contexts for addressing mental disorder. Over time, this formed a catalogue of mental disorder categories which served as a discussion basis – and was further clarified – in later phases of the field research. In the successive research phases, a number of interviewee groups were included on the basis of their professional and/or personal background. All along, follow-up interviews were conducted in order to both clarify and deepen the data received earlier, and on a number of occasions, field trips throughout the Southern Region were made to ensure cross-regional comparability, thus giving a clear picture of the wider, national validity of the field research information received. All through the research period, close connections to Chancellor College of the University of Malaŵi were maintained.

The largest part of field research data was collected by means of interviews, frequently including follow-up interviews in order to attain a higher degree of in-depth information. Further accounts – e.g. on the social interaction within communities, therapeutic rituals, and the like – are derived from etic data received through participant observation. Overall, research has been conducted on the basis of a complex method that examines a given phenomenon throughout the different levels of cultural representation. Here, emic concepts – as expressed in traditional laws and behavioural rules, proverbs, classificatory as well as explanatory systems – have acquired considerable importance due to *(a)* the scarcity of previously published material as well as *(b)* the high relevance of this intentional data (Mühlmann 1938) for the overall question. Nonetheless, etic data was incorporated as well – by means of participant observation, or the study of primary as well as secondary literary sources – in order to control, complement, contextualize, and correlate otherwise unchecked field information.[29]

28 Among the NGOs, the Malaŵi Council of the Handicapped (MACOHA), Malaŵi Against Physical Disabilities (MAP), Feed The Children Malaŵi (formerly Cheshire Homes) or the Parents' Organization of Disabled Children in Malaŵi (PODCAM) need to be mentioned, while government organizations included the Federation of Disability Organizations in Malaŵi (FEDOMA) as well as the Office of the Minister of State Responsible for Persons with Disabilities (OMSPWD). Additionally, government health facilities such as Zomba Mental Hospital (ZMH) or Queen's Hospital in Blantyre, among others, were also contacted and interviews conducted.

29 Following the terminology as presented by Mühlmann (Mühlmann 1938: 108-114), László Vajda questions the practicability of clear distinctions between intentional and functional data due to the fact that cultural phenomena as – as perceived and explained from an emic perspective – may not always be directly traceable from an etic perspective. Here, the cultural construction

The data presented and analysed in this study was obtained through intensive literature review in both German and Malaŵian archives, and through undertaking twelve months of anthropological field research as carried out February 2004 and April 2005. The actual research was preceded by preliminary field stays in Malaŵi in 1998 and again in 2001.

Interviews were conducted in the form of qualitative, semi-structured interviews, and especially well-informed interview partners were consulted on consecutive occasions to further elaborate on former statements. Some interview partners hereby assumed the position of a key informant. Language skills improved during the course of the research due to private language training with a local instructor as well as by its everyday in-field application. Still, most of the interviews conducted in Chicheŵa involved the participation of a research assistant in counteracting potential language problems and facilitating social contact. Whenever applicable and agreed to by the participants, interviews were tape-recorded and transcribed into bilingual Chicheŵa/English documents at an early stage of the research by linguistically trained personnel as contacted via Chancellor College, thus eliminating the biggest part of the possible translation-related challenges.[30] Interview data was complemented significantly by further findings made by means of participant observation.

As the primary research setting, the district of Zomba in the Southern Region of the country was selected. This choice was encouraged not only by direct cooperation with the University of Malaŵi's Chancellor College located there, but also by the specific character of the wider area. Forming a minor urban center, Zomba municipality attracts some extent of regional labour migration – partly due to the presence of Chancellor College, the social sciences branch of the University of Malaŵi. At the same time, rural communities of the district are poorly accessible and therefore offer good samples for comparative analysis within a relatively small geographical area. Zomba District allowed the inclusion of both urban and peri-urban settings as well as rural locations into the research, while other districts were also accessible due to favourable infrastructural conditions. As an in-depth setting for intensive data collection in a rural context, long-term field research was conducted in Nkagula Village, Sakata Trading Centre, in the area of SubT/A Nkagula, T/A Kuntumanji, in rural Zomba

---

of a given phenomenon may reflect historical processes in a way that, as Vajda put it, a society may still regard the horse as the most important animal even though the sheep has long since have obtained a much more central economic position (Vajda 1964: 770-771). It is therefore the inclusion of different types of data that allows a clearer understanding of a given phenomenon within its cultural setting.

30 The transliteration applied here has been double-checked in cooperation with staff members of Kachere Series publishers, Zomba. Frequent reference has been made to the linguistic standards established by Steven Paas in his recent Chicheŵa dictionaries (Paas 2005; ibid. 2004).

District. Due to personal acquaintance with a subsistence farmer and father of a child with severe disabilities in the area, a small network of parents with children with disabilities could be accessed. In addition, repeated research trips were conducted to other rural communities of Zomba District – such as Namirongo Village in T/A Mlumbe, Govala Village, T/A Jali, or Jali Village itself. Many other areas were included in the form of more extensive field research and interview sessions, providing multi-sited ethnographic data. Developing a bigger picture of the cultural conditions of persons with mental disorder throughout the Southern Region, interviews were also conducted in adjacent districts – including Blantyre, Chiradzulu, Machinga, and Balaka. Moreover, extended field trips were made in order to obtain comparative data from more remote districts of the Southern Region.[31]

Due to historically defined settlement areas as well as more recent migration processes, Zomba District – as well as many parts of the country as a whole – is an ethnically heterogeneous district. The ethnic groups most highly represented in this area are Yao, Lomwe, Mang'anja, and Nyanja. Due to migratory effects – and also by extending the range of research into other districts of the Southern Region –, persons from a Cheŵa, Ngoni, Tumbuka, Sena, Tonga, and Shona background were also among the interviewees, thus creating room for additional insights into the specific cultural notions in their respective home communities. The exact ethnic composition of the interview partners is given in the appendices attached to this study (see *Appendix 4*).

Due to its focus on medical anthropology, the current study endeavours to provide room for interdisciplinary discussion between the faculties of medicine and social or cultural anthropology. While the qualitative research techniques as depicted above demonstrate a clearly anthropological methodology, basic medical categories are nonetheless applied in order to provide a basic terminological structure for the otherwise extremely complex notions of medicine in Malaŵi. Therefore, it is necessary to make some efforts in differentiating systematic – i.e. etic – categories which are not clearly distinguished in their emic context in order to clarify the conceptual logic of medical processes. The necessity of introducing analytic tools in order to give a better understanding of Malaŵian medical concepts is supported by Brian Morris who states that

> "Although no rigid demarcation can be made between nosology, the principles behind disease classification, and etiology, the underlying causes of the affliction, it is conceptually important […] to consider those separately. A failure to do this has led to a lamentable tendency, reflected in the writings of many scholars, to

---

31 These included Nsanje, Chikwawa, Mangochi, Mulanje, and Phalombe.

view all illness as caused by witchcraft or other mystical forces" (Morris 1996: 104).

Accordingly, the analysis of issues of mental disorder in Malaŵi paradoxically operates on the basis of central, basic biomedical concepts in order to reveal their benefits and limitations.

2. Introducing Mental Disorder in Malaŵi

In every given culture, mental disorder challenges society in terms of medical and economic support strategies as well as mechanisms of social inclusion. In spite of explicit governmental efforts to improve the situation of persons with mental disorders in Malaŵi, a severe lack of integrative success must still be attested. With substantial anthropological data missing, the cultural background of the problem itself remains unclear up to the present day, reducing hope for more effective approaches to questions of mental disorder. Recent statistical research has substantiated the significance of disability issues in Malaŵi, revealing that the problem is disproportionately prevalent in rural areas (Loeb & Eide [eds.] 2004).[32] In spite of government programs designed to alleviate the prevalence of disability in Malaŵi – such as the installation of a Government Ministry Responsible for Persons with Disabilities –, little change for the better is visible. With a million persons with disabilities and an even higher number affected indirectly nationwide, the question of disability is an issue of highest national and international importance in terms of the medical, political, economic and social problems it causes in Malaŵi.

2(a) Setting Presentation

Some basic data about the setting of this study is required in order to comprehend the embedding of the present study. As elementary knowledge, the geographical, historical, political, ethnic, and demographic background of the country shall therefore be depicted in brief. Particular consideration will be given to the Southern Region of the country, reflecting the fact that the field data forming the ethnographic basis for this study originates from this area.

The Republic of Malaŵi is a land-locked country situated along the South of the Great Rift Valley in South-Eastern Africa, bordering on the neighbouring

[32] Due to the low degree of urbanization in Malaŵi, 93 percent of the disabled population lives in a rural setting (NSO 1987: 4).

states Tanzania, Zambia, and Mozambique.[33] Out of its 118,484 km^2 of national area, only 94,276 km^2 are dry land, the rest being taken up by its various lakes – the largest being Lake Malaŵi (formerly known as Lake Nyasa). As one of the most densely populated countries in sub-Saharan Africa, Malaŵi's population is estimated at about 13 million, indicating a population density of more than 130 inhabitants per square kilometre (WHO 2006b: 172). By comparison, the Southern Region is the most densely populated area with close to 6 million inhabitants, with population density approximating 180 persons per square kilometre. An estimated 88 percent of the population live in rural environments, and for most, farming represents the main source of livelihood. Particularly in the South, maize (*chimanga*) is by far the most important food crop – predominantly used in the form of *ufa* (maize flour) and prepared into *nsima* (a stiff maize porridge) or *phala* (maize gruel), the main ingredient of virtually every Malaŵian meal. Some cash crops are also planted and sold on local markets to provide small income. With 78 percent of the economically active population being smallholder subsistence farmers (*mlimi*) and others living from fishing or forestry, more than 90 percent of Malaŵian households' livelihoods rely directly on natural resources. National export trade is dominated by cash crops such as tea, tobacco, sugar cane, and coffee (Munthali, Konyani & Loeb 2004: 28; NSO 1998: xix).

In 2005, the country's development index was ranked on position 165 out of 177 nations worldwide. 65 percent of the Malaŵian population lived in dire poverty, with the Southern Region having the highest regional poverty rate.[34] The ensuing developmental challenges are manifold. As one of them, education levels are also low. While 64.1 percent of the adult population are literate nationwide, the Southern Region has the lowest literacy rate of the three national regions, and only 44 percent of Malaŵian grade 1 students reached grade 5 education in 2003 (NSO 2005a: 139; UNDP 2005; NSO 1998: xv).

The population of Malaŵi falls into a number of different ethnic groups which are generally defined by common descent, language, cultural representations and/or history. While most of these groups have their historical population centers, many areas in Malaŵi feature a highly heterogeneous ethnic composition due to factors such as labour migration, considerable regional mobility, and high population density. At present, about one third of the national population belong to the historically related groups of the Cheŵa, Nyanja, and

---

33 Malaŵi stretches between the latitudes of 9 degrees 45 minutes to 17 degrees 16 minutes south, and from the longitudes of 32 degrees 40 minutes to 35 degrees 51 minutes east.

34 Poverty is closely related to reoccurring food crises in Malaŵi. In 2002 and 2003, 33 percent of the population was considered undernourished and directly affected by famine and starvation (UNDP 2005: 243). In 2005 AD, food shortages affected an estimated five million Malaŵians.

Mang'anja – while Lomwe, Yao, Ngoni, and Tumbuka constitute other strong ethnic units of the population; smaller groups such as the Sena, Tonga, or Nkhonde are of more regional importance (NSO & ORC Macro 2005: 26).[35] In the Southern Region where the field research for this study was conducted, the Mang'anja, Nyanja, Yao, Ngoni, Lomwe, and Sena are the most prevalent ethnic groups.

Both originating from the historical Maravi ethnic cluster (see below), the Mang'anja mostly live in the Lower Shire area in the extreme South while the Nyanja inhabit parts of the South-West (Lienau 1981: 85; Crosby 1980: 46).[36] Like all other ethnic groups in Malaŵi, the rural majority of the Mang'anja and Nyanja engage in agriculture, and their social organization consistently recognizes a matrilineal system of descent and uxorilocal, segmentary forms of settlement. The Chicheŵa language spoken by all these ethnic groups is recognized – along with English – as the national language of Malaŵi.[37] The former homeland of the matrilineal Yao, in contrast, lies in the Niassa Province of North-Western Mozambique. Due to their involvement in trade with Arab trading posts on the Indian Ocean, the Yao migrated into Malaŵi around the 1860s where they engaged in slave-trade as well as other mercantile activities. At present, most Yao also practice subsistence farming, and they apply their own Bantu language, the Chiyao (Peltzer 1987: 3; Alpers 1972: 168-170).[38] The patrilineally structured Ngoni, in turn, left Natal and Swaziland during the *mfecane* period (c. 1815 to 1835) after military conflicts with the ruling confederation of the Zulu king Shaka (1787–1828 AD) in 1819 AD. From the 1840s onwards, they established themselves in parts of Central and Southern Malaŵi, and presently, their main centers lie in Mzimba District (Northern Region) as well as in Ntcheu, Dedza, and Dowa Districts of Central Region. Their original Bantu language, closely related to isiZulu, has largely disappeared so that most Ngoni now use Chicheŵa as their first language (Phiri 2004: 79; ibid. 1982; Read 1979: 132; Pachai 1972: 179). The likewise patrilineal Lomwe formed as a loose federation of clans in Western Mozambique as late as the 19th century AD. While some units migrated into South-Eastern Malaŵi in the late

---

35 For full numbers see *Table 1*.

36 Along with the Cheŵa, smaller groups such as the Chipeta or Nsenga are also mentioned as descendants of the Maravi (Kubik 1987: 7; Bruwer 1955: 113). Matthew Schoffeleers, however, identifies the Chipeta with the pre-Maravi clan Banda which was later incorporated into the Cheŵa. By intermarriage with the powerful Maravi clan Phiri, the Banda formed a moiety of the royal Cheŵa lineage (Schoffeleers 1992: 27-32).

37 Also called Chinyanja, Chicheŵa is a Bantu language which, according to linguistic classification, belongs to the Benue-Congo branch of the Niger-Congo language family which, in turn, constitutes part of the Niger-Kordofanian super-family (Greenberg 1963).

38 Prior to their migration, the majority of the Yao converted to Islam. At present, the areas with the largest Yao population are Mangochi, Machinga, and Zomba Districts in the Southern Region.

19th and early 20th centuries AD, significant numbers of Lomwe still live in Mozambique (Phiri 2004: 100; Schoffeleers 1997: 34; Peltzer 1987: 3).[39] The Chilomwe, a Bantu language closely related to the Makhuwa used in parts of Mozambique, is also widely spoken (Phiri 2004: 107; Soka 1999). The Sena, in turn, reached Southern Malaŵi from the Zambezi valley of Mozambique in the 19th century (Schoffeleers 1997: 34; Peltzer 1987: 3). Today, the patrilineally structured Sena make up a considerable part of the population in the districts of Chikwawa and Nsanje in the Lower Shire area, and they apply their own Bantu language, the Chisena.[40]

It is important to note here that, in spite of their historical distinctiveness, the different ethnic groups represented in this study do have a history of close inter-ethnic contact and exchange. Consequently, not all results discussed in this thesis do merit a distinction according to a given ethnic affiliation; many representations of culture in Southern Malaŵi have, in fact, developed the character of shared cultural representations (Morris 2000: 13-19). In this perspective, Brian Morris refers to differences between ethnicity and culture, pointing out that

> "[…] many cultural ideas and beliefs – with respect to the divinity, medicine, witchcraft, ideas about bodily humours and the dangers of 'heat', disease concepts, human/animal relationships, and beliefs relating to the spirits of the dead (*mizimu*) – are widely shared and common throughout the country. […] The important point, however, is that in Malawi 'culture' cannot be equated with 'ethnicity', and that cultural representations, as noted earlier, are diverse and exist on many different levels, one of which reflects the common cultural heritage shared by all the matrilineal people of Malawi. Given the fact that all these matrilineal people have common origins and historical traditions, and that there have been complex and long-standing cultural, economic and linguistic interrelationships between all the matrilineal people of Malawi, it is hardly surprising that common social institutions and cultural representations are evident" (Morris 2000: 18).

This observation is shared by a number of scholars who also report the consent between different ethnic groups with respect to various areas of cultural representation (Vail & White 1989; Alpers 1975: 7; Gamitto 1960: 63; Mitchell

---

39 Most of the Malaŵian Lomwe live in Mulanje, Phalombe, Thyolo, and Chiradzulu Districts of the Southern Region.

40 Numerous studies have addressed Malaŵian historical developments, and this issue shall therefore not be elaborated at length. For more concise studies on different eras of Malaŵian (pre-)history see Rotberg 2005; Phiri 2004; Welling 2000; Shepperson & Price 2000; Muyebe & Muyebe 1999; Phiri 1999; Booth 1998; Schoffeleers 1997; ibid. 1992; ibid. 1979; Englund 1996; Lwanda 1993; Kubik 1987; Crosby 1980; Linden 1979; Phiri 1976; Langworthy 1973; Ntara 1973; Clark 1972; Gamitto 1960; Bruwer 1955; Young 1950.

1956: 14; Young 1950: 37). Especially due to increasing population density and high spatial mobility, cultural discourse is no longer necessarily restricted to a given ethnic context, but it discusses issues on a wider, inter-ethnic level. Cultural concepts travel fairly easily and may be adopted among different ethnic groups.[41] Brian Morris thus observes that

> "Many contemporary scholars, however, still write of the Chewa or Tumbuka as if they constituted ethnic enclaves with their own specific bounded culture or cosmology. Yet to stress this intermingling and common cultural heritage is not to deny that ethnic affiliation and ethnic identity are not important in Malawi. But it is probable that ethnic consciousness itself came to be fully articulated only during the colonial period, partly through the system of indirect rule and the ethnic stereotyping of the European colonialists, and partly through the struggles of local people themselves, for political autonomy, for economic and educational advance, and as a form of resistance against the missionaries and the colonial state" (Morris 2000: 18-19).

It may be regarded as a result of historical processes to categorize people in Malaŵi according to numerous ethnic communities, each of which have their own distinctive cultural heritage and regional provenience. This notion, however, has been identified as misleading, rather reflecting the quintessentially Western – and, historically speaking, colonial – idea of ethnicity as some kind of 'primordial' and monolithic concept. The struggle of political elites for power, as Brian Morris argues, may also have contributed to the acceptance of ethnic units as a means of collective identification (Morris 2000: 15-16). As a result, field research indicates that for many Malaŵians, ethnicity may have a situational, changeable, or even ambiguous character and be negotiated according to the given social occasion. Therefore, many persons characterize their own ethnic affiliation by statements such as being 'half Mang'anja and half Yao' or as 'being Nyanja but also Lomwe'. This more complex concept of ethnic specificity also expresses itself in terms of the representations of traditional culture. At present, a broad cultural common ground transcends ethnic affiliation and forms the basis for public discourse, and it is by far not uncommon to hear the ethnic origin of a given concept disputed among the local population. This interplay between ethnically distinctive and shared representations of culture is a complex process that is reflected in the way data is presented in this study.[42] And it is,

---

41 On a grassroots level, the population of a given Southern Malaŵian village frequently composes of more than one ethnic group, and due to the high occurrence of inter-ethnic marriage, the question of defining affiliation – and thus the ethnic identity of future offspring – is frequently open to negotiation.

42 It is in recognition of this condition that the current thesis does not focus on one ethnic group alone but, as elaborated in the methodology section (see *Chapter I.1.d*), investigates cultural

after all, exactly this wide ongoing discourse and its specific character of consenting, conflicting, and negotiating cultural notions – along with its different discernible elements including ethnic factors in the same way as gender, religious, social, or regional affiliation – that forms the dynamic layers of the complex cultural process of construction in question here, and it is therefore at the very bottom of this thesis' objective.

The historical dimension of the various Malaŵian cultures as outlined here provides the basis for a wider understanding of the setting in general terms, but it also highlights some more specific factors that are directly relevant for the more specific question of this thesis. The migratory movements mentioned represent the direct cause of the rich cultural pluralism prevalent in Malaŵi today. Geographic factors relate to some of the most pressing challenges in Malaŵian development including its economic weaknesses, and the political processes mentioned here further clarify that, in spite of its national independence in the 1960s, truly democratic political structures are still a comparably recent introduction into Malaŵian society. Moreover, the importance of certain legal measures has already been emphasized, and it will be shown that Malaŵian law plays a particularly considerable role in the context of questions of mental disorder.

2(b) Legal Framework

National policy can be seen as a result from both international guidelines and pre-colonial, cultural notions of morally right behaviour, shaping a specific sense of justice at the grassroots level of society. The inclusion of persons with disabilities and the protection of their rights have a broad ethical basis of international laws and conventions. As a first fundamental guideline, the Universal Declaration of Human Rights issued by the United Nations General Assembly in 1948 set the humanitarian standards in the treatment of persons with disabilities as well. Accordingly, civil as well as political rights are guaranteed to people with disabilities (UN 1948).

As another milestone, the United Nations developed the World Program of Action (WPA) concerning Disabled Persons in 1983, marking the beginning of a United Nations Decade of Disabled Persons from 1983 to 1992 (UN 1983).[43] By

conditions both on their specifically ethnic level as well as on a larger, inter-ethnic scale. In this thesis, the specific relevance of ethnic affiliation – and of the similarities and dissimilarities of cultural concepts – will be pointed out on numerous occasions. For that purpose, all interviewees directly related to are specified with their ethnic group.

43 This program promoted the prevention of disability as well as the rehabilitation and equalization of opportunities for the affected persons, aiming to provide persons with disabilities with full

the end of this decade, the United Nations General Assembly adopted a resolution on the Standard Rules on the Equalization of Opportunities for Persons with Disabilities, corroborating their statements as formulated in the 1983 WPA and mapping a toolbox for achieving equality for persons with disabilities which could be applied by organizations working on national and international levels alike (UN 1993).[44] In 2006, the United Nations Ad Hoc Committee on a Comprehensive and Integral International Convention on the Protection and Promotion of the Rights and Dignity of Persons with Disabilities finally issued a draft convention on the rights of persons with disabilities. Being the result of year-long endeavours and intensive negotiations between government officials and disability organization representatives from around the world, the agreement, reached at the eighth session of the Ad Hoc Committee was applauded among the disability community. With the treaty still requiring ratification on the respective national levels, it focuses on the fight against discrimination against persons with disabilities, protecting their civil rights, their access to justice, as well as other basic rights such as education, health care, and means of transportation (UN 2006).

Expectedly, the global concerns about persons with disabilities as well as mental health issues have major impact on national policies and legislative measures. While, during the colonial period, British legislation had been applied, Malaŵian independence in 1964 directly led to the freedom as well as the necessity of structuring national law in accordance with a Malaŵian understanding of society. In the year 1971, the national government started issuing legal regulations meant to increase the care and protection for handicapped persons. This text, known as the Handicapped Persons Act, underwent minor changes until its final issue in 1973. This act, marking the founding stone of a national Malaŵian disability policy, defines itself as

> "An Act to make provisions for the improvement of the care, assistance and education of handicapped persons in Malaŵi; to establish a Council for the handicapped; to provide for the voluntary registration of handicapped persons; to provide for the registration, direction, control and regulation of associations whose objects include the welfare of the handicapped; and further to provide for

---

participation and equality in social life and personal development. In the same year, the International Labour Organisation (ILO) issued Convention No. 159 in Geneva which concerned the vocational rehabilitation and employment of disabled persons. Calling states around the world to establish appropriate vocational training and rehabilitation facilities for persons with disabilities, the ILO Convention 158 emphasizes the need to support disabled persons in developing their personal skills and employment opportunities (ILO 1983).

44 In the context of mental health issues, the year 2001 marked the launch of the WHO Mental Health Global Action Plan (mhGAP), coming as a reaction to the results of the 2001 World Health Report which focused explicitly on mental health issues (WHO 2001c).

matters incidental thereto and connected therewith" (Government of Malaŵi 1971: Preamble).

By this act, associations and organizations for persons with disabilities are encouraged to operate in Malaŵi, and cooperation with governmental institutions is also welcomed (Government of Malaŵi 1971). A second important measure implemented by the 1971 Handicapped Persons Act is the establishment of the Malaŵi Council for the Handicapped (MACOHA) in the same year. This newly founded governmental organization acts as an implementer of all government disability programs. These measures include providing and coordinating rehabilitation services as well as awareness-raising towards a better integration of persons with disabilities into Malaŵian society.[45]

In the time before multi-party democracy – especially between 1971 and 1994 –, the active services for persons with disabilities had a strong focus on charity while personal development or human rights were not primary motivations. At the same time, no official policy had yet been implemented to provide guidance for activities (Munthali, Konyani & Loeb 2004: 35). Following the first multi-party elections in 1994, another significant step in terms of the legal situation of persons with mental disorders – and here, more explicitly of persons with disabilities – is the Constitution of the Republic of Malaŵi as implemented in 1995. In full accordance with international standards, the Malaŵian constitution gives recognition to the situation of persons with disabilities and demands the implementation of programs based on the principle of non-discrimination (Munthali, Konyani & Loeb 2004: 35; Government of Malaŵi 1995). In 1998, the office of the Minister Responsible for Persons with Disabilities was established by presidential directive as a coordinator institution for all issues pertaining to persons with disabilities. Before that, disability issues had been under the responsibility of changing ministries such as the Ministry of Health or the Ministry of Community Services (Munthali, Konyani & Loeb 2004: 35-36).[46] It can be seen as one of the main achievements of the mentioned Ministry to develop a National Disability Policy which is meant to provide a

45 Up to the present, MACOHA also acts as an advisor to the government on all questions touching persons with disabilities. Currently, a number of Community Based Rehabilitation programs are run by MACOHA nationwide, and some Institutional Based Rehabilitation centers are also part of MACOHA strategy. The Institutional Based Rehabilitation projects resemble vocational training facilities for persons with mainly physical limitations, such as the Kamuzu Vocational Rehabilitation and Training Center in Magomero in Zomba District. Additionally, a few outreach services and some workshops for persons with disabilities are also under MACOHA coordination.

46 By 2004, this office was restructured into the Ministry of Social Development and People with Disabilities (MSDPWD), thereby becoming independent from the Office of President and Cabinet it was formerly affiliated to.

closer legislative basis for the inclusion of persons with disabilities into society (Government of Malaŵi 2006). As the new National Disability Policy argues,

> "It is now widely accepted that disabled people have a right to live a dignified and independent life-style within the community; to take an active part in the general, social and economic development of the country; and to receive education, medical care and social services within the ordinary structures of their societies. The new approach stresses abilities, not disabilities. It promotes disabled persons' rights, freedom of choice and equal opportunities" (Government of Malaŵi 2006: xii).

The necessity to legally protect the rights of persons with disabilities is frequently emphasized and commented on in the public discourse of present-day Malaŵi. Therefore, court cases against someone violating the rights of persons with mental disorders are covered at some detail in national media.[47]

While national legislation constitutes the main body of Malaŵian jurisdiction,[48] rural communities have the opportunity to negotiate minor legal conflicts internally, by the power of so-called traditional courts. A traditional court (*bwalo*) is under the responsibility of traditional authorities on different hierarchical levels. While minor issues on grassroots level may fall under the competence of a village headman (*mfumu yaing'ono* or *nyakwawa*), he or she usually brings all cases of higher public interest to the attention of the group village headman (*mfumu yaikulu* or *grupu*) who has the duty of acting as a traditional judge. If a lawsuit is seen as being of even greater importance, the Traditional Authority (T/A, *mfumu* or *chalo*) of the area is called upon as supreme judge. In addition to referring touchy cases to a higher level of jurisdiction, headmen and headwomen can also turn to their own superiors for advice and instructions on how to negotiate a particularly difficult court case.

The legal tradition frequently reiterated implies that all persons must be regarded as equal in the face of traditional law. This explicitly includes persons with mental disorders, so that every case of abuse against such a person would be brought to the *bwalo*, as the *mafumu* of different ethnic groups point out. In the event of such a court case, though, opinions are split about the question whether or not a person with a mental disorder has the right to speak in front of the

---

47 As an example, a 27 year-old Malaŵian was sentenced to a three years' prison charge for sexually abusing a 12 year-old girl described as mentally retarded. In reaction, the Ministry of Social Development and Persons with Disabilities was quoted as demanding "stiffer penalties for such [...] horrendous crimes" and "barbaric behaviour", reminding the general public of the equal right to security and participation on the side of persons with disabilities (Kasunda 2005: 3).

48 The judiciary is structured hierarchically, ranging from Magistrate Courts (located in every larger population center of every district) to the four High Courts (located in the cities of Lilongwe, Blantyre, Mzuzu, and Zomba) and to the Supreme Court situated in Blantyre.

bwalo.[49] In the event that a person is found guilty of committing an offence against a person with a mental disorder, he or she is usually sentenced to pay a fine equivalent to the value of livestock, i.e. of a chicken or, in more severe cases, a goat. If a person with a mental disorder, in turn, is convicted for violating somebody else's rights, he or she cannot be punished or even blamed according to, e.g., Yao customs. The family guardians would usually try to explain the situation to the unfortunate wrongdoer, but the only viable punishment in such a case is sending them to the next District Hospital or Zomba Mental Hospital for more specialized Western treatment.[50]

While local courts therefore constitute an important addition to the national legal system, their recognition is also subject to processes of cultural change. A Yao *mfumu* therefore laments the fact that the behavioural rules towards persons with mental disorders do not have a legally binding character anymore, and that traditional courts are losing some of their cultural standing. Legal measures mostly apply only in cases of physically violent behaviour, but all other forms of misconduct cannot be prosecuted by law. Rather, they are a matter of good manners (*khalidwe*) and politeness (*ulemu*) only, making it unlikely for people to consult the *bwalo* for clarification.[51] Moreover, though, the *bwalo* is the only legal institution in Malaŵi where cases will be heard that are seen as being related to magic practices. Given the high prevalence of magic – especially *ufiti* – in Malaŵi and its equally great importance in the context of the causation of mental disorder, traditional courts still cover an enormously important field of jurisdiction in Malaŵian society.

The Malaŵian legal system gives a direct and emblematic impression of the challenges posed by modern state structures superimposing traditional African ones. While being part of the state jurisdiction and therefore forced to comply with government policy and law, the *abwalo* still constitute a governmental

---

49 Therefore, a Mang'anja *mfumu* clearly supports this principle while a Yao *mfumu* expresses his opinion that such persons must be generally considered unfit to personally address the court. Clearly implying a changing state of mental disorder, the former *mfumu* assesses that any person with *misala* or *kuzerezeka* (see *Chapter III*) who does not comply with behavioural rules of the *bwalo* would have to be tied up and removed. When negotiating a case without the direct participation of a person with a mental disorder, a Yao *mfumu yaikulu* explains that he would conduct personal inquiries and investigations about the actual proceedings in order to make up for the claimant's inability to speak for himself or herself.

50 While this lenience of the law against persons with mental disorders bears some resemblances with conditions of diminished responsibility, it is also subject to critical verification. A Mang'anja *mfumu* thus mentions his habit of conducting interrogations within the community in order to assess whether the condition of the accused truly justifies clemency of the law or whether it is a case of pretence.

51 Furthermore, the cooperation between these governmental courts and the traditional *bwalo* is frequently difficult. While cases of alleged murder have to be tried before the respective Magistrate Court, national law does not acknowledge *ufiti* as a count of indictment.

concession to the limited applicability of a largely European legal system to the cultural conditions of a Malaŵian setting. This gap between mainstream political practice – as evolved from colonial notions – and traditional culture represents a considerable disruption within Malaŵian culture, questioning the socially binding character of both legal systems by providing a potential alternative that argues on the basis of different basic assumptions. This illustrates the difficulties in implementing national and/or international legal concepts into a largely traditionally defined setting. Here, global health strategies and their correlation with traditional legal concepts and institutions are of particular importance for the actual health situation in Malaŵi.

2(c) Health Conditions

Public health care is among the most pressing issues the national government and international aid organizations in Malaŵi face. In spite of ongoing involvement of both national and international agents, health conditions remain difficult in many parts of the country. Like many other countries in Southern Africa, Malaŵi faces some considerable health challenges.

Due to severe infrastructural problems throughout the country, the availability of psychiatric institutions in Malaŵi is minimal. As depicted by the National Statistical Office, the country has two official institutions for mental health care nationwide. While one of these facilities – St John of God's Hospital located in Mzuzu, Mzimba District (Northern Region) [52] – is a religious institution run by the Christian Health Association of Malaŵi (CHAM), the other and much larger one is the government-owned Zomba Mental Hospital. Together, these institutions officially provide 153 beds for mental in-patients, 25 of which are at St John of God's (NSO 2005b). For persons with disabilities, private institutions – such as Feed the Children Malaŵi, an organization formerly known as Cheshire Homes and based in the suburban areas of both Blantyre and Lilongwe Districts – are frequently seen as an alternative to hospitals. At the same time, their programs focus on rehabilitation services and vocational training for special needs children. As considerable drawbacks for potential patients, their services are comparatively pricey and only available to those situated in the immediate vicinity of the institution.[53]

---

[52] This facility is an institution of the Hospitaller Order of Saint John of God, a Catholic order with headquarters in Ireland.

[53] Thus, for instance, institutions such as Feed the Children Malaŵi in Ndirande, Blantyre, have an estimated catchment area of 20 km from where students can commute for a couple of days of training per week. The biggest part of the estimated 700 students trained throughout a year are identified as suffering from cerebral palsy, but also learning difficulties, mental retardation,

Due to its relative distance from the research area, St John of God's does not have an immediate impact on the therapeutic options for people in the Southern Region of Malaŵi. Zomba Mental Hospital with its *quasi* nationwide catchment area, on the other hand, represents an institution with significant relevance to this study. As already indicated, Zomba Mental Hospital provides an official 128 beds for in-patient treatment as well as out-patient services for a varying number of persons.[54] While the explicit policy focuses on referring persons with disabilities to rehabilitation institutions, a considerable number of them still remain in the rehabilitation wards of Zomba Mental Hospital for lack of suitable alternative treatment facilities. As a general average, in-patients are said to stay for a period of at least one to two months, but cases of long-term institutionalization of ten or more years are no exception either. Due to the relative age of the facilities in Zomba as such, the regrettable condition of the institution – especially with regard to its architectural structure – is presently a source of criticism and worry.[55] In addition to the structural inadequacies of the building, Zomba Mental Hospital is also facing frequent shortages of supplies and medical equipment.[56]

The national health system in Malaŵi is controlled by two separate agencies. While governmental institutions – under the supervision of the Ministry of Health – constitute the largest part, a significant number of additional institutions are also provided by the Christian Health Association of Malaŵi (CHAM). The health care system has a hierarchical structure, with district and regional hospitals providing the widest range of medical services. Primary health centers exist in smaller towns, offering basic facilities on the level of smaller population centers, and local dispensaries provide additional aid in remote places

---

physical disabilities (such as hearing or speech impediments), emotional and behavioural problems, and visual impairments. As another example, Kamuzu Vocational Rehabilitation and Training Center for Disabled Persons in Magomero, Zomba District, is a center run by the Malawi Council of the Handicapped (MACOHA). While offering vocational training for students with mainly physical challenges, they also offer accommodation to students in the fashion of a boarding school.

54 According to interview data obtained from former Zomba Mental Hospital staff, the hospital consists of two Acute Male Wards (of c. 40 beds each) and an Acute Female Ward (c. 30 beds) as well as a Children's Ward (which doubles as Female Rehabilitation Ward, c. 15 beds), an Infirmary Ward (c. 10 beds), and a Male Rehabilitation Ward (c. 20 beds). According to these numbers, Zomba Mental Hospital thus features an estimated 155 beds altogether.

55 A Malaŵian health worker with professional experience in Zomba Mental Hospital thus describes the situation, explaining that "the problem is that our hospital is very old so most of our patients abscond the institution because the hospital is rotting down. So patients stay while some go out – maybe without us knowing" (Vivian Changata, a Mang'anja nursing officer).

56 Thus, as a nursing student working at Zomba Mental Hospital explained, the hospital possesses neither electroencephalography (EEG) nor electrocardiography (ECG) facilities, and even a thermometer could not be provided.

(Sommerfeld 1987: 82). With regard to the Southern Region, this situation translates into a total of 29 hospitals,[57] 135 primary health centers and 53 dispensaries, providing a grand total of 6,575 beds for an estimated 6 million inhabitants (NSO 2005b: Table 3.2).

The amount of personnel working in these facilities is likewise insufficient to meet everyday demands.[58] According to national statistics, on average there is one physician for every 61,817 persons in Malaŵi – notwithstanding the much higher concentration and availability of doctors in urban areas as compared to the more rural, medically less accessible 88 percent of the country's population. To compensate for that, nurses have an increased responsibility in maintaining the country's health care services, but there are 2,228 patients per nurse nationwide (NSO 2005b: Table 3.12), and the lack of qualified medical personnel is recognized as a key shortage in the Malaŵian health care system – as it is in many other countries of the world, and in sub-Saharan Africa in particular (Lwanda 2008).[59] Due to the severe difficulties in meeting the basic medical demands of the Malaŵian population by biomedical means, the medical landscape of the country offers a number of therapeutic alternatives. Traditional healers (*asing'anga*) provide a wide variety of services, traditional birth attendants (*azamba*) provide maternity care, and different kinds of religious specialists offer faith healing rituals.

So far, very little information exists to provide an outline of mental disorder in Malaŵi.[60] The historical dimension of mental disorder is not very well-documented, and earliest reports on the issue include colonial records as found in the National Archives in Zomba, illustrating British attempts to address the

57 The numbers given here refer to a 1998 survey. With some exceptions, most of these hospitals are confined to the respective district capitals. While the districts of Zomba and Mangochi boast four hospitals each, the districts of Chiradzulu, Mwanza, and Chikwawa (three each) follow before Blantyre, Thyolo, Mulanje, Phalombe, and Nsanje (with two hospitals). Both Balaka and Machinga Districts only feature a single government hospital (NSO 2005b: Table 3.2).

58 2004 figures indicate the following numbers for medical staff personnel. Nationwide, 179 doctors are working along with 4,966 nurses as well as numerous clinical officers (738), medical assistants (693), health assistants (263), and health surveillance assistants (8,241). According to the National Statistical Office, this leads to national ratios of 61,817 inhabitants per doctor and 2,228 persons per nurse (NSO 2005b: Table 3.12).

59 According to the World Health Organization, "Staffing in Malawi's health service is inadequate to maintain a minimum level of health care, and is particularly low even by regional standards. It is also insufficient for the delivery of antiretroviral therapy and other HIV/AIDS-related services in response to demand. Of 27 districts, 15 have fewer than 1.5 nurses per facility, and five districts do not have even one each, while four districts have no doctor at all. HIV/AIDS-related attrition among the workforce compounds the shortage. In addition, up to 800 qualified nurses living in Malawi choose not to work in the health sector" (WHO 2006b: 22).

60 Here, terminology is of course an issue that must be recognized. While none of the sources mentioned below apply the term mental disorder as defined here, their results still resemble the closest indicators for the prevalence and nature of the phenomenon.

problem of mental disorder among the Malaŵian population. The little statistical information available is closely connected to the medical situation in Zomba Mental Hospital. It was only after achieving independence in 1964 that the recognition of disability as a national health concern increased significantly, and by now, different agencies operate in order to raise awareness and create political leverage on the issue.

In 1983, the National Statistical Office of the Government of Malaŵi conducted a first systematic *Survey of Handicapped Persons* in the country. Its results in the form of quantitative data paint a fairly positive picture, identifying only 2.9 percent of the Malaŵian population as disabled. According to these numbers, a total of 11 percent of the households nationwide have at least one member living with a disability, and the regional variability of the disability rate is comparably low (NSO 1987: 4) (see *Table 3*). Furthermore, the occurrence of disabilities indicates that a full 46 percent of the cases appear before the age of five years of age (see *Table 4*). In full compliance with biomedical concepts, the study differentiates mental illness from disability, consequently indicating that cases of mental illness do not occur congenitally but are only diagnosed from the age of 5 years onward. Likewise, mental retardation always occurs early in a person's life, appearing at the latest at 14 years of age (NSO 1987: 22-23). Education was identified as a considerable problem for the affected persons' social situation, while their integration into work processes was described as comparatively favourable.[61] In the context of this study, the numbers given for epilepsy as well as for mental illness or retardation may be emphasized. At the same time, it is important to note that these numbers might require re-reading with regard to mental cases due to the fact that the study explicitly leaves the inmates of prisons, schools, and hospitals unconsidered (NSO 1987: 1) – which is the place where a considerable number of persons with serious mental disorders may be expected.

In a more recent study, the Federation of Disability Organizations in Malaŵi (FEDOMA) in cooperation with the Foundation for Scientific and Industrial Research at the Norwegian Institute of Technology (SINTEF) provide a more comprehensive account of the prevalence of disability in Malaŵi (Loeb & Eide [eds.] 2004). While the percentage of households with members with a disability

61 School education as well as vocational skills training was therefore reported as low. Only 42 percent of persons with disabilities had over 5 years or school education while secondary school was attended by a total of 4 percent of the affected persons. Only 36 percent of persons with epilepsy and 41 percent of the mentally ill attended any kind of formal school training. Still, disabled persons were generally found to be integrated into cultural work processes: only 30 percent of the disabled population of Malaŵi stated to do no work at all, whereas 39 percent were occupied with farming and/or fishing and 26 percent performed household duties (NSO 1987: 6-8).

is virtually unchanged at 10.6 percent in this second survey, the overall picture still indicates significant differences to the 1983 census (see *Table 3*).[62] In contrast to the earlier survey, the various districts now show considerable variations in terms of the prevalence of disabilities among the population (Loeb 2004a: 82-83). The mental health situation of persons with disabilities was investigated by means of patient self-evaluation. Due to their results, the self-perception of poor mental health frequently goes along with a more severe case of disability, indicating that

> "In other words, and not unexpectedly, physical and mental health and disability are correlated. Those who experience poor physical or mental health also experience higher levels of need for assistance in carrying out daily activities as well as more activity limitations and participation restrictions" (Loeb 2004a: 135).

This study also gives some indication of the assumed reasons for the condition, alluding to the width of explanatory models as well as their relative prevalence (Loeb 2004a: 108).[63] Further on, the educational and professional background of persons with disabilities receives some special attention, indicating that disability severely exacerbates the already difficult economic situation of people in Southern Malaŵi.[64] Here, the category of 'mental and/or emotional disabilities' stands out, indicating the cases to be the most severe with regard of the persons'

---

62 Once more, the southern Region stands out with the highest percentage (11.4 percent) of households with disabled household members (Loeb 2004a: 82). In the overall identification of the phenomenon, the definition of disability is clearly a crucial issue. Arne Eide and Mitch Loeb address this problem, giving official numbers according to which high-income countries like Norway (17.8), Spain, the USA (both 15.0), Canada (14.7) or Germany (8.4 percent) have a much higher prevalence of disability then low-income countries such as Kenya (0.7), South Africa, Zambia (both 0.9), Zimbabwe (1.9), or Malaŵi (2.9 percent). This underlines the fact that statistical numbers on disability tend to lack comparability due to diverging definitions and research techniques applied (Eide & Loeb 2004b: 51).

63 In systematic order of their assumed prevalence, the causes mentioned include physical illness (48.3), 'natural' (17.2), accident (10.6), witchcraft (3.8), mental illness (3.2), animal related (1.0), violence (0.6), alcohol and drug abuse (0.3) as well as other reasons (14.9) (Loeb 2004a: 108). Due to the high importance of explanatory models within the framework of the present research and the dire need for further clarification, this complex will be elaborated at greater length in a following chapter (see *Chapter IV*).

64 34.8 percent of the persons with disabilities in Malaŵi reportedly do not receive formal education, compared to 19.7 percent of the non-disabled population. Here, persons with psychological disabilities are disproportionately represented with more than 36 percent. Over 61 percent of the disabled population are illiterate, and accordingly, the employment conditions for persons with disabilities are critical. 58.8 percent of persons with disabilities attested to have no professional skills, and 57.7 percent described themselves as unemployed while 47.6 percent of the disabled persons aged 15 and older even attested never having held any employment position. Vocational training as well as welfare services are reported to be not appropriately available, with only 5 percent of the respondents who expressed demand actually had access to such facilities (Loeb 2004a: 86-93, 117; Loeb & Eide 2004: 16).

activity limitations and participation restrictions. Accordingly, the affected people show the highest dependency in performing daily activities and the highest need for specialized services. At the same time, the condition of persons with mental/emotional disabilities is shown to be worse than that of all other types of disability with respect to activities such as learning and knowledge, communication, self care, domestic life, interpersonal behaviour, major life areas, as well as community and social life (Loeb 2004a: 129-130).[65]

In spite of formal and methodological differences, a careful comparison of the two surveys leads to a number of important results. A rise from 190,000 persons or 2.9 percent of the total population in 1983 up to 480,000 and 4.2 percent in 2003 clearly represents a conundrum. It may either be seen as a highly concerning development in itself or as an additional indicator of the lacking ontological clarity as to what disability represents and, hence, should be counted as one. Still, an increase of the occurrence rate of about 30 percent over a twenty years' period, and a growth of 150 percent in terms of the persons affected by disability clearly suggests that the phenomenon demands immediate attention on the political, medical, and social levels. While different definitions of disability and activity limitations restrict direct comparability, these numbers underline the high – yet continually growing – importance of disability in Malaŵi. At the same time, it has been illustrated that national health facilities do not have the appropriate means to effectively tackle the challenges set out for them, leaving the thus unsatisfied medical demands to be met by other, alternative practices of medical service which thereby take an increasingly important position within public medical discourse. But while infrastructural, political, and developmental conditions undoubtedly form a crucial obstacle for the general well-being of persons with mental disorders in Southern Malaŵi, other, more internal factors have an equally considerable impact on the issue. It is these cultural issues that are of central interest in an anthropological line of argument, and they must be seen in the context of the cosmological, religious, philosophical comprehension of the world as a whole and of health problems in particular.

In part, the challenges affecting persons with mental disorder in Malaŵi are located on a structural level. While issues of biomedical public health care and its accessibility certainly have a considerable impact on the living conditions on the ground, it would be highly misleading to consider this as a singular contributor to the situation as such. Accommodating its anthropological

---

65 Here, Mitch Loeb states that "Generally speaking this indicates that individuals with mental/emotional disabilities experience significantly greater difficulty in performing day to day activities without assistance and are to a greater extend unable to perform daily activities in their current environment. In other words they experience more barriers to full participation in society" (Loeb 2004a: 131).

orientation, this thesis focuses on the diverse cultural factors that influence – or, essentially, define – the conceptualization of mental disorder in Southern Malaŵi. A more in-depth understanding of the cultural notions connected to issues of mental disorder is required in order to comprehend its complexities.

Map 1: District Map of Malaŵi (SAHIMS 2002)

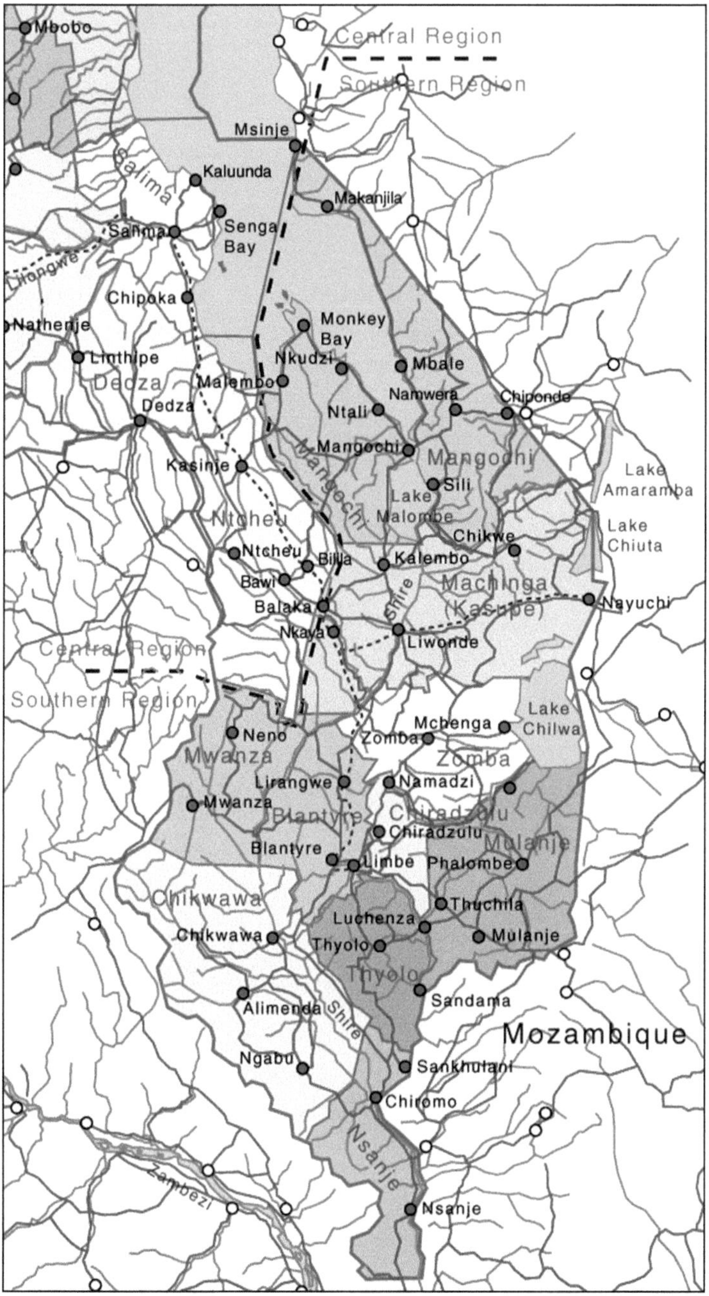

Map 2: Map of Southern Malaŵi (White Fathers 2007)

II.

Cultural Conditions

As in any given culture, mental disorder is a part of social life in Southern Malaŵi, and it is represented by – and incorporated in – different cultures on various levels. The construction of this phenomenon reflects sets of values which are specific to a cultural setting which is determined by a pluralism of social processes, thus incorporating traditional representations as well as issues of Western science, mainstream cosmopolitan religion, or international legislation. The living conditions of persons suffering from mental disorders within the complex cultural framework of Southern Malaŵi are therefore defined by diverse factors of cultural representation which require closer clarification and analysis. Presenting the cultural basis for the study as a whole, the present chapter explicitly considers its heterogeneity, cultural dynamics, and historical genesis, offering results of in-depth field research as concerning the representations of mental disorder within the different spheres of cultural life.

1. Mental Disorder in Oral and Ritual Tradition

A cultural concept of mental disorder is not an isolated idea. Rather, the emic construction of such a phenomenon manifests itself on various levels of cultural life and is part of a rich social discourse. The various societies in Southern Malaŵi represent and reflect mental disorder in different social spheres, and it becomes manifest in cultural contexts such as initiatory teachings, ritual performance, and oral literature.

1(a) Normative Traditions

Cultural norms are an integral part of any form of social life, expressing underlying values which, in essence, constitute the core structures of society as a whole. If made explicit – in the form of behavioural guidelines of either positive (instruction) or negative (avoidance) character –, such normative rules may serve as indicators for the general cultural conception of a certain phenomenon within its emic frame of reference. In Chicheŵa, the term *mwambo* (pl. *miyambo*) is applied for a wide variety of normative rules of social conduct, encompassing both positive and negative directives.[1] In other words, they predefine what a person should and should not do – and, for obvious reasons, instructions in some way referring to mental disorder are of particular interest here.

As a central part of cultural life, the basic dos-and-don'ts provided through the *miyambo* create a fairly tightly knit structure of cultural norms which, if observed correctly, constitute socially accepted and validated behaviour. While initiation rituals may be the classical setting for formal cultural education, many *miyambo* are also part of a more general understanding of appropriate social conduct, being therefore conveyed in a more informal context, e.g. from parents onto their children. It is, however, difficult to classify *miyambo* according to the specific time and space of their conveyance as their knowledge transcends the secrecy of a given ritual instruction and circulates freely through the different spheres of society. Examining the representation of mental disorder within traditional *mwambo* norms, the present section therefore distinguishes different kinds of cultural norms according to functional criteria.

As one of their most basic and obvious functions, the *miyambo* form an elementary regulatory force within Malaŵian society, re-creating the connection between the social *status quo* of personal lives and the cosmological order – as, in a traditional framework, represented by mythic tradition and the ancestral spirits (*mizimu*) who are seen as the guardians of the *miyambo* (see *Chapter II.1.a*). After all, these traditional norms are said to exist

> "Because of the ancestors, people who began this a long time ago. We also try to follow, and even if it fails, we have still observed it" (Olive Pilimiti, a Nyanja *mzamba*).

The violation of *miyambo* is seen as a serious offence which may lead to punishment by the spirits, but also by the Supreme Being itself – thus underlining the strong structural connection between the *miyambo* and traditional cosmological concepts. The applicability of a given *mwambo* may, at the same time, vary immensely. While some *miyambo* are recognized *quasi*-universally among the ethnic groups of the Southern Region, others may have a more specific character, and many Malaŵian clans (*chiwongo*) or kinship groups (*chibale*) have their own additional sets of behavioural prescriptions – e.g. food

---

1 The semantic field of the term *mwambo*, in fact, encompasses meanings such as tradition, ceremony, custom, and function (Paas 2004: 306). For the scope of this study, 'tradition' or 'custom' may be pointed out as core meanings.

restrictions – which only apply for this small group of people.[2] The basic function underlying all *miyambo* on some level is therefore the embodiment of cosmological structure and social group identity. More particularly, a number of immediate functional categories may be distinguished according to the rules imparted by them, creating the link to questions of social conduct.

The maintaining of social structures is, as mentioned already, a key function underlying all traditional teachings,[3] and numerous *miyambo* taught especially in a ritual context focus on the protection of the socially deprived. In this context, the demand for considerate behaviour towards persons with mental disorders – and persons with health disorders in general – are a typical feature of initiatory teaching across the various ethnic groups of Southern Malaŵi. Many Mang'anja and Lomwe likewise remember such instructions as part of their own past initiations, and a Yao *mfumu* reports that traditional instructions in his community always include teaching youngsters not to insult or abuse persons suffering from mental disorders.[4] The latter statement alludes to a well-documented *mwambo* which, due to its wide cross-ethnic occurrence, represents an almost commonsensical idea in Southern Malaŵi. This most frequently mentioned *mwambo* with respect to mental disorder advises people never to mock or ridicule persons with mental disorders – especially by means of pointing and laughing. Typically, this kind of abuse against a person with a mental disorder is said to bring about the same condition to the mocker or a member of his or her own kin-group. Here, the behaviour of pregnant women is particularly significant as their misconduct is expected to cause mental disorder to their unborn children.[5]

---

2 Accordingly, "each clan has got its own rules, so to say. Things they follow, their own beliefs. [...] You can be punished so that you follow the *miyambo*" (Miriam Namanja, a Yao disability organization representative).

3 Therefore, "you should respect the elders but also kneel down to the chief if he wants to speak to you – these are teachings that help that the children should give respect to the elders" (Josephine Maboma, a Lomwe *mzamba*).

4 Accordingly, "This [i.e. mental disorder] is a sickness, so people do not laugh. Can a person laugh at someone who is suffering? No!" (Doreen Masamba, a Yao *mzamba*).

5 As a variation of this motif, a Yao *mzamba* instructs people "that they should not laugh about *kupunduka* because of being afraid just to stay laughing ceaselessly. But also not to stare at them going by, for fear of getting a twisted neck" (Joyce Chawa, a Yao *mzamba*). Another Yao *mzamba* shares this notion, adding that pointing at a person with a mental disorder would make the finger always point in the respective direction like a compass – e.g. North. On some occasions, people express the notion that persons with mental disorders might also possess secret magical powers, and that behavioural rules demanding respect for the disadvantaged are a measure to avoid provocation. Therefore, "You should not laugh about the *opunduka* persons [...]. They fear that if you would laugh about them, they would happen to give birth to an *opunduka* child, but they are also told not to stare for a long time, fearing that they could bewitch [*kulodza*] them to look the same as them" (Josephine Maboma, a Lomwe *mzamba*). This notion refers to some proverbs analysed elsewhere (see *Chapter II.1.c*).

While the socially protective function of *miyambo* mentioned in this context aims at alleviating social pressure from people suffering from mental disorder, their function may, at the same time, also focus on the prevention of mental disorder. Like the aforementioned cases of social prohibition against ridiculing disadvantaged persons, a large number of the *miyambo* relevant in the context of this study are connected to behavioural rules affecting the sphere of human reproduction – this being female menstruation, sexuality, pregnancy, and childbirth. Therefore, a whole set of *miyambo* regulates the appropriate times for sexual contact between marriage partners, their violation usually resulting in death, mental disorder, or related conditions – such as *tsempho-mdulo* contamination (see below).

All of the ethnic groups in Southern Malaŵi recognize certain cultural rules (*miyambo*) which regulate sexual behaviour, and mental disorder is one of the most frequently mentioned outcomes of sexual misconduct. Yao notions, therefore, indicate that mental disorder as well as physical impairments may be caused by parents performing culturally disapproved forms of sexual intercourse.[6] Among the Sena, it is expressed that parents can cause mental as well as other kinds of disorder to their children by having intercourse while the child is outside the house. This action is compared to abandoning the child, or 'like throwing it away'. The general rule of abstaining from sexual contact at times when the children are outside the house applies up to six years of the child's age.[7]

In the traditions of the ethnic groups of Southern Malaŵi, the observation of certain periods of sexual abstinence play an important role – this being during menstruation as well as sometime before and after the delivery of a child. The knowledge of these instructions is part of initiatory teachings and shows some variations between the respective ethnic groups. In general agreement between Cheŵa, Nyanja, Mang'anja, and Ngoni data, parents must abstain from sexual activity from the seventh month of pregnancy until six months after the delivery or the child would suffer from severe mental disorder. Many Sena likewise confirm this general notion[8] while Yao tend to concede that a child would be

6 Here, one account graphically relates to *coitus a posteriori* or sexual intercourse 'from behind'. According to him, this position would be considered as 'twisted and the wrong way round' so that a child conceived in this fashion would show signs of deviation reflecting its 'twisted' mode of conception.

7 According to a Yao *shehe*, premarital intercourse may be a reason for receiving a child with a mental disorder. This is caused by angry ancestral spirits who would be addressed as *mazimu mwa atsempha* in Chiyao, thus referring directly to the notion of *tsempho* or *mdulo* contamination (see below).

8 A discourse among a Sena group, however, addresses the question whether or not a couple had to abstain during or after pregnancy at all. While a professional health worker insists that a child would be born with a mental disorder if the parents had intercourse after the fifth month of

born with a mental disorder if the parents have intercourse during the prohibited time – lasting from the sixth month of pregnancy to the sixth month after birth according to Yao tradition.[9] A Lomwe healer also explains that a woman should not be sexually active after the fifth month of pregnancy. Before that, though, frequent intercourse would have a strengthening effect on the unborn child.[10] After childbirth, parents have to abstain for eight months according to Lomwe *miyambo*, or the child would start suffering from mental disorder.

Apart from sexual activity, it has been mentioned that the observation of special *miyambo* is also perceived as being particularly important during critical periods of life such as pregnancy. Among all the ethnic groups of Southern Malaŵi, women with children frequently have knowledge of a number of these behavioural rules, and it is common for a pregnant woman to strictly observe those *miyambo* she knows or regards as relevant for her. The prescriptions that may require adherence are manifold:

> "That is, they say that while you are pregnant, […] do not stop at the doorstep, do not sit on the doorstep or you would deliver a child with *kupunduka*. But they also say not to laugh at a disabled person, not even to point a finger, not to drink water while standing, also not to laugh at the elders while you are pregnant or you will deliver an *opunduka* child" (Iselda Tchema, a Yao *mzamba*).

Pregnant women – or rather, their unborn offspring – are seen as particularly easy prey to the evil deeds of *ufiti* magic (see *Chapter IV.1.a*). Therefore, women are advised not to wander around during pregnancy in order not to be targeted, and not to eat market food in order to avoid magic attacks. Also, the unchecked spiritual power summoned during the dance ceremonies of the *nyau* secret society (the *gule wamkulu*, see below) is considered potentially dangerous to pregnant women. Therefore, Sena women are advised not to watch these dances

---

pregnancy, a *mfumu* emphasizes that no period of abstinence is required before birth. Nonetheless, he elaborates that a man having sexual contact with a woman during the first six months after delivery – or abortion – would die on the same day. This sickness would be considered as *chitayo* (see *Apendix 1*). According to him, Sena parents usually tell their daughters when to resume sexual relationships with the husband after delivery. The new beginning of sexual activity is initiated in a ritual performance during which the wife's parents bring some *ufa* flour to the couple's house, and the mother puts a bit of it under the child's mat. While the couple can now commence sexual activity again, all her relatives in the village have to abstain on this first day or be punished by the ancestral spirits.

9 As a Muslim leader explains, a woman is considered impure during the mentioned period after delivery, and sexual activity would cause post-natal damage – especially in the form of mental disorders – to the child.

10 Here, the excess semen inside the womb is described as increasing the child's strength. When ceasing sexual activity, a Lomwe woman is advised to eat lots of *terere* (i.e. okra or *Abelmoschus esculentus*) to substitute it – which might be interpreted as symbolic due to the *terere*'s slippery texture and its vaguely phallic form. When lacking semen or *terere*, miscarriages or mental disorders on the side of the child are given as possible consequences.

during pregnancy in order “to avoid giving birth to something wild”, i.e. resembling the mask characters.[11] During pregnancy, Yao women are also advised not to attend funerals, indicating that their children would be either stillborn or otherwise suffer from mental disorder. Among the Lomwe, a *mwambo* demands pregnant women not to stay seated in one spot for a longer period of time “for fear that if you stay where you are, so would your child” – thus trying to counteract the risk of delayed birth, a condition closely associated with the occurrence of mental disorder. At the same time, certain *miyambo* also address the behaviour of a pregnant woman’s husband. Therefore, the members of different ethnic groups agree that a man should not physically abuse his pregnant wife for fear of causing mental disorder in the unborn child. A pregnant woman should also be fed well so she can give strength to the child, and husbands should avoid quarrelling with their pregnant wives in order not to upset the ancestors who might punish the unborn children with mental disorders. Unfaithfulness of the husband during his wife’s pregnancy is a frequently reported explanation for mental disorder in a child.

Among the Yao, a pregnant woman is advised to wear a string around her waist in order to ‘stabilize’ the child inside the womb, and to remove the string right before birth in order to ensure safe delivery. Among the Sena, a mother is told not to press her baby too close while breastfeeding in order not to suffocate the child or cause mental disorder, and pregnant women should not sleep on their bellies to prevent the brain of the child from being damaged.[12] Sena women are told to avoid using the pit latrine during pregnancy because bad smells could enter her body and cause problems such as mental disorder to the unborn child.[13] According to a Mang’anja *grupu*, women are advised never to take honey during pregnancy because honey is known to make a person salivate excessively. This condition could be transmitted unto the unborn child, causing it to salivate ceaselessly – a typical symptom of mental disorder. Likewise, pregnant Yao women used to be told to avoid eggs so their children should not be born with a small head, a condition associated with mental disorder.

A whole set of *miyambo* serves to avoid a condition that is described as *mdulo* or *tsempho* – two broadly equivalent categories which are associated with

---

11 All in all, “people are told never to point at a grave – if you do, you are going to have the fingers disabled. When you are pregnant, never watch *gule wamkulu* – or you will give birth to a disabled child. When you see the elderly, you have to kneel down – otherwise they might curse you and you will give birth to a disabled child” (Miriam Namanja, a Yao disability organization representative).

12 Likewise, Sena mothers are advised to safeguard that none of the mother’s milk touches a baby boy’s penis – which would cause him to become impotent.

13 A health professional explains that Sena women would therefore go into the bush to defecate during pregnancy – which he considers a health issue with respect to a high cholera risk.

the occurrence of various life-threatening situations including mental disorder.[14] In spite of the complexity of these emic categories, it may suffice here to specify that *mdulo* implies a notion of symbolic temperature that is widely recognized among the various ethnic groups of Southern Malaŵi.[15] Due to the idea that direct contact with a symbolically 'hot' person poses considerable danger to the life and wellbeing of a 'colder' one, a number of *miyambo* restrict and regulate social interaction in situations associated with 'hot' symbolic conditions – such as menstruation, (especially adulterous) sexual intercourse, or bloodshed.[16] The potential consequences of contamination with symbolic 'heat' include different kinds of health problems – including forms of mental disorder – as well as death. The prevalence of the idea of *mdulo* is considerable. Especially in some rural contexts, the violation of *miyambo* social rules for the avoidance of *mdulo* contamination is among the first assumptions made if the development of a young child does not progress as expected.

Among the various culturally recognized lines of transmission, sexual intercourse, the eating of salt (*mchere*, see below) as well as close body contact constitute the most typical notions. What is crucial in the understanding of *mdulo* is that it's negative, contaminating effect is not necessarily limited to a direct contagion, but that it incorporates more complex social mechanisms. Children are generally considered as symbolically cold and extremely vulnerable to 'hot' states, and they may be easily affected by their parents' violations of *miyambo* for *mdulo* avoidance. Once a child is thus contaminated with *mdulo*, its condition may develop into different forms of mental disorder. The most common notion of *mdulo* causation is that of a wife adding salt into her husband's relish during menstruation or pregnancy, thus causing severe health disorder to the spouse and potential mental disorder to her unborn child.[17] Likewise, committing adultery during pregnancy or shortly after the birth of a child bears severe danger of producing *mdulo* contamination.[18] It should be outlined that, according to the

---

14 For the sake of easy reference, this complex will be addressed here under the more commonly applied term *mdulo*.

15 Sometimes interpreted as an originally Cheŵa notion, the concept of *mdulo* is also mentioned by members of Nyanja, Yao, Lomwe, Mang'anja, and Ngoni ethnic groups – thus claiming a considerable degree of cross-ethnic validity in the Southern Region.

16 Accordingly, "*mdulo* is not a rigid, clear cut system of encoded prescriptions for behaviour but rather something highly ambivalent and ambiguous" (Probst 1995: 10). Nonetheless, certain behavioural norms do find widespread cultural recognition in the attempt of avoiding *mdulo* contamination.

17 As a practical solution, mothers usually ask their small children to add salt to the dishes.

18 The condition of a child suffering from *mdulo* may hence be a consequence of a father being unfaithful to his wife during pregnancy. If either marriage partner involves in extramarital sex after the death of their child, they also produce ritual 'heat' that can cause *mdulo* when transmitted by either salt or sexual contact. Moreover, a husband may involuntarily kill his child during the first six months after birth if he touches his child after engaging in extramarital

data presented here, regulations concerning the prevention of *mdulo* closely correspond with other sets of behavioural norms as depicted above. Despite its specific temperature symbolism, *mdulo* contamination follows the same cultural structures as other *mwambo* violations.

Among the different ethnic groups of Southern Malaŵi, traditional normative rules of behaviour invariably act as important markers for the cultural interpretation of ontological reality and as standards for socially validated behaviour. Their importance is underlined not only by a number of case samples but is also emphatically supported. When asked about potential reasons for their given case, many parents of children with mental disorders emphasize that all the *miyambo* they were aware of had been followed. In turn, this corresponds with the frequently expressed notion that mental disorder in a newborn child occurs more frequently in first-born children – due to the parents' unfortunate ignorance of all the appropriate *miyambo*.[19]

1(b) Ritual Embedding

Rituals – in the sense of "stereotyped sequence of activities involving gestures, words, and objects, performed in a sequenced place, and designed to influence preternatural entities or forces on behalf of the actors' goals and interests" (Turner 1989: 55) – are a central part of cultural life within the various ethnic groups in Southern Malaŵi. Ritual activity may be seasonal, but it may also be contingent in the way that it, in particular, relates to the life cycle and to the veneration of ancestor spirits as well as the Supreme Being.

Numerous rituals are held in honour of the ancestor spirits (*mizimu ya makolo*), and they are conducted periodically in order to maintain mutual consent with the spirit world. Among the Lomwe, it is considered necessary that every village performs an annual beer brewing fest during which the ancestor spirits receive copious offerings. By thus perpetuating good relationships with the *mizimu*, the community means to avert potential misfortune – including droughts and floods, but also the birth of children with mental disorders. Maintaining harmonic relationships with the ancestral spirits is considered crucial in any period of life but, most especially, in the context of rites of passage, including

intercourse – a period that is defined as the time required for the child's navel to heal. Likewise, a woman having sexual contact during the prohibited time after delivery can cause *mdulo* in her newborn child.

19 In some cases, parents take a pseudo-empirical perspective by pointing out that a given case of mental disorder occurring in a second-born or subsequent child cannot be caused by *mwambo* violation due to the fact that they observed the same rules as during previous pregnancies – which went without complications.

not only marriage but also pregnancy and birth.[20] Rites of passage provide the basic structure not only for a person's life but for society as such. Malaŵian concepts of the person as such are based on the notion of human development as a continuous process of growth and status accumulation, expressing itself in different stages of initiation that mark the various levels of progressing humanization.[21]

While the various ethnic groups of Southern Malaŵi have different initiatory rituals, the patterns underlying these are comparable in the way they identify the main passages in social life – such as the first recognition of pregnancy (*chiyembekezo*)[22] transforming persons into parents-to-be, birth (*chikuta*), or a child's initiation into society (*chinamwali*) by which "a new human being is born out of the symbolic womb of the values and ideas of a particular tradition and culture" (Chigona 2002: 39). Most initiatory rituals are conducted by initiation specialists, with titles like *namkungwi* or *mulangiza* indicating a senior adviser or initiator while the *ngaliba*, responsible for supervising male initiation ceremonies among the Yao, may also act as a circumciser.[23] In other communities, the elders are responsible for performing initiation rituals.

The following section does not attempt to compile exhaustive descriptive data on initiatory rituals as performed among the different ethnic groups of Southern Malaŵi. By providing concise information on the general structure of ritual life, it rather aims to exemplify the framework within which cultural knowledge is being transported, thereby creating the logic context for the accounts of traditional instructions (*miyambo*) as mentioned earlier as well as for the section on Malaŵian concepts of the person (see *Chapter III.1.a*). At the same time, the relevance of particular rituals within the cultural discourse of mental disorder will also be illustrated.

---

20 As a common ritual among the Cheŵa, Mang'anja, and Ngoni in Malaŵi, the relatives of a pregnant woman bring a sacrifice of *ufa* to the ancestral spirits under an *akesha* tree. When the flour is gone after some time, it is assumed that the *mizimu* are content and grant their protection for the unborn child. According to a Ngoni pastor, other trees can be used alternatively, including the Baobab (*Adansonia digitata*) and the *ngongomwa* tree. As he rationalizes, all of the trees mentioned are usually inhabited by ants which, according to his suspicion, may be responsible for eating the *ufa* flour – although their activity is ascribed to the ancestral spirits.

21 The great importance of initiation in Lomwe society, e.g., is well demonstrated by Francis Bonongwe who states that "In most traditional African societies, not birth, but socialization and initiation, made the person a member of the community" (Bonongwe 2005: 9).

22 Gerard Chigona, however, describes the *chiyembekezo* stage of pregnancy as being connected to hope for the growth of family and community, but also with fears "about whether the woman will survive especially at delivery, or whether what will come out of her will be something other than a human being" (Chigona 2002: 40). This shall be discussed later on (see *Chapter III.1.a*).

23 In Chiyao, the alternative title *nakanga* applies to both female and male initiation specialists.

Birth Rituals

Birth always marks an important initiatory step in the life of a person – for most obvious reasons of its physical emergence from the mother's womb, but equally so in social terms –, and the birth of a child is therefore a frequent focus of ritual activity. In Southern Malaŵi, varying ritual traditions surround childbirth, but all these important rituals are invariably surrounded by behavioural rules (*miyambo*) which have to be followed in order to ensure the well-being of the newborn child. The compliance with the behavioural rules as depicted earlier are partially under the responsibility of traditional birth attendants (*azamba*) who, doubling as ritual specialists, impart the respective *miyambo* to a pregnant woman.

In general, birth rituals such as the Cheŵa *kudabwa kwa mwana* are a female domain, being conducted in a delivery house (*chikuta*) and observed exclusively by women.[24] Yao ceremonies are structurally similar to those of the Cheŵa even though some ritual sequences indicate Muslim influence,[25] and other groups – such as the Ngoni and Lomwe – also have comparable traditions.[26] In essence, the delivery itself as well as its preparation is usually connected to considerable

---

24 The exodus of mother and child from the delivery house (*kutulutsa chikuta*), happening some days after the delivery, is accompanied by the washing of the child (*kusambitsa mwana*) which is seen as the first initiation of the newborn child into society (Bruwer 1955: 121). At this point, the child is shaved, named, and handed over an open fire. After one to three months, the first smile of the child indicates the right time to introduce the child into the extended family by performing the *kutenga mwana* or 'taking in the child' (Marwick 1965: 66). At this point, the parents resume their sexual relations, the child is no longer considered fragile, and in case of its death, it receives a normal burial.

25 A Yao mother and child are confined to the delivery house (*chilowero*) until the naming ceremony (*kupereka lina*) and the subsequent coming-out ritual (*kuposiya chilowero*) are conducted about one week after birth. By shaving the child's head, it becomes a full member of the kin- group. Muslim influence is incorporated in the washing of the child (*kusingula*) which takes place at the point of the mother leaving the maternity house. In case that the ritual cannot be held at this day – due to the bad condition of the child, the mother, or other eventualities –, the ceremony is held at a later point, but always a full week after birth, i.e. 14 or 21 days after the event. In Islamic tradition, the *akika* ritual must also be observed seven days after the birth of a child. Parallel to the *kupereka lina*, it constitutes the initiation of the newborn into society as demonstrated by a naming ceremony. Male children frequently receive circumcision at this point. The celebration accompanying the *akika* is described as implying the slaughtering of goats for communal meals.

26 In Ngoni tradition, the women attending to the birth remove the husband's belongings from the house. After delivery, the mother – as well as her child and the house – remains secluded until being ritually purified from the pollution caused by the process of birth. About ten to 14 days after birth, the child is received into society in a coming-out ritual, is named and introduced into the mother's family by visiting her home village. Among the Lomwe, the birth of a child also requires some ritual actions to place it under the protection of the ancestral spirits (*mizimu*). In this case, disobeying the traditions of giving *mankhwala a zisamba* (or 'medicine for the firstborn') to the infant would put it into great danger of contracting a mental disorder. Soon after birth, the Lomwe also perform a ritual dance called *likwata*.

ritual efforts to safeguard the health of mother and child, and the birth is always followed by a fragile liminal period which ends with the formal ritual introduction of the child into society.

Cosmopolitan religions also provide rituals for the formal introduction of a child into society. While Islam offers initiation to any child, it has been observed that children with mental disorders are sometimes excluded from this due to the wish of the parents who do not see the necessity for their child to get baptized. In a Christian context, the introduction of the person with mental disorder into the community of the faithful by means of baptism is described as equally indiscriminate – while facing the same problems of parent response. A Lomwe Catholic priest addresses the applicability of this ritual initiation, explaining that

> "People who receive baptism are those who have asked for baptism. When it is a child, we look into the religious background of the parents, and when it is a mad person, we look into the level of madness. If it is the kind of madness which comes and goes, then no problem – we can even anoint the person. And if not, then we first of all find the reason for the madness. And if the reason is there, then no problem – we anoint and baptize the person" (Evans Cholo, a Lomwe Catholic priest).

Maturity Rituals

Marking the transition from childhood into adulthood, maturity rituals have a particular high cultural importance in Southern Malaŵi. As a general function, the initiation into adult life focuses on preparing young men and women for their future position – especially concerning sexuality, gender roles, and parenthood – in society, and this is achieved mainly by conveying behavioural norms during extended periods of social seclusion. Accordingly, the first female initiation among the Cheŵa – called *kangali* – prepares young girls for puberty while the following *chinamwali* marks the first menstruation of a girl.[27] For Cheŵa boys, initiation into the male secret society (*nyau*) constitutes the most important passage. The Yao girls' initiation called *chiputu* is also conducted before the first menstruation,[28] and it is followed by the *chabulika*, a one-day ritual that takes place immediately after a girl's first menstruation. Yao boys undergo the *jando*

---

27 Over a period of two weeks, girls stay at a secluded house without contact to anyone but their *anamkungwi*. They have to observe strict rules of hygiene and avoid salt in their diet. At the final day, the girls, only wearing a loin cloth, appear among the initiated women. Their heads are shaved and subsequently painted with white and red dots. Lastly, the elder women carry the newly initiated through the village and to the *dambwe* (or gathering place), where singing, dancing, and ululating follow.

28 Recently, the *chiputu* ritual is sometimes replaced by the *msondo* ritual which is performed around the age of eight years. The *msondo* is performed during a two-week seclusion in the initiation house (*ndagala*).

at an approximate age of 15 years,[29] and are encouraged to find a partner for their first sexual experiences shortly afterwards.[30] Among the Ngoni people, female maturity rituals have a more private character so that, during a seclusion period of up to three months, girls are instructed by their father's mother at the beginning of their menstruation while Ngoni boys receive instructions from elder boys as well as their father. For the Lomwe, the *dzoma* boys' initiation marks the transition from childhood to adulthood (Bonongwe 2005: 7), and Sena puberty rites take four days for both girls and boys alike.[31]

While different forms of maturity rituals have been performed by the different ethnic groups, endeavours are presently made to bridge these gaps and introduce more generalized initiation rituals. Therefore, some Christian churches in Malaŵi – such as the Presbyterian CCAP or the Roman Catholic Church – are encouraging the newly-created *chidototo* male initiation. This ritual, independently from ethnic affiliation, is meant to replace traditional initiations which still display a strong connection to traditional, non-Christian religions.[32] Analogously, the female initiation ritual of *chinamwali* is presently described as being widely independent from creed or ethnic background.[33] Maturity rituals are among the most central occasions for imparting *miyambo* rules of conduct. While the instructions taught in this ritual context may vary widely – e.g. including advice on child care and nurturing along with prescriptions meant to avoid magic attacks or offending ancestor spirits[34] – many of these *miyambo*

---

29 Unless already circumcised, the circumcision of Yao boys is performed during the *jando*, hereby formally introducing them into the adult world. During a full month's seclusion in the initiation house (*ndagala*), they receive teachings to prepare the young men for sex and married life. Equivalent to the female *msondo*, they receive lessons about how to conduct sexual intercourse as well as the need to remain faithful to a wife during and after her pregnancy. The *jando* combines Muslim influences (e.g. circumcision) with traditional elements – such as drumming and dancing. At present, even Christian Yao frequently participate in it. After the *jando*, the boys should not be washed by their mothers anymore, thereby keeping up a ritual secrecy of the circumcision.

30 This is referred to as *kuchotsa fumbi* or 'removing the ashes'.

31 During this female *kuvinira* initiation, the girls are kept in seclusion for three days, and while walking naked all through this time, they receive teachings on adulthood. The ritual culminates in the reintegration of the girls into society, being accompanied with excessive public dancing

32 The initiation includes a whole month of seclusion during which the boys stay in a house near a river. Similarly, a male initiation called *lupanda* is mentioned as being held independently from ethnic group or religion, and which is associated with high status.

33 The introduction of a Christian female initiation ritual overcoming ethnic boundaries is addressed by a study on the *chilangizo* ritual in Malaŵi (Longue 2003).

34 With respect to the girl's initiation or *chinamwali*, a Nyanja birth attendant illustrates this difference by stating that "These women [i.e. teachers at *chinamwali* initiations] advise them not to wear tight clothes for fear of squeezing the child which can cause the child not to be born alright. But also, they are told not to eat food that is bought on the market, ready-cooked, but to eat what they cooked themselves at home" (Olive Pilimiti, a Nyanja *mzamba*).

tackle the question of mental disorder and its avoidance. A Yao *mzamba* describes her role accordingly:

> "I am also an instructor at the girls' initiations [*mulangiza wa chinamwali*], therefore we advise them not to laugh at *opunduka* persons because they do not want to be like that either. [...] We also teach them that they always have to help these persons who cannot work for themselves, and that they should always respect these persons as well as those with *kupunduka*" (Gift Makata, a Yao *mzamba*).

Marriage and Parenthood Rituals

In the context of marriage and procreation, another complex of rituals is observed by the different ethnic groups of the country, and many sets of behavioural rules that were already taught in maturity rituals are expanded, emphasized, and elaborated in marriage rituals. Among the Chewa, e.g., wedding arrangements are made by the representatives (*ankhoswe*) of both kinship groups – usually the elder brothers (*mchimwene wamkulu*) or maternal uncles (*malume*) – before the wedding proper introduces the husband into his wife's matrilineage. Before pregnancy, a Chewa woman is then instructed by her mother, her mother-in-law (*mpongozi mwa akazi*), and the female instructors (*anamkungwi*) from both communities. Towards the end of a woman's first pregnancy, the *litiwo* (or 'first born') ritual is performed to educate her on the delivery and the subsequent birth rituals as explained earlier. In Ngoni tradition, only girls with a high status undergo the pre-marriage *umsindo* ritual meant to display the wealth of the family and prove the virginity of the bride-to-be. The marriage formalities are arranged by go-betweens – usually the paternal uncles of both the future spouses –, and a bride price (*lobola*) is agreed on.[35] Sena marriages also include the institution of *lobola*, but the bride is instructed on her future role as wife and mother through the *kulowa banja* (or 'entering the family') ritual.[36]

The observation of *miyambo* rules is crucially important in the context of marriage rituals, and the ancestral spirits serve as guardians of these traditions. Among the Yao, it is therefore stated that a wedding ritual that is not performed according to traditional norms may lead to the bridal couple receiving offspring with a mental disorder – the idea being that the *mizimu* punish the newlyweds for their wrongdoing.

---

35 For the wedding proper (*mtimba*), the bride receives additional instructions on right behaviour in her future family, and would then be received in the bridegroom's village with singing and dancing.

36 After the groom-to-be and his future wife reach agreement to get married, the man contacts the woman's family and agrees with them on a *lobola* which depends on the bride's family – and which can easily exceed 20,000 MwK.

Funerary and Commemorative Rituals

A somewhat difficult case of mental disorder being related to ritual performance addresses the Malaŵian tradition of *kulowa kufa*. This ritual – literally translated from Chicheŵa as 'entering death' but usually explained as 'chasing away death' – is traditionally associated with the Sena but also partially practiced by a number of other ethnic groups. *Kulowa kufa* is held a day after the funeral of a married man when his patrilineage holds council and discusses the future of the widow and the orphaned children. If it is agreed that the widow may have difficulties finding a new partner, the lineage may decree that she shall perform *kulowa kufa* – i.e. having sexual intercourse with her late husband's brother (*mlamu*). At the same time, a woman is expected to ritually resume sexual activity six months after her delivery. If the husband has passed away in the meantime, *kulowa kufa* may be the only way for the mother to honour the *miyambo* regarding the end of her abstinence. If the mother does not perform sexual intercourse at this prescribed time, her newborn child is expected to get sick, develop mental disorders, or even die.

According to Sena data, the ritual is perceived as putting the spirit (*mzimu*) of the deceased husband at rest. Local knowledge implies that, due to the sexual act performed during *kulowa kufa*, a widow dispels death out of the immediate proximity of her affinal patrilineage.[37] In this context, it is assumed that a woman conceiving during the *kulowa kufa* ritual would give birth to a child with mental disorders. Likewise, even the brother-in-law (*mlamu*) who performs *kulowa kufa* with his late brother's widow faces similar consequences. Thus, a *mlamu* having sexual intercourse with his own wife without undergoing ritual cleansing would cause mental disorder in his own offspring thus conceived.[38]

Due to its cosmological importance as marking the transition from a human being (*munthu*) to an ancestor spirit (*mzimu*), funerary ceremonies (*kumeta maliro*) are of crucial importance (Bruwer 1955: 121). The ritual procedures observed here show numerous cross-ethnic similarities. As a typical part of the funeral rituals of many local ethnic groups, the bereaved shave their heads as an expression of mourning and in order "to avoid the deceased spirit tormenting them" (Paas 2004: 197). Among the Cheŵa, a dying person passes in the

---

37 A widow who keeps living without ritually performing this sexual act of renewed procreation is therefore described as 'inviting death into the family' (Paas 2004: 234).

38 A recent report assesses that it may now occur that no relative is willing or able to conduct *kulowa kufa* with the widow due to processes of cultural changes – which, in turn, have lead to the introduction and hiring of semi-professional 'sexual cleansers'. At present, the Malaŵi Human Rights Commission is therefore campaigning to stop 'harmful cultural practices' such as *kulowa kufa* with regard to the high risk of HIV infection or the transmission of other STIs, and because of the violation of the personal freedom and dignity of the women involved (Mumba 2006: 5)

company of the immediate kin-group who then prepares a rectangular tomb in the graveyard (*manda*).[39] In the presence of the assembled village community, the corpse is carried to the graveyard and buried. Three months after the burial – or, for the widowed spouses, twelve months –, mourners usually undergo a second shaving ceremony (*mpalo*) indicating the end of the mourning period and of behavioural regulations such as sexual abstinence. Here again, *miyambo* are closely connected to the ritual occasion – illustrated in the already quoted case that pregnant women are advised not to attend funerals due to the risk of birthing children with mental disorders. But the above outline of a typical funerary ritual also serves to address another intimately relevant issue. According to numerous sources, the traditions of various ethnic groups in Southern Malaŵi recognize conditions in which a person may be denied the merit of a full ritual funeral. People dying of leprosy or smallpox, e.g., may not receive a burial according to traditional ritual patterns, but rather

> "They were not buried in the ground but left hanging from a tree in the graveyard so that the earth would not be contaminated by the disease. Nowadays they favour burial of these persons but they leave the grave open so that the evil can come out without contaminating the soil" (Breugel 2001: 120).

Evidence provided by field research as well as by previously published sources confirm this notion, indicating that the 'evil' dead are not buried as usual, but that they are disposed of by throwing the corpses into a river or hanging them into trees (in the case of epidemic victims), leaving them in the bush (for people dying of leprosy or *mdulo*) – or, in case of practitioners of anti-social magic (*afiti*), by burning them (Schoffeleers 1968a: 297-298).[40] As these accounts demonstrate, a wide range of persons may be, for different reasons, excluded from society to the degree of receiving severely reduced respect after death. The same applies in case of stillborn children (*nsenye*) or those not fully introduced into society due to, e.g., the aforementioned *kutenga mwana* ritual (see above). As Daniel Soka substantiates with respect to the Lomwe people, such a

---

39 At night, a *manda* is considered to be haunted by spirits (*mizimu*) as well as *afiti*, and every single branch cut down in a graveyard challenges the spirits' wrath. When burying a person, graves are usually about two meters deep in order to warrant that the corpse does not fall prey to wild animals. For some further information on death rituals among the Cheŵa, see Brian Morris (Morris 1996: 55-58).

40 This corresponds with contemporary data. On the slopes of Chinguni Hill in Machinga District, a hollow Baobab tree was reportedly used to dispose of leprosy victims by the local Yao population in the past. A Yao *mfumu* agrees that people using *ufiti* magic "were not buried at the graveyard, they managed to throw them into a cave or maybe into the forest". With reference to the notion of *mdulo*, Matthew Schoffeleers reports that "Persons died of smallpox or wounds were considered 'hot', and burial in the ground would have caused a drought. Therefore they were hung into a tree or committed to a river" (Schoffeleers 1968a: 189).

ceremony is carried out by women only, the respective children are not buried at the regular graveyard (*manda*), and they may be entombed in a shallow grave (Soka 1999). This observation has some direct connection to the issue of mental disorder in Southern Malaŵi as a whole and will be addressed in the final section of this chapter. In a Muslim context, it has been said that children born with a mental disorder may not be initiated on some occasions. In such a case, no religious prayers are performed during their funerals, putting their spiritual purity at risk.

All ethnic groups in Southern Malaŵi agree that death is not the end of a person's involvement in society. Commemoration rituals are a common means of perpetuating society beyond the limits of human life. In the context of the present study, the most central of these rituals is the *sadaka* as performed among the Yao. As a ritual that focuses on the remembrance of a particular person, the *sadaka* is conducted one to three months after his or her death when the bereaved and the village community celebrate with drinks and food in honour of the deceased.[41] Strong behavioural rules (*miyambo*) regulate the performance of *sadaka*, and if these *miyambo* are violated – by either omitting the *sadaka* entirely or performing it in a dissatisfying fashion –, mental disorder is the typical consequence. In such a case that the *sadaka* does not meet the demands of the deceased person it is performed for – some important guests were not invited, food and drink were not appropriately provided, or the dead person was not honoured accordingly –, the respective *mzimu* takes action against the own descendants, attacking them by causing mental disorder. Due to its crucial importance in the causation of mental disorder, this complex will be examined more closely in a later chapter (see *Chapter IV.2.d*).

Nyau Dance Rituals

As an additional ritual example that lies beyond the sequence of life cycle initiations, some mentioning shall be made of the dance rituals of the *nyau*. While the *nyau* male secret society has been documented to some extent already (Birch de Aguilar 1996; Kaspin 1993; Mvula 1990; Kubik 1987; Lindgren & Schoffeleers 1985; Linden 1975), its representation of mental disorder may still merit its mentioning here. This society's most important cultural expression, the *gule wamkulu* ritual – performed publicly in the wider context of initiation ceremonies including the funerals of honoured members – applies a large variety

41 On a cosmological level, the *sadaka* serves as a meal of reconciliation, reuniting the living with the dead and renewing the bonds among the extended family and the community alike. As mentioned earlier, the different Muslim schools in Malaŵi may have varying attitudes towards the celebration of the *sadaka* – and towards the exact form in which this ritual should be performed.

of masks, each of which display a distinctive character (*kapoli*) furnished with particular cultural relevance. While it has been mentioned that the mystic powers of *gule wamkulu* dances do in themselves bear dangers that may lead to mental disorder, some of its mask characters also embody states of mental disorder in themselves and convey cultural knowledge and *miyambo* values on the respective condition to the audience.[42] *Nyau* characters deliver their messages in the form of songs performed by the respective masked dancers. As an example of *nyau* characters showing a distinctive relationship towards mental disorder, Steven Chimombo gives the following illustration:

> "*Mwam'na wa Chilonda* depicts the lame, crippled or deformed. The mask sings that the unfortunate people should not be laughed at or despised for one might have children similarly afflicted" (Chimombo 1988: 141).

When featuring at *gule wamkulu* performances, the mask of *Mwamuna wa Chilonda* sings several songs which in themselves resemble *miyambo* on the culturally validated behaviour towards persons with mental disorder, instructing viewers not to ignore the respective persons and explaining their emotional hardships.[43] Further mask characters which also display conditions of mental disorder include the mask *Chitsiru*, resembling a pitiable yet unintentionally comical woman with a mental disorder,[44] and *Akuchilekwa* – who impersonates a man in rags, incapable of singing its songs, dancing uncoordinatedly and falling over, much to the amusement of the audience. At the same time, the didactic message associated with his performance is that

42 Due to its secretive character, any in-depth research on the society requires membership in the *nyau* itself. While the *nyau* is more relevant in the Central Region of Malaŵi (thus having only limited relevance in the research area under discussion here) and touches the issue of the present research only marginally, no initiation into the society was sought. The present description therefore relies on unpublished data provided by one of the most remarkable connoisseurs in questions of the *nyau* secret society, Fr. Claude Boucher. Most of the sample characters mentioned here belong to the unique collection of original *nyau* masks at the Chamare Cultural Museum at the KuNgoni Center of Culture and Art at Mua Mission in Mtakataka, Dedza District (Central Region). As the collection is unpublished due to traditional norms of secrecy, explanations as provided by Fr. Boucher in Chamare Cultural Museum and documented in the process of an interview session are indicated here.

43 The name of the mask is translated as a 'man covered with sores' (Chimombo 1988: 141). The respective songs are cited as "*Mwam'na wa chilonda / Toto kundiitana / Undiitanila chiani? //* The man covered with sores / Don't call me / Why do you call me? (with Mwam'na wa chilonda taking the position of a woman refusing to respond to a disabled person's needs) and *Leka kundipenya / Mtima uli pa iwe / Pa iwe toto pa iwe. //* Don't look at me / My heart is on you / Is on you, is on you (where the mask addresses a beloved woman)" (Chimombo 1988: 141-142).

44 Johann van Breugel describes that "*Chitsiru* (the mad woman) has the pitiful appearance of an old woman in rags who does all sorts of unbecoming things, like appearing to relieve herself, etc. [...] She rather seemed to be some sort of clown" (Breugel 2001: 166).

> "Even if he behaves strangely he is genuine and completely innocent. He means no harm to anyone. Through this character the ancestors want to teach that the community should accept him as one of their own. They should put up with him and show him kindness" (Display text, Chamare Cultural Museum).

Two other masks – called *Apundula kwa Chikanga* and *Chilomo lende* – represent men who have acquired mental disorder due to their illicit use of anti-social forms of magic (see *Chapter IV.1.c*). The songs accompanying their performance indicate an underlying *mwambo* that deters onlookers from "greed and warns them against its terrible effects".[45] Another *nyau* character named *Chiuli* symbolizes mental disorder in the form of *khunyu* (see *Chapter III.2.e*) by falling down in apparent seizures and showing frustration about the disrespect and mockery he experiences, thus teaching that

> "[...] a disabled husband should show perseverance and accept many hardships if he wants to continue enjoying the company of his wife and children. [...] Such a person has to accept his handicaps with resignation. [...] The character of Chiuli not only encourages the disabled husband to show more determination and steadfastness but also invites the in-laws to show more sensitivity to their mkamwini, treating them more humanely by respecting their qualities. Through the mask of the badger, the ancestors condemn the derision of the lame and the handicapped" (Display text, Chamare Cultural Museum).

Traditional culture makes very direct reference to issues of mental disorder, and as a central element of every ethnic group in Southern Malaŵi, ritual performance serves not only to introduce and socialize the phenomenon as such. Rather, traditional culture addresses mental disorder on its various levels and that normative rules about culturally appropriate behaviour are conveyed in the single most powerful way – i.e. by means of ritual performance – in order to secure general recognition. Traditional culture therefore attributes considerable importance to the phenomenon and its social discourse – and reacts due to rules of interaction and social cohesion.

---

45 "The song [...] explains, »He was normal when he was born. You children, all this happened when he became older«. The women's song adds »Is it because he practiced witchcraft or because God made him so? We do not know! God created him normal but he crippled himself«. [...] The songs suggest that there are various reasons for his deformation. He may have mocked the infirmity or the poverty of a neighbour. Therefore has encountered the wrath of the ancestors. He may have practiced witchcraft and eaten human flesh. He may have consulted a diviner with the intention of bewitching or increasing his own powers. All of these practices show that he is motivated by uncontrolled ambition and greed" (Display text, Chamare Cultural Museum). The different lines of causation mentioned here will be addressed later (see *Chapter IV*).

1(c) Proverbial Expressions

In social anthropology, proverbs are a classical source for traditional notions and values as reflected and perpetuated in everyday culture, and specific analysis may be used to discover its reference to issues of mental disorder or, more broadly, of disability.[46] With respect to Malaŵi, a small number of studies – most of all the formidable collection presented by Joseph Chakanza (Chakanza 2000a) – provide an outlook on the proverbs (*miyambi*, sg. *mwambi*) used in different parts of the country. David Mphande also adds to the available material, emphasizing the social importance of proverbs (Mphande 2003). With some validity for the Southern Region, Mphande states that

> "The proverbs collected have shown the Tonga philosophical outlook, religious and moral conceptions for revealing their values, philosophy, character, wisdom, beliefs and practices. In some cases they clearly express the deepest-set values of the Tonga people, showing the drive that motivates moral behaviour in the people. They reveal concepts of a human being, society, the world and God. Like folktales, they address several themes such as unity and cooperation, responsibility, conflict, obedience and disobedience, good and evil" (Mphande 2003: 13).

This section focuses on proverbs referring to health conditions which constitute representations of mental disorder as defined previously. A large number of Malaŵian proverbs refer to the complex of sickness and human suffering, providing a broad picture of the cultural conception of mental disorder.[47] While depicting a more general understanding of the condition as such, their message simultaneously articulates cultural prescriptions and recommendations on socially appropriate behaviour.

> "*Kupepera kulibe mankhwala.* / To be ill-conditioned or foolish has no remedy" (Chakanza 2000a: 141).[48]

---

46 This has already been demonstrated by Patrick Devlieger who provides examples from the Songye of Southern Congo (Devlieger 1995: 96-97) as well as the Zimbabwean Shona. From the latter, he provides examples such as "*Chirema chiripacho kucherera daro.* / A person with a disability is at his place to get beer from the beer pot" or "*Ane benzi ndeane rake udzana unopurudza.* / If one has a child who is an idiot, if it dances to drums, one ululates at its performance" (Devlieger 1998: 60).

47 Some of the terms mentioned in the following proverbs will be defined in the chapter on terminology (see *Chapter III*). It becomes apparent that the translations given by the quoted authors for some of these disability terms applied do not fully coincide with the more lengthy interpretations provided in this study. While not attempting to question the translations as provided by these Malaŵian authors, this definitions allude to the wider linguistic background as given in the mentioned chapter.

48 As an alternative version of this same proverb, Joseph Chakanza also gives "*Kupusa kulibe mankhwala.* / To be foolish has no remedy" (Chakanza 2000a: 143-144).

As the above cited Chicheŵa proverb puts it, certain cases of mental disorder are regarded as being beyond cure – a question that will be addressed later (see *Chapter V.1.c*) for more thorough reflection. At the same time, many proverbs define general cultural standards concerning the mental as well as physical development of a child. Here, a number of sayings emphasize the importance of early experience for a child's later behaviour and condition.[49] More specifically, some Malaŵian proverbs make a direct statement about the onset of mental disorder and the logic of its occurrence. One such example therefore states:

> "*M'mimba ndi m'chipala.* / What is in the womb is only seen after birth (Salifu Nkanda, a Yao Muslim practitioner).[50]

In this case, the proverb conveys immediate didactics, stressing the volatile incidence of cases of mental disorder: it is only at the end of pregnancy that the condition of the newborn child is revealed – or, more generally: while people may be born without recognizable imperfections, they might still develop them later in life.[51] Implicitly, such accounts demand people to show consideration and discretion when dealing with cases of mental disorder because their family could be likewise affected. This strong socially regulative quality of Malaŵian proverbs is also expressed in the following example:

> "*Chitsiru chili ndi mwini.* / Even the fool has an owner" (Chakanza 2000a: 65).[52]

A general message of a whole category of proverbs touching the wider question of mental disorder in Malaŵi may be identified as an admonition not to judge a book by its cover, and to acknowledge the social involvement of persons with mental disorders. In some cases, traditional proverbs convey messages that are immediately relevant in the context of mental disorder in terms of ugliness.[53] At

---

[49] This may be illustrated by proverbs such as "*Kuwongola m'tengo mponyamba.* / A tree is straightened when it is young" or "*Madzi saiwala khwawa.* / The water does not forget its bed" (both from Serpell, Mariga & Harvey 1993: 5).

[50] Joseph Chakanza translates this proverb as 'The womb is like a blacksmith's forge,' explaining that children are always different, and no-one could ever tell what comes out at birth (Chakanza 2000a: 161).

[51] Proverbs with a similar message include the following: "*Lungalunga n'kubadwa, chilema chichita kudza.* / Better at birth, deformity follows later" (Paas 2003: 104).

[52] Here, the translation of *mwini* as 'owner' might be somewhat confusing; it should be understood as a person who is responsible and caring. Steven Paas gives his interpretation of this same saying as "if your child is a mutt, you will still regard him as your child even if he is neglected by others" (Paas 2004: 74). A similar adage from the Tonga of Northern Malaŵi says that "*Nyoko ndi nyoko chingana wapunduki.* / Your mother is your mother even if she is disabled" (Mphande 2003: 59).

[53] Appealing to overcome criteria of physical appearance, one proverb thus states that "*Chiyipira achaje amake n'kumati ndi mwana.* / It is nasty to outsiders, yet its mother still calls it her child" (Chakanza 2000a: 66).

the same time, Malaŵian proverbs encourage persons to overcome their limitations and create their own special skills. Therefore,

> "*Ukaipa nkhope, dziwa nyimbo (gule).* / If you have an ugly face, learn how to sing (to dance)" (Chakanza 2000a: 307).

This quote directly refers to culturally accepted coping strategies – like, in this case, conquering social marginalization by developing artistic and creative skills that are socially validated. It encourages the development of inventive strategies to overcome obstacles presented due to mental as well as other kinds of deviation.[54] The special social position held by these persons is expressed in the form of

> "*Nyumba ya chitsiru sikupsa.* / The house of a mad person does not get burned" (Chakanza 2000a: 264).[55]

Some examples of Chicheŵa proverbs indicate that a person with a mental disorder may still have important abilities which deserve social recognition. The socially integrative notion of ascribing potential competence to the apparently incompetent is a recurring pattern in Malaŵian proverbs and displays an explicit connection to states of mental disorder. Some sayings therefore insinuate secret abilities hidden in a person with a mental disorder – against all social expectations and to the advantage of the community.[56]

> "*Wamisala adaona nkhondo.* / A madman saw war" (Chakanza 2000a: 334)

The above proverb may therefore be interpreted as either alluding to the gift of foresight or, more basically, as demanding the openness to "lend even the simple your ears" (Chakanza 2000a: 334). The idea of the unknown capabilities of persons with mental disorders and their good use for society is further expressed by sayings such as

> "*Chitsiru chinaomba ng'oma ochenjera navina.* / The fool beat the drum and the clever ones danced" (Chakanza 2000a: 65).

Here, the proverb not only displays a person with a mental disorder as possessing socially valued capabilities but also as performing culturally important tasks and

---

54 This corresponds with Shona proverbs as presented by Patrick Devlieger. As he quotes, "*Chirema chenmazano chinotamba chakazendama kumadziro.* / People with disabilities are clever, they have strategies, they dance whilst leaning against the wall" (Devlieger 1998: 59).

55 Joseph Chakanza explains this proverb's message as "Do not interfere in other people's affairs. Keep out of it. Mind your business" (Chakanza 2000a: 264), thus adverting that it may indeed be the social detachment of persons with mental disorder that not only protects them from community strife but that also represents a laudable characteristic.

56 Alternatively, Joseph Chakanza also gives the version "*Chitsiru chinaona nkhondo.* / The fool (imbecile) saw the approaching war" (Chakanza 2000a: 65-66).

participating in collective activities in an unexpectedly high position of responsibility. Further proverbs remarkably exceed the slightly protective attitude expressed in these sayings to an almost confounding degree, granting unexpected social graces to the mentally disordered person. A Chicheŵa proverb therefore boldly postulates that

> "*Wopunduka n'Chauta, mpembedzeni.* / A crippled person is God himself, adore him" (Chakanza 2000a: 343).

While it may be assumed that this notion does not actually ascribe special divine qualities to persons with mental disorders, it may nonetheless be understood as inverting social conditions for the sake of emphasizing the spiritual importance of the person, indiscriminate of his or her mental condition.[57] Nevertheless, it will be shown that there are still some metaphysical qualities to be traced which are attributed to persons with mental disorders. As a common feature, many proverbs concerning mental disorders show the dichotomy between apparent foolishness and special mental capacities far exceeding those of normal persons.[58] But Malaŵian proverbs demand social acceptance and tolerance towards persons with mental disorder not only by pointing out their hidden qualities but also by pointing out the unpredictable occurrence of the condition as such.[59]

In his study on Tonga proverbs, David Mphande portrays the protection and introduction of social deviants as a major motif of Malaŵian proverbs. In this context, he defines his notion of such outsiders as

> "[…] unknown travellers, the needy, aging parents, children, the infirm, orphans, madmen and women. Thus, as noted earlier the traveller calling at the home should always be well treated because, *Mulendo ndi dungwi*, in crude translation, a visitor is dew. The traveller or stranger or visitor is compared to dew because in the tropics, dew is seen in the mornings of certain months only for a short spell of time. The traveller was likewise not a permanent bother to the host" (Mphande 2003: 13).

It may be concluded that proverbs that touch issues of mental disorder have an important normative character. While they clearly demand respect for persons

---

57 Accordingly, Joseph Chakanza interprets this proverb as meaning that "All people are made by God, even the disabled ones. See God in the deformed" (Chakanza 2000a: 344).

58 As an example, persons with mental disorders may be depicted as having prophetic powers – a notion reflected in numerous other records which mention 'madness' as a frequent symptom of spirit possession – and prerequisite for becoming a religious specialist (Breugel 2001: 85).

59 This corresponds with Patrick Devlieger's assessment on Shona proverbs on disability. Here, he offers examples such as "*Seka urema wafa.* / Laugh at disability when you're dead" or "*Nirenwe zuva gava richadimbura muswe.* / One day, the wild dog will break its tail" (Devlieger 1998: 59-60).

with mental disorders on the basis of pointing out their accomplishments and hidden capabilities, it is also implied that affected persons have to either accept or actively overcome their limitations. Only by recognizing their special condition, one might deduct, can persons with mental disorders develop their own special fields of competence in the community (Devlieger 1998: 59; ibid. 1995: 97).

2. Conflicting Cosmologies and Mental Disorder

In the previous section, the relevance of behavioural norms (*miyambo*) for the cultural construction of mental disorder in Southern Malaŵi and its occurrence throughout various spheres of cultural life have been outlined. Throughout this presentation, it has become apparent that recognition and applicability of these cultural instructions is not universal, but that it depends on numerous factors. Here, the importance of the different cosmological systems must be taken into consideration. While most of the *miyambo* displayed above are more or less deeply rooted in traditional cosmology, they may in part be represented by other philosophical frameworks such as Islam, Christianity, and scientific discourse – all of which, at the same time, compete for dominance over the public discourse.

In addressing the different cosmological conceptions prevalent in Malaŵi, the wider context of religion and medicine comes into play. Religious factors – or, more generally, questions of cosmology – have an important impact on the semantic framework in which a person perceives a medical phenomenon and the medical procedures he or she thus engages in. A person strictly rejecting the basic assumptions of a given religious system is unlikely to resort to them for therapeutic services, but another person who – not even part of a certain religious group – feels more indifferent about their particular cosmological model may, on the other hand, consider the services provided as a useful addition to the treatment options available. Religious affiliation and, more importantly, cosmological mobility therefore gain crucial relevance by predefining preferences and/or prescriptions – i.e. by either suggesting or ruling out – of certain forms of treatment which imply a specific cosmology.

2(a) Traditional Discourses

Talking about 'traditional' – as opposed to 'modern' – cultural phenomena is notoriously problematic, bearing the flaw of artificially creating a monolithic, seemingly primeval order where none has ever existed.[60] But society can never be perceived as a fixed structure as it is, by definition, a complex process of continuous change (Turner 1989: 58). Therefore, the use of the term traditional should not be limited to idealized notions of an assumed primordial *ur*-culture, but it may serve as an analytic category that has its value in the distinction of different historic processes of cultural change as well as in the identification and classification of the respective influences. In Malaŵi, traditional forms of medicine constitute a vital part of everyday basic health care. Especially in the rural context – and therefore, for the vast majority of the population –, traditional medical practices constitute the main health care services, and recent numbers indicate that traditional health specialists are still by far the most frequently accessed form of the medical service for persons with mental disorders.[61]

Frequently, even persons without any specialized medical training have a basic knowledge of treatments for everyday complaints, thus forming the popular sector of Malaŵian medicine. Accordingly, health specialists are not usually involved in the treatment of well-known health problems such as a cold or a sore throat. More serious but common diseases such as *malungo* (commonly identified with malaria) may be dealt with according to medical lay knowledge as accessible within the immediate social network. In the event of unusual, prolonged, or obviously dangerous health problems, specialists (*asing'anga*) are frequented in order to regain control over the health situation. This section provides the general structures of traditional medicine in Malaŵi, putting a special emphasis on the therapeutic techniques relevant in the context of mental disorder. The main categories of traditional treatment will be depicted and their application illustrated. Due to the direct interrelation between traditional medicine and traditional religious thought, it is elementary to first develop a basic understanding of the elementary structures of traditional religion in Southern Malaŵi.

---

60 This problem has recently been addressed by Marleen de Witte who agrees that "The notion of African traditional religion is a problematic one, as it suggests a static, unchanging and clearly bounded set of beliefs and practices, and is itself a historical construction that placed these beliefs and practices in opposition to modern Christianity" (Witte 2005: 333). In an attempt to give greater consideration to processes of cultural change in Malaŵi, Karl Peltzer distinguishes between a traditional and a transitional cultural discourse. This differentiation conflicts with a general understanding of culture as an axiomatically transitional process and of the emic discourse as reflecting different – i.e. parallel and, in part, contradicting – cultural influences.

61 According to the aforementioned 2004 disability survey, a full 59.7 percent of the persons identified as disabled had actually received treatment by at least one traditional healer, and 84.4 percent of them were aware of the availability of their services. The various forms of biomedical services were known to smaller parts of the disabled community, and medical rehabilitation, the most commonly available Western health service, was only accessed by 23.8 percent of them (Loeb 2004a: 110).

Malaŵian Cosmology

Traditional forms of medicine bear a direct connection to traditional religious notions as well as other cultural concepts referring to Malaŵian cosmology.[62] Due to this, traditional medicine stands in constant implicit or explicit conflict with both of the major, cosmopolitan religious denominations, i.e. Islam and Christianity. But while the continuity of traditional religious representations is therefore partly supplanted from the public discourse, its basic notions persist especially in the context of traditional medicine, one of the last domains of traditional culture that endures largely due to its embeddedness within medical services. At the same time, traditional notions also find their way into or around the exclusiveness of cosmopolitan religions, surviving under the surface of proclaimed Islam and Christianity. While very few people in Southern Malaŵi therefore declare themselves as sole adherents to traditional religion, an assumed majority of the population maintain certain elements of traditional representations by either incorporating them into their religious concepts in a syncretistic process – which can be assessed in the case of some non-cosmopolitan churches (see *Chapter II.2.c*) – or by accentuating the conflicting representations of two different religious systems on a situational level.[63]

The religious traditions of the various ethnic groups in Southern Malaŵi differ in many respects, but a number of significant similarities have also developed. Thus, the traditional religious concepts of the various ethnic groups generally imply the existence of a Supreme Being and creator deity who is addressed by different, ethnic-specific names – the most widely applied one among them being *Mulungu*.[64] Generally, Malaŵian notions of the Supreme

---

62 As a central part of Malaŵian cosmology, the different concepts of legitimate and illegitimate magic –known by the Chicheŵa terms *matsenga* and *ufiti* – will not be discussed here. They are depicted at greater length in a later chapter (see *Chapter IV.1*).

63 As an indication for the rare occurrence of declared followers of traditional religion, the National Statistical Office of Malaŵi asserts that less than half a percent (0.3 among female, 0.4 among male) of the population indicated to adhere to 'other' – i.e. non-Muslim and non-Christian – religions in a 2004 survey. At the same time, a larger part of the population (0.9 female, 3.0 male) stated to have 'no religion', supposedly reflecting the interviewees' reluctance to directly express their adherence to traditional belief systems (NSO & ORC Macro 2005: 26). Bregje de Kok provides a highly illustrative cultural psychological study on the competing traditional and Christian realities as acknowledged by the individual believer (Kok 2004).

64 This term is derived from Yao and Nsenga tradition while *Chauta* is identified as originating from the Cheŵa (Linden 1979: 202; Ntara 1973: 39). Other words for the Supreme Being include names such as *Chisumphi*, *Namalenga*, *Mlengi*, *Mleri*, *Mtanga*, *Leza*, or *Mphambe*. These names can in part be interpreted as resembling honorary titles applied to the Supreme Being, but also as denoting originally separate religious entities from the different ethnic groups which, due to intensive cross-cultural contact, are now difficult to distinguish (Marwick 1965: 63-64). Therefore, the name *Chauta* is translated as the 'big bow', putting a strong symbolic focus on hunting as well as the rainbow (Linden 1979: 203). For more information on these

Being have the character of a *deus otiosus* – a 'hidden God', withdrawn from the immediate affairs of the world and mankind – with slightly ambivalent qualities. Combining benevolent and punitive characteristics at the same time, the Supreme Being is therefore associated with attributes such as fertility, rainfall, and the sky, but also with natural disasters, floods, lightning, sickness, and destruction. It resembles:

> "God, God in space and the rainbow across, God the creator, God as rain provider, and God as the destroyer manifesting himself in earthquakes, lightning and epidemic diseases" (Schoffeleers 1997: 59).

The different societies of Southern Malaŵi distinguish subordinate categories of religious entities, and these spirit agents (*mizimu*) generally play a highly prominent role due to the detached character of the Supreme Being itself. Acting as advocates for the concerns of man, spirits form the crucial link between the spheres of the living and the divine realm. As the individually most powerful ones among them, territorial spirits form a very wide category of spiritual beings whose worship is bound to geographical factors. The most well-known example of territorial spirits is the spirit Mbona,[65] and like him, many territorial spirits are associated with serpents, rainfalls, and water (Schoffeleers 1992; ibid. 1968a).[66] Less powerful but much more common is the wide category of ancestral or lineage spirits (*mizimu ya makolo*) which are recognized and venerated in the context of a given kinship group. Acting as guides, guardians, and representations of cultural values, the *mizimu ya makolo* are the main mediators between the living and the Supreme Being, and due to their former human status, they are conceptualized as being frequently involved in the affairs of their living

---

concepts, refer to specialized studies (Amanze 2002: 125-146; Chakanza 1987).

65 Mbona's mythical character as a bringer of rain is supported by the fact that any visitor who receives permission to approach his secret shrine in the Lower Shire has to wear black clothes, resembling dark rain clouds. The wearing of rubber boots is also recommended, and those without them wrap up their trouser legs as to avoid them getting wet. Historically, the Mbona cult is traceable from the year 1866 onwards (Heintze 1970: 77), while its origins are dated back to historical developments in the 16th century AD. His cult, developing around a mythical figure of the Lundu dynasty, has its center in Nsanje District in the Lower Shire valley. Genesis and history of the Mbona cult in Malaŵi have been described in full detail by Matthew Schoffeleers (Schoffeleers 1992) while an additional, colourful version of its mythical origin is given elsewhere (Schoffeleers & Roscoe 1985: 43-48).

66 Similarly, the serpent spirit Thunga has been mentioned to act as a mediator for the Supreme Being (Linden 1979: 188-192; Schoffeleers 1979: 155), and in the Lower Shire valley as well as around Zomba Plateau, a snake-shaped spirit called Napolo is associated with dangerous landslides and floods (Schoffeleers 1968a). Territorial spirits are also conceptualized as the spirits of particularly powerful human beings, e.g. associated with the royal graveyard of Mankhamba where the deceased kings are venerated as protectors of the land and its people (Linden 1979: 188). This demonstrates the strong conceptual ties between territorial spirits and the wider category of ancestral spirits (*mizimu ya makolo*).

descendants. Other categories of spirit agents may and will be distinguished in the context of their involvement in the causation of mental disorders.

All these spiritual entities are manifested in a number of ritual contexts. In particular among the Mang'anja and Sena people of the extreme South of the country, rain cults are an important part of religious tradition, and in many cases, territorial spirits – such as Mbona – are the focus of such rituals (Schoffeleers 1992). Within these cults, spirit mediums have the crucial position of a go-between, negotiating between man and spiritual entity. Especially among the Chewa, the *nyau* secret society also constitutes a central element of traditional religion, providing a hierarchically organized cult structure that performs periodic dance rituals. More generally, religious rituals are frequently performed by local chiefs or *mafumu*, with official prayers (*mapemphero*) and offerings (*nsembe*) being directed to the ancestor spirits in their function as protectors of the kinship group and as representatives of the Supreme Being.[67] All ancestral spirits are entitled to receive periodic worship, and they are known to articulate their interests and needs in a number of ways which are directly connected to the occurrence and conceptualization of mental disorder and human health in general, and which will receive more consideration later on in this study (see *Chapter IV.2*). More so, direct contact with the spirit entities of Malaŵian cosmology is also intimately related to the person and position of the traditional healer (*sing'anga*).

Local Medical Specialists

In ethnographic literature, various attempts have been made to develop a closer classification of African medical specialists according to their exact working procedures and professional background.[68] With reference to research in Malaŵi, Rupert Pöschl provides his own typology, specifying the main categories of medical specialists as

---

67 While specialized rain cults usually cluster around particular cult shrines, ancestor worship usually does not require a man-made structure as a religious center. According to Lomwe data, sacrificial rituals in honour of the ancestors may therefore be conducted under a *mtengo wa mpoza* or custard-apple tree (*Annona reticulata*) where a white circle of *ufa* flour is laid out around the tree before communal prayers are performed. Graveyards are also associated with the presence and – potentially harmful – activity of spirit ancestors.

68 As an example, Paul Hinderling develops a highly stratified model according to which the various types of healers can be distinguished according to criteria of their medical responsibility – these being either primarily diagnostic or therapeutic – as well as their cosmological world view as representing either a magical-religious or a para-scientific system (Hinderling 1981: 127). Accordingly, he classifies different healer categories – such as the seer, oracle medium, cult leader, shaman, witch doctor, *nganga*, herbalist, priest, and medical doctor – into a model of responsibility and cosmology.

"Der Medizinmann (*sing'anga*), der Exorzist oder *witchdoctor* (Zauberdoktor: *nfiti*), der Divinator (*nchimi*) und der Herbalist" (Pöschl 1987: 130).

Many other, similar typologies could be added here.[69] Personal field accounts, however, do not provide comparable distinctions,[70] and it appears justified to question whether these categorizations reflect genuinely emic notions – or if they represent strictly analytic tools. In response to this question, Brian Morris elaborates that

"The appellation sing'anga or mnganga (plural asing'anga), like that of 'traditional healer' is very much a blanket term covering a number of different types. Although early writers [...] drew a distinction, particularly amongst the Yao, between the herbalist ng'anga and the diviner (amisengo or mchisango), contemporary usage does not seem to make this explicit and sing'anga is often used as a broad term to cover midwives, village and market herbalists, as well as doctor-diviners; and apparently, [...] when Jesus is referred to in Christian hymns as a greater healer, he is also called a sing'anga" (Morris 1986: 368).[71]

This observation is strongly supported by the findings of the research presented here, and thus, the term traditional healer (or *sing'anga* in Chichewa) will serve as a broad category of professional non-biomedical specialists in Malaŵi in the context of this study. They will here be distinguished from neighbouring categories such as traditional birth attendants (*azamba*), primarily religious specialists (such as *ashehe* or *abusa*), and Western-trained biomedical personnel such as clinical nurses and psychiatrists.[72]

---

69 Karl Peltzer, e.g., differentiates traditional healers in Malaŵi into a number of categories which he terms as *(a)* the diviner, *(b)* the herbalist, *(c)* the diviner/herbalist, *(d)* the traditional pharmacist, *(e)* the specialist – consisting of the spirit healer, the traditional birth attendant and the traditional surgeon – as well as *(f)* the faith healer (Peltzer 1987: 72).

70 Within the scope of this research, other terms such as *nchimi* (frequently identified as a diviner) or *namkungwi* (as a spirit medium) were not commonly applied. Traditional healers, on the other hand, alternatively introduced themselves as *asing'anga* or as herbalists (*maherbalisti*), thus indicating that no general distinction between the two was recognized. The term *mfiti* – sometimes translated as 'witch doctor' – was clearly reserved for an anti-social magic specialists (see *Chapter IV.1.a*).

71 Rupert Pöschl agrees, pointing out that the practices of the Bantu *nganga* or »great healer« typically include divinatory techniques for diagnosis as well as exorcism therapy (Pöschl 1987: 131), thereby contradicting Hinderling's approach of differentiating traditional healers according to the diagnostic or therapeutic services offered (Hinderling 1981: 127). While Brian Morris explicitly includes midwives under the blanket term *sing'anga* (Morris 1987: 368), own data suggests that, in the respective research area, a distinction is made between *asing'anga* and *azamba*. Only one *mzamba* claimed to be experienced in *using'anga* as well, and this double qualification was described as uncommon.

72 At the same time, the term *sing'anga* is still subject to further specification in Southern Malaŵi. Therefore, it may be a matter of cultural negotiation and recognized status whether or not a given medical specialist is regarded as a 'real' or 'proper' healer (*sing'anga weniweni*) or if he/she is regarded as a mere herbal specialist (*sing'anga wa mitengo*). The different subcategories or

In European tradition, it seems self-evident to distinguish between religious and medical specialists due to the basic assumption of them representing two separate spheres of social life. In a Malaŵian context, however, this distinction is only partially applicable. While historic accounts do mention the existence of highly renowned religious specialists – usually the spirit mediums and/or guardians of a given shrine –, this professional group has all but disappeared in present-day Malaŵi. Traditional healers, in contrast, are a very common part of cultural life, and their position as well as their professional work is connected to explicitly religious representations. Even though their responsibilities may encompass spirit mediumship, divination, and the keeping of traditional culture, medical services are still central to the status and office of traditional healers among the different ethnic groups of Southern Malaŵi. According to Steve Chilivumbo,

> "*Ng'anga* means a healer. Many people know a few herbs as medicine for common simple ailments such as headache, etc. They are not *ng'anga*. The term is reserved and applied to more specialized medicine men who claim some degree of expertise" (Chilivumbo 1976: 70).

As stated above, the Chicheŵa term *sing'anga* is the most commonly applied expression for a traditional medical specialist or healer.[73] The beginning of a traditional healer's career is marked by spiritual initiation, revealing the strong bond linking the office of a *sing'anga* to a concept of spiritual mandate and vocation. As a typical account, most traditional healers share a history of mental disorder which, after a long and complicated process of identification, results in them acquiring knowledge about the art of healing (*using'anga*),[74] with the respective techniques being obtained by a form of spiritual training offered by ancestral spirits. The respective *using'anga* instructions usually take place at night in the form of dream encounters and imply a moral obligation of accepting this vocation (Morris 1986: 370; Kapapa 1977: 59).[75] Due to these strong ties to

---

specializations of *asing'anga* will be depicted in the following chapter (see *Chapter II.2.a*).

73 Other variations of this term include *ng'anga* (Chitumbuka), *mganga* (Kiswahili), as well as *umuganga* (Kinyarwanda), *nganga* (Chishona) and *inyanga* (isiZulu). See Kivuto Ndeti for further linguistic parallels in Bantu languages of Eastern Africa, and Brian Morris' study on the linguistic genesis of the term (Morris 1996: 68-69; Ndeti 1976: 12).

74 This issue will be elaborated in a different context (see *Chapter IV.2.d*). For a classical example of the education of a Lomwe *sing'anga*, refer to Brian Morris (Morris 1986: 370-371). Additionally, a mythical account of the initiation of a Sena healer is given by Matthew Schoffeleers and Adrian Roscoe (Schoffeleers & Roscoe 1985: 61-63).

75 As we shall see later on, these spirit instructors may be replaced by the apparitions of angels or saints in an Islamic or Christian context (see *Chapter II.2.b* and *II.2.c*). Remarkably, Paul Kapapa reports that nocturnal encounters between persons and their deceased ancestors are interpreted differently among the diverse cultures of Malaŵi. Therefore he recounts that dreams about ancestors are seen as a first step towards *sing'anga* initiation among the Yao of Chipoka,

the sphere of the spirits, the observance of – partially personalized – *miyambo* rules is particularly important for *asing'anga*, and their violation could be punished with mental disorder.

In many cases, an initial training by *mizimu* spirits is followed by additional instructions as received from a senior *sing'anga* who acts as a teacher. In part, *using'anga* trainees cover long distances to find an appropriate master, sometimes even migrating into a neighbouring country, and the overall duration of the *sing'anga* training varies between two and ten years. Once fully initiated as a *sing'anga*, a person attains a number of social functions in the respective community, acting not only as a medical specialist, but also taking on informal responsibilities as a mediator within the community as well as between the living and the ancestors, and as an advocate of tradition (Kapapa 1980: 205-207; ibid. 1977: 59-60). As Brian Morris puts it,

> "In a sense, as Cullen Young and Banda long ago remarked, »nothing is beyond the sing'anga and his medicine«. Life itself, health, love, politics, agriculture, hunting and fishing, all are departments of life and fields of human activity which fall within the scope of the sing'anga art" (Morris 1986: 376).[76]

As in wide areas of Southern Africa, healer associations are a common phenomenon in modern-day Malaŵi. While the foundation of the first African Sing'anga Association of Nyasaland dates back to the late 1950s, many other Healer Associations came into being during the 1960s and '70s AD. With the standardization of treatment expenses being one of their foremost concerns, many Healer Associations issue price lists so patients would have a clear reference of the appropriate payment, thus eradicating accusations of exploitation and arbitrary billing on the side of some *asing'anga*.[77] In addition to that, Healer Associations fight professional problems by designing and implementing traditional treatment standards in order to avoid false treatment or by facilitating further education of traditional healers (Morris 1996: 95-98; Peltzer 1987: 82).[78]

Salima District (Central Region). At the same time, the neighbouring Ngoni of Dedza District (Central Region) regard that same phenomenon as a symptom of mental disorder and sanction it with social isolation, considering it as a result of divine punishment (Kapapa 1977: 59-61).

76 The cross-reference alluded to in this context refers to Young & Banda 1946: 19. Joseph Chakanza emphasizes the spectrum of traditional medical competence by stating that "Traditional healers claim success in treating such diseases as cancer, diabetes, insanity, asthma, epilepsy, sexually transmitted diseases, conditions of impotence in males and of infertility in females" (Chakanza 1998: 101)

77 For examples of such price lists see Pöschl 1987: 142; Morris 1986: 370.

78 Some of these Healer Associations known in a Malaŵian context are the Herbalist Association of Malaŵi (HAM), the African Herbal Association, the Traditional Doctors Association of Malawi, the African Herbalist Traditional Medicine Association of Malawi, the Traditional Mediciners of Central Africa (TMCA), or the True African Nganga Herbalist Association of Central Africa (TANHACA) (Morris 1996: 95-102; Peltzer 1987: 81-82; Morris 1986: 370;

While some of these organizations have a small-scale, regional character, other Healer Associations have a highly professional structure with a clearly defined agenda, mission statements, annual budgets and general annual meetings. As a *sing'anga* and former chairperson of the Herbalist Association of Malaŵi explains, the HAM currently boasts an approximate 12,000 members nationwide, being founded during the era of Hastings K. Banda who explicitly supported *using'anga* medicine. Among other strategies, HAM officials use their meetings to encourage local *asing'anga* to increase their cooperation with government institutions. For some time, the HAM also spearheaded interdisciplinary research on traditional medicine in cooperation with departments of the University of Malaŵi. Collecting their knowledge on the usage of medical plants, HAM members discussed their results in joint seminars with government representatives, Western-trained medical specialists, and research biologists (Morris 1996: 99-100; Msonthi 1983c).

While the stereotypical picture of a *sing'anga* healer would be that of a primarily rural specialist offering his or her services to visiting patients as well as on the weekly village market, some traditional healers have started to build up medical centers modeled after Western hospital institutions. Providing accommodation for in-patients on the healer's compound, these entrepreneurs in traditional medicine not only increase the number of people that can be accommodated simultaneously, but they also provide remarkably well-structured and systematic training facilities for their apprentices.[79] In addition, traditional healers have attained some degree of professional organization due to the foundation of numerous healer associations.

Msonthi 1983c). The International Traditional Healers Council or the International Traditional Medicines Council of Malawi – a Healer Association with members in adjacent countries such as Mozambique – are also common in the Southern Region. The last two seem to be identical as both names appear on printed membership cards, with their respective headquarters having corresponding P.O. Box numbers in Blantyre.

79 As an example for such an institution of traditional medicine, Rupert Pöschl describes a *using'anga* clinic which provides room for the stationary treatment of 120 patients, with a staff consisting of an additional eight assistants and students and equipment which includes, among others, two Land Rover vehicles. The symbolic content used by such institutions frequently combines the imagery of traditional medicine with biomedical symbols. Thus, *asing'anga* frequently bear the title of 'doctor' (or *dokotala*) and employ waiting rooms as well as receptionists while traditional amulets (*zithumwa*), animal horns (*nyanga*) or gourds (*nsupa*) used for divination feature as central parts of the interior in the examination room (Pöschl 1987: 135-138). Smaller institutions of traditional medicine likewise apply symbolic allusion to biomedicine. Thus, the consultation room of a Lomwe *sing'anga* may be decorated with a white blanket bearing a red cross while she is wearing a white cap with a similar Red Cross symbol, resembling a classical nurse outfit. At the same time, she expresses her explicitly Christian approach by wearing a red stole and beginning her consultations with prayers in front of the cross on the wall.

Traditional Therapy

Traditional healers in Malaŵi apply a number of different techniques for various therapeutic purposes. In order to create a basic understanding of their medicinal actions, it is important to distinguish a number of different medical tools or appliances. Therefore, the wearing of specially prepared amulets (*zithumwa*) – sometimes referred to as *nkhata* or 'wreath' – is usually part of protective or preventive medicine applied for a very specific purpose. Most commonly, such a *chithumwa* has the form of a small cushion of fabric or leather, sown up and worn on a string around the neck or waist. Some special kinds of *zithumwa* are directly connected to the occurrence of mental disorder in an infant, and they are also worn around the neck in order to unfold their preventive qualities.[80] In all these cases, the particular medical value of a given *chithumwa* depends on the effects attributed to the substances hidden inside of it – these mainly being herbs (*masamba*) or roots (*mitsitsi*) which are associated with certain medical effects. At the same time, the position of a given *chithumwa* is also crucial for the success of the treatment.[81] As a general rule, *zithumwa* are worn over a long period of time as specified by the attending *sing'anga*, and their therapeutic efficiency develops gradually. An even more typical form of medical treatment applied for all sorts of complaints is the use of medicines meant for drinking (called *mankhwala akumwa*) – and this also applies for the treatment of mental disorders.[82] Here, plant substances are pound, soaked in water or other liquids and imbibed by the patient.[83]

For the treatment of many forms of mental disorder, medicine is also applied by washing (*mankhwala a kusamba*) either the entire body or those parts of the person identified as significant for his or her respective condition. In many

---

[80] Made in the form of a small ring of roots and cloth, this amulet (called *phula*) is used to prevent children from developing *mutu* (see *Chapter III.2.d*). Its use is a common part of traditional medicine even though its protection may not always be required. As a traditional birth attendant explains, "This thing is a tradition, because it was started by our ancestors that whenever a child was born, they would get medicine and tie it on to it. But if you have not applied it and it stays like that, it may still be alright all by itself. Then you should not tell anyone because if people know they might attack it by ways of *ufiti*" (Olive Pilimiti, a Nyanja *mzamba*).

[81] A Yao *sing'anga*, for instance, prescribes a *chithumwa* to rest upon the heart as an element of his *kupepera* treatment.

[82] Thus, an infusion made from the bark of the *mkundi* tree (*Parkia filicoidea*) mixed with the roots of *chesa* grass (*Cyperus alternifolius*) has been mentioned as a drinking medicine against *misala* (Williamson 1955: 91). A Lomwe *sing'anga* describes that he successfully treats cases of *misala* by some medicine produced from pieces of *karingo* (a *mitengo* yet unidentified) which is soaked and then administered by ingestion.

[83] It should be marked here that the mode of administration of these *mankhwala* does not necessarily comply strictly with the mentioned procedure. Rather, the phrase *kumwa mankhwala* or 'to drink medicine' is used generally for the internal use of medicine – which might include swallowing pills, chewing down more solid substance, or eating *phala* porridge.

reported cases of mental disorder, the head is the focus of this *kusamba* treatment. The recipe for the production of this medicated water is, as in the case of concoctions meant for drinking, variable. Also, many kinds of traditional medicine are administered in the form of *mankhwala ofungatira*, i.e. by fumigating the patient with medical vapour. This form of treatment is frequently mentioned in the context of mental disorder, and it can be described as immersing suitable *mitengo* or *masamba* into boiling water with the patient inhaling the fume. At the end of this steam treatment, the same water may be used again in order to wash the patient as described above.[84] In other cases, *asing'anga* apply medical fumes by blowing the smoke on to the patient for more specific application. Therefore, it is emphasized that *mankhwala ofungatira* enter the patient's head through the ears, continuing straight to the brain where they develop their therapeutic effects.[85] Yet other *mankhwala ofungatira* are administered by a slightly different technique, with patients inhaling the treatment in the form of snuff. A female Lomwe specialist explains this procedure as follows:

> "For *misala*, we have a different medicine which is in the form of a powder, and we make the patient inhale it through the nose, and when the patient belches and sneezes, he/she falls and goes to sleep, and then everything is finished, he/she is cured" (Doris Petroyo, a Lomwe *sing'anga*).

In addition to its already mentioned uses, plant material is also burned with the purpose of obtaining medicinal ashes. This ash is applied by rubbing it into skin scarifications which are referred to as *mipini* (sg. *mphini*).[86] As these *mipini* are considered to have a limited period of effectiveness, they may be applied repeatedly in order to achieve a longer lasting or even permanent effect. The

---

84 Convincingly, the background of this procedure is described as the sweat of the patient opening the pores in the skin so 'bad things' come out with the sweat. Thus, washing the patient afterwards would be applied to close the pores again.

85 The effectiveness of this form of treatment for mental disorders is explained due to the notion that the respective condition may be regarded as an irritation located in the brain. Therefore, medication is mainly applied to the head, being blown into the ears and inhaled by the airways. It is stressed that "This smoke is very important and helpful, and we even believe that without the smoke getting into the ears, there wouldn't be any healing. The smoke gets into the ears, then into the brain, and when this happens, the patient feels much better – faster than maybe when putting the medicine in the food for the patient to eat. When the smoke gets into the ears and when the patient also breathes the smoke from the burnt medicine while covering his/her head with cloth over the fire, the patient feels better quickly, the brain relaxes well" (Francis Muramu, a Lomwe *sing'anga*).

86 The process of making the *mphini* skin incisions is called *kutemera*. Usually, the *sing'anga* uses a razorblade in order to make a number of incisions in parallel lines, and the prevalence of this form of treatment is recognizable due to the high percentage of persons in Southern Malaŵi showing marks of old linear scars on their visible skin.

exact location of the scarifications is equally relevant as the composition of the ashes applied thereon.[87]

A number of results may be emphasized with respect to the present section. Firstly, the symbolic and organizational flexibility of traditional medicine in Southern Malaŵi has been outlined. Instead of opposing new – e.g. biomedical – influences, traditional healers make use of their particular symbolisms by introducing them into their own professional context. Traditional medicine thus presents itself as a penetrable, inclusive cultural system that, while maintaining a specific basis of medical and cosmological logic, displays considerable formal flexibility. Additionally, the use of different substances as traditional *mankhwala* – as depicted above – may require some further clarification. In general, it may be subsumed that the choice of plants used in order to produce therapeutic substances indicates the medical potential of the remedy, while its locale of application on the patient's body stands in direct connection to the physical location of the complaint. Making a direct reference to the emic interpretation of the problem under discussion here, some Lomwe *asing'anga* agree that, for the treatment of mental disorder in the form of *khunyu* (see *Chapter III.2.e*), *mphini* incisions would only be made on the patient's temples, indicating a close association of the problem with the head.[88] Along with further indications mentioned above, these observations clearly support that mental disorders are usually located in the head (*mutu*) of the patient, and that this is the locus that the appropriate medicine is primarily applied to.[89] Furthermore, field data clearly indicates that the choice of plant material used in the context of traditional healing is defined by two general mechanisms of semantic attribution. Firstly, a plant can be considered suitable due to a *quasi* analytic appraisal of its inner properties – such as a strong smell which is meant to have a therapeutic effect on the patient's brain.[90] At the same time, plants may also be allocated to the

---

87 In order to create ashes for *misala* treatment, Karl Peltzer mentions the roots of certain plants (*Afzelia quanzensis* and *Dalburgia nitidula*), being applied in the form of *kutemera* therapy (Peltzer 1987: 205).

88 With reference to a different kind of mental disorder, a Yao *sing'anga* mentions that *kutemera* treatment against *misala* focuses on the ankle joints, the back, and the chest area around the heart. As an explanation, he elaborates that "our blood circulates in this direction, so when I make incisions here, the blood takes the medicine and brings it here to this side and then cleans this particular place", also referring to the person's head. A Yao *sing'anga* insists that, due to *maula* diagnosis (see *Chapter II.2.a*), he could assess whether a given case of *misala* would affect the left or the right side of the brain, indicating the appropriate location for his *mipini*. For the treatment of *kuzungulira mutu*, a Sena *sing'anga* recommends *mipini* to be applied on the forehead and one the legs, sometimes backed by more incisions on the shoulders, the knees, and on the anterior fontanel.

89 The connection between mental disorder and the concept of the head in Malaŵi has already been assessed by Brian Morris (Morris 1996: 119).

90 As one example, this is the case for *mpungabwe* leaves, identified as *Ocimum canum* (Morris

treatment of a given health disorder due to exterior criteria such as colour, shape, or more complex processes of symbolic allocation of meaning.[91] This analogy between material quality and therapeutic effect follows classical models of magic which will be addressed in a later context (see *Chapter IV.5*).

It is also important to note that, while the above mentioned forms of applying traditional medicine may seem easy to distinguish and largely materialist in nature, the actual therapy for mental disorder usually consists of more than just one of these medical techniques and will necessarily be embedded into a larger ritual framework. A full course of treatment may combine a large number of different elements, developing a complex structure that, in itself, acquires the characteristics of a healing ritual. Therefore, a Sena healer describes his way of treating mental disorder – in the form of *misala* (see *Chapter III.2.a*) – as

> "[...] a one day treatment only. The second day, his/her head starts working again. [...] They bring the patient here. We take some medicine to boil, other medicine we put in a bathing basin and wash his/her head with that. Then after washing the head with the medicine, we make incisions on him/her. After making the *mipini*, we give the patient the boiled medicine in a cup to drink, after drinking we blow some more medicine on him/her. After three hours, the patient stops whatever abnormal things he/she was doing. All the abnormal things from his/her head disappear" (Lexon Kondwani, a Sena *sing'anga*).[92]

In addition, not all forms of traditional medicine derive their effectiveness solely from plant materials. Rather, a *mitengo* treatment can be combined with other substances such as a "chicken whose blood we mix with the bundle of wood to treat the patient" or similar substances. The exact location in or around the house

---

1996: 330).

91 Therefore, a Yao *sing'anga* mentions that, in order to cure a form of mental disorder that is associated with physical instability and deformed limbs, the patient should be treated with the seeds from a straight tree. These seeds, taken in the form of a *mankhwala akumwa*, would straighten the patient out due to their immanent characteristics.

92 A similar description refers to the treatment of mental disorder in the form of *kuzerezeka* (see *Chapter III.2.b*). In agreement with his present Yao colleague, a Lomwe healer explains that "about *kuzerezeka*, there are also signs like the brain not working properly, and so when people bring this type of patient we do welcome them and take them inside the house. [...] Then we take a certain type of medicine and boil them. [...] Then we take the medicine and wrap them in a piece of cloth. [...] Then we start blowing into this ear, and the other ear also. [...] Then there is also need for extra fire on a piece of iron-sheet on which we burn some more medicine while the patient has covered his/her own head with a cloth over the fire. [...] Thus, the smoke from the burnt medicine on the fire should get the patient and work together with the medicine blown into the ears. [...] After three days we make scarifications on the patient. [...] We make three *mipini* on the left breast, another three below and also close to the ears. [...] The patient feels better, or I should say he/she stops talking nonsense. Everything stops after four days, and on the fourth day of administering the medicine which is actually the last day, the patient completely changes and feels better" (Francis Muramu, a Lomwe *sing'anga*).

where a given medicine must be administered may also have a crucial impact on the desired therapeutic effect.[93] It should therefore be obvious that traditional Malaŵian medicine follows a number of different therapeutic lines at the same time, incorporating symbol and substance into ritual performance designed specifically for the cosmological categories within which the case of mental disorder is located.[94]

2(b) Muslim Concepts

Not surprisingly, traditional medicine is not the only form of therapy in Malaŵi that follows certain ritual procedures. So far, only a limited amount of research has been conducted investigating the specific structures of Islamic medicine. Due to the history of its introduction through trade and proselytizing, Islam in Malaŵi is less directly connected to international biomedicine then, e.g. Christianity. At the same time, traditional medicine and their inherent reference to pre-Muslim religious thought also impedes its acceptance in a more devout Muslim framework. The existence and the structure of therapeutic concepts genuinely derived from Islam, thus seeming self-evident, must therefore be examined more closely. The following outline will focus on the treatment of mental disorder, but it will also provide a general overview on more general Muslim healing practices as found in the Southern Region. Before addressing these questions, it is also necessary to provide an introduction into the historical dimension of Islam in Malaŵi.

Islam in Malaŵi

In Malaŵi, the historical process of introducing Islam followed a number of separate lines of geographical distribution. While it is argued that the area of modern-day Malaŵi first got in contact with Islam through traders from the influential Kilwa Kisiwani Empire which began to flourish in the Southern coast of Tanzania by the 12th century AD, Arab traders had established more substantial relationships with Malaŵi by the 1530s AD, operating from their trading posts along the Zambezi river in the Tete area of modern-day

---

93 A pregnant woman afraid of miscarriage is therefore advised to imbibe the *mankhwala a kumwa* provided by the *sing'anga* on the doorstep of her house. In analogy to her blocking the exit of the house she is said to thus prevent the child's exit out of the uterus.

94 As shall be elaborated later on, the variation of therapeutic procedures according to the aetiological categories ascribed to the individual case is decisive (see *Chapter IV*). Therefore, every therapy implies a direct reference to emic categories of cosmological order and cultural identity.

Mozambique.[95] By the 1890s, a phase of active proselytizing followed, being carried by dedicated individual teachers or <u>sh</u>ay<u>kh</u>s. Ever since their migration into the areas South of Lake Malaŵi, the Yao constitute an important force in Malaŵian Islam and the largest national group of predominantly Muslim faith that represents a rough 13 percent of the national population (NSO & Orc Macro 2005: 26; Hofmeyr 2000).[96] Apart from Yao and Swahili groups as well as converts with yet other ethnic backgrounds, Indian as well as other Asian families have become the most influential and economically powerful Muslim community, immigrating into Malaŵi primarily in the 1880s and since the late 1920s AD (Panjwani 2000: 181).[97]

The approximate representation of Islam within the Malaŵian population is difficult to assess, and available publications provide only comparably imprecise numbers. While it may be affirmed that a rough 12 to 18 percent of the population are Muslim, the largest part of the Muslim community is situated in the Southern Region of the country due to its strong Yao population (NSO & ORC Macro 2005: 26; Matiki 2000: 153; Statistisches Bundesamt 1992: 28; Bone 1987: 28; Crosby 1980: 60). In present-day Malaŵi, three main Muslim subgroups can be distinguished that represent different theological schools. These divisions are addressed under the names Ķādiriyya, Shādhiliyya, and Sukuti, all of which belong to the larger Sunni denomination of Islam (Bone [ed.] 2000; Mahomed 2000; Bone 1987: 28). In the following, a brief outline of the respective character and history of these Muslim schools shall be given.

The Ķādiriyya brotherhood is the dominant Muslim group in Malaŵi and the strongest *ṭarīka* in the whole of Eastern Africa.[98] Reaching Zanzibar and Somalia

---

95 Another line of introduction developed from the late 17th century onwards. By that time, continental trade routes connected the area of what is now Malaŵi to the East African coast. While a Northern route, again, linked the Lake Malaŵi region with the Kilwa area, a second one went East to the coast of Mozambique. These trade routes became highways of migration. From the East, Muslim Yao groups traveled inland by the 1850s, settling in the South of Lake Malaŵi between Mangochi and Blantyre (Panjwani 2000: 181). Coming from North-Eastern Mozambique, the Yao had already been engaged in continental trade – including slave trade (Schoffeleers 1997: 34). Meanwhile, Swahili and Arab traders entered Malaŵi from the North, arriving in the 1840s and establishing lake shore settlements such as Nkhotakota, Karonga and Salima (Panjwani 2000: 184; Lienau 1981: 88).

96 The first conversion of a Yao chief to Islam is recorded around the year 1870 AD when Makanjila Bonali made Islam the state religion of his entire chiefdom (Bone 2000a: 13; Mahomed 2000: 19-20).

97 For a more concise outline on the history of the expansion of Islam in Malaŵi and neighbouring Africa see Alpers 2000.

98 This school of Islam traces its origins back to the Persian teacher ʿAbd al-Ķādir al-Djīlānī (1078–1166 AD) (Mahomed 2000: 21). The organization developed into a Ṣūfi *ṭarīka*, and at present, the Ķādiriyya is widely distributed throughout the world. It has been described as the oldest Muslim mystic order in existence. Ever since its beginning, a descendant of the founder acts as keeper of ʿAbd al-Ķādir's tomb in Baghdad, thus representing the formal head and

around the 1880s AD, the powerful phase of its conversion took place in the first decades of the 20th century AD by individual shaykhs such as the Yao Sabiti Ngaune in Jalasi (Mangochi District) or Mtumwa bindi Ali in Nkhotakota District (Mahomed 2000: 21). Ḳādiriyya theology stresses values such as moderation, modesty, human kindness, tolerance and charity. Its specific character expresses itself in a number of rituals which, at the same time, do not form an exclusive system of representations (Margoliouth 1978: 381-382).[99] In a Malaŵian setting, the Ḳādiriyya is described as strongly opposing prayer healing while supporting the *dhikr*, accompanied by the use of coloured flags and banners, as a central ritual practice. The importance of the post-funeral memorial ceremony or *sadaka*, accompanied by communal eating and drinking, is also emphasized. Their rite also displays minor differences in the Friday prayers, combining two of the five *salāt* prayers into one.

The Shādhiliyya, secondly, are the most widely represented Muslim school in the Swahili-influenced areas of the Central Region, especially around Nkhotakota and Salima Districts.[100] Its introduction into the area of modern-day Malaŵi by Arab traders and/or Yao migrants took place in the early 20th century AD due to the proselytizing of highly devoted shaykhs such as Haridi Amlani (Mahomed 2000: 22). Their theology focuses on a strict obedience to the Sharīʿa law as well as a strong position of the shaykh within the community. At the same time, their approach has been described "in the sense that a greater accent is placed on practice rather than doctrine" (Lory 1997: 174), and music as well as dancing are tolerated. The Shādhiliyya understanding of asceticism explicitly includes cherish for the beauty of God's creation, thereby allowing followers to enjoy the comforts of wealth while showing their gratitude (*shukr*) for it (Lory 1997: 174). In Malaŵi, the Shādhiliyya are the only Muslim group practicing hands-on healing, which is accompanied by prayer. They are depicted as strongly resembling the Ḳādiriyya in many respects – e.g. also combining two Friday prayers and practicing the *sadaka* and including specific *dhikr* prayers into the Friday *jumaa* (Mahomed 2000: 21-22).

The Sukuti movement, the third school in Malaŵian Islam, developed as a reformist offshoot from the mentioned Shādhiliyya order.[101] Being an originally

---

leading authority of the Ḳādiriyya order (Margoliouth 1978: 380-382).

99 One of its most striking features is the fact that women have a comparably strong position in this brotherhood, being allowed to become *walimu* or shaykhs, and teaching the Islam to other women.

100 They derive their religious custom from the teachings of Abu 'l-Hasan al-Shādhilī (1196–1258 AD), a Moroccan scholar who founded the Shādhiliyya order during his exile in Egypt as a Ṣūfi brotherhood with an emphasis on ascetic mysticism (Lory 1997: 172-175). Being introduced into Eastern Africa via the Comoros around 1850 AD, the Shādhiliyya has a strong following along the Swahili coast while its largest communities are found in Northern Africa.

101 According to Mawil Izzi Dien, they were split off in the year 1934 AD over a dispute whether or

Malaŵian phenomenon, the influence of the Sukuti movement is limited mainly to the Yao-dominated areas. The Sukuti are characterized as strictly rejecting both the concept of prayer healing and the performance of the *sadaka* memorial ceremony. Chanting, singing, dancing, and the use of flags during religious ceremonies are frowned upon, and food restrictions are observed around funerals. Their theology focuses on the teachings of the Qur'ān, thus questioning some practices observed by the other Malaŵian *ṭarīka* (Mahomed 2000: 22).

Even though the differences between these three Muslim schools are frequently stressed, the unity of Islam is likewise emphasized as overcoming these minor exegetic variations.[102] This is stressed by the fact that Muslim dignitaries such as *ashehe* (see below) frequently express their conviction that they cannot be considered as members of one of these groups once they attain their elevated status. Rather, as many *ashehe* stress, their high spiritual position takes them beyond these minor differentiations, possible sectarianism, and favouring a certain school of Islam.

Muslim Therapeutic Specialists

Especially in rural areas of Southern Malaŵi, the representatives of Muslim organizations have a considerable impact on the health seeking behaviour of the believers in their area. Here, not only their spiritual counsel is of crucial importance to the understanding of a given health problem, but some Muslim dignitaries also consider medical services as part of their religious office. It is, at the same time, a question of some dispute whether the notion of a specifically Muslim healer conflicts with Islam or not. A Yao *shehe* thus elaborates that

> "[...] in Islam, a person cannot call himself a healer, and God says every disease has got medicine. This simply means it is not someone who belongs to Katriya or Sukuti who can give medicine. Any Muslim can do it, provided he knows how to prepare the medicine. Talking about myself, I don't know how to prepare medicine but I have been to Sudan for five years. But my other friends who had been in Sudan know how to do it because they learned. [...] They use verses from the Qur'ān" (Lazim Khananji, a Yao *shehe*).

---

not singing and dancing should be permitted on certain ritual occasions. The followers of shaykh Ali bin Salimu, who was in opposition to Ṣūfi tradition, acquired the name Sukuti as an expression of the silence – with the Arabic *sukūt* meaning 'quiet' (Izzi Dien 1997: 806) – they maintain during prayers and funerals.

102 In addition to the mentioned clashes between these groups – being about the post-funerary celebrations or *sadaka*, singing and dancing at funerals or the carrying of flags, the combination of separate prayers as well as the exact text of the *dhikr* – Imuran Mahomed also mentions questions concerning issues like the eating of hippopotamus meat as causes of religious dispute (Mahomed 2000: 22-23). For additional information on the differences between the different Islamic schools in Malaŵi see Panjwani 2000: 190.

Regardless of this more theological discussion, a variety of persons offer medical services with an explicitly Muslim frame of reference. Within all of the above mentioned Muslim communities, these persons are usually holders of official positions which may be differentiated according to a number of hierarchical levels of status.

As the most widely applied term in this context, the Chiyao term *shehe* – derived from the Arabic shaykh – denotes a scholar of the Qur'ān and the Muslim faith. The qualification necessary for obtaining this prestigious title is comparably loosely defined: the most common prerequisite for being recognized as a *shehe* is to undertake a religious quest called *daha*[103] which lies in reading the Qur'ān to the rural people for a number of years as a means of proselytizing. Due to his religious authority, the *shehe* is an expert in the realm of spirits who is experienced not only in contacting spirits (*majini*) as well as in finding ways of treating disorders induced by them. As a subcategory of the *ashehe*, some parts of the population distinguish the group of the *ashehe aduni* as denoting those *ashehe* who acquired their elevated spiritual status after having worked as a traditional healer (*sing'anga*) before, therefore having an even stronger medical background. The title of a *mwalimu*, the Kiswahili term for a 'teacher,' is applied for a Muslim instructor. Usually, this position ranks below the authority of a *shehe*, but like *ashehe*, some *walimu* are known to have certain medical abilities due to their knowledge of the Qur'ān and their habit of conversing with the sphere of the spirits. As a third major category, the *ngaliba* resembles an initiation specialist among the Muslim Yao. He is in charge of carrying out the Yao boys' initiation rituals (*jando*) in a special circumcision shelter (*ndagala*), and in the more remote areas of rural Malaŵi, he frequently takes the responsibility of conveying behavioural rules (*miyambo*) as a religious instructor. Some traditional healers (*asing'anga*) also adhere to the Muslim faith, thus observing certain faith-specific *miyambo* when executing their medical profession. They are referred to as *asing'anga a matalasimu*, indicating the use of *matalasimu* (see below) as their distinctive therapeutic characteristic. Deriving their healing powers directly and exclusively from the Supreme Being, they consider themselves as a mere tool of divine will, and due to their close bonds to the spiritual realm, *asing'anga a matalasimu* condemn the use of non-Muslim, traditional insignia – such as the divinatory gourd (*nsupa*) or the flywhisk (*mchira*).[104]

---

103 The concept of *daha* can be regarded as the Yao-ized version of the Arabic word *dā'i*, denoting a 'propagandist' of the faith.

104 Therefore, a *sing'anga a matalasimu* is in constant contact with the agents of his spiritual cosmology who act as mediators between him/her and God. While these spirit entities are sometimes defined as angels (*angelo*), they may also belong to the *majini* category of spirits. In order to emphasize the strong connections to the spirit world, a Yao *shehe* explains that it is not

These abovementioned specialists apply a number of therapeutic techniques as part of their medical responsibilities. While some of these show strong similarities with other, e.g. Christian, forms of therapy, some attitudes towards healing can still be considered as specific for the Muslim Yao. The following paragraphs will outline basic principles of religious healing as advocated and carried out within the sphere of Malaŵian Islam.

Muslim Medicine

When performing religious healing, Muslim specialists among the Yao frequently rely on the spiritual authority – and therefore, therapeutic value – of the Qur'ān. While the Qur'ān consists of 114 sūra or chapters – each of which is comprised of a varying number of āyāt or verses –, the passages applied in the context of religious healing typically constitute a small part of the full sūra only, and their knowledge depends on the personal expertise of the given religious specialist. In Southern Malaŵi, the verses which are identified as therapeutically relevant are frequently referred to as *sūra ya sini*, and they unfurl their medical potential due to recitation and/or transcription. While many of the therapeutic sūra are reported to be specific for the treatment of a particular kind of health disorder, the general idea underlying this concept of healing is comparably unspecific. By reciting the Qur'ān, a person asks for divine support for and protection against some kind of distress which is defined by the choice of verse that is applied.[105] In the context of this present research, some sūra and their particular medical uses have been specified.[106] While most of them imply a protection against the attacks of *majini* spirits, the sūra used against mental disorder include the following:

> "We have got sūra *te-thlas*, sūra *te-lanas* and sūra *te-tharak*, and sūra *tu-jinni*. The first three are short so you can recite them and sing during the day, and later during the night you can recite sūra *tu-jinni* and *ayatu-kursi*" (Lazim Khananji, a Yao *shehe*).

---

considered unusual for a male *matalasimu* healer to establish a close relationship to a female *jinni* in the form of actual marriage. To an outsider, the spirit agent would appear as a perfectly normal woman at all times. The concept of *maula* divination is discussed elsewhere (see *Chapter II.2.a*).

105 As a basic prerequisite, only the prayers of a true believer living according to the culturally recognized Muslim norms is expected to find divine attention, but a person endued with such a strong faith can also focus his or her prayers onto a third person, asking God to help them.

106 Due to slight linguistic contortions of the names given for the respective verses, their identification may not always be accurate even though some expert assistance was fortunately available. At this point, Professor Heinz Grotzfeld from the Institute for Arabic Philology and Islamic Studies at the University of Münster shall once again be gratefully mentioned for his support.

This short account of Qur'ān verses may serve to exemplify the character of the sūra which are applied in Muslim religious healing in Southern Malaŵi. While the so-called *te-thlas* therefore is of a more general nature that does not provide an immediate therapeutic specification,[107] the subsequent chapter – rendered in the context of the quoted interview as sūra *te-lanas* – is specific in its reference to the protection against the attacks of spirit agents.[108] The mentioned sūra *te-tharak*, on the other hand, emphasizes divine guardianship that protects every faithful from the actions of disbelievers,[109] while sūra *tu-jinni* reiterates cosmological structure and divine order with a focus on God's spiritual supremacy. The last-mentioned sūra named *ayatu-kursi* is described as being widely applicable, providing divine help against all kinds of health disorders when recited.[110] In addition to these, a sūra called *te-falas* is memorized and then recited before going to sleep in order to obtain divine protection during the night. This procedure is supposed to help against thieves and the magic attacks of *afiti* likewise.[111] As a special form of healing prayer, some interviewees mention a formula called *dowa*. It is described as a prayer used for those suffering, traveling, in danger or distress. By reciting a *dowa* prayer, a person expresses

---

107 This may be identified as sūra 112 (*al-ihlās*) which states "Say: He is Allah, the One! / Allah, the eternally Besought of all! / He begetteth not nor was begotten. / And there is none comparable unto Him" (Pickthall 1930: sūra 112).

108 The mentioned *te-lanas* may be interpreted as referring to the six verses of sūra 114 (*an-nās*), saying that "Say: I seek refuge in the Lord of mankind, / The King of mankind, / The God of mankind, / From the evil of the sneaking whisperer, / Who whispereth in the hearts of mankind, / Of the jinn and of mankind" (Pickthall 1930: sūra 114).

109 This may refer to sūra 86 (*aṭ-ṭāriq*) whose 17 āyāt will be given here in full length: "By the heaven and the Morning Star / Ah, what will tell thee what the Morning Star is! / The piercing Star! / No human soul but hath a guardian over it. / So let man consider from what he is created. / He is created from a gushing fluid / That issued from between the loins and ribs. / Lo! He verily is Able to return him (unto life) / On the day when hidden thoughts shall be searched out. / Then will he have no might nor any helper. / By the heaven which giveth the returning rain, / And the earth which splitteth (with the growth of and plants) / Lo! this (Qur'an) is a conclusive word, / It is no pleasantry. / Lo! they plot a plot (against thee, O Muhammad) / And I plot a plot (against them). / So give a respite to the disbelievers. Deal thou gently with them for a while" (Pickthall 1930: sūra 86).

110 Presumably, the Yao-ized expression *ayatu-kursi* refers to āyāt 255 of sūra 2 (*āyāt u-kursi*). This verse serves the general glorification of divine power, and it is rendered as follows: "Allah! There is no God save Him, the Alive, the Eternal. Neither slumber nor sleep overtaketh Him. Unto Him belongeth whatsoever is in the heavens and whatsoever is in the earth. Who is he that intercedeth with Him save by His leave? He knoweth that which is in front of them and that which is behind them, while they encompass nothing of His knowledge save what He will. His throne includeth the heavens and the earth, and He is never weary of preserving them. He is the Sublime, the Tremendous" (Pickthall 1930: sūra 2).

111 With some caution, *te-falas* may be interpreted as sūra 113 (*al-falaq*) of the Qur'ān whose five āyāt read as follows: "Say: I seek refuge in the Lord of Daybreak / From the evil of that which He created; / From the evil of the darkness when it is intense, / And from the evil of malignant witchcraft, / And from the evil of the envier when he envieth" (Pickthall 1930: sūra 113).

gratitude for his or her own fitness and well-being, asking for divine support for those who are less fortunate.[112]

As a central feature of Muslim forms of therapy, prayer healing is a common way of curing all kinds of health disorders, being especially relevant in the treatment of mental disorders.[113] In Southern Malaŵi, local Yao *ashehe* address this technique as *kusoma* – an originally Kiswahili term meaning 'to read' or 'to study' – which denotes the reading and/or recitation of passages of the Qur'ān. Certain sūra are known for their properties to appease as well as drive out spirit agents (*majini*) responsible for the mental disorder of a given patient (see *Chapter IV.2.a*). This practice requires a certain degree of religious expertise, as only some Qur'ān sūra hold medical powers, and all of them are effective for a specific purpose only, e.g. for the cure of a given kind of sickness. The specific efficiency of specific verses is expressed in expressions such as the following:

> "In Islam, when a person has *majini* we recite the sūra. This is done in presence of the person. We use the Qur'ān and this is called sūra *tu-jinni* – meaning, to a person who has been attacked by *majini*. [...] The *majini* leaves the person. [...] If he was talking a lot, he stops, and if he was feeling headache, it stops" (Lazim Khananji, a Yao *shehe*).[114]

Even though prayer is frequently applied for the treatment of mental disorders, opinions about its medical efficiency were still divided among Muslim faith specialists. Thus, a traditional Islamic leader expresses his position that prayers are not meant to cure a person, but only served to save the patient's soul while other *ashehe* agree that healing by recitation of Qur'ān verses is possible. At the same time, it is expressed that strong personal faith is a prerequisite for prayers to be answered, as they only ask God for help.[115] As a general rule, healing

---

112 As an example, the Yao chairman of a Muslim organization recommends the use of the *dowa* in order to treat a patient suffering from *misala* caused by *majini*. The *majini* leave the person immediately, and unsuccessful treatment would only be conceivable in case the condition is caused by something other than *majini* spirits. Reportedly, the prophet Muhammad himself used *dowa* – a term derived from the Arabic *duā'*, meaning a personal prayer as opposed to the strictly formalized service of worship, the *ṣalāt* (Dorpmüller 2005: 247) – in order to do miracles, and they can be applied in order to ask divine forgiveness for a third person.

113 Even among local Muslims it is debated whether practices of prayer and recitation can be seen as therapeutic steps in themselves. Particularly educated Muslim leaders tend to claim that prayer can be used to ask for divine grace. At the same time, prayers performed for children with severe mental disorders are said not to focus on healing, but have the sole purpose of safeguarding the child's spiritual wellbeing.

114 This Qur'ān chapter has been identified as sūra *al-djinn* (sūra 72). While its 28 verses make it too elongated to quote in full, it may suffice in this context to assess that the chapter in question focuses on the cosmological fact that no *jinn*, whether good or evil, can contest the power of God (Pickthall 1930: sūra 72).

115 Therefore, prayer healing strongly implies asking for divine support. At the same time, these prayers can also seek for divine mercy, with persons repenting their sins in the hope of healing.

prayers can be conducted by the affected persons themselves as well as by third parties who pray on their behalf. In many cases, a person recites Qur'ān verses in search of divine help in a personal health problem. This process of individual prayer healing is described as follows:

> "There are some verses, *sūra*, in the Qur'ān which talk about healing, so they copy them onto a paper and recite them for several times. And again, even when you are feeling headache or anything else, you can also recite the same verses for two or three times and you get healed" (Lazim Khananji, a Yao *shehe*).

As some *ashehe* explain, prayers for the sick are an elementary part of Islamic teaching. The Qur'ān requests every believer to visit the sick, and prayers for their well-being are a customary element of these visitations. Likewise, relatives or even Muslim specialists can say their prayers for a person suffering from mental disorder, which is usually conducted in the presence of the respective patient. Prayers meant to cure conditions such as mental disorders caused by *majini* spirits may need to be conducted five times a day or must be undertaken over a prolonged period of time – e.g. a number of days. In addition to that, recitation of Qur'ān verses can also serve as a prophylaxis against the attacks of malevolent spirits such as *majini*.[116]

As a less prominent feature of Muslim Faith Healing, some groups practice prayer healing accompanied by hands-on healing. As mentioned above, only the Shādhiliyya group in Malaŵi supports hands-on healing as part of their healing ministry. Non- Shādhiliyya *ashehe* describe this technique as a part of unofficial or folk-Islam, at the same time disclosing that these practices are reported to prove successful for minor health disorders such as headaches.

The Power of the Matalasimu

According to Muslim historiography, the Qur'ān was laid down by the prophet Muhammad himself when receiving the words of God through the angel Jibrīl – who is equivalent to the Christian archangel Gabriel. A considerable number of the sūra provide explicitly therapeutic instructions which have a high degree of cosmological validity and authority within a Muslim discourse due to their directly divine source. According to these instructions, Muslim healers with the necessary expertise of the Qur'ān prepare concoctions (*mankhwala akumwa*) for their patients. The therapeutic use of the Qur'ān, however, is not limited to its

---

This concept implies a model of divine punishment which will be elaborated elsewhere (see *Chapter IV.2.b*).

116 Therefore, as a Muslim specialist explains, "as a protection I just recite the verses from the Qur'ān. It is a good thing to recite during the night and in the morning" (Lazim Khananji, a Yao *shehe*).

direct medical contents. Rather, many local Muslims agree that the use of a therapy called *matalasimu* must be recognized as the central non-biomedical technique in Muslim Malaŵi.

> "In Islam, we believe that any disease has got its medicine. So people are asked to go to the hospital whenever they are sick. In case of failing to get healed, they then use *matalasimu*" (Lazim Khananji, a Yao *shehe*).

In short, the Kiswahili term *matalasimu* subsumes the therapeutic use of religious texts in a pseudo-magical way of contagious transmission.[117] It usually takes the form of a small, handwritten document with clear reference to Islam which is, in itself, put to direct medical use. Due to the fact that the choice of religious texts written onto a *matalasimu* – as well as their mode of administration – is crucial to its effect, their preparation and application is bound to a specialist's knowledge of the Qur'ān or other religious texts suitable for the given occasion.[118] Any person who has acknowledged expertise in the use of *matalasimu* is usually attributed with the dignitary title of a *shehe* or shaykh.

Matalasimu therapy may be applied in a number of different ways. The most widely known technique used to treat mental as well as other forms of disorder is oral ingestion, also described as *kumwera matalasimu* (i.e. 'drinking *matalasimu*'). Thus, a *matalasimu* expert writes an appropriate Qur'ān sūra onto a piece of paper on behalf of a patient and his or her given health disorder. This patient, in turn, receives the slip of paper – usually folded and tied up with string in to keep its written contents secret – along with instructions for its application. The exact procedures specified here usually involve soaking the piece of paper in a given liquid and subsequently imbibing it.[119] The drinking of the fluid in question constitutes the central therapeutic act. Alternatively, the sūra may be written onto a blackboard with chalk and then squashed with water which is

---

117 This term converges with the English 'talisman', both being derived from the Arabic *ṭilasm* (pl. *ṭalāsim*) as an "inscription with astrological and other magic signs or an object covered with such inscriptions" (Bosworth 2000: 500). The form applied in the Malaŵian context represents the Kiswahili *talasimu* (pl. *matalasimu*) for a "talisman, charm, magic diagram" (Johnson 2003:447).

118 Surprisingly, a Yao *shehe* contradicts this notion, saying that the true source for learning the *matalasimu* lies in different kinds of books written in Arabic. According to him, "people mistake them, saying it is the Qur'ān because the books used are written in Arabic numerals. [...] There are some books that have names. For example *al-ufak*, *shams-mari*, a lot of books" (Lazim Khananji, a Yao *shehe*). With all due caution, the latter of these books may be identified as *Shams al-ma'ārif al-kubrā wa-laṭā'if al-'awārif,* a tome of magic written by the Algerian Ṣufi and writer Abū 'l-'Abbās al-Būnī who died in 1225 AD (Dorpmüller 2005: 232; Dietrich 2004: 156).

119 Such instructions may e.g. define that the *matalasimu* must be boiled up with tea for ten minutes, or that it needs to be immersed in water for 24 hours before being imbibed on three consecutive days.

collected and, again, ingested as medicine. Not all forms of *matalasimu* are applied by drinking though. They may also be written on paper, folded up and put into a small leather pouch (*chithumwa*) to be worn around the neck, thus gradually developing its therapeutic properties on its bearer.[120]

The preparation of *matalasimu* follows sophisticated rules known to and prescribed by the acting medical professional. The palpable preparation of *matalasimu* for a patient typically involves two consecutive consultations. On the first meeting, patients express their medical needs to the *matalasimu* specialist. The time between the first and second session is needed for preparations. In order to ban the divine power onto paper, the *sing'anga a matalasimu* first undergoes cleansing rituals performed before prayer service, and puts on clean clothes. By means of the following prayers, he or she obtains knowledge about the verses that need to be applied against the complaints of the specific patient. Only then can the *sing'anga* start writing. In some cases, it is reported that the name of the respective patient needs to be added to the medically efficient Qur'ān text, and that the specialist himself or herself observes certain rules of ritual purity when writing them down.

The effectiveness of a *matalasimu* treatment is not only determined by the choice of religious text applied, but it also depends on the composition of the ink used to transcribe the respective verses. Here, specialists usually have personal recipes specific for a given medical purpose.[121] On the following day, a second meeting is held when the *matalasimu* are handed over to the patient, along with precise prescriptions for their application. It should be noted that *matalasimu* do not necessarily consist of a single piece of paper only. Rather, the whole course of medication may require combinations such as three small, tied-up square paper bundles which have to be carried close at all times, while four other slips of folded paper are meant to be immersed in water and drank on four consecutive occasions.[122] In the treatment of mental disorder, *matalasimu* are only regarded

---

120 The daily recitation of *matalasimu* texts is likewise mentioned, resembling the more general use of religious texts for therapeutic purposes as depicted above and requiring considerable personal expertise.

121 The preparation of the ink used for writing *matalasimu* is therefore part of the therapeutic process. A Yao *sing'anga a matalasimu* mentions different kinds of ink, one of which he refers to as *wino*, a black ink consisting of the ashes of special plants and maize seeds. For the treatment of *misala*, he uses a different kind of ink, being produced from mixing saffron (*Crocus sativus*, obtained from local traders) with animal blood. This, he explains, would have an additional, calming effect on the spirit causing the disorder, acting as an oblation. At the same time, he expresses that, when mixing his inks in the proper way, the healing power comes straight from God.

122 This case study refers to a previous field research and was recorded on August 11th and 12th 2001 in Senga Bay, Salima District (Central Region). Here, a Muslim Yao *sing'anga* from Makanjila, Mangochi District, prescribed this *matalasimu* treatment as a love charm – thus substantiating the fact that *matalasimu* practices can be applied for a variety of magic purposes.

as effective if the respective case is directly connected to the cosmological sphere – being caused either by spirit agents (*majini*), by *ufiti* magic, or by structural reasons (see *Chapter IV.3*). While some cases – such as those induced by drug abuse – are therefore regarded as being beyond its capabilities, most other forms of mental disorder are considered to be curable by the use of *matalasimu*.[123] These specific cases differ in the choice of sūra applied, with some of these being highly efficient against *majini* spirits while others counteract evil magic or may be used to invoke divine mercy. In spite of the high importance of *matalasimu* for Muslim healing among the Yao, some interviewees still have a very critical attitude towards this medical practice. Especially persons with a higher degree of Islamic education protest that the use of *matalasimu* is not part of original Islam and pointing out its similarities to non-Muslim, traditional practices.[124] Accordingly,

> "A shaykh who does this is a witchdoctor himself, and he charges a fee for the work done" (Lazim Khananji, a Yao *shehe*).

Admittedly, the division between *matalasimu* and more conventional *using'anga* is not always as clear-cut as this depiction might suggest. Rather, this specifically Muslim form of therapy is sometimes combined with plant elements – in the sense of *mtengo* or *masamba* medicine – which indicate the direct connection to traditional Malaŵian medical systems.[125]

Muslim religious healing in Southern Malaŵi follows a multi-layered rationale. Unambiguously, the cosmological authority required to achieve therapeutic success is derived from the Qur'ān.[126] The process of Muslim faith healing works on different levels, all of which pursue the general goal of establishing a close spiritual connection to supreme religious authority. Firstly, religious texts are used in a strictly analytic way by directly extracting positive

---

123 A rather graphic account of successful treatment with *matalasimu* is provided by a Yao *shehe*.

124 The wearing of *matalasimu* as a necklace therefore parallels them with *zithumwa* (see *Chapter II.2.a*). Many *ashehe* express their concern about the non-Islamic implications of this procedure, stating that "When you take paper as your God, that is totally against Islam. People of course use these verses to protect themselves. Sometimes they work and sometimes they don't. What you do is you ask God, like »I am doing this in your name, and I am asking for your protection«. Do not take this paper as your protector, but take God as the protector. The paper cannot protect you. People do not understand: they take this paper, put it around their neck and say this is my protector – meaning a piece of paper" (Lazim Khananji, a Yao *shehe*).

125 Thus, Yao *ashehe* relate that *asing'anga a matalasimu* possess certain texts about the use of plant medicine which may be administered as such or in combination with a *matalasimu* treatment.

126 As indicated, other, less common texts associated with comparably strong spiritual power may also be used. Obviously, non-experts tend to identify all scriptures applied in this context as originating from the Qur'ān while specialist knowledge indicates that other texts composed by different, highly valued Islamic authorities also act as sources of faith healing power.

norms of conduct – i.e. therapeutic instructions – from the religious text in order to avoid or treat personal health complaints. On a second, more symbolic level, reading and reciting certain parts of religious scripture is seen as evoking divine power to prevent or cure sickness – including mental disorder. In this context, the sacred text is conceptualized as manifesting the superior cosmological order from which it originates, thus possessing protective as well as therapeutic properties as granted by the Supreme Being to the truly faithful. Thirdly and even more complex, the sacred writing itself may be associated with therapeutic qualities which penetrate the material medium it is written on. The transcription of religiously potent texts onto a piece of paper thus transfers their medically utilizable power onto the profane object and thereby transforms it into powerful medicine. This process of analogous transfer of spiritual power represents the part of Muslim faith healing that is most fiercely rejected by the majority of Islamic authorities, being considered inconsistent with Islamic teaching and closely representing traditional Malaŵian forms of medicine. Nonetheless, the application of these *matalasimu* is frequently described as the most common form of Muslim healing in a rural context, and it therefore underlines the considerable influence of traditional, non-dogmatic practices within the religious discourses of medicine in South Malaŵi. Along with the other mentioned forms of therapy that derive its medical potential from sacred texts, *matalasimu* represent one of the most important techniques to treat mental disorder in an explicitly Muslim frame of reference. The wider cosmological conception of the phenomenon as such will be addressed at the end of this chapter.

2(c) Christian Approaches

Christian faith encompasses a wide scope of different religious denominations, and other than the Christian mainstream in Western Europe, many Christian communities in Malaŵi regard religious healing as a major part of their spiritual responsibility and dedicate considerable effort to this mission. Among the wide variety of Christian churches found in the Southern Region, a large number have an implicit or explicit focus on faith healing practices. Attributing great efficiency to these techniques in the treatment of virtually any health complaint, a wide public discourse surrounds reported cases of successful faith healing within the social environment of both rural and urban Malaŵi. For the sake of their particular therapeutic commitment, large numbers of Christian believers perceive Pentecostal churches as an attractive alternative to the cosmopolitan mainstream – a branch of Christianity that gains growing influence in the local health discourse. Considering these conditions, the therapeutic significance of Christian churches in Southern Malaŵi clearly seems to be increasing.

In order to allow a better understanding of Christian notions of faith healing in the context of mental disorder in Southern Malaŵi, this section will provide a short historical summary of the genesis of Christianity in the region before introducing the various Christian groupings that interest us in this context. Defining the religious agents performing these medical duties and outlining their therapeutic actions, this section will finally substantiate the relevance of different Christian currents within the public discourse of mental disorder.

Christianity in Malaŵi

In many African countries, Christianity and Christianization are closely connected to the period of colonialism. The gradual introduction of Christianity into the area of present-day Malaŵi followed in the footsteps of the British explorer-missionary David Livingstone (1813–1873 AD) who took a leading role in the formation of the Universities Mission to Central Africa (UMCA) in 1857 AD.[127] Establishing the first Christian mission in the Southern of the country, the mission center at Magomero, Zomba District, operated from 1861 onwards while UMCA installed a second mission post in Cape Maclear, Mangochi District, in 1875 AD (Phiri 2004: 136; Panjwani 2000: 185).[128] In the following decades, both Catholic and protestant churches – e.g. the Catholic White Fathers or the protestant Dutch Reformed Church – engaged in evangelization of Malaŵi, maintaining considerable influence within the country (Marwick 1965: 64). According to recent surveys, an estimated 86 percent of the national population in Malaŵi is considered to adhere to Christian faith. Strikingly, the largest single category within this Christian scale – a rough 36 percent of the overall population – is specified as 'other Christian' (NSO & ORC Macro 2005: 26).[129] A high percentage of Christian communities in Malaŵi are part of non-

---

127 In the honour of this Scottish explorer's birth place in South Lanarkshire, the Church of Scotland named its first mission station in the Shire Highlands, founded in 1876, the Blantyre Mission which developed into what is now the municipality of Blantyre (Phiri 2004: 113).

128 The Magomero post had to be abandoned by 1863 due to its unfavourable climatic conditions as well as frequent clashes between local Yao and Nyanja groups. Therefore, the UMCA mission station was temporarily transferred to Zanzibar. In 1875 AD, the Livingstonia Mission – yet another tribute to the Scottish missionary who had died two year previously – was established near Cape Maclear before moving to Bandawe, Nkhata Bay District, in 1882 and finally settling in Karonga District of Northern Malaŵi by 1894 (. Phiri 2004: 116-119).

129 Recent numbers indicate that the Roman Catholic Church (22.2 percent of the population) as well as the Church of Central African Presbyterian (CCAP, with 18.7 percent) represent the most considerable communities in Malaŵi. Seventh Day Adventist or Baptist (6.3 percent jointly) as well as Anglican (2.4 percent) denominations still have a solid representation, while 36.3 percent of the population belong to other Christian denominations (NSO & ORC Macro 2005: 26). Many other statistical surveys disregard a more thorough differentiation of Christian groups. However, Peter G. Forster already alludes to the growing importance of born-again Christians in Malaŵi (Forster 1998: 538).

cosmopolitan Christian organizations but rather churches with national or even regional distribution. Research data suggests that great numbers of these church communities coexist within a given area, creating a very dense and heterogeneous network of partially cooperating, partially competing religious units (Chakanza 1979).[130] Currently, the most influential Christian groupings constituting the vast amount of non-cosmopolitan Christian denominations in Malaŵi belong to the broad category of Pentecostal Churches, and their explicit faith healing theology makes them an even more important focus for this study.[131]

Pentecostalism is not an African phenomenon – even though, as closer observations below shall indicate, its characteristics show some parallels with traditional African concepts of religion which facilitate evangelization. As soon as 1908 AD, North American missionaries exported the idea of Pentecostalism to South Africa, spreading throughout Southern Africa in the following decades.[132] Today, those Pentecostal churches active in Malaŵi can be distinguished into three major groups – these being the Classic Pentecostal Churches, the Younger Charismatic groups, and the Zionist denominations. For all of these, faith healing constitutes an important part of their theology, and a bewildering multitude of different persuasions exists simultaneously, amassing a considerable amount of followers.[133] However, fixed numbers can only provide a fairly broad impression, as these communities are subject to continuous changes – with new denominations breaking off from existing churches and forming new ones, or small ones merging into larger religious bodies. Especially older and more mature denominations develop a more differentiated understanding of sickness, along with the respective, highly sophisticated healing ministry.

---

130 As a sample survey illustrates, 28 different Christian denominations have recently been identified as operating in Balaka Parish, Balaka District, alone (Tilisho 2003: 23-24).

131 The high relevance of Pentecostalism is not a Malaŵian peculiarity. Rather, the considerable cultural impact of Pentecostal churches and their influence on neo-traditionalism in Ghana has recently been investigated by Marleen de Witte (Witte 2005).

132 Some short remarks may illustrate the historical genesis of the Pentecostal movement. While Pentecostalism shares some similarities with conservative Methodist as well as Baptist theology, the distinct development of Pentecostalism is connected to a number of founders. Here, the Scottish evangelist and faith healer John Alexander Dowie (1847–1907 AD) as well as the Canadian theologian Albert Benjamin Simpson (1843–1919 AD) are of importance. The first public manifestation of a Pentecostal movement is the almost legendary Azusa Street Awakening in Los Angeles which stood under the guidance of the African American preacher William Joseph Seymour (1870–1922 AD) in 1906.

133 Current research indicates that over 200 Classic Pentecostal and Younger Charismatic groups as well as an additional 27 Zionist denominations can be distinguished nationwide. Klaus Fiedler provides some estimate numbers, stating that the Assemblies of God (see below) might total a rough 80,000 members at present while the Apostolic Faith Mission is reckoned at 25,000 faithful (Fiedler 1999: 32).

As indicated above, Classic Pentecostal churches form an influential religious movement.[134] Forming the mainstream of Malaŵian Pentecostalism, they have a considerable impact in both urban and rural communities, and the different Classic Pentecostal congregations represent an ever-growing factor in the religious geography of Southern Malaŵi.[135] As a typical example of a Classic Pentecostal church, the Assemblies of God (AoG) may be mentioned which, due to the missionary efforts of migrant converts, expanded their influence into Malaŵi by 1934 AD (Fiedler 1999: 31). Following the principal faith in the Holy Spirit (*Mzimu Woyera*) and the Holy Trinity, the theology of the AoG embraces healing prayers for the sick as a vital part of their religious agenda and as the universal tool to solve personal problems by achieving divine deliverance.[136] Evidently, the approach to medical issues is crucial within the framework of the present study. With special reference to the healing ministry of the Apostolic Faith Mission (AFM) in Malaŵi, Ulf Strohbehn points out that

> "Pentecostalism teaches that there is an ongoing spiritual battle between the heavenly and evil forces. Curses, chants and bewitchment are not »explained away« in Pentecostalism [...]. Pentecostals view sickness oftentimes as if the devil has a foothold in the life of the afflicted. This does, however, not automatically mean that the person is also blamed for the sickness or even accused of secret sins. [...] Demonisation is not assumed unless certain manifestations have been observed. Signs of demon possession are fainting, falling down, ecstatic and uncontrollable shouting, cursing and even physical violence" (Strohbehn 2000: 2).

As the second main category, the Younger Charismatic churches have been mentioned.[137] Based on classic Pentecostal representations, the Charismatic

---

134 As examples of these Classic Pentecostal communities in Malaŵi, the influential Assemblies of God (AoG) and the Apostolic Faith Mission (AFM) shall be mentioned. The AFM, established in 1933 AD and thus commonly considered as the oldest Pentecostal denomination in the country, currently boasts about 200 local congregations nationwide (Strohbehn 2000: 1). Smaller Classic Pentecostal churches include organizations such as Christ Citadel, Harvest Rock Ministries, Free Love Ministries, Built on the Rock Church, or the Bible Believers.

135 Within Zomba municipality, the Assemblies of God have an estimated 500 members. In contrast to complex and stratified organizations such as the AoG, smaller Classic Pentecostal churches have an entirely different setup. Due to their more dispersed following typically found in rural or suburban areas – the priest of a small Classic Pentecostal church describes his flock as "18 members in Namadidi Trading Center, 15 members in Chinsusi, and 25 members in Sadzi" –, communities such as Free Love Ministries are undertaking outreach activities on a regular basis in order to increase their impact. These prayer missions are frequently a magnet for persons living with mental disorders who consider Pentecostal churches as a potential therapeutic option – but also as a whole new approach to making sense of their respective life situation.

136 An AoG official formulates her conviction that "Church is about war against evil. [...] God is the solution for any problem" (Mariam Mwale, a Nyanja Church administrator).

137 This category is not identical with the wider term of Charismatic Churches. Among these

Movement took its origin in the United States in 1960 AD, reaching Malaŵi in the 1970s and spreading immensely throughout the 1980s (Fiedler 1999: 33).[138] At present, typical Younger Charismatic churches are a primarily urban phenomenon, offering English services and including issues like professional and economic success as an important focus into their ministry. Prayer services held by Younger Charismatic churches frequently have the character of suit-and-tie occasions, with professionals from the corporate sector with a comparably high degree of Western cultural orientation forming one of the main target groups. The theology of Younger Charismatic churches also puts a strong emphasis on faith healing, generally considering sickness – and, likewise, mental disorder – as a necessary consequence of personal sin.[139]

Finally, Zionist churches also belong to the wider complex of Pentecostal churches in Malaŵi, reaching the country in 1923 AD (Fiedler 1999: 29). Tracing their origin to the Christian Catholic Church in Zion, Illinois, Zionist denominations in Southern Africa were under considerable initial influence from the American Pentecostalism before breaking away from them in the early 20th century AD. Even though the Zionist churches may primarily appear as small local communities, the 27 different Zionist groups reported so far have an estimated support of 80,000 followers throughout the country.[140] Many of the

---

Younger Charismatic churches, the following as examples may be mentioned: Living Waters, Charismatic Renewal Ministry, Faith of God International, Universal Church of the Kingdom of God, Amazing Grace, Calvary Family Church, All For Jesus Church, Wide Alive Ministry (formerly Blantyre Christian Center), Agape Life, Deeper Life, Mastered Seed, Forward in Faith Church, Revival Ministry, or Wells of Revival.

138 At present, more than 30 Charismatic churches are reported in Blantyre alone, estimating the total Charismatic community at 20,000 nationwide (Fiedler 1999: 33).

139 Among the Younger Charismatic churches, the Living Waters Church can be considered to be one of the most prominent ones. Having started as a branch of the Apostolic Faith Mission (AFM) in 1985 by Stanley Ndovi, it now boasts an estimated following of over 50,000 believers nationwide. Services conducted by Apostle Ndovi and his fellow preachers are frequently broadcast on Malaŵian state television, emphasizing their focus on a young, Western-oriented target group (Anderson 2002). Their local communities are structured as loose prayer groups within which members meet at their private homes and take it in turns to head the gatherings and prepare prayer and sermon. Joint yet individual prayers are also part of the meetings, usually followed by prayer healing.

140 As an example for Zionist denominations, the Holy Apostolic Church in Zion (HACZ) may be mentioned. Introduced in Malaŵi as early as 1925 AD, its branch in the suburbs of Blantyre City is headed by a *mlevi* – a 'Levite' or local leader – who conducts local services held on Sunday afternoons. The overall leader of the HACZ bears the title of a bishop or *bishopo*. Because of customs such as of praying over their drums before service – thus creating 'sacred' objects –, other apostolic churches (like AFM) disassociate from the HACZ, criticizing their exegetical approach. The Zion Christian Church (ZCC), as another example, has it's headquarter in Lilongwe District (Peltzer 1987: 54). One of the most renowned Zionist denominations in Malaŵi is the African Apostolic Church of John Maranke (AACJM) with its regional headquarters in Balaka District. Its founder, the Zimbabwean Shona apostle John Maranke (c.

smaller Zionist communities have only regional distribution. In Malaŵi, Zionist denominations frequently express themselves as a rural phenomenon, and they combine a strong Pentecostal heritage with traditional elements such as drumming and dancing performances integrated into church services. Male church officials as well as many male members are typically encouraged to grow long beards and wear long white robes during the services. For Zionist churches, healing testimonies also have crucial importance – being frequently perceived as representing a deliverance from the satanic influence of *ufiti*. Mostly, medical treatment is provided by communal prayers, the use of Holy Water, and Holy Communion – which is seen as being in line with Biblical tradition.[141]

While these numerous denominations are divided by some important differences, many parts of their respective theology show similar structures. As mentioned earlier, their attitude towards religious healing is one of the most important factors – not only for the scope of this current study, but also within public discourse in Southern Malaŵi.

Christian Healing Specialists

Many of the above mentioned non-mainstream churches share an explicit emphasis on the idea of faith-healing. Many representatives of these non-cosmopolitan churches define their religious duties as explicitly including medical services. Though these representatives are typically organized in hierarchical models that are specific for every single one of these denominations, certain terminological categories are accepted so generally that they may be introduced here in order to outline the overall structures of non-cosmopolitan Christianity and the duties associated with its offices.

Typically, the highest positions in the hierarchical structures of many non-cosmopolitan churches in Malaŵi are taken by a so-called *mpostoli* (pl. *apostoli*). The honorary cognomen of an apostle is reserved for a preacher who has acquired sufficient independent religious authority and therefore represents the

---

1912–1963 AD), had started his missionary work after a divine revelation in 1932. He spent the following thirty years spreading his message into the modern-day states of Malaŵi, Zambia, Botswana and even South Africa and the Congo, reaching an estimated global membership of more than one million in 1996 (Tilisho 2003: 23; Daneel 1998; Jules-Rosette 1975).

141 According to the King James Version of 1 Corinthians 11:27-32: "Wherefore whosoever shall eat this bread, and drink this cup of the Lord, unworthily, shall be guilty of the body and blood of the Lord. / But let a man examine himself, and so let him eat of [that] bread, and drink of [that] cup. / For he that eateth and drinketh unworthily, eateth and drinketh damnation to himself, not discerning the Lord's body. / For this cause many [are] weak and sickly among you, and many sleep. / For if we would judge ourselves, we should not be judged. / But when we are judged, we are chastened of the Lord, that we should not be condemned with the world" (Cogliano 2004: 659).

leading figure for an entire religious grouping. Below this level, the local heads of a given Pentecostal church typically bear the title of a bishop (*bishopo*), indicating an elevated position of power that exceeds the scope of a single church community. As one of the most common terms applied for a senior church representative, the word *mbusa* (pl. *abusa*) signifies a 'pastor' in its most literary sense, denoting a minister as well as a shepherd. Within the framework of the more administrative and institutionalized Christian communities, the title of *mbusa* is reserved for an official member of the clergy. At the same time, non-cosmopolitan churches have a more liberal use of the title and its associated elevated position of religious authority.

In addition to these specifically Christian offices, a number of traditional healers (*asing'anga*) also follow an explicitly Christian approach to their therapeutic activities – a development that has been described as a comparably recent innovation (Chakanza 1998: 101).[142] Among the *asing'anga* interviewed throughout this research, a remarkable number directly refers to Christian concepts and/or symbols within their therapeutic work, establishing a highly syncretistic field of Christianized *using'anga*. Basically, all Christianized *asing'anga* establish their own personal relationship to the spiritual forces, and usually, their interaction with angels, saints and apostles is directly analogous to traditional notions in which ancestral spirits (*mizimu ya makolo*) play the exact same part.[143] On the outside, these *asing'anga* typically show their religious conviction by using specifically Christian symbolism – e.g. using the Bible as a divinatory device, decorating consultation rooms with Christian cross symbols, wearing specifically ornamented attire, and the like.

In the light of this development, some Healer Associations in Malaŵi as described above also define themselves in clearly Christian terms and can therefore be seen as an expression of the growing influence of Christianity within traditional medicine. As one such example, the Traditional Mediciners of Central Africa reject divinatory practices as well as practices of spirit possession as part of their work, promoting a stronger focus on plant medicine (*mitengo* and *masamba*). These requirements are seen in the context of Christian ideas of spiritually legitimate medicine, and at the same time, the TMCA explicitly encourage their members to cooperate with governmental health institutions as a necessary supplement to their own medical services (Morris 1996: 98-99). Other

142 Joseph Chakanza characterizes these healers as "spirit mediums who claim to heal not by being possessed by ancestral spirits, but by personalities mentioned in the Bible as well as by Christian saints, thereby giving their healing ministry a Christian flavour" (Chakanza 1998: 102-103).

143 The abovementioned Christian spirit agents therefore act as messengers of divine wisdom. They are the ones who impart medical knowledge to the chosen person in terms of dream inspiration, and they are contacted during patient consultations in order to obtain the required medical knowledge.

Healer Associations promote their particular notions of Christian faith healing – such as the African Ngangas Association of Rhodesia (now Zimbabwe) and their clearly Biblical approach to diagnosis and medication, declaring in 1972 that

> "We fear God and work with the Bible. Our work is blessed by God. [...] We practice proper medicine as shown in Jeremiah 46:11.[144] We are proper traditional African doctors and physicians. We don't guess anyone's course of illness. Our sole duty is not to stir up strifes among brothers by pointing to another person as the cause of illness. We admit that illness is natural, but we believe it can be healed up. So we try to give what we consider is true remedy, e.g. for boils, 2 Kings 20:7;[145] fractures, Ezekiel 30:21;[146] stomach ache, Timothy 5:24;[147] use of oil in curing ailments, Luke 10:34;[148] James 5:14.[149] [...] We believe and maintain that we are just as good as any European doctor in as far as we are able to do according to our knowledge of herbalism" (quoted from Chavunduka 1978: 83).

In general, Christian therapeutic specialists agree on the basic notion that healing powers represent a manifestation of divine grace, being bestowed upon a person by God. Therefore, priests and other thus gifted therapeutic specialists see themselves in an immediate connection to the divine sources of health, and they offer their services to pray for others, conducting home visits to their believers and supporting them in hospital.[150] In many cases, Christian faith healing requires a direct link between a gifted individual and God Himself. In order to

---

144 The Bible reference of Jeremiah 46: 11 is identified as follows, using the King James Bible translation: "Go up into Gilead, and take balm, O virgin, the daughter of Egypt: in vain shalt thou use many medicines; [for] thou shalt not be cured" (Cogliano 2004: 473).

145 According to 2 Kings 20: 7, "And Isaiah said, Take a lump of figs. And they took and laid [it] on the boil, and he recovered" (Cogliano 2004: 228)

146 Ezekiel 30: 21 is given as "Son of man, I have broken the arm of Pharaoh king of Egypt; and, lo, it shall not be bound up to be healed, to put a roller to bind it, to make it strong to hold the sword" (Cogliano 2004: 499).

147 Here, the preacher quoted by Gordon Chavunduka may be victim to a minor misquote of the Bible. While the mentioned verse – 1 Timothy 5: 24, reading "Some men's sins are open beforehand, going before to judgment; and some [men] they follow after" (Cogliano 2004: 686) – fails to provide the sought medical information, the previous verse (i.e. 1 Timothy 5: 23) indicates: "Drink no longer water, but use a little wine for thy stomach's sake and thine often infirmities" (Cogliano 2004: 686).

148 In Luke 10: 34, Jesus narrates the incidence of a Samaritan who approached a wounded traveler, "And went to [him,] and bound up his wounds, pouring in oil and wine, and set him on his own beast, and brought him to an inn, and took care of him" (Cogliano 2004: 599).

149 The verses of James 5: 14-15 read as follows: "Is any sick among you? let him call for the elders of the church; and let them pray over him, anointing him with oil in the name of the Lord: / And the prayer of faith shall save the sick, and the Lord shall raise him up; and if he have committed sins, they shall be forgiven him" (Cogliano 2004: 700).

150 At the same time, the members of different Pentecostal churches express their belief that if prayer healing for a given patient stays fruitless over a longer period of time, it is due to the lack of belief on the side of the person suffering. This indicates that he/she is no true believer, or even a particularly bad sinner.

clarify the background of a given health disorder, the spirit of a person with such particular abilities communicates with the divine spirit and thereby reveals the true reason for a person's suffering. As one such gifted individual describes this spiritual experience,

> "You can hear it in your ears, or it just comes straight out of your mouth" (Andrew Chisadza, a Lomwe Pentecostal priest).[151]

This connection to the divine sphere is characterized as a gift from God which, albeit not necessarily given as a reward for being faithful, requires the recipient to meticulously observe the Christian values as defined by the respective church community in order not to lose these powers again. A divine mandate is described as crucial for conducting healing practices. Especially with respect to the frequently satanic origin of sickness, a healer is said to need the power provided by the Holy Spirit in order to differentiate and overcome the different forms of devilish influences including the works of evil spirits as well as *ufiti*.

While the religious specialists who engage in Christian faith healing are thus invariably defined and legitimized by their access to direct communication with the Supreme Being, the forms of medical services they apply differ according to the particular religious doctrine as well as the individual person. In this context, a number of concepts can be regarded as typical elements of Christian religious healing in Malaŵi, and they will be depicted in the following.

Healing Ministry

Prayer is the technique most commonly applied in the context of Christian faith healing in Southern Malaŵi, and it is also particularly relevant for the treatment of mental disorder. In general, prayer healing rituals seem to fall into two broad categories – that is, into those performed by non-specialist lay individuals praying on their own accord, and those conducted by professional faith healing specialists offering prayer services for others. In actual fact, all cases share the same logical framework for therapy. Most commonly, prayer healing is performed within a prayer group consisting of both lay persons seeking cure, and religiously specialized facilitators. Accordingly, many Christian churches offer personalized healing prayers which are frequently scheduled as concluding a regular Sunday service. After the gospel, the sick and suffering queue up in front of the altar, indicating their personal problems to the pastor and/or elders who lay on hands (see below) and pray for the healing of the person.[152] At the same

---

[151] This account also indicates the particular importance of glossolalia within Pentecostalism. This notion will be elaborated below.

[152] This religious practice has been explained as deriving from the Biblical quote in Mark 16: 17-18 which states: "And these signs shall follow them that believe; In my name shall they cast out

time, even the weekly meetings of a local Pentecostal church may include communal prayers during which one participant spontaneously performs prayer healing on the rest of the group. Even though such an individual may not be generally considered a specialist – and therefore, e.g., a *mbusa* –, he or she still experiences a personal spiritual bond with the divine which predestines him or her for a future religious career.

Independently of the number of individuals present at a given prayer healing session and their religious status, the faith of a praying individual constitutes the essential factor to the success of the prayer healing. As the healing effect is ascribed entirely to divine grace, a person praying can only receive this gift by strength of faith. At the same time, it is crucial that the recipient of faith healing – i.e. the patient – justifies the divine intervention by strict obedience to the religious norms supported by the respective Christian church. It is frequently stressed that, if a person does not truly believe, no prayer can change his or her condition. Within this context, there are some indications that a lack of spiritual strength in a patient can be levelled by the religious power of another person praying for him or her. This issue becomes essential when considering the capabilities of people with mental disorders because, as the Lomwe minister of a small Malaŵian Pentecostal church states, their lack of insight into their own actions makes it impossible for them to repent by themselves. In recognition of this fact, prayers conducted by relatives or faith-healing specialists can also be effective to cure patients from mental disorder in case their own faith is too feeble. In simple cases of mental disorder, faith healing experts describe the necessary prayer treatment as easy and quick to perform. On such occasions, the extensive prayers could be replaced by simply using the 'word of God' known to the gifted religious specialist. A Lomwe Pentecostal priest elaborates that, when treating persons with mental disorders,

> "[…] we only speak a word of authority and the demon will come out" (Andrew Chisadza, a Lomwe priest).

More complex cases of mental disorder, at the same time, may require an equally sophisticated ritual treatment and more time to take effect. Therefore, prayer healing can include full-time prayers and fasting on the side of the respective priest who continues his prayers for a number of days.[153] In many Christian

devils; they shall speak with new tongues; / They shall take up serpents; and if they drink any deadly thing, it shall not hurt them; they shall lay hands on the sick, and they shall recover" (Cogliano 2004: 590; see also Kiev 1972: 126-129).

153 As some of their representatives lament, though, many small Pentecostal congregations lack the required personnel to provide these full-time services for individual patients. In the case of Zionist churches, these services are performed in so-called healing homes. Here, in-patients are welcome to stay for a number of days while preachers perform constant – i.e. 24 hour – prayers over the patient. With reference to mental disorders caused by spirits (such as *misala ya mizimu*),

groups, communal prayers for the sick and suffering represent the first therapeutic measure taken. An Evangelical pastor of the Ngoni ethnic group, for instance, advices his congregation to always address God in prayers before seeking other forms of medical support. In case of epidemics or comparable threats to the communal health situation, some churches call their followers together in order to overcome the situation by collective prayers. At the same time, some churches even offer free healing services for the in-patients of government hospitals.[154]

In the religious framework of non-cosmopolitan Christianity in Malaŵi, all forms of religious healing also involve ritualized elements that may, in part, be considered as culturally accepted evidence for divine vocation. Here, glossolalia or 'speaking in tongues' (usually referred to as *kulankhula malilime*) has the most vital importance. Conceptualized as the ultimate expression of divine presence within the human person through which the Supreme Being speaks, the central role of glossolalia is particularly evident – or even self-evident – in the context of Pentecostal churches and their specific theology.[155] While being explicitly banned among many of the mainstream churches, it is seen as a manifestation of divine presence in a human being, and it bears a high resemblance with more traditional practices of spirit possession (see *Chapter IV.2*). As stated above, prayer healing is frequently accompanied by hands-on healing. Even Catholic priests recommend it as a means of transferring divine healing power onto an individual. On the occasion of prolonged prayer sessions dedicated to the healing of a given individual, the respective priests and/or lay persons may be compelled to observe certain food restrictions, and these rituals can take the form of "two days of fasting, praying and laying hands on him". Some Pentecostal adherents describe this technique as the key practice in their concept of faith healing, frequently leading to instant recovery on the side of the respective patients. At the same time, it is argued that the particular spiritual power of this therapeutic technique derives from its Biblical origin.[156] The

---

a prayer healing treatment is described as a prolonged process, with the patient only starting to show signs of amelioration one week after the end of the prayer treatment.

154 As one Evangelical pastor recollects, he once initiated a communal praying and singing session on the premises of a hospital in Nsanje District. Attracting of a considerable number of patients, he then told every patient to lay their own hands onto the location of their respective health problems while singing and praying along with the priest. After a couple of days, some former patients visited him, telling that they had been cured by him. They had suffered from asthma, malaria and comparable disorders for a long time.

155 The term Pentecostalism itself is derived from a Biblical account of glossolalia. According to the King James translation of Acts 2: 2-4, the apostles had gathered for the Pentecost celebration, "And suddenly there came a sound from heaven as of a rushing mighty wind, and it filled all the house where they were sitting. / And there appeared unto them cloven tongues of like as of fire, and it sat upon each of them. / And they were all filled with the Holy Ghost, and began to speak with other tongues, as the Spirit gave them utterance" (Cogliano 2004: 627).

156 As a slight modification of hands-on healing, the abovementioned African Apostolic Church of John Maranke (AACJM) practices a so-called *kutyuna* ritual, consisting of laying hands on the patient and rubbing the skin. This is meant to prepare the patient for receiving divine inspiration

importance of hands-on healing in the context of Christian faith healing is unquestionable. In essence, it represents a direct symbolic action aiming to transmit divine healing energy onto a given patient in order to reach the desired therapeutic effect.

Additional forms of Christian faith healing also exist. Some Christian groups in Malaŵi also utilize Holy Water in the context of their healing ministry.[157] It may be applied on a person as well as on a given location, e.g. a house, with the implicit intention of achieving spiritual purification and, subsequently, therapeutic success. Zionist groups, in particular, favour the therapeutic use of Holy Water. Similarly, the sacrament of anointing the sick may also be applied within a clearly therapeutic context, and its use is also common among some of the mainstream churches. As a Catholic priest in Chikwawa District explains, the anointment of suffering persons

> "[...] is a power type of healing that depends on the acceptance of the sick person. If he accepts, saying »Let the will of God happen«, then he gets healed. This works on all types of diseases, either natural diseases or whatever" (Evans Cholo, a Lomwe Catholic priest).

Faith healing, therefore, is generally embedded into a larger ritual context in which a wide variety of culturally recognized symbols are applied. While the abovementioned forms of religious therapy may be conceived as fairly typical, a countless number of other notions reflect the individual yet spiritually inspired character of therapy development. Standing under the direct spiritual influence of angels, apostles, or saints, many Christian *asing'anga* thus develop their own, highly personalized forms of religious healing which, due to their diverging symbolism, show some contradictions to cosmopolitan Christian doctrine, and small church communities take the liberty of establishing their own healing ministry.[158]

It has been argued that the success of many Pentecostal communities in Malaŵi is related to their free healing services which serve as a key factor in the evangelization of new followers. It is common policy among Pentecostal

---

due to expelling the influence of evil spirits (Peltzer 1987: 54-55).

157 Other denominations, though, clearly reject the use of Holy Water. A representative of the Pentecostal AoG thus insists that faith healing does not require any certain substances, and neither would priest or patient have to follow ritual rules such as gestures or postures. Likewise, another Pentecostal church representative points out that, from his religious perspective, faith healing does not involve Holy Water or anything else but laying on hands.

158 A Christian Lomwe healer hence describes one of her techniques as hitting a patient with the Bible while reciting prayers. With reference to a given patient's case, she explains that "If a patient with *kuzerezeka* is unable to eat, to walk or whatever, we just instruct the guardian to bring the patient here. Then we stay with him/her and fight hard, singing and beating him/her with the Bible, and he/she can even walk off cured. There was one patient [...] who came here unable to walk, the whole body was inactive, but right now he/she is farming again – by the power of the Bible" (Doris Petroyo, a Lomwe *sing'anga*).

churches to accept patients from other denominations to participate in their healing prayers, emphasizing that faith healing must be considered a gift from God to be offered even to members of competing religions.[159] This form of evangelization by advertising one's spiritual achievements due to therapeutic efficiency is described in statements such as 'mobilizing the kingdom of God' or 'working with the blood of Christ'.[160] In order to increase their catchment area, a considerable number of Pentecostal churches undertake Healing Crusades or Faith Healing Ministries. On such occasions, a certain faith healer – usually a *mpostoli* – travels a given area, holding prayer healing services at towns and villages along the way. By word-of-mouth-advertising, the arrival of a Crusade spreads easily, and people take considerable efforts to assemble in one of the prayer locations in order to receive healing prayers.[161] Independent from these mass rallies and their relevance in both therapy and conversion, the undeniable growth of especially Pentecostal churches within both urban and rural settings in Southern Malaŵi is, to a large extent, connected to the success ascribed to their faith healing ministries. Their attraction, at the same time, is not limited to medical services, but it reflects more general representations of traditional culture and ongoing processes of inculturation.

As a whole, the theological discourse on the particular success of Pentecostal churches in Malaŵi frequently implies their benefit of having a higher degree of acculturation into society – as opposed to the mainstream churches. Due to a process of Christian transformation of traditional religious elements – i.e. spirit possession into demonic possession, or *ufiti* into Satanism –, Pentecostal churches introduce culturally significant categories into their teaching and, at the same time, provide a therapeutic model for overcoming them.[162] Even though the

---

159 While reliable statistical evidence is difficult to obtain, field data clearly indicates that Pentecostal churches in Malaŵi have expanded significantly over the last years. Local theological discourse supports the assessment that a high degree of Pentecostal evangelization is conducted due to faith healing. Even Muslims or the adherents of other religions may participate in prayer healing, and it is stated that such occasions are used to make Muslim visitors susceptible to the Christian faith.

160 Accordingly, a given Classic Pentecostal church in Zomba District receive approximately 30 new persons per week, most of which come in search for medical treatment. While most patients attend Sunday services which reserve a large part of the session for prayer healing, healing prayers are performed daily at their local church.

161 Therefore, the parents of children with mental disorders sometimes express regret about the lack of Pentecostal churches within their immediate neighbourhood, expressing their readiness to go as soon as a healing crusade arrives.

162 This factor is seen as the key feature explaining the tremendous evangelization success of Pentecostal churches in Malaŵi today, as "They truly bridge the gap between ancestor worship and the Internet age". In the same way, some local Pentecostal churches also comply with other cultural demands. Therefore, some local Pentecostal churches are notorious for their liberal attitude towards beer drinking as well as their approval of polygyny.

general effectiveness of prayer healing is debated in many cases, the notion of divine power as the universal and ultimate therapy is widely shared. While being unpredictable and unreliable due to its dependence on internal factors such as divine will, the powers of prayer healing are nonetheless considered unlimited, offering a potential solution for any health problem.[163] Many Christians in Malaŵi agree that God offers the gifts of health and healing to the faithful,[164] and this notion is also relevant in the context of mainstream Christianity.

> "As some churches have said, it is true that priests can heal because we believe that Jesus Christ has given us power. And again, it depends on the faith the person to be healed has. If he or she comes open and says I have this problem, may you please help me, we lay hands on him and pray. Eventually, sometimes the person is healed and sometimes he is not. It depends on what Christ has wished to do" (Evans Cholo, a Lomwe Catholic priest).

At the same time, the idea of Christian faith healing is closely connected to the necessity of behavioural change and adherence to religious values. Not only is therapeutic success usually described as reserved to the truly faithful – i.e. those showing the highest degree of value conformity –, it may also be reversed in case Christian behavioural values are no longer observed.[165] Therefore, Christian communities provide their own sets of rules equivalent with the traditional *miyambo* in form, function – and in their immediate reference to the occurrence of mental disorder.[166] In many cases of prolonged human suffering, faith healing is mentioned as a last hope for therapeutic success, and many case studies support the great and growing importance of Christian faith healing within the health seeking behaviour of persons suffering from mental disorder.[167]

---

163 Not only Pentecostal or other non-mainstream Christian communities, but wide parts of the Christian population certainly concur that prayer – and the divine powers thus activated – has the potential to overcome any kind of health disorder. Therefore, "some people do get healed through prayers. But even when doing the same prayers – if you pray in truth, you get healed, but if it's not in truth, then you can't get cured" (Doris Petroyo, a Lomwe *sing'anga*).

164 A Mang'anja *mfumu* expresses his critical agreement. While supporting the notion that due to divine choice, a person can receive the power to heal, he reminds that not even all the apostles of the Bible were blessed with this gift. Therefore, he explains that healing powers occur far less commonly than they are claimed.

165 The Nyanja spokesperson of a Pentecostal Church thus emphasizes that successful faith healing should go hand in hand with behavioural changes. Any person who seeks healing is required to lead a life agreeable to God – i.e. complying by a particular set of norms of conduct – in order to acquire divine help. If relapsing to their old ways after being cured, their old health disorders will come back to them as well.

166 Thus, a Christian *sing'anga* claiming inspiration by Christian saints has to observe closer rules of behaviour in the form of personal *miyambo*. In one such account, the drinking alcoholic beverages would – as a violation of Christian norms – be punished by mental disorder.

167 From his own professional experience, a Pentecostal church official explains that patients with mental disorders tend to show some improvement immediately after healing prayers, and that

2(d) Biomedical Paradigm

As pointed out earlier (see *Chapter I.2.c*), the availability of biomedical services in Malaŵi is restricted by infrastructural limitations, and serious efforts are taken – by national government and non-governmental institutions alike – to further expand the reach of biomedical support into the remote rural areas.

While it may be assumed that the professional background of biomedical specialists is known to the reader, it is important to make some remarks about the availability of training facilities inside the country. While medical staff had to be trained abroad until very recently, medical colleges for both medical doctors and nurses are now available at the University of Malaŵi – such as the College of Medicine (CoM) in Blantyre or the Kamuzu College of Nursing (KCN) in both Lilongwe and Blantyre. In spite of these welcome training facilities, the country still faces a dire need for qualified medical personnel.[168] Governmental health facilities notoriously struggle with staff shortages, and rough numbers have already been indicated in order to illustrate the dimension of this challenge. Due to this fact, many local health institutions operate with the support of external health workers – especially in highly specialized fields of biomedical services.[169] As representatives of the international biomedical model, they constitute an additional link to European and North American concepts of medicine, and even though a considerable parts of these expatriate healthcare specialists express their interest in genuinely Malaŵian concepts of health and sickness, their working conditions frequently limit their opportunities for a full mutual exchange of cultural ideas.

It may not come as a surprise that the availability of specialized biomedical health services – especially in the treatment of mental disorder – is limited in Southern Malaŵi. Pharmaceutical products are therefore the central tool of biomedical therapy. In the urban centers of the country, specialized pharmacies make a greater number of products accessible for paying customers, and in smaller population centers such as district capitals, grocery shops usually still provide a fair selection of pharmaceuticals. Even in rural communities, Western pharmaceuticals are available from so-called drug peddlers, but their unrestricted business with otherwise prescription drugs has been marked as a serious health

---

they keep recovering gradually. The father of a child with a mental disorder knows about a case similar to his son that was successfully treated by faith healing, feeling encouraged to try out other sources.

168 Unfortunately, over the last years, a disproportionately large number of college graduates have emigrated out of Malaŵi, searching for more promising job opportunities and better payment in other countries such as the UK.

169 Hence, it is not uncommon to have foreign staff members – a German surgeon, an English paediatrician, or a Belgian psychiatrist – working in Malaŵian health institutions for a limited period of time.

concern politics and media.[170] With respect to the biomedical treatment of mental disorder, a number of pharmaceutical drugs are in frequent use and comparably readily available. The anti-epileptic sedative barbiturate Phenobarb, therefore, is frequently applied, and the anti-psychotic sedative Chlorpromazine (CPZ) is also in use for the treatment of mental disorder.[171]

In addition to pharmaceutical treatment, electro convulsive therapy (ECT) is also frequently applied as mental disorder therapy in the respective specialized institutions. Patients receive a muscle relaxant before electroshock treatment, and the results are rated as supporting the improvement of the patients.[172] Moreover, basic rehabilitation services also represent therapeutic measures. Therefore, organizations for persons with disabilities frequently supply rehabilitation tools such as wheelchairs, crutches, and various kinds of chairs, supports, and racks. Even though such essential rehabilitation articles can be produced locally, they may still be in dire need in some more rural areas.[173] Within the limits of difficult Malaŵian infrastructure, biomedical health institutions try to make services available for patients with mental disorders. Some organizations for persons with disabilities – such as MAP – offer monthly visits of outreach teams to some rural health stations where new patients are diagnosed and known cases may receive pharmaceutical as well as advocacy support. Sometimes, these outreach services are also available as an after-treatment for patients who have been hospitalized in one of the few specialized institutions and released to return to their home communities (Kalmanash 1968).[174]

Complementing the initial depiction of Malaŵian health conditions (see *Chapter I.2.c*), this section gives additional information on the different kinds of health services available. The structural difficulties of the biomedical health

---

170 The origins of these drugs sold by market vendors remain something of a mystery. In a newspaper interview, the representative of a national TB control program speculates that "These drugs come from our own health facilities. They are stolen by our health workers and sold to the vendors" (Ntonya 2005: 13). The problems arising from the free trade with controlled substances will further be mentioned below.

171 Some accounts lament its side-effects as extreme sleepiness and hypotension (i.e. low blood pressure) so that sedated patients may be found sleeping all day.

172 Even though being discussed controversially in the Western discourse, ECT is still an important form of Western psychiatric treatment. In Malaŵi, ECT treatment was described as eight guards holding a patient down while he/she receives treatment. Even though patients are given a carton to bite on, they frequently suffer minor injuries in the process. Common dosages are given at 6 treatments of 200 Volts each.

173 Thus, a Mang'anja farmer expresses his appreciation for the pharmaceutical drugs he receives for his son in a local dispensary while he still admonishes the availability of a wheelchair.

174 A Mang'anja farmer reiterates being institutionalized in Zomba Mental Hospital for two months due to a *khunyu* condition (see *Chapter III.2.e*) before finally being dismissed. Learning how to identify approaching seizures and to deal with them, he has been in monthly treatment with the anti-epileptic sedative Phenobarb for 20 years now.

system become even more apparent in recognition of the previously depicted alternatives and their sophisticated networks. In essence, the present section directly leads to the question of interaction between biomedical and other health care services. This issue, though, cannot be examined in isolation but requires the inclusion of data from the previous sections. Due to the more general relevance of this complex, the pluralism of medical systems and their compatibility will therefore be discussed at greater length in the final section of this chapter.

3. Discussing Medical and Cosmological Pluralism

Concluding the present chapter with a discussion of the findings, one of the most fundamental deductions from the material presented here is that the overall cultural discourse on mental disorder in Southern Malaŵi is strongly represented in various spheres of culture. As the first section of this chapter has demonstrated, mental disorder is part of a very rich emic discourse that is conducted on various levels. Its strong embedding within the various ethnic traditions illustrates that mental disorder is not a marginal phenomenon that is avoided and concealed. Rather, it plays a role in oral tradition and the conveyance of cultural knowledge, values, and norms about the condition forms an integral part of ritual culture. The second above section provides the broader context within which the public discussion is embedded, establishing medical pluralism as a central factor not only for the health conditions in Malaŵi in general, but particularly in the way mental disorder is conceptualized within this cultural framework. The following summary will conclude this chapter not only by means of recapitulation, but also by presenting and analyzing additional data necessary for the comprehension of the larger context.

The Dead and the Deviant

In the context of funeral rituals in Southern Malaŵi, some attention was given to the modified ritual procedures as carried out in case of stillborn children (*nsenye*). Research data, however, indicates a direct connection between these practices and different conditions of obvious infant deviation. Accounts from different ethnic groups – including Lomwe, Cheŵa, Tumbuka, Sena, and Yao – agree that children born with obvious mental disorders may fall victim to infanticide.[175] In such a case, a child identified as deviant is killed right after the

[175] Comparable practices on infanticide in the context of disability have been reported. Among the Songye of the Kasai Region of Southern Congo, the birth of a disabled child has been interpreted

delivery within the group of present women – i.e. traditional birth attendants and some female members of the mother's kin group – who, subsequently, declare it a stillbirth.[176] These children are buried by women only who dig a shallow grave in a special graveyard (*manda a nsenye*), it is never referred to as *munthu* but only as *nsenye*, and the child's condition is kept secret from the wider public. With reference to the general funerary procedures observed within Cheŵa society, Johann Breugel states that

> "A stillborn child or one which has survived for less than a week is carried by a few women (the grandmother and some others) in a broken pot and put down somewhere near the graveyard at the foot of a tree. [...] The same procedure is followed in the case of a completely deformed child. While still alive it is put in a pot, carried to a tree in the bush near the graveyard, and the pot is closed with a clod of earth. Afterwards the women go to bathe at the river. There is no wailing, except for the mother herself who weeps 'silently' so as not to be heard. Nowadays the child's corpse is often put wrapped in a cloth and put in a shallow grave dug by the women" (Breugel 2001: 119).

Data from throughout the various ethnic groups of Southern Malaŵi stresses the conviction that this custom is practiced in remote rural areas of the country up to the present day, and accounts of such incidents are frequently reiterated.[177] A traditional birth attendant recalls such a story:

> "I first heard about this in the year 1978. A certain mother was giving birth to children with small heads. She kept delivering children like this for five times, and she killed all these children right when they were born. She told people that there was a problem and that she had received a dead child. The mother was delivering at her own house. At the sixth time her husband wanted to find out for himself, so he stayed outside the room where his wife delivered the child. When the child was born she did not manage to kill it because she knew that her husband had heard the child crying. This child grew up, but its head is still small" (Josephine Maboma, a Lomwe *mzamba*).

---

in terms of a spirit manifesting itself in a 'wrong' or 'non-whole' body. Therefore, the spirit could be sent back to the spiritual realm by a thus justified act of killing in order to be born again whole (Devlieger 2000: 159-167).

176 Some myth surrounds the role of *azamba* in such cases. One speculative – and male – account describes the *azamba* as responsible for inspecting a child thoroughly at birth. If the child is regarded as having any deficits, the *mzamba* may decide to poison the child – even without the mother's knowledge who may also be told that the child was either stillborn or died right after birth. This way of 'creating a miscarriage' is said to be a secret among the *azamba*.

177 In some cases, organizations for persons with disabilities are called upon to intervene and investigate such incidences by order of community neighbours or village *mafumu*. Some cases of severe wilful neglect with fatal consequences for the children are also reported.

Records such as this one show a close connection to mythical tradition.[178] On a larger scale, the question of reduced funeral services for the stillborn and, even more so, of deviant infants being conceptualized as dead within their cultural context constitutes a direct connection to the larger question of social deviance and personhood (see *Chapter III.1.a*).

Negotiating Truth and Superstition

It has been demonstrated that oral as well as ritual traditions in Malaŵi provide rich sources for the study of the cultural incorporation of mental disorder, and while the depicted examples are far from exhaustive, they still give a useful overview. As condensed, pragmatic manifestations of cultural norms, the importance of traditional *miyambo* as a social regulatory tool has been outlined. Due to their protective function, they are crucially important for the living conditions of persons with mental disorders while the depiction of different cosmological models in Southern Malaŵi reveals the dependence of these normative traditions on a given cosmological system. Here, cultural pluralism and processes of cultural change gain social momentum. At present, the observation of *miyambo* is no longer a social imperative that is beyond critique due to their allegedly sacrosanct character. While traditional norms are generally highly validated in a rural context, they are increasingly subject to critical evaluation and rationalization.

> "In the past the mothers of *wopunduka* children[179] knew themselves what to do with their children. [...] There was a lot of advice and beliefs on what can happen to you if you behave badly towards a person with disabilities, for example: first, laughing at someone, which was associated with laughing that will never cease, and second, pointing at someone, which was associated with your finger staying like that – if you pointed to the North it will always stay pointing Northwards. These things were applicable in those days because a person could become lame just because of laughing or teasing someone who is lame. Even though these things are not true nowadays, parents still advise their children. The only change and difference is that children now do laugh at them since they've realized that it is not true" (Doreen Masamba, a Yao *mzamba*).

---

178 This story applies motifs of a Cheŵa myth in which the repeated birth of half-persons – in this case in the form of a human head – finally ends with the fourth one turning into a fully able-bodied albino. This myth mentions the elders advising the mother to kill the abnormal children by throwing them into the river – in the hope of finding divine mercy for an implicit offence. Finally refusing to continue doing so, she is exiled from the village (Schoffeleers & Roscoe 1985: 106-108).

179 The term *wopunduka* designates a person suffering from a particular kind of mental disorder which will be depicted below (see *Chapter III.2.f*).

Numerous accounts express this more critical approach to the observation of *miyambo*, pragmatically questioning their cause-and-effect rationale and considering them as means of protection and social control within the community.[180] Increasingly, *miyambo* are seen as a mere didactic tool applied to control behaviour within the community, and younger age groups are notorious for challenging these traditions.[181] At present, ritual instructors express that *miyambo* on the culturally validated behaviour towards persons with mental disorders are no longer part of her initiation curriculum, and when asked about the justification for these *miyambo*, it is concluded that

> "[...] parents always say that but this is not true, no. As for me, at our place there is a person who cannot see and another one who has *kupunduka*. We people still point at them but we do not deliver disabled children, no. These teachings are just useless" (Iselda Tchema, a Yao *mzamba*).

This critical, *quasi*-empirical evaluation of traditional normative rules is a frequently documented approach.[182] Representing signs of cultural disruption, this critical approach to *mwambo* instructions indicates cultural change. The loss of socially binding norms of behaviour is a process that coincides with fewer young people undergoing traditional initiation due to their changed living situations and their modified cosmological views.[183] Cosmological pluralism has to be addressed at greater length in order to comprehend the basic cultural mechanisms that generate the conditions outlined here.

Culture of Pluralism

Not only with regard to mental disorder but in a wider medical context, Malaŵian patients apply different forms of treatment at the same time. What is crucial in this is the fact that the different treatment options thus accessed all represent conflicting cosmological structures that are, at least in part, mutually exclusive. This assertion shall be substantiated with the aid of additional material.

---

180 As an example, children may be told that they would die if acting up around a funeral ceremony – in order to make them respect funerals.

181 Therefore, "These days, the children do not listen any more, compared to the times of the past".

182 A Lomwe TBA likewise states that "These things are not true, no. They are useless stories because if mothers go out they may always meet with *opunduka* persons. And they can laugh about them but they do not give birth to *opunduka* children" (Josephine Maboma, a Lomwe *mzamba*).

183 In response to this perceived loss of morally binding rules, recent publications as provided by Rachel Nyagondwe Fiedler and Molly Longue focus on the recent introduction of initiation ceremonies in Malaŵi which are modified in order to comply with a Christian – or, more specifically, Baptist – cosmological frame of reference while maintaining its socially supportive functionality (Fiedler 2005; Longue 2003).

It is a typical practice within a Malaŵian hospital setting that in-patients leave the premises in order to consult a traditional healer – just like local food hawkers and soda vendors, *asing'anga* are among the typical professionals offering services outside a hospital entrance –, and many times hospital staff 'catch' these *asing'anga* practicing secretly on the institution grounds. While this simultaneous treatment reveals some form of unwelcome coexistence of these different health institutions, some rare cases show that medical pluralism in Malaŵi can develop genuinely cooperative structures.[184] In general, traditional healers have a fairly differentiated perception of the accomplishments of biomedicine in relation to their traditional medical practices, and they act accordingly. Among the *asing'anga*, cooperation with biomedical health facilities on an equal footing is considered prestigious, and transferrals from traditional to biomedical institutions are well-reported.[185] Even cooperation between the specialized Zomba Mental Hospital and traditional healers is documented – usually in the form of meetings on the case of a specific patient. But while a number of *asing'anga* mention referring their patients to institutions like ZMH, this is much more unlikely to occur the other way round. Accordingly, *asing'anga* express some dissatisfaction about their lacking involvement in the therapeutic process at Zomba Mental Hospital. A Yao *sing'anga* therefore declares that

> "[...] if we were allowed to go there, we would go and examine all of them [i.e. the patients], and we could tell whether the *misala* of those ones can be healed or not. If not, then we would give them traditional medicine because there are some who are there with *misala* because of *chamba*. But for most patients it is because they wanted to become rich, so to them we can reverse everything, and they can be healed" (Vincent Chitete, a Yao *sing'anga*).

At the same time, some traditional healers claim that hospitals explicitly refer patients with mental disorders to them if no appropriate therapy can be found. Such accounts, rare as they may be, are an indicator of the sporadic yet existing

---

184 In one such account, a Sena healer explains that "We try our best to heal the patient, but if we fail we refer the patient to others to try and heal the patient, because prescription differs. [...] It happens that a person has been sick for a long time and has been going to the hospital, getting medicines and injections, but does not get better. Then the patient comes here to us traditional healers, we help the patient and he improves. But there are other diseases like TB or malaria for which we advise patients to go to the hospital. When the hospital personnel fails to treat a patient, they send the patient to us and we know that it's from *ufiti*" (Siyani Walala, a Sena *sing'anga*). A recent study reports cooperation between biomedical doctors and *asing'anga* in Balaka parish – with hospital doctors sometimes referring their patients to local *asing'anga* (Tilisho 2003: 37-52).

185 A Sena *sing'anga* therefore emphasizes that "I have letters of credence, they even invite me to meetings at the hospital. I have credential letters which allow me that if I fail to treat a patient, I should not delay but immediately refer him/her to hospital" (Siyani Walala, a Sena *sing'anga*).

recognition of the medical potential of traditional medicine on the side of biomedical service providers. In general, though, the cooperation between biomedical and other forms of treatment – i.e. traditional and other religious therapies – is marred by a lack of trust.[186] While *using'anga* must, in many areas, be regarded as the most immediately available form of medicine, biomedical specialists frequently disapprove of the health seeking behaviour prevalent in the population. Relying on the *sing'anga* as the primary source of healing, it is assessed, frequently leads to patients accessing biomedical services when all other therapeutic options have failed, thus arriving at the hospitals when their condition has already progressed beyond therapy.

Biomedical health services are, at the same time, by far not uncontested in Malaŵian discourse. While many sources express the need for better availability of biomedical services in the rural areas, a considerable degree of distrust surrounds local perceptions of Western biomedicine. As a general attitude, the biomedical standard of demanding payment for services provided, regardless of their outcome, is frequently described as ethically questionable and cash-hungry by traditional standards – which are derived from *using'anga* medicine which is usually paid only in case of an experienced therapeutic success. Moreover, the cost for treatment is independent from the financial situation of the patient which is considered discriminating and unjust. Other issues such as long-term therapy that does not lead to an instantly recognizable effect of relief also challenge the faith of Malaŵian health care seekers in biomedical procedures, and if they see no improvement after some days, patients leave hospitals in search for alternative treatment options.[187] This critical outlook on biomedicine is, moreover, aggravated by improper use of pharmaceutical drugs. By common opinion, various available pharmaceuticals are associated with and applied for therapeutic effects that conflict severely with those specified by producing companies and prescribing doctors alike, leading to potentially dangerous practices of unwitting substance abuse.[188] Suspicion also exists around

---

186 Some biomedical health specialists therefore criticize that, according to their perception, most Malaŵians foolishly consider their *asing'anga* capable to cure just anything (see *Chapter V.1.c*). Many of the biomedical professionals interviewed express their disrespect for the work of the *asing'anga*, labelling their services as pure charlatanry only meant to provide them with a good income and high social status by the use of basic psychological skills, common sense, traditional symbolism, and theatrical performance.

187 J. Kalmanash therefore laments that "people do not trust the medicine that can cure Epilepsy [...]. The patients take the medicine for a short time and then stop attending the clinics. Even if they notice some improvement in their condition, they hardly ever admit that this is due to their medicine, and naturally, with their fits recurring, their beliefs are reinforced and they go to seek advice and treatment from the traditional healers" (Kalmanash 1968: 3).

188 Therefore, articles in national newspapers mention the use of the bactericidal antibiotic Rifampicin – usually administered on tuberculosis patients – against complaints such as

unwelcome side effects of pharmaceutical products. Contraceptive pills as well as abortifacients are mentioned as causing mental disorder in a child if the mother becomes or remains pregnant in spite of using them, respectively.[189]

Yet, traditional and biomedicine are not the only health systems that clash in their attempts in reaching reciprocal compatibility. With respect to the faith healing practices of either Muslim or Christian communities in Malaŵi, the degree of acceptance on the side of biomedical professionals depends largely on personal religious conviction. While the majority of the staff in biomedical institutions certainly favours biomedical means over all other forms of treatment, some remarkable exceptions follow a more integrative approach. Explicitly welcoming religious healing in the context of rehabilitation services, the representative of an organization for persons with disabilities states that

> "I always feel that they should combine what we do and also when we go to church and hear what the church people are saying. […] It's the same as the one who wants to go to a *sing'anga*. They say O, you want to go to a *sing'anga*. But you should also combine it with what we are doing as therapy. You should not separate them. [...] I think that is very good because of what they preach in the church, like »With God, nothing is impossible – everything is possible with God« […]. So maybe when we train we also have our ideas like when we teach them how to do the exercises and with belief that they have in God and that courage, I think they get the maximum improvement that they can have. […] because you believe and have that faith, they improve quite a lot because of the relationship of that church background and the exercises that we have taught them" (Francis Genamu, a Lomwe disability organization representative).

The acceptance of different medical cosmologies is also a crucial issue in the religious discourse led within both Christian and Muslim communities in Southern Malaŵi. Many representatives of Muslim organizations provide recommendations on the choice of treatment suitable for members of the local community. Frequently, Islamic officials discourage their communities from consulting local *asing'anga* and advise them to avoid any contact with them, explaining that their concept of medicine and their reference to traditional

---

diarrhoea, gonorrhoea, and other sexually transmitted diseases. Sought-after by persons suffering from sexually transmitted diseases, its liberal use creates a drug resistance due to which cases of tuberculosis may become even more difficult to treat (Ntonya 2005: 13).

189 The explanation given refers to the notion of the contraceptives influencing the female menstruation so women lose more blood – which is needed inside the mother's womb for the normal development of the child. As examples of abortifacient agents, Penbritin tablets – an antibiotic contain 250 mg of Ampicillin per capsule – have been mentioned. Being recognized as a very strong drug against infections, it can also be used by a woman to trigger abortion. As elaborated, even the husband may cause a woman to abort by taking a Penbritin tablet and having unprotected intercourse with her. The man's sperms are said to transmit the substance into the woman's womb, instantly destroying the foetus and causing abortion.

symbolism is incongruous with Islam.[190] While traditional medicine is thus rejected fairly generally in a strictly Muslim discourse, most *ashehe* agree that believers are welcome to access biomedical institutions for their health care needs. As a general tendency, non-cosmopolitan churches in Malaŵi – and, more especially, Pentecostal communities – reject traditional medicine as an expression of non-Christian hence reprehensible cultural values. Like Muslim communities, most Pentecostal churches disapprove of their followers using traditional medicine, and may even threaten members who are found consulting a *sing'anga* with excommunication. In spite of their claim of working through direct inspiration and possession by the spirits of Biblical saints and/or apostles, Christianized *asing'anga* also have an ambiguous standing as not all Christian communities acknowledge the spiritual legitimacy of this 'new breed' of traditional healers. The administrator of one such Pentecostal community hence expresses that

> "In truth, they [i.e. the Christianized *asing'anga*] work with spirits of divination [*mizimu ya mbwebwe*], which is not like ancestral spirits [*mizimu ya makolo*]. These *mbwebwe* are part of the satanic forces. Satan has many evil spirits, and many harmful ways" (Miriam Mwale, a Nyanja church representative).

While *using'anga* is therefore generally more or less severely rejected by most Christian denominations, very few of them bar their members from consulting biomedical health institutions. At the same time, biomedical services may still be regarded with some concern due to their conflicting worldview, and the relationship between Christian faith and biomedicine is frequently marked by mutual distrust. Some Pentecostal churches therefore recommend their followers to avoid hospital treatment and exclusively rely on faith healing instead, associating biomedicine and its institutions with a lack of morality and religious values or even amoral corruption.[191] Hence, it is expressed that

---

190 Malaŵian Muslims tend to associate traditional medicine with *ufiti* beliefs which conflict with the Qur'ān. Other interpretations regard treatment provided by *asing'anga a matalasimu* as befitting to Muslim or argue that, while *maula* divination (see *Chapter II.2.a*) would certainly contradict Islamic teaching, medicine made from *mitengo* or *masamba* may be acceptable. As a justification for his use of plant medicine – and in order to encompass this technique into an explicitly Islamic cosmological framework – a *matalasimu* specialist elaborates that every therapeutic effect derives from divine power and not from any potency inherent to a given plant. Accordingly, the medical potential of certain plants is considered as a direct result of divine intervention that provides substance with spiritual power.

191 Here, the dismissal of spiritual models for the explanations of sickness on the side of Western-trained medical personnel appears to be a crucial point. A Pentecostal priest therefore characterizes the diagnostic means provided by local government hospitals as unacceptable and morally inferior to his own spiritual powers "because of all these evil forces at work in the hospitals nowadays".

> "[…] you do not have reliable medicine anymore these days, because witchdoctors and scientists have joined forces. The witchdoctors have worked very hard to be allowed access, or maybe the scientists were afraid of being bewitched. […] healing power is declining now. There is no help even in the hospitals" (Andrew Chisadza, a Lomwe Pentecostal priest).

Accordingly, a number of Pentecostal churches in Southern Malaŵi – most especially Zionist denominations – permit their followers to access neither traditional nor biomedical health institutions. Following their theological approach, divine power is considered as the only legitimate source of healing, thus indicating the one acceptable form of therapy.

These facts confirm the conclusion that positive cooperation between the different health care providers in the country is rare and constricted by conflicting worldviews. So far, the competing cosmological concepts have not established a mutually respectful dialogue, and their continuous conflict has an immediate impact not only on the metaphysical orientation of the Malaŵian population, but also on their access to medical options. The structural challenges connected to biomedical health care and its usage go beyond the mere accessibility of the respective services. Rather, even more substantial problems refer to its lacking cultural embedding which lead to the misuse of its therapeutic tools, the rejection of its medical philosophy, and other inadequacies resulting from a considerable lack of mutual understanding. This affects the issue of mental disorder in many ways. Due to the difficult treatment, patients with mental disorders usually undergo particularly long processes of health seeking behaviour, and by accessing different health facilities they are forced to work with most contradictory and inconsistent explanations for their condition.

Structures and Actors

The present chapter has provided an abundance of material that should be evaluated carefully in order to comprehend its vital importance for the general discussion on the cultural construction of mental disorder in Southern Malaŵi. As a useful tool for analysis, the presented data may be looked at in categories of structure and agency. The whole social conceptualization of mental disorder as developed so far may be analyzed as reflecting a conflict between personal decision-making and culturally binding rules, further complicated by their relativization due to pluralistic frames of reference.

Behavioural norms create structures meant to define the cultural conception of a phenomenon such as mental disorder while, at the same time, its occurrence is ascribed to the agency and/or ignorance of e.g. a parent. Processes of cultural change, moreover, eliminate the binding character of structure, create cosmological pluralism, and provide additional room for actors questioning the relevance of these cultural normative structures that used to regulate the discourse on mental disorder. Ritual activities and proverbial expressions likewise represent and recreate structures that convey cultural meaning, and it is within the scope of personal agency to validate or dismiss its normative content. But only in understanding the cosmological basis of this cultural discourse can the complexity of the context be understood. Cosmological systems and their respective health discourses certainly constitute a highly sophisticated cultural structure, and their partially dogmatic character has been demonstrated by their systematic incompatibility. The pluralistic situation of various, mutually independent and incoherent sets of cosmological structure, at the same time, creates considerable room for agency – not only in the affected actors' choice of treatment, but also in the generalized selection of explanatory models and respective social attitudes. As will be elaborated more circumstantially in a later chapter (see *Chapter IV.5*), cosmological orientation and flexibility are decisive factors for the social perception of the phenomenon and the allocation of cultural meaning.

In spite of its wide cultural recognition in Southern Malaŵi, the phenomenon of mental disorder is not met with appropriate therapeutic and social care. The situation appears paradoxical: in spite of the fact that society apparently realizes both the potential and the needs of those persons affected, the necessary support is still not fully available. Yet, an analysis that explains the emic conceptualization of a given health problem solely as depending on cultural processes of change or infrastructural conditions does not reach far enough. Deeper knowledge of the wider cultural framework is required in order to comprehend the categories that determine, simplistically speaking, what mental disorder really is in Southern Malaŵian societies – and to understand the processes that define, again in plain terms, why someone has a mental disorder in the first place. Such considerations will provide a more substantial insight into the way in which mental disorder is constructed within the various cultural contexts.

Figure 1: The Lomwe *sing'anga* Amanda Ndala amidst a selection of her herbal remedies, consulting the Bible

III.

Nosological Tradition

When dealing with questions which, according to Western standards, are categorized as mental in nature, it is crucial to be aware of the ethnocentrism of the implicit cultural bias. The dualism of mind and body as re-introduced into European philosophical thought by René Descartes (1596–1650 AD) – compartmentalizing human existence into all things mental and their physical counterparts – certainly does not have universal validity within a non-Western or, for that matter, Malaŵian cultural framework (Morris 1996: 109). In order to reach a more substantiated understanding of the different cultural notions connected to mental disorder in Southern Malaŵi, it is essential to examine the exact categories defining – and defined as – mental disorder in the framework of the present study. It is necessary to ask what mental disorder really is in order to reveal the classificatory models applied for categorizing 'normal' from mental conditions and distinguishing different conditions of mental disorder according to specific criteria. This chapter therefore depicts the terminological categories which are applied to denote different kinds of mental disorder and investigates their cultural contents.

1. Mental Disorder as a Terminological Concept

When conducting research on a certain health disorder within a non-Western society, the first obstacles that need to be surmounted are of a terminological nature. The vocabulary applied in Western culture – and, therefore, in biomedical philosophy – represents notions that find more or less unchallenged recognition within their own cultural context – or rather, that are subject to continuous debate on the solid foundation of common ground assumptions. In the context of a society in sub-Saharan Africa, on the other hand, the intercultural transferability of basic terms such as 'disease' or 'medicine' are already disputable – let alone more specific concepts such as 'epilepsy', 'psychosis', or even more debatable terms of 'disability' and 'handicap.' As a means of discovering the underlying cultural principles in a given society, it is important to analyse the indigenous terms applied to denote the respective phenomena, thus addressing emic systems of classification. This terminological approach gives access to implicit cultural evaluations prevailing in the respective languages – which are of particular importance in order to comprehend social acceptance and cultural valuation of a given phenomenon.

1(a) Concept of the Person

The study of mental disorder within a given cultural context can only be comprehensive if the specific, culturally defined notions of personhood are considered. Based on the fundamental assumption that mental disorder is not, after all, an objective, ontological state but a cultural category, this set of ideas represents the key model for that specific human condition which is regarded as normal, healthy, and non-pathological – and without which no concept of mental or other disorder could be formulated. By developing a notion of personhood that is applicable for Southern Malaŵi as a whole, it will be possible to locate persons with mental disorder within this framework and finally assess which allowances and/or limitations are culturally allocated to their respective conditions. Among the central questions of interest here, issues like the emic conceptualization of mental normality and the relationship between mental disorder and personhood will receive particular attention.

Notions of Life and Personhood

Life in itself is a complex concept that is highly culture specific due to its recourse on cosmological categories. With respect to Malaŵi, the notion of life as such has been described as sacred due to the idea that its "origins are beyond the bounds of human understanding" (Chigona 2002: 40). Accordingly, the Cheŵa concept of life, e.g., attributes vital force (or *moyo*) to a number of entities which may be considered inanimate according to Western biological models – identifying not only human beings (*anthu*), mammals (*nyama*), snakes (*njoka*), and birds (*mbalame*) as holders of life force, but also trees (*mitengo*) and mushrooms (*bowa*), the soil (*nthaka*), the spirits of the ancestors (*mizimu*) and other kinds of spirit agents (Morris 1998: 141).

In the context of this study, two different concepts are distinguished as denoting different aspects of 'life' as an abstract category. The aforementioned vital force or life energy (*moyo*) may be regarded as a fairly basic concept which is associated with the blood (*magazi*) as well as other bodily humours. An abundance of these fluids and the raw vital energy they represent indicates vitality, liveliness, and health (Kaspin 1996: 568-569). It develops during a person's lifetime – an unborn child may already express its emerging *moyo* by physical movement and vividness while the unreproductive condition of the elderly, metaphorically speaking, is conceptualized as a gradual process of clotting, shrivelling, or drying up (*kuwuma*), all indicating a decrease of a person's *moyo* (Paas 2004: 496). In contrast to *moyo*, the heart (*mtima*) is described as representing a person's vital principle – encompassing consciousness, temper, will, decision-making, experience, and knowledge.[1] *Mtima* emerges at birth – not, like *moyo*, at conception – and disappears with the death of a person's body. Due to its strong link to the development of the person, *mtima* has the quality of growing and changing during a lifetime. Both of these categories of life are associated with particular categories of spirit or soul which will be addressed below, constituting vital components of the human person as such.

In Malaŵi, no single, monolithic definition exists to describe the human person. While some differences may reflect ethnic specificities, some details concerning the notion of personhood are a matter of discussion and constant re-evaluation even within a given community. At the same time, the various ethnic groups in the Southern Region have comparably coherent notions about personhood, and in order to overcome the minor contradictions that may arise, it may be useful to use Gerard Chigona's approach of interpreting Malaŵian notions of the person as metaphoric rather than factual categories (Chigona 2002: 28-56). When identifying the specific concept of the person, Brian Morris refers to the Chicheŵa category *munthu*. As he elaborates,

> "'Muntu' (person), defined as a living force with intelligence and will, is not conceived by the Bantu as a dualistic being split between body and soul, as in the Cartesian metaphysic derived from Plato; it is rather a more complex notion" (Morris 1994: 121).

It may be helpful to think of Malaŵian conceptions of the person not as a dualistic model but as a complex spiritual-somatic unity (Morris 1994: 144). The category *munthu* (pl. *anthu*) is described as encompassing human characteristics such as "vigour, vitality, sound morals, health, strength, and virility" (Chigona 2002: 40). With respect to childhood development, Sylvia Kambalametore and others argue that personhood (*umunthu*) defines a human being as a philosophical category. According to them,

> "*Umunthu* makes a child behave. *Umunthu* gives the child the ability to demonstrate all the attributes of social responsibility. According to the concept

---

1 This distinction is supported by Matthew Schoffeleers who elaborates that "The principle of life is the heart (mtima), which also denotes the totality of a person's cognitive and effective functions. The heart is said to be 'black, white, cool, hot or stupid'" (Schoffeleers 1968a: 296).

> *umunthu* further distinguishes the child from other species by giving the child intelligence/logical thinking. One respondent referred to the opposite of *umunthu* as, 'despite counsel the child behaves like an animal'" (Kambalametore et al. 2000: 806).

Umunthu (personhood) therefore is an attribute that is acquired very early in a person's life, usually connected to his or her introduction into society such as by the *kutenga mwana* ritual (see *Chapter II.1.b*). Social competence and involvement play a crucial role for a full person (*munthu*), and Fr. Claude Boucher emphasizes this social component by defining *anthu* as social beings that are supposed to honour the *miyambo* and act responsibly for the benefit of their kin-group and the larger community. *Anthu* are motivated by culturally validated values, and they become ancestor spirits (*mizimu ya makolo*) after death.[2] Moreover, the notion of *munthu* also positions the person within a larger cosmological context of the human life cycle. According to one account,

> "A person is called by three different names, according to the condition. He is *munthu* when everything is fine, he is *matenda* when sick, and he is called *maliro* when dead" (Gerard Mdindire, a Mang'anja farmer).

With slight modification of the aforesaid statement, a Yao account explicitly describes persons with mental disorders as *munthu*, the only difference being that they are *anthu odwala matenda*, or persons suffering from sickness. A Lomwe account relates to a dogmatic *mwambo* learned in the context of maturity initiation, stating that the suffering (*odwala*) are human persons (*anthu*) in spite of their condition, and that they therefore deserve to be treated kindly and respectfull.

Composition of the Person

It has been argued before that Cartesian notions defining the person as a dualism of body and soul do not apply in the cultural context of Southern Malaŵi. Rather, more complex categories comprise a human person (*munthu*), and it is therefore

> "[...] not uncommon to hear a person being conceived, thought and defined as mthunzi (shadow), moyo (life itself), fumbi (dust), mphamvu ya abambo (power from the father), or magazi (blood from the mother). A human being is even defined as mpweya (wind/air)" (Chigona 2002: 37).

---

2 Matthew Schoffeleers likewise defines death as the transition from *munthu* to *mzimu* (Schoffeleers 1968a: 296). As the antithesis to *anthu*, Fr. Claude Boucher describes *afiti* (see *Chapter IV.1.a*) as violating the *miyambo*, leading an individualistic, ego-centric, anti-social existence and, accordingly, living from human flesh.

These somewhat confusing notions, of course, require some clarification. Following the argument of Gerard Chigona, the shadow (*mthunzi*) of a person usually indicates personality which one loses at death and which is strongly associated with a certain part of the human spirit (Chigona 2002: 102). The physical shape, on the other hand, is subject to growth, change, and decay, decomposing after the person's death. In total, the body (*thupi*) is closely connected to the aforementioned life force (*moyo*) and its vehicles, the body fluids.[3] *Magazi* (blood) is a highly important category in traditional Chewâ, Nyanja, and Mang'anja cosmologies, defining a person's kinship affiliation as well as the strength, health, and endurance of a person as manifest representations of *moyo*. In general, the *magazi* is passed on from mother to child and can therefore be perceived as an inherited quality connected to the matrilineal kin group (Morris 2000: 53).[4] While blood (*magazi*) loses its qualities with increasing age, it is considered as a sign of particularly 'strong blood' if this development is delayed. Therefore, with age,

> "The blood does not have power anymore, and it is nothing but good fortune that I inherited some strong blood [*magazi amphamvu*] from my parents because I was born in the year 1919. Up to now, I could still run a race against you, I am strong. You might see that this sister of mine is old and that she cannot hear anymore, but she is still the younger one" (Usanene Kwela, a Yao *mfumu*).

In his early work on Mang'anja religion, Matthew Schoffeleers observes that the notion of the spirit (*mzimu*) represents the closest Mang'anja equivalent to a Western concept of soul.[5] *Mzimu* (pl. *mizimu*) is described as an integral part of human existence which is set free upon death, but in contrast to Western notions, the *mzimu* of a person grows over the years – in accordance with local principles of seniority (Schoffeleers 1968a: 296).[6] The *mzimu* is located in the head (*mutu*) – or, as sometimes specified, the brain (*ubongo*) – of a person. Malaŵian notions of the spirit, however, imply an additional distinction:

> "About the spirit of earthly life [*mzimu wa pansi pano*] you need to know that there are two different spirits, one from the heavenly father and another, earthly one" (Usanene Kwela, a Yao *mfumu*).

---

3 Some accounts suggest a close connection between the movement of these body fluids and the causation of mental disorder (see *Chapter III.2.b*).

4 Even Yao interview partners tend to agree that the category of *magazi* used to apply to matrilateral kinship ties. Recently, he continues, even kinship relations on the father's side are sometimes referred to as *magazi*.

5 "The Mang'anja have no noun which expresses the concept of 'soul' in the sense of an immaterial, formative and causal element of life" (Schoffeleers 1968a: 296).

6 Reportedly, the human spirit leads an "embryonic existence" during lifetime. Its power of activity can be seen during sleep, when it visits the spirits of deceased persons and receives visits from them in return (Schoffeleers 1968a: 296).

On many occasions, people in Southern Malaŵi mention the human spirit or *mzimu* without giving any further specification. Upon closer inquiry, people from different ethnic backgrounds widely agree that the human person is endowed with two different *mizimu*, both of which represent necessary parts of his or her personhood (*umunthu*). These two spirits do not conjoin, nor are they thought of as an integral whole, but they constitute separate categories which, in Chicheŵa, are described as the divine spirit (*mzimu wa umulungu*) and the personal or human spirit (*mzimu wa umunthu*), respectively.

The *mzimu wa umulungu*, spirit of divinity, represents the spark of life which is received during conception and which returns to the Supreme Being after death, and which is associated with the vital force (*moyo*) as well as the conscience of a person (Chigona 2002: 102). It is utterly divine and unchanging, and – due to its strong bonds to body and blood – it only leaves the person at the point of his or her physical death.[7] Therefore, the divine spirit leaves a dying person for the celestial realm, and the former human person (*munthu*) is henceforth attributed as *mtembo*, *chitanda*, *maliro*, or *thupi* – that is, as a body or corpse (Chigona 2002: 102).

> "Yes, one [*mzimu*] stays down here on earth, the other is for God [*Mulungu*]. The earthly one is the one that comes wanting *nsima* when a person is dreaming, that stays waiting" (Usanene Kwela, a Yao *mfumu*).

The *mzimu wa umunthu* or spirit of personhood is the faculty that controls a person's decision-making processes and voluntary actions. Sometimes referred to as the shadow or image (*mthunzi* and/or *chithunzi*) of a person, it represents personal fortune (*mwayi*) and character, and it is associated with the heart or *mtima*. The *mzimu wa umunthu* is a variable entity that changes throughout lifetime and grows by personal experience and age. It is received at birth and is identical with the part of a person's metaphysical existence that transforms into an ancestral spirit (*mzimu wa makolo*) after death, therefore lingering on in the world of the living.[8] Being endowed with considerable independence and agency, the *mzimu wa umunthu* temporarily leaves a person during sleep – in the state of dreaming that is sometimes described as 'being half dead,' and that makes the person vulnerable to magic attacks such as *ufiti*.[9] By magic means, the

---

7 It is regarded as the privilege of the Supreme Being to withdraw a person's *mzimu wa umulungu* and thereby end a human being's worldly existence. Accordingly, "when a person dies and people hold prayers, they pray for the spirit [*mzimu*] and not the body [*thupi*]".

8 In a Christian context, the *mzimu wa umunthu* is also identified as the part of the human being that awaits divine punishment on judgment day. From the point of view of the Catholic dogma, the existence of a *mzimu wa makolo* among the living could therefore be identified with purgatory.

9 It is, actually, the personal spirits who are the main protagonists within this concept of magic. For the performance of anti-social acts, Malaŵian *afiti* (see *Chapter IV.1.a*) send out their own

mzimu wa umunthu may be removed from a person (see *Chapter IV.1.c*), thus causing a condition that – due to the loss of personal reasoning, comprehension, control, and coordination – leaves the person acting unreasonably and wandering idly in a state of mental disorder.

Defining Mind and Intelligence

Within the ethnically diverse context of Southern Malaŵi, the cognitive processes that underlie mental activity are explained with reference to various different models. More generally, the close association of human cognitive activity with the human head (*mutu*) may be considered common knowledge.[10] Accordingly, a Sena healer agrees that

> "The head [*mutu*] is where human thinking is formed, but the desire comes from the heart [*mtima*]" (Manueli Matundwe, a Sena *sing'anga*).

While the brain (*ubongo*) is the locus of thinking and judgment, its processes are expressions of the spirit of a person, leaving all decision-making and voluntary action in the control of the aforementioned *mzimu wa umunthu*. The idea of intelligence, at the same time, has been described by the principle of *nzeru* – a superordinate concept encompassing cognitive alacrity (*kuchenjera*, an ability demanded and fostered by contemporary schooling) as well as social responsibility and cooperativeness (*kutumikira*, denoting both trustworthiness and compliance).[11] Without *kutumikira*, cognitive alacrity (*kuchenjera*) is described as a negative social force in Cheŵa society (Serpell et al. 1993: 8). With reference to a rural Cheŵa community in the Central Region of Malaŵi, Sylvia Kambalametore and others have likewise conducted research on notions of child intelligence. According to their results,

> "Intelligence was defined as cleverness, smartness, increasing knowledge and understanding and developing discernment. It was also defined in terms of social skills, for example, being able to anticipate parents' needs, being able to run the home by the age of 12" (Kambalametore et al. 2000: 806).[12]

---

mizimu ya umunthu to harm others by magic means – while their physical bodies (*thupi*) can be found sleeping in bed. By *ufiti* victims, the *mzimu wa umunthu* is usually described as the pale white image of a person's physical shape.

10 Brian Morris therefore argues that "Although the Chewa have a concept of brain (*ubongo* or *uwongo*) and often us the term in the sense of the mind [...] all afflictions of a mental nature are described in terms of the head (*mutu*)" (Morris 1996: 119).

11 Steven Paas accommodates the wide semantic field of the verb *kuchenjera* by translating it as 'beware, mind, care for, be brave, be artful, be cautious, be clever, be acute, be sly, be circumspect' (Paas 2004: 33-34). *Kutumikira*, on the other hand, is given as to 'serve, work for, perform duties for' (Paas 2004: 448).

12 For children of the age group of about 4 to 5 years, it is reported that children were expected to

In Chicheŵa language, the terminological category that comes closest to Western notions of intelligence or wisdom is *nzeru*. It is defined as representing

> "[...] several aspects of personality, including cognitive alacrity, social responsibility, and wisdom, in ways that only partially overlap with the English concept of intelligence" (Kathuria & Serpell 1998: 229).[13]

In many accounts, the reasoning that is perceived as lacking in the behaviour of a person with mental disorders is referred to as *nzeru*. In one such case, a traditional healer among the Sena explains that

> "At any time what you just have to know is that a person with *kuzungulira mutu* has no *nzeru* and also thinks without *nzeru*. [...] A person's *nzeru* escapes him/her according to how his/her brain [*ubongo*] was protected. A person like this is such that you can even send him/her to fetch water with a broken bucket, and he/she really goes" (Manueli Matundwe, a Sena *sing'anga*).

Nzeru is, at the same time, conceived of as a variable concept that increases by age, therefore reflecting the personal development of a child and its progress in the age set system.[14] The loss of *nzeru* is therefore equivalent with mental disorder, which can also be expressed as a "change into a *wamisala*" (see *Chapter III.2.a*). But while the faculty of human reasoning – the *mzimu wa munthu* – represents a necessary part of *munthu*, every person receives the gift of *nzeru* in different amounts.

> "*Nzeru* is given by God [*Mulungu*]. When those children are born with little *nzeru*, it means that God created them this way. Therefore it is difficult for a *sing'anga* to help with these things, because a *sing'anga* can succeed against what another *sing'anga* did, but not against God. Many times the children of one family do not differ in their *nzeru*. Those children who come first usually have less *nzeru*

---

be "active, curious and to learn by imitation, distinguishing good from bad, wanting to go to school and being keen to please parents. Examples of skills anticipated around this age are washing up, making clay figures, carrying water on the head, running errands and carrying messages (with full recall), knowing one's name and the names of relatives, bathing without help, telling stories to friends and parents, playing games, make believe play (wedding was an example given) reporting back on what has been said in church, knowing folk stories, songs and dances" (Kambalametore et al. 2000: 806).

13 In this article, Ravinder Kathuria and Robert Serpell develop a culturally appropriate method of assessing intelligence in Zambia, the so called Panga Munthu Test or PMT (Kathuria & Serpell 1998). Elsewhere, Robert Serpell describes *nzeru* as the superordinate concept of intelligent wisdom encompassing both the previously named principles of cognitive alacrity (*chenjera*) and of social responsibility and cooperativeness or *tumikira* (Serpell 1993: 73-74).

14 This is supported by Robert Serpell and others who state that "In rural communities, where chronological birthdates are accorded very little significance, their behavior indicative of growing *nzelu* is an important index of general maturation. Indeed it may carry more weight in arriving at the decision that an adolescent is »ready« for formal initiation into adulthood than do the organic signs of reaching puberty" (Serpell, Mariga & Harvey 1993: 9).

> because they were in a hurry to get born, and children following after that usually have more *nzeru*" (Manueli Matundwe, a Sena *sing'anga*).

Therefore, the concept of *nzeru* is described as a divine gift which, at the same time, has some hereditary aspects. Poor performance of a schoolchild is seen as an expression of weak *nzeru,* and a child failing to make progress as the other classmates would is described as being *opanda nzeru,* lacking intelligence.[15] Such a condition is not conceived as pathological, and there is nothing that either traditional or biomedicine can do about it. While some people may therefore be endowed with a larger or smaller amount of *nzeru* due to birth and/or hereditary factors, its loss during lifetime is considered a pathological situation. It may therefore be subsumed that cognitive processes as well as social responsibility (*nzeru*) are given to each person as expressions and functions of human personality (i.e. the *mzimu wa umunthu*).

Personhood and Social Structure

The above depiction of the concept of *nzeru* has already alluded to the social embedding of Malaŵian concepts of the person, and the connection between a person's cognitive faculty and the ancestral spirits likewise integrates the human person into the cosmological structure. In a traditional Malaŵian setting, the person is therefore defined as

> "[...] socialized from birth to death into the authority dimension, which is based on the principles of age and seniority and which consists of the mother, elder siblings, father, elders, ancestors (<u>mizimu</u>) and God (<u>Mulungu</u>)" (Peltzer 1987: 12).[16]

Among the different ethnic groups of Southern Malaŵi, the principle of seniority is of central social importance, and it provides a direct connection to the cosmological hierarchy through the ancestral spirits (*mizimu ya makolo*) of a respective lineage. In this context, the initiatory stages mentioned above play a

---

15 Other accounts describe this situation as *ubongo watopa* – laziness of the brain – on part of the student.

16 According to Karl Peltzer, the person is embedded into the cosmic hierarchy in a very early stage of his or her personal development, and it happens by a structural identification of spiritual authorities with the respective parents. These 'ideal-parents-patterns' (Peltzer 1987: 13) are later on completed by other relatives – as the mother's brother (*malume*) in the case of the matrilineal Cheŵa – who take over a crucial position in the development of the person, with the ancestral spirits (*mizimu*) and the Supreme Being (*Mulungu*) functioning as superior authorities. With concern to the notion of the person as embedded within its social and cosmic sphere, the system of seniority implies that "The ancestral cult can be compared with the »ideal-parents-images«: both ancestors and »ideal parents« are believed to be omnipotent, so the ancestor-parent relationship is the ritual equivalent of the parent-child relationship" (Peltzer 1987: 14).

major role in the social location of the individual. According to the principle of seniority, a condition of human completeness is only achieved with old age, attributing almost ancestral status to elders even in their living days (Sow 1980: 126). Thus, death is not identified as the end of human existence, but as a final transformation and initiation into the spirit world (Kubik 1987: 21; Peltzer 1987: 15). The moral prescription to pay respect and honour seniors is an important part of traditional culture. Their representation in normative traditions has already been depicted (see *Chapter II.1.a*), and a Chichew̋a proverb likewise emphasizes the high social status of elders, declaring that

> "*Wamkulu salakwa.* / An elderly person is never wrong" (Chakanza 2000a: 334).

In spite of this proclaimed infallibility, the effects of old age may, at the same time, display some similarities with cases of mental disorder. It is therefore important to examine the relation between the socially prestigious position of the elders and the – at least – challenged social situation of persons with mental disorder in Southern Malaŵi. According to these differences in cultural perception, it may not be surprising that people generally make a clear distinction between the various forms of mental disorder on the one hand and old age on the other. Therefore, society strictly differentiates between old age and pathological states, expressing that

> "[...] they talk nonsense and even forget what they are talking about. It is not *misala*, not a sickness at all. [It is] deterioration of the brain, a tired brain" (Francis Muramu, a Lomwe *sing'anga*).

The connection between mental disorder and old age is therefore described as being entirely limited to its external manifestation, and usually, the condition is associated with the person's blood losing strength (see above). Therefore,

> "When a person reaches 70 [...] or more, he/she can do those things. It's not just that the person is getting old, his/her blood becomes weak, and when walking, his/her steps become weak and different from the way he/she was walking, but without any strength. [...] If someone becomes like this, we help him/her by treating the patient again and again. We give him/her special medicine to drink because the person has grown old in a normal fashion. We give him/her medicine for the body to keep strong" (Lexon Kondwani, a Sena *sing'anga*).[17]

---

17 These cases of mental deterioration due to old age are therefore considered non-pathological in traditional terms and no treatment is sought – even though it is conceded that biomedical treatment may exist: "[...] there is old age which exceeds just getting old, but that the brain fails to work properly, forgets things easily and also does abnormal things. For that type of old age, there is no traditional medicine, no medicine for forgetfulness. I do not give medicine for that, but maybe if one goes to the hospital, there they would maybe find a way to deal with this. [...] The big issue is when a person is old and the way he/she does things because there are some old

On a number of occasions, in contrast, people agree that certain states occurring at old age may be referred to in mental disorder categories. At the same time, even such a condition is described as normal and non-pathological – which has a direct effect on health seeking behaviour. If a given case is considered to be age-related, relatives usually do not seek any kind of medical treatment for that patient, but "they just look after him/her".[18] The understanding of age-related conditions in Malaŵi implies a somewhat cyclic model of individual development due to which the old persons' condition is compared with childish patterns of behaviour.[19]

The category of *munthu* is generally applied for every living human being, and it is emphatically agreed that even the most severe cases of mental disorder are considered as *anthu.*[20] While *umunthu* is thus conceptualized as an integrative concept that means to attribute equal moral status to everybody – indiscriminate of their abilities and/or limitations –, certain criteria that define personhood according to emic notions clearly conflict with conditions of mental disorder. Taking social responsibility, contributing to the wellbeing of the community, or observing the *miyambo* are declared as distinctive features of the concept of *munthu* – characteristics that not every person with a mental disorder may be able to adhere to. At the same time, it is obvious that strong cultural norms (*miyambo*) demand categorizing even the most deviant members of society as *anthu*, and the notion of losing the personality spirit (*mzimu wa umunthu*) by magic means is depicted as an unfortunate yet temporary state that explicitly does not influence the *umunthu* status of the victim. It is, nonetheless, justified and necessary to consider the interaction between the concept of *umunthu* and mental disorder very closely in this context. In fact, the all-

---

people whose brains act normally, but there are other old people who become abnormal and for these, the brain is not working properly" (Gordon Chitsulo, a Lomwe *sing'anga*).

18 More especially, cases that may otherwise be diagnosed as mental conditions – such as *kuzerezeka* (see *Chapter III.2.b*) – due to their particular symptoms may be labelled as normal cases of old age once the treatment against the mental disorder fails to take effect. As a traditional healer puts it, "[…] as for me, I have the medicine which I use to help people according to the type of *kuzerezeka* and also the age, how old the person is. Then I do help. If I fail, it is because of the intelligence of an old person" (Luka Dzaone, a Lomwe *sing'anga*).

19 Incidents of age-related cases of mental disorder – here identified as *kupepera* – are explained by a reduced functionality of the brain (*ubongo watopa*, a tired brain) which thus returns to childish thinking. A Lomwe *sing'anga* emphasizes that "when someone is old we say he/she has gone back to childhood". Likewise, a Yao chief describes that "Most times when people get old they change into being *ozerezeka* because they do not hear what their relatives say, because their brain does not work anymore. So that person returns to childhood" (Usanene Kwela, a Yao *mfumu*).

20 According to the assessment of a Mang'anja *mfumu*, the perception of persons with mental disorders has not changed significantly over the last 50 years. They are considered as human beings (*munthu*), but they cannot be held responsible for their actions for lack of consciousness.

embracing, egalitarian concept of personhood paints a picture that does not go unchallenged. The representatives of organizations for persons with disabilities in Malaŵi therefore express their involvement in this debate on a daily basis, expressing that

> "[...] there is actually that one [attitude] that a person with a disability is maybe a half-being. That's why we as an organization come up with some slogans like 'Each individual is a human being no matter how disabled', and there is a saying that 'No thin person is half a being, and no fat person is two beings'. As an individual you are a human being, whether disabled or not. And we try to advocate through our field officers for a change of attitude. Yes, but of course there is a philosophy behind that. A person with a disability, because of the shortfalls one has, gets considered as to be an incomplete being" (Peter Ngomwa, a Sena disability organization representative).

In spite of the far-reaching philosophical concept of *umunthu*, persons with mental disorders are evidently located on the very edge of the culturally defined sphere of personhood in Southern Malaŵi.[21] The conflicts with the ideal criteria constituting the person in its social framework have been outlined, and it may be suggested here that the general inclusion of persons with mental disorder under the category of *munthu* is based not on the literal applicability of its emic definition but on the compliance with normative traditions (*miyambo*) forbidding their classificatory exclusion. Here again, traditional norms of conduct have a crucial impact on defining the social positioning of persons with mental disorders.

1(b) Diagnostic Processes

Among the different ethnic groups of Southern Malaŵi, the ascription of a specific category to the mental – or general health – disorder of a given person works on two distinct levels of diagnostic allocation. First, a broad common knowledge of cultural health disorder categories allows lay persons to classify a given case according to outward symptoms. On a second level, more in-depth professional medical knowledge is required in order to provide specialized background information about the respective mental disorder, locate its causative agent (aetiology), and identify appropriate therapeutic means. Here, diagnostic

---

21 The concept of *umunthu* as depicted here also clarifies an observation made in an earlier chapter (see *Chapter II.1.b*). The integration of a newborn child into the community of *anthu* happens in the ritual soon after delivery. A stillborn child (or *nsenye*) – or one dying before this formal introduction into society – is buried with reduced ritual effort because it is regarded as strictly not *munthu*. It is referred to as a stillborn (*nsenye*) instead of a child (*mwana*), and its shallow grave is prepared in a field called *manda a nsenye* – or graveyard of the stillborn.

procedure cannot be examined independent from the social context in which both the given health problem and its examination occur.[22] Thus, the symptoms presented by a given patient as well as the inter-subjective perception through the immediate social environment have an impact on the diagnostic process. In some cases, external factors – e.g. the economic situation of the patient's family, the kinship position of the patient, or a particular family situation – can predefine a certain explanation for the disorder.[23] Therefore, traditional diagnosis is embedded into a highly sophisticated cultural framework and part of a larger social discourse. In essence, most cases of mental disorder in Southern Malaŵi are referred back to a social context, identifying the reasons for the condition as the rational actions of personal or spiritual forces.

Generally, the terms applied for mental disorder in Southern Malaŵi are associated with a comparatively well-defined canon of symptoms. These nosological categories are not part of an insider code that can only be understood and applied by a specialized few, but they belong to the common sphere of the respective local languages. Accordingly, a given person in Southern Malaŵi usually has a fairly clear comprehension of the different terms culturally applied for the different forms of mental disorder – such as *misala* or *kuzerezeka* – and their specific presentation. Virtually any person in a rural market setting can offer basic definitions for these terms, and they are applied freely when pointing out an allegedly affected person or narrating past personal experience. On the basis of this wide-spread knowledge, the different terms for mental disorder are easily attributed even to passers-by without requiring any more in-depth information about a given case than what a casual glance can tell.[24] Within this process of classification, basic cultural notions of normative behaviour play a central role. Even slight aberrations from the social norm are easily interpreted in

---

22 With reference to disorders associated with the head (*mutu*) of a person, Brian Morris therefore argues that "What is diagnosed depends both on the nature of surrounding social circumstances, and on the nature of associated symptoms" (Morris 1996: 119).

23 The relatives of a Yao boy with severe mental disorders are therefore convinced that his condition cannot be related to anti-social magic (see *Chapter IV.1.a*) even without consulting a traditional healer (*sing'anga*). Elaborating on their persuasion, the mother explains that the affected child is her fourth-born, and that any deliberate attempt to harm her family would either target the first-born or prevent the parents from having more children. The same logic applies in the case of a Sena family. A Mang'anja mother explains that, even without the help of a *sing'anga*, her decision to live in the compound of her husband's kin-group – violating the rule of matrilocal residence – led his family to apply *ufiti* against her daughter. According to her, the relatives are motivated by jealousy, fearing that the child may – again, in conflict with the matrilineal system of inheritance – take over the parents' house, and so the child's mental disorder is meant to prevent her from claiming her inheritance.

24 On some occasions, requests concerning how a certain person could be labelled as *womisala* (see *Chapter III.2.a*) on first sight may lead to some amusement among a group of interviewees, describing the character of this patient's condition as perfectly obvious – 'just look at him'.

terms of mental disorder, and distinctive, culturally defined behavioural patterns therefore form the basis of every process of lay diagnosis.[25]

In contrast to lay categorization, a diagnosis carried out by a medical specialists – including *asing'anga* healers or *azamba* midwives, but also biomedical personnel such as doctors, nurses, or special needs staff – involves some more sophisticated techniques as defined by the respective medical system. Here, again, the connection between the particular presentation of the given mental disorder and its social context and perception plays a crucial role. While diagnostic findings conflicting with common assumptions about the background of a given disorder may, on the one hand, modify public opinion, every diagnosis – whether coming from traditional or biomedical authorities – is also subject to scrutiny and doubt. The pluralistic character of the medical system in Malaŵi entails that contradicting approaches to a given health disorder coexist, and that it is a question of individual as well as group preference which explanatory model is favoured in a given case. As diagnostic procedures usually take social circumstances into consideration, some details of the patient history or the occurrence of the health disorder may contribute significantly to the identification of sickness causation.

Traditional Specialist Diagnosis

As a first diagnostic procedure, traditional health specialists frequently claim to apply their more sophisticated knowledge in visual diagnosis.[26] While visual examination as well as narrative accounts of relatives are commonly the first steps taken in traditional Malaŵian diagnosis, it is important to note that well-reputed and more spiritually specialized *asing'anga* reject any form of direct verbal patient-healer interaction. Accordingly, patients frequently assess it as a sign of high qualification and exceptional competence if a *sing'anga* ascertains the nature, cause and/or treatment for a given complaint without receiving any explicit information from patients or their relatives. This appreciation implies the assumption that a *sing'anga*, treating a patient without any further details, has a vital bond to the world of the spirits (*mizimu*) – as it is the spirits who provide all necessary knowledge about the given case.

In order to obtain the required expertise about the relevant case history from spiritual sources, traditional diagnosis in Southern Malaŵi operates with

---

25 A Lomwe *sing'anga* accordingly states that a person's behaviour should be moderate and reasonable at all times. Whenever a person is seen as being overly agitated, his/her condition is easily interpreted in terms of mental disorder – more especially as *misala*.

26 With reference to that, a Lomwe *sing'anga* points out that an experienced traditional healer can diagnose cases of mental disorder – more especially of *khunyu* (see *Chapter III.2.e*) – in a newborn child due to the weak expression in its eyes.

divinatory techniques which are commonly referred to as *maula* (sg. *ula*).[27] *Maula* divination is considered as part of the healers' art (*using'anga*) and an integral part of the medical services provided by traditional healers.[28] *Maula* is conducted by the use of different divinatory items which possess certain spiritual properties. A typical *maula* consists of a calabash gourd (*nsupa*) – combined with other objects such as animal horns (*nyanga*), conch shells (*kankhono*), pieces of leather (*chikopa*), or strings of beads (*zipote*) – that obtains its special powers by the time it is manufactured. In most cases, one part of the *maula* device functions as a communicative unit through which spiritual knowledge is imparted to the diviner.[29] Typically represented by a small glass mirror (*galasi*) that is attached to the *maula*, this 'display' of the divinatory device is said to provide *sing'anga* with the necessary information by displaying visual images.[30] For this purpose, the *nsupa* may also be applied to significant parts of the patient's body in order to show the interior condition. On a more technical level, it should be noted that the principle of *maula* divination – as the classical technique of traditional diagnosis – implies the acquisition of spiritual knowledge due to direct communication with spirit agents (*mizimu*). The *maula* is not 'charged' with magic power, but rather opens a connection to the ancestral spirits (*mizimu ya makolo*) which provide otherwise inaccessible information.

What is crucial in this context is that these elaborated diagnostic procedures are typically not applied in order to reveal which health disorder category should be applied in a given case. Rather, divinatory techniques serve to examine the cause of a given health disorder, and their application frequently leads to remarkably complex diagnostic statements. In case of mental disorder, for instance, a *maula* may not only indicate whether or not a given condition is

---

27 The process of divination due to *maula* is also mentioned as *kulosa* or *kuwombeza*.

28 Due to its inherently religious implication, the concept of *maula* is seen as clashing with both Muslim and Christian philosophies. Therefore, it is rejected by many *asing'anga* with either of these religious orientations, depending on the dogmas acknowledged by their respective denominations.

29 These objects may be conceptualized and applied as analogous to a telephone receiver, and therefore the *sing'anga* receives communication by holding the respective device – such as a shell or *chithumwa* – to his or her ear. In order to apply such a divinatory device, "We make some noise and sing, asking the *nsupa*. And the *nsupa* responds through the shell which is there. From there, we sometimes also use the *zithumwa*, putting them to our ears and listening to what they say" (Henry Mwambo, a Yao *sing'anga*).

30 The *maula* devices used by local *asing'anga* are generally manufactured according to the individual needs and knowledge of the healer. A given Lomwe *sing'anga* therefore uses a *nsupa* gourd, partly covered with leather and decorated with a round mirror. A glass hip flask is connected to it by a string of beads, and flywhisks (*mchira*) as well as animal horns (*nyanga*) are attached to form a vaguely anthropomorphic shape, with the mirror signifying the face. The *sing'anga* refers to the *maula* as his *tivi* (or 'TV'), showing whatever he desires to see due to him manipulating the hip flask which he considers as the corresponding 'remote control'.

caused by spirit agents (*mizimu*), but it may also facilitate the identification of the responsible spirit.[31] If a given case of mental disorder can be established as being caused by magic reasons such as *ufiti*, on the other hand, *maula* divination may serve to ascertain the name and/or kinship position of the respective person. Moreover, *maula* techniques are not only applied to analyse the aetiological causation of a given disorder, but they may also provide information needed in order to identify the adequate medication for a given case. Thus, as a Yao healer explains,

> "We use a *nsupa* and a mirror [...] which work hand in hand. [...] When they bring a patient here, we find out the problem through the *nsupa* and the mirror. Then we might know that this patient has been attacked by *ufiti*. Then, with the same mirror, we find out the medicine to treat the patient with, and the mirror tells us to give him/her such-and-such a medicine. Then we come here and take different types of *mitengo*, and we boil it and give it to them. When the patient drinks, he/she feels better" (Linga Nasawa, a Yao *sing'anga*).

Muslim, Christian, and Biomedical Diagnostics

Recently, increasing numbers of *asing'anga* in Southern Malaŵi apply diagnostic – as well as therapeutic – techniques which refer to Muslim as well as Christian notions. While the representatives of many Muslim and Christian communities emphasize their disapproval of their followers engaging in *maula* divination, the diagnostic techniques of Muslim or Christian *asing'anga* follow a similar line of thought. Here, direct spiritual inspiration is a common feature applied in the diagnostic process in order to diagnose health problems and prescribe medication.[32] Likewise, nocturnal visions and visitations inspired by these spirits can reveal the identities and complaints of future patients. As opposed to the more traditional use of lineage spirits (*mizimu ya makolo*) as the source of spiritual inspiration, *asing'anga* with a strong Muslim or Christian background frequently cooperate with entities from the Qur'ān or with Biblical characters – e.g. having a *malā'ika* or *jinn*, an apostle or saint act as a spirit mentor. Usually, these spirits establish long-lasting relationships with the *asing'anga* who, as an expression of their strong spiritual affiliation, may even

---

31 A Sena healer explains *maula* divination as a binary try-and-error inquiry, stating that, when trying to identify a given spirit agent, "I trace all the ancestors of the person by advising my *maula* to start with one person after the other. So we begin with the father, and if I find nothing, I go to the grandparents" (Manueli Matundwe, a Sena *sing'anga*).

32 A Christian Yao healer explains this relationship, saying that "Even if I am seated like this, during daytime or while doing my work, as soon as a patient comes, I pray and tell the patient why he/she has come here, what his/her problem is. [...] I pray to God, to the spirits of prophecy [*mizimu ya m'neneri*]" (Joseph Kamwendo, a Yao *sing'anga*).

take on a new personal name.[33] In any case, diagnostic prayer and the use of Holy Scripture – both meant to induce spiritual or divine inspiration – serves as a central divinatory method meant to impart secret knowledge to the *sing'anga*.[34] As a Christian Lomwe healer explains:

> "I always use the Bible. At that time, the spirits come and choose the words from the Bible, and when I read them out I usually know what that person is suffering from, but also the treatment that I should give to him/her. From that Bible, I can also deduct if that person will get better or not" (Mose Chingale, a Lomwe *sing'anga*).[35]

The power of these Christian *mizimu* can be utilized in a number of different ways. In addition to their potential in diagnosing health disorders and finding appropriate treatment, the helping spirits of a *sing'anga* can also act to facilitate the examination of a violent patient, and they may also prescribe the appropriate payment expected for their diagnostic services.[36] In a Muslim context, several other divinatory techniques are in use, most frequently applying the Qur'ān in order to diagnose a given health disorder.[37] In this context, passages of the

---

[33] Accordingly, a Lomwe *sing'anga* has adopted the name of the Virgin Mary, and a Yao healer calls himself after Saint John, denominating their respective spirit allies.

[34] A Christianized *sing'anga* explains her diagnosis thus: "When we go into a house, we take a Bible, the patient's clothes, and we also take a head cloth [*mpango*] because we use all these things. As soon as we wipe the patient with the head cloth, numbers appear on it. Then I start praying, and we examine him/her using the Bible. When I finish praying, I start speaking and the spirit comes into my tongue, my whole body feels as if it is paralyzed, and the spirit takes over. Saint Luke comes through the spirit and starts talking in tongues, and then I translate into Chicheŵa that this sickness is so-and-so and the medication should be like this" (Doris Petroyo, a Lomwe *sing'anga*).

[35] In a statement underlining the tradition of not having patients talk about their complaints upon first consultation, this same *sing'anga* continues: "When a person comes, I start praying. Then, I take the Bible to read, and the *mizimu* tell me the problem of that person who just came. Once we have done this, we organize his/her problems systematically. If he/she approves, we administer the treatment. If persons come, they do not tell me about the problems they are having, but I tell them after hearing it from the *mzimu*. Sometimes these *mizimu* can just come, telling me which problem the person has I am just examining" (Mose Chingale, a Lomwe *sing'anga*).

[36] Thus, a Lomwe *sing'anga* describes that whenever a person entering her consultation room is possessed by potentially dangerous spirits, her own Christian *mizimu* attack these intruding spirits and subdue them – making especially violent *misala* patients (see *Chapter III.2.a*) easier to handle. As a sign of this spiritual struggle, such patients would usually break down upon entering her shrine. Later on, the spirits inform her about the adequate payment for her diagnostic services – usually a sum of about 25 MwK.

[37] Special forms of divination include a method disclosed by a rural Yao healer, which he refers to as 'chicken oracle' (*ulosi wa nkhuku*). When searching for treatment for a given health problem, the *sing'anga* reads different *dowa* prayers from the Qur'ān – effective in the treatment of different kinds of disorders (see *Chapter II.2.b*) – to a chicken. The chicken, as he continues, stays motionless in case that the prayer read is suitable for treating the respective patient due to the power of God holding the chicken in place. If the respective su>ra is inappropriate for the given case, the animal would keep on running around the yard.

Qur'ān as well as the Hadith are used to examine character and background of health disorders, with the identification of a therapeutically suitable sūra representing the diagnostic process itself.[38] While a number of Muslim *asing'anga* also apply traditional divinatory methods, others express that, according to a closer observation of the Qur'ān, elaborate diagnostic procedures are not an indispensable part of their medical philosophy. Rather, it is expressed that divine power is the sole key to cure all sorts of disorders – mental and physical. Because of their universal applicability, these therapeutic measures do not require a clearly defined diagnosis but utilize spiritual power to overcome health disorders regardless of their exact causation. This notion is also supported in the context of numerous non-cosmopolitan churches in Southern Malaŵi.

It would not seem inconsistent to omit biomedical procedures from this portrayal of diagnostic systems as they show no cultural characteristics that would structurally distinguish them from European or North American approaches. What is important, however, is that the results of biomedical diagnostic procedures are usually conveyed to the patients or their respective guardians by the use of Western – that is, in the case of Malaŵi, English – medical terminology which has no direct equivalent in local languages. Due to their very limited transferability, biomedical concepts are therefore not suitable to replace cultural notions as applied by lay diagnosis, rather offering an additional, alternative model of explanation that, even on a simple linguistic basis, is difficult to communicate. Thus, a child with a remarkably large head may be considered to suffer from *mutu* or *khunyu* according to the assessment of a rural community even after a check-up at the next Health Station has indicated hydrocephalus or, in indigenous terms, water in the head (*madzi m'mutu*). It is crucial to observe the lacking negotiability of the conflicting diagnostic findings resulting from the different medical categories. Therefore, a factual coexistence of diagnoses can be attested, which leaves ample room for reinterpretation and personal opinion.

This observation stresses the cultural importance of emic systems of mental disorder classification. The present summary, at the same time, also needs to point out the structural differences between lay and specialist diagnostic procedures. Lay diagnosis is an informal, public discourse focussing on the labelling process (nosology), and considerations about the causation of the condition are common but regarded as largely speculative. Specialized –

---

38 A Yao healer explains his procedures as ritual washing – as customary before prayers –, putting on a clean dress, and intensive praying. During these prayers, divine forces provide the *sing'anga* with instructions on the suitable Qur'ān passages to apply. Due to the duration of this procedure, patients usually come on two consecutive days – explaining their complaints on the first, and receiving the prepared treatment on the second. The sūra medication mentioned here is applied in the form of *matalasimu* medicine (see *Chapter II.2.b*).

especially traditional – diagnosis, on the other hand, focuses primarily on unveiling the hidden causative agents (aetiology) while ignoring discussions about terminological categorization. Religious procedures as applied in the context of many Muslim and Christian communities, on the other hand, tend to have an even more condensed approach. While the categories used to denote a given mental disorder have no impact on the therapeutic process, its precise causation may – e.g. in identifying therapeutically suitable parts of the respective sacred texts – or may not – e.g. in Christian discourses that attribute all suffering to satanic forces and all healing to divine grace – be the focus of diagnostic examination. It may therefore be assessed that the mental disorder terminologies presented in this chapter are not part of any specialized concept. Rather, the nosologies applied in Southern Malaŵi reflect a broad public discourse whereas specialized diagnosis focuses on aetiological factors – which will receive more attention in a following chapter.

2. Nosology of Mental Disorder

In order to obtain some cultural understanding of the perception of mental disorder in the context of Southern Malaŵian societies, this section will outline the terminological categories applied for the respective forms of health disorder, and it will provide the respective definitions as well as basic information about their culturally recognized backgrounds. In addition, a number of nosological categories cannot clearly be identified as mental disorders themselves, but a closer understanding of these conditions constitutes an important part of the bigger picture concerning the phenomenon of mental disorder, and therefore they will be incorporated as well in this chapter. Thus, the category of *khunyu* for instance will be depicted in some detail, as *khunyu* represents a very common side-effect and epiphenomenon of other forms of mental disorder. Accordingly, the nosological category *kulumala* will also be examined even though its character appears to be of a mainly physical nature.[39]

All through this section, the description of Malaŵian nosological categories of mental disorder follows an explicitly emic perspective. Therefore, the depictions of aetiologies, pathogenesis and other aspects of the respective disorders represent local notions as presented in the cultures of the different

[39] It does not appear viable to elaborate on all concepts applied for the classification of mental disorder in Southern Malaŵi at equal length. Therefore, the present selection of nosological categories has been made according to the prevalence of the term throughout the period of the research and may therefore represent the most important nosologies. Additional categories will be addressed less circumstantially in the glossary (see *Appendix 1*).

ethnic groups that were incorporated. These depictions necessarily conflict with Western medical notions, and these conflicts will not be argued away for the sake of an artificial clarity of terminological analogy. The order in which the different categories of mental disorder are discussed here loosely reflects the frequency of its occurrence during interview session as well as their relevance to the overall argument of this study.

From a biomedical perspective, it appears all but self-evident to differentiate physical from mental complaints – maybe including a third, combined category of multiple cases. This notion clearly reflects the Cartesian dualism of distinguishing mind and matter, and it can claim very limited validity in a non-Western cultural context. In Southern Malaŵi, the distinction between mental and physical health disorders is not as strictly defined. Rather, traditional notions identify a direct connection between categories which, according to biomedical standards, would qualify as mental and physical health disorders, respectively. It is a common notion that a person's physically discernible disorder – be it a limping leg, or a dysfunctional hand – also has a mentally disordering effect on the affected person. On numerous occasions, slight deviations from normative behaviour as perceived in a person with a primarily physical disorder are interpreted as indicating a general mental disorder – or rather, categories applied in this context attribute mental symptoms to conditions that could, from a Western perspective, be regarded as entirely physical.[40] The present study therefore applies a wide definition of mental disorder which, according to emic notions, has to include various cases which do not appear to constitute mental cases at all. The justification of this approach shall be discussed in the context of the respective terminological categories (see *Chapter III.2.f*).

---

40 A group of Mang'anja subsistence farmers, e.g., therefore conclude that a person with an obvious physical challenge must also be mentally affected as well. As an example, one farmer points at a group of children gathered around during our interview. While most children sit down – which is considered appropriate behaviour in order not to disturb the adults' discussion –, one child keeps standing, not showing the demanded amount of consideration and respect. This ten year-old girl, he explains, was born with a slightly deformed hand, and her behaviour is used to exemplify that even her condition is, at least in part, a mental problem that making it difficult for the person to perform within the limits of the cultural norm. In a different line of thought, a well-known Lomwe *sing'anga* points out that limping can also be a sign of *khunyu* (see *Chapter III.2.e*). Likewise, the effects of primarily physical and mental cases of disorder – *kulumala* and *kuzerezeka* – are described as being interrelated. In this sense, a Yao *sing'anga* uses the expression of *kulumala mozerezeka*, thus creating a joint term combining physical and mental disorders.

2(a) Madness, or Misala

Among the nosological categories applied for mental disorders, *misala* is the most central concept in Chicheŵa language, and it is widely known and applied throughout Malaŵi as part of a very general, non-specialized vocabulary. Chicheŵa dictionaries as well as anthropological studies usually translate *misala* as 'madness' (Paas 2004: 269; Schoffeleers 1997: 143; Botne & Kulemeka 1995: 70), and its character as a severe challenge of human cognitive capabilities has been suggested previously.[41] In some cases, the term *misala* is substituted by the synonymous Chicheŵa expression *kupenga*, or in the composite form of *kupenga misala* (Kalipeni 1981: 109-110).[42] In addition, Steven Paas offers the alternative version of *kuchita misala* or 'to be mad' (Paas 2003: 226-227), and a number of alternative expressions are also regarded as synonymous with *misala*.[43]

The onset of *misala* can differ widely, with some patients showing symptoms early on in childhood and others developing *misala* at any later point of their lives. There is some disagreement about whether *misala* may occur from birth onwards: while some people assess that a child may be born with inherent *misala*, others insist that *misala* could only start during early childhood.[44] Apart from this open question, it is generally consented that *misala* occurs at any point during a person's life – and that the point of its occurrence may be an indicator for its causation (see *Chapter IV*). Throughout Southern Malaŵi, it is a frequently shared sentiment that *misala* is very easy even for a lay person to diagnose. A traditional healer describes his first assessment of a *misala* patient, saying that

---

41 Accordingly, a Malaŵian *sing'anga* has been cited as stating that "With misala, a person's mind loses its way, as the tendons are destroyed" (quoted from Morris 1996: 121). Accordingly, Ezekiel Kalipeni defines *msala* as the common Chicheŵa notion of 'madness' in its most general sense, while Paul Kapapa mentions *wamisala* as a term used among the Ngoni of Dedza District (Central Region) for a mad person (Kapapa 1977: 60).

42 Translations for *kupenga* include 'insane', 'lunatic', 'to be mad, become mad/insane' or 'insanity'. It also appears in derived forms such as *kupengetsa* or 'to madden, drive mad by means of medicine' (Paas 2003: 226; Moxley 2001; Botne & Kulemeka 1995: 70; Zambezi Mission [eds.] 1986).

43 Sometimes, *misala* is also identified with the Chitumbuka term *kufuntha* meaning "to be mad" (Turner 1996: 30). While some people consider these categories as interchangeable, others differentiate *kufuntha* symptoms as the rude and violent behaviour in children, molesting adults and 'being troublesome' in general. Brian Morris states that *misala* "is normally spoken of in terms of a 'spinning' head (*mutu umazungulira*)" (Morris 1996: 121). Field data however suggests a distinction between *misala* and *kuzungulira mutu* which will be clarified in the depiction of the latter notion itself (see *Chapter III.2.c*).

44 A Yao *mzamba* explains her idea about this question, stating that *misala* would manifest itself in misbehaviour (*mphulupulu*) which obviously could not emanate before the child achieves the appropriate age to show personal action.

> "People suffering from *misala* come here together with their guardians. For me to know that the person is *misala* – the guardians bring the patient in chains, tied up, which indicates that if they let him loose he would probably beat up people" (Linga Nasawa, a Yao *sing'anga*).

In general, a condition of *misala* is defined as a state of apparent confusion, often accompanied by the use of abusive language and unpredictable as well as violent behaviour. Moving from place to place with no apparent destination or reason is also a common indicator due to which the condition is sometimes referred to as *kuthamanga misala* or 'to run *misala*'. As opposed to other mental disorders such as *kuzerezeka* (see *Chapter III.2.b*), it is frequently emphasized that *misala* patients are incapable of any form of sensible reasoning. Many accounts describe *misala* as the most prominent and harshest form of mental disorder that leaves the patient not only unproductive but a potential threat to its respective community. Arson – as well as the destruction of property such as crops – and more general aggressive behaviour is regarded as a typical symptom of *misala*, and "people with *misala* do wild things like cutting people with a panga knife or quarrelling with others for no reason". In their destructive vigour, *misala* patients are described as being particularly uncompromising. As a rough description of his *misala* patients, a traditional healer states that

> "We know the patient from the things he/she does, like beating up people, always standing up, sometimes running away, sometimes walking around without any destination. Then we know that this person has gone *misala*" (Lexon Kondwani, a Sena *sing'anga*).

The presentation of *misala* is associated with a number of additional symptoms. Certain behavioural patterns, therefore, are described as classical indicators of *misala* – such as a general lack of comprehension, apparently meaningless talk, wearing rags or public nudity, sexual behaviour, collecting and eating garbage, inadequate personal hygiene including eating feces, defecating or urinating in public. From a patient perspective, the condition of *misala* is reported to be accompanied by sensations of heat or dizziness, and of an itching head. Moreover, *misala* is connected to a general loss of self-control – and an increased degree of sexual desire (Morris 1996: 121-122; Peltzer 1987: 201). Traditional healers frequently differentiate between slight and severe conditions of *misala*.[45] In total, the symptoms of *misala* therefore have an explicitly anti-social character due to the violation of elementary social values such as personal

---

45 In pragmatic terms, a Sena person distinguishes between those *womisala* who can look after themselves in terms of body hygiene and clothing from those who cannot. This dual distinction is shared by Western psychiatry. From their perspective, the slight variant is interpreted as an organic psychotic disorder whereas severe cases of *misala* are seen as functional psychotic disorders (Peltzer 1987: 200).

cleanliness, sense of shame, affect control, or respect of property. No monolithic explanation provides the conceptual basis for *misala*. Rather, a number of rivalling notions coexist, frequently prompting discussions among medical experts (*asing'anga*) or other guardians of traditional culture (*mafumu*). One explanatory model for the background of *misala* refers to the notion of the brain. According to a Yao *sing'anga*,

> "[…] there are three types of *misala*, so we examine the back of the head because that's where *misala* comes from. […] When the brain mixes up with blood, it boils. […] When it boils, he/she does unthinkable deeds" (Linga Nasawa, a Yao *sing'anga*).[46]

Therefore, a possible explanation of *misala* implies a physiological modification within the human brain which can be excited by different factors such as substance abuse.[47] The logical background behind *misala* is, at the same time, described as depending on the causation of the condition. Thus, many *asing'anga* rationalize that the occurrence of *misala* is frequently related to the abuse of *chamba* (see *Chapter IV.3.c*), and in such a case, the fumes inhaled by the smoker are perceived as entering the brain of the person and driving out the personality spirit or *mzimu wa umunthu*. Without this controlling agent, the behaviour of the person necessarily lacks understanding and reason – a condition representing *misala*. In itself, *misala* is sometimes depicted as the potential long-term effect of *khunyu* or *kuzerezeka* as well as being caused by *majini* spirits (see *Chapter IV.2*).[48] In addition to that, cultural sickness categories such as *mutu waukulu*, *tibi*, *malungo* or – more severely – *malungo aakulu* are mentioned as potentially resulting in *misala* (see *Chapter III.2.a*). Reversely, it is stated that *misala* could lead to *mutu* or even *kuzerezeka* over a long period of time.[49] A

---

46 The general idea of the 'boiling brain' is shared by other traditional healers who state that "*Misala* really starts in a person when his/her head does not work because the brain starts boiling [*ubongo wachita boilo*]. That's when a person starts becoming *misala*" (Lexon Kondwani, a Sena *sing'anga*). The notion that boiling liquid in the brain leads to *misala* is said to apply especially in connection to drug abuse (see *Chapter IV.3.c*) because "smoking *chamba* or drinking beer excessively […] makes the brain boil".

47 As another model of explanation, a Lomwe *sing'anga* points out that human intelligence should be conceived as a worm (*kachimbozi*) in the brain which gives sense and thought to the human person and whose activities are also directly related to mental disorder. Blood clotting in the brain, for instance, may send the *kachimbozi* to sleep, thus provoking a condition that is identical with a state of mental disorder. Likewise, the *kachimbozi* of a person may be caused to move in some parts of the brain only while leaving out others. Such an imbalance may lead to socially inadequate behaviour and senseless action which, in itself, also fulfills the criteria for mental disorder – especially in the form of *misala*.

48 In some references published earlier, *misala* also appears as the final and critical state of *ufiti* and as a potential follow-up to states of spirit possessions like *vimbuza* or *madzoka* (Morris 1996: 121; Peltzer 1987: 181).

49 In some cases, *misala* and *kuzerezeka* have been described as being interconnected. Singular

wide number of different reasons are recognized as causative agents for *misala*. Most frequently, *misala* is explained by *ufiti* or other forms of magic including *kukhwima* practices. In rare cases, *misala* is also traced back to spiritual intervention in the form of spirit retribution or divine punishment – e.g. in the case of a Muslim *shehe* neglecting his religious duties. The concept of *misala* as caused by spirit agents – hence sometimes classified as *misala ya mizimu* – is mentioned frequently, indicating a strong link between *misala* and different kinds of spirit possession. In a number of cases, the occurrence of *misala* is also traced back to purely structural reasons, with drug abuse featuring as a particularly prevalent explanation.[50] In addition to that, hereditary reasons are also mentioned on some occasions (see *Chapter IV.3.b*).

2(b) Being a Fool, or Kuzerezeka

In Chichewa terminology, *kuzerezeka* is the most frequently mentioned term for disorders that would be categorized as disabilities from a biomedical perspective, and it is defined as denoting retardation or "somebody who is mentally challenged".[51] The verb *kuzerezeka* itself has been translated as 'to be insane, lunatic, or foolish' (Paas 2004: 512).[52] As an alternative expression, the term *kupepera* is almost equally prominent. Even though appearing as an independent category at first, the majority of accounts identify *kupepera* as identical with *kuzerezeka* while others declare the former either as a regional variation or a more severe condition of the latter.[53] Even though the expression *kuzerezeka* has slightly derogatory connotations, it is still considered as more respectful than alternative terms, and local organizations for persons with disabilities therefore

---

records even depicted these two complaints as identical, while the vast majority of sources make a clear distinction (see *Chapter III.2.b*).

50 Karl Peltzer also mentions inheritance or divine will as possible causes for *misala*, along with the abuse of drugs such as *chamba* or *Cannabis sativa* (Peltzer 1987: 203). Accordingly, Brian Morris also judges *misala* as "a natural, organic disorder due to some brain malfunctioning" (Morris 1996: 121-122). In some cases, the condition of structural *misala* is referred to as *kusokonekera*, a term otherwise equated with *kuzungulira mutu* (see *Chapter II.2.c*).

51 While some accounts identify *kuzerezeka* with *misala*, the larger part of the data identifies a significant difference between the two, thus supporting *kuzerezeka* as an independent nosological category.

52 The term *kuzerezeka* is used identically in both Chichewa and Chitumbuka languages, with translations identifying *kuzerezeka* as 'to be silly, to be mentally deficient'. Derived Chichewa forms include nouns such as *wozerezeka* – denoting a 'mad person' or 'maniac' (Paas 2004: 496) – and *kuzerezeka* or 'insanity, foolishness' (Paas 2004: 214). Additional Chitumbuka forms include *mzerezeka* or 'fool, simpleton' as well as *uzerezeka*, 'folly, stupidity' (Turner 1996: 163).

53 As neither the symptoms nor the aetiological background show any significant differences, *kupepera* will therefore be interpreted as synonymous with *kuzerezeka* in the context of this study.

advocate its use for the lack of better terminological means. Many accounts emphasize the highly offensive connotations of *kupepera*, finding it exceptionally spiteful and insulting.[54]

Cases of *kuzerezeka* predominantly occur when patients are still in their infancy, and the notion that it can develop from birth onwards is widely shared and accepted. Due to the fact that *kuzerezeka* – such as most other mental disorders as well – expresses itself mainly in terms of behavioural changes, though, the exact onset within the earliest phase of a child's life is not easily defined by Malaŵian diagnostic means.[55] At the same time, some reported cases of *kuzerezeka* also developed when persons had grown up – e.g., at a time when they were already married. As general signs of *kuzerezeka*, patients display severely reduced mental abilities which leaves them absent-minded, lacking initiative and comprehension, or "somehow stupid or dull". The facial expression of a person suffering from *kuzerezeka* is characteristically described as weak, and some accounts describe the condition as "acting as if you are not human".[56] Other typical symptoms include uncontrolled salivating (*kutuluka dovu*), wandering aimlessly, picking up garbage and eating it. In some cases, patients appear to be dizzy and weak, rendering their limbs partially useless. Defecating in public is also a classic sign of *kuzerezeka*, and patients are said to have reduced command over their hands, refuse food that is offered, and need to be hand-fed. When infants are affected, it is considered characteristic for them to bite their fingers or lick their hands.

In sharp contrast to *misala*, persons with *kuzerezeka* are characterized by passive, apathetic behaviour marked by "sitting idly on the *khonde* [i.e. veranda]". Communicative skills are generally described as poor, and when talking at all, the articulation of persons with *kuzerezeka* is unintelligible. *Kuzerezeka* implies slow learning and slow physical actions compared to those of an old person.[57] In most cases, affected persons are considered unfit for school

---

54 In some cases, other circumlocutions are applied for the same or very similar conditions. As one example, the idiom *kuchepa nzeru* – translated as 'being narrow-minded' (Paas 2004: 34) – may be mentioned, describing a 'dull' person whose mental capacities are poorly developed. A more verbatim translation, though, could also describe this expression as 'being short on intelligence' or 'having little wisdom'.

55 The problem of clarifying this question is addressed by a traditional birth assistant who argues that "We cannot manage to discover if a newborn child has *kuzerezeka* at the time just after birth, but only when it grows up like that. That is why it is a problem for us to tell whether it is inborn or not, but this is sometimes possible" (Gift Makata, a Yao *mzamba*).

56 As a Lomwe *sing'anga* explains, socially normative behaviour demands meekness, politeness as well as mental balance. Thus, being overly aroused is considered abnormal just the way passiveness is. The latter even results in isolating oneself from the community, which is considered even more abnormal.

57 It has been argued earlier that age-related disorders may in some cases be categorized as *kuzerezeka* or *kupepera*, and that an elderly person's brain stops working properly, going back to

education, vocational training, and marriage due to a lack of basic capabilities required in order to be economically productive or even lead an independent life. Some accounts report slight cases of *kuzerezeka* that include sudden moments of clarity when the behaviour of an affected person follows comprehensible lines of reasoning. A patient may even appear completely normal in some respects while having greatest difficulties in others, leading some people to agree that patients may be able to fulfill minor household chores while other accounts explicitly deny this ability. Colloquially, the expression *kuzerezeka* is also used figuratively in order to depict a generally non-normative albeit non-violent behaviour including disregarding social obligations or incomprehensible actions.[58]

A high number of cases of *kuzerezeka* are conceptualized as being connected to a loss of an integral spiritual part of the human person depicted as the spirit of personhood (*mzimu wa umunthu*) or the heart (*mtima*) (see *Chapter III.1.a*).[59] Most frequently, this notion refers to the idea of *kukhwima* causation which will be elaborated more fully in the following chapter. In the present context, this idea of magically stealing a person's *mzimu wa umunthu* may be described as the loss of control along with the spiritual agent representing personal cognitive faculties. Other magic explanations – which describe the situation as the destruction of some part of the patient's head or brain – refer to parallel concepts.[60] As a different explanation, a Yao *sing'anga* refers to conflicting body fluids, stating that

> "[…] what really happens is when the child is still breastfeeding. As you know, we people have blood, water and foam [*thovu*] in our bodies. And so when the

---

childish thinking (see *Chapter III.1.a*). Accordingly, *kuzerezeka* is sometimes described as childish behaviour, and the term is also applied for children whose personal development is significantly slower than that of their age-mates.

58 As an example, not attending a close relative's funeral might be perceived as a sign of *kuzerezeka* in its broadest sense. Likewise, a husband giving all this salary to his wife can be a slight case of *kuzerezeka* due to the influence of some love magic (*matsenga*) bringing about a lack or loss of own will. In this same context, a number of Malaŵians independently agree that European as well as Northern American persons (*azungu*) would usually qualify as slight cases of *kuzerezeka* as well – never really complying to Malaŵian cultural notions. Likewise, a medical professional working with mentally sick patients expressed that, in his home community in the Northern Region, he was widely regarded as mentally affected. This would be seen as the reason why he can treat other patients.

59 Some statements express the notion of stealing the spirit (*mzimu wa umunthu*) or heart (*mtima*) also as sacrificing the intelligence (*nzeru*) of a person.

60 Some accounts support the idea that in most cases, *kuzerezeka* is a simulated condition. A Ngoni priest explains that *kuzerezeka* patients only pretend to be abnormal even though they are completely fine. Similarly, a Yao *sing'anga* argues that the thought processes of persons with *kuzerezeka* are completely normal, but that they only lack the physical strength to act accordingly.

water and foam meet, then the child becomes *opepera*, his/her heart beats very fast and that weakens the body. And so, he/she becomes weak because the high blood pressure blocks the neck, then he/she faints and becomes *opepera*" (Vincent Chitete, a Yao *sing'anga*).

Kuzerezeka is described as a possible long-term effect of *khunyu* or *misala*, or likewise of *mutu*. It is also stated that other severe and/or prolonged conditions – such as infant *chikasu*, or *mdulo* – may lead to *kuzerezeka*. At the same time, some accounts stress that *kuzerezeka* may lead to *misala* in turn as well, and fits of *khunyu* are also depicted as potential side-effects of *kuzerezeka*. Many accounts ascribe *kuzerezeka* to magic manipulation. While *ufiti* may also play a role, the notion of *kukhwima* is of even higher significance in this context. In some cases, *kuzerezeka* is also seen as being caused by the intervention of spirit agents – which include evil spirits (*ziwanda*) as well as ancestral spirits or *mizimu*. At the same time, it is stressed that *kuzerezeka* may also be related to structural reasons – including accidents such as pregnancy complications. Some accounts also identify heredity as well as drug abuse as reasons for a *kuzerezeka* condition.

2(c) The Spinning Head, or Kuzungulira Mutu

As a comparatively mild case of mental disorder, the condition of *kuzungulira mutu* is frequently mentioned and may therefore be identified as an independent category. While bearing some resemblances with *misala*, *kuzungulira mutu* is described as being a far less severe condition. Nonetheless, it is considered a pathological state, and medical treatment is sought and applied to remedy this condition.[61] The idiom *kuzungulira mutu* has been translated as 'being mad, insane, lunatic' (Paas 2004: 521). The explanations given suggest interpreting it as a state of mental confusion, and linguistically related expressions exist in great numbers, and they create a bigger picture of the ideas related.[62] Here, the basic meaning refers to a circling, rolling, or revolving kind of movement related to a person's head, and literally, *kuzungulira mutu* denotes a 'spinning head', or a 'head going round.' The expression *kusokonekera* or 'being confused or disturbed' (Paas 2004: 408) is applied and defined very similarly to *kuzungulira*

[61] Confusingly, the distinction between *kuzungulira mutu* and *kuzunguzira* [sic] *mutu* has also been emphasized. This last condition is described as a more temporary confusion or loss of self-control. As an example, one interviewee is depicted as unpredictable, and it is disclosed that he had attacked and wounded a neighbour with a panga knife when losing his temper in the discussion of some minor disagreement. Even at court, this person displays bad behaviour by insulting judge and jury – consequently being convicted to a prison sentence and proving his reputation as suffering from *kuzunguzira mutu* in his home community.

[62] The verb *kuzungulirazungulira* e.g., is thus translated as to 'walk aimlessly' (Paas 2004: 521).

mutu, and it will therefore be treated as synonymous here.[63] The expression *kuzungulira mutu* – as well as *kusokonekera* – is neither described nor received as particularly derogatory, and it bears only slight derisive connotations.

This condition is frequently described as being inborn, but due to the wide range of its potential aetiologies, it can nonetheless develop at any stage of a person's later life as well. As general symptoms, persons suffering from *kuzungulira mutu* are described as acting "like being dumb [*ngati kupusa*]", which may manifest itself in extremely poor performance at school. As classical presentations of *kuzungulira mutu*, many accounts support that affected persons may talk incomprehensibly or soliloquize, show unusual behaviour such as inappropriate dressing, and have minor eruptions of unprovoked violence. A lack of etiquette – such as impolite, rude behaviour or other kinds of personal peculiarities – are also conceived as qualifying criteria for *kuzungulira mutu*. In contrast to the more severe condition of *misala*, persons suffering from *kuzungulira mutu* are described as being capable of comprehending and interpreting situations even though their judgment may still be faulty and they may find it difficult to make connections. In addition, states of *kuzungulira mutu* may be described as sporadic, repeatedly occurring and vanishing.

Apart from some accounts of a specific reason responsible for *kuzungulira mutu* as depicted below, no in-depth explanation is given describing the physiological and/or metaphysical materialization of the problem. What is evident with respect to *kuzungulira mutu*, though, is the notion of a pathological disturbance of a person's mental processes. Thus, a traditional healer describes the general condition of persons suffering from *kuzungulira mutu*, stating that

> "At any time what you just have to know is that a person with *kuzungulira mutu* has no *nzeru* and also thinks without any *nzeru*" (Manueli Matundwe, a Sena *sing'anga*).

With respect to the synonymous term *kusokonekera*, some explanations relate to heat developing in a person's head due to conflicting humours – not unlike the model that has been applied in the context of *kuzerezeka*.[64] The notion of *kuzungulira mutu* can be subsumed as implying a temporary loss of brain functionality. In some accounts of a small child being affected by *kuzungulira*

---

63 Frequently, this expression appears in the form of *kusokonekera mutu* or *kusokonekera ubongo*, indicating a state of confusion 'in the head' or 'in the brain', respectively. On a single occasion, the condition of *kusokonekera* in young children was equated with *kuzerezeka* rather than *kuzungulira mutu*.

64 A Yao healer therefore describes that "It is *kusokonekera* of the brain, the brain mixing with the blood, that is all. […] That is why we use this mirror and gourd [*nsupa*] so we find out that in one case, the head just heats up without a reason, but in the other, it is because of magic [*matsengsa*]" (Linga Nasawa, a Yao *sing'anga*).

mutu, sores on the body of the child are mentioned as possible side-effects while others describe *kuzungulira mutu* as a potential epiphenomenon of *polyo*. Also, some accounts disclose that pregnant women suffering from *kuzungulira mutu* may cause serious complications during delivery, posing a special danger to the child. While various reasons may cause *kuzungulira mutu* in a given patient, the different forms of magic are specified as being most common. More specifically, a large number of cases are attributed to anti-social *ufiti* practices while a comparatively high amount is also connected to the notion of *kukhwima* which will be addressed later. In addition to that, the attacks of spirit agents (*mizimu*) are also mentioned as causing *kuzungulira mutu*, including those belonging to the *majini* and *ziwanda* spirit categories. At the same time, structural reasons – accident such as premature delivery, inheritance, or substance abuse – are also regarded as possible reasons for *kuzungulira mutu* (see *Chapter IV.3*).

2(d) The Head Issue, or Mutu

Among the most dreaded disorders of mental disorder there is a state unanimously referred to as *mutu* and explicitly depicted as a child disorder occurring at a very young age. A considerable amount of traditional norms (*miyambo*) surround the avoidance of *mutu* in a newborn child due to the fact that it represents a remarkably prominent condition.[65] As a nosological category, though, *mutu* poses some problems with respect to its terminological consistency. Literally, *mutu* must be translated as meaning head (Paas 2004: 301), and the term is widely applied for a large number of head-related health disorders such as headaches.[66] Even though the mental disorder under discussion here is definitely distinct from these more general conditions of head-complaints, this form of *mutu* is never referred to by a non-ambiguous term – people usually specify what is meant by ways of closer description.[67]

Due to its particular pathogenesis (see below), this form of *mutu* necessarily occurs in children at a very young age, and it cannot emerge any later than at two

65 A notable proportion of the research accounts refer to families with children suffering from *mutu*.

66 Many previous authors have mentioned *mutu* as 'headache'. In addition, Paul Kapapa mentions the term *wammutu* – which he translates as "jemand, der was im [sic] Kopf hat" – as a generally disqualifying term applied for persons with mental disorders among the Ngoni of Dedza District, Central Region (Kapapa 1977: 60). At the same time, this post-natal *mutu* is explicitly different from *mutu waukulu* (the 'large head', or 'splitting headache') which has been interpreted as "extremely painful or chronic" headache (Morris 1996: 118).

67 On one occasion, a *sing'anga* referred to one such case as *mutu wa manda* (literally a 'head of the grave') – but none of the relatives of the patient present could do anything with this term nor receive a helpful explanation from the healer. Finally, the mother of the patient assumed that it meant the condition was lethal.

years of age. As one of the first signs for an early stage of *mutu*, an affected child is said to produce a lot of *nthongo*, or eye discharge. As the disorder progresses, the child's cranium starts swelling, thus causing accompanying symptoms such as eye complaints – i.e. visual impairment and, later, blindness – or severe diarrhoea. At a more advanced and critical stage, the continuous growth of the child's head can develop visible cracks or deformations such as the splitting of the skull. In the long run, *mutu* is generally considered to have a fatal outcome.[68]

Unlike other forms of mental disorder, the causation of *mutu* follows a remarkably coherent model. According to accounts from diverse ethnic groups in Southern Malaŵi – including Mang'anja, Yao, Lomwe, and Ngoni –, the fontanel (*liwombo*)[69] of a child is open at the time of its birth. Soon after, this additional opening starts breathing through the skin, thus providing the body with extra air which is considered as necessary, as the child's lungs are seen as not yet powerful enough to supply the required respiration.[70] A child's *liwombo* starts its breathing activities about two months after birth, and it may keep operating up to the age of two years without causing any trouble.[71] Ideally, the fontanel closes at the same time when the pumping of the *liwombo* ceases and the lungs are strong enough to take over (Drake 1976: 202). Problems arise whenever the mutual adjustment of these processes fails. Thus, if the fontanel closes too early or the breathing of the *liwombo* is too intensive, excess air gathers within the – now closed – skull, creating pressure on the child's brain as well as within the cranium and causing the condition described here as *mutu*. Difficulties can also emerge if the *liwombo* closes late – with the now active lungs and the undiminished fontanel breathing building up an equally dangerous pressure on the brain. In such a case,

> "If the head of a child continues to breathe and the parents have not tied some medicine to it, the head might crack in the middle. […] When a child is born, it is appropriate to tie it with a medicine called *likambako*, for fear of things like these" (Olive Pilimiti, a Nyanja *mzamba*).

---

68 In many cases of *mutu*, Western medical services diagnose the respective children as suffering from *hydrocephalus*, *microcephalus*, and comparable disorders.

69 I.e. the anterior fontanel, *Fonticulus anterior*. Brian Morris mentions the close association of the *liwombo* with headaches, the fontanel thus being "a focus of concern in head ailments, particularly with children" (Morris 1996: 124).

70 Some accounts show a remarkable conviction that a child's fontanel has an important function for breathing. A Mang'anja farmer thus insists that, due to the *liwombo*'s respiration, a child of the appropriate age could not drown as long as the top of the head is above water, offering to substantiate the accuracy of his statement by immersing his newborn son into a large pool of water.

71 This breathing is demonstrated on the cranium of a one-year old child as a small hollow under the skin, showing a slight pulsing movement.

It is due to this increased pressure within the cranium that the child produces the excess eye discharge (*nthongo*) as mentioned above, and the occurrence of these so-called '*mutu* eyes' (*maso a mutu*) indicates that the closing of the fontanel (*liwombo*) does not proceed in due course. If not treated in time, the cracks in the child's cranium may lead to other mental disorders such as the severe *kuzerezeka* as explained above as well as death. The time during which the child's fontanel is still open is regarded as an especially vulnerable period in its life where it is particularly susceptible to negative influences. A Lomwe *sing'anga* points out that therefore, no 'hot' person[72] should be allowed into the *chikuta* delivery house in order to avoid secondary complaints. Otherwise, the child could develop fits, its eyes become yellow and it starts salivating – a description reminiscent of *chikasu*. Once this happens, special treatment is urgently required to stop the child from developing fits of *khunyu* as well (see *Chapter II.2.a*).

Magic measures can be the reason for the manifestation of *mutu*. *Ufiti* may be applied to implant substance into the child's head, causing disorders which can be mistaken as an ordinary *mutu* condition. Also, *ufiti* can be used in order to weaken the medicine used to help the fontanel close and can therefore be the real originator of a given problem. In more rare cases, divine intervention is also considered to cause *mutu* in a patient. Spiritual intervention – in the sense of evil spirits (*ziwanda*) harming a child – is likewise mentioned as a potential reason for *mutu*. As depicted above, however, the fundamental medical background for *mutu* implies a normal disposition that may always develop into a pathological state, indicating that the main reason for *mutu* is considered as structural (see *Chapter IV.3*).

2(e) Falling Disorder, or Khunyu

In Malaŵi, a whole number of local categories exist which, in dictionaries of the respective local languages as well as in studies of medical anthropology, are directly translated as epilepsy. Within the framework of the present study, *khunyu* is identified as the most commonly applied term for such disorders, and it shall therefore serve as the major category.[73] As mentioned already, the term

---

[72] In this context, the mentioning of a 'hot' condition refers to the concept of symbolic temperature as relating to *mdulo* (see *Chapter II.1.a*).

[73] It is, strictly speaking, difficult to define *khunyu* as a form of mental disorder in its own right as it also occurs as a symptom, side-effect, or even a causative factor for others. Many references mention it as part of the presentation of another category of mental disorder, or as related to it in any other way. On the other hand, many accounts explicitly mention *khunyu* when itemizing the most common forms of mental disorder. It is therefore suggested that *khunyu* combines characteristics of all the above-mentioned qualities, being a mental disorder that is highly interrelated with other forms of mental complaints as well. This emphasizes the high relevance

khunyu is translated as 'epilepsy' – or sometimes, more broadly – as 'irritableness' in dictionaries of Chicheŵa language (Paas 2004: 171; Moxley 2001; Zambezi Mission [eds.] 1972). Alternatively, the Chicheŵa term *chifufu* is applied and frequently treated as synonymous with *khunyu* in all respects.[74] A number of other alternative terms occur, and among them, the Chicheŵa term *njirinjiri* is one of the more widely applied (Paas 2004: 327).[75] Other synonyms – such as the Chisena term *mfayi* – are also mentioned.[76] The seizures marking the typical manifestation of this mental disorder are described by verbs such as *kudzidzimuka* ('to startle'), as *kukomoka* or 'collapsing', or as *kututumuka* or 'shock' (Paas 2004).

Signs of *khunyu* may manifest themselves at different points of a person's life, but most reported cases first occur during early childhood. The general consensus is that most cases of *khunyu* are congenital, while more sporadic evidence denies this notion and considers every case as acquired. At the same time, it is undisputed that *khunyu* may also appear at an adult age. The symptoms for *khunyu* are generally depicted as "consistent with those to be found in any medical dictionary under epilepsy" (Morris 1996: 123). In particular, frequent seizures, the sudden loss of consciousness, sudden signs of anxiety and panic, and talking unrelated or unintelligibly are mentioned.

> "*Khunyu* comes when a person faints and the whole body trembles. [...] it is as if a person dies temporarily. The patient can be walking and all of a sudden he/she faints and falls to the ground. The patient can even fall into a fire and burn completely. If people are around they rescue him/her, but if there is no one around, the patient can die and burn in the fire. The problem is that he/she cannot tell when he/she is going to faint and where" (Siyani Walala, a Sena *sing'anga*).

---

of *khunyu* within the bigger context of mental disorder in Malaŵi. For some biomedical accounts on the prevalence of epilepsy in Malaŵi see Kalmanash 1968.

74 This identification of *khunyu* with *chifufu* is in accordance with Brian Morris (Morris 1996: 511). Sporadic evidence distinguishes *chifufu* from *khunyu*, depicting the former as the most severe manifestation of the latter. In Chicheŵa dictionaries, it is translated as 'convulsion' or 'epilepsy' (Paas 2004: 40).

75 Matthew Schoffeleers mentions this disorder in the context of a person being possessed by a deceased chief's spirit, the victim showing "signs of mental disorder or epileptic fits and after the initiation he is credited with the power to cure epilepsy (unjirinjiri)" (Schoffeleers 1968a: 166-7). The same condition is also mentioned in the form of *linjiri-njiri* (Breugel 2001: 240), *minjilinjili* (Moxley 2001), or *manjirinjiri* (Zambezi Mission [eds.] 1972). Its identification with *khunyu* is frequently emphasized.

76 Some accounts make minor distinctions, characterizing *mfayi* as a less severe case than *khunyu*. In some cases, the Chicheŵa term *chihinduhindu* is used as another synonym for *khunyu*, being equally identified as 'epilepsy' or 'convulsion' (Paas 2004: 43). Likewise, the term *nthenda ya kugwa* occurs, its literary translation explicitly characterizing it as a 'falling sickness'. The synonym *kugwa mutu* ('falling head') – translated more generally as to 'be confused' or 'be hysterical' (Paas 2004: 128) is also applied.

During the fits, patients are also reported to be yelling or crying, and uncontrolled salivating and the production of foam on the mouth are also mentioned as important symptoms (Morris 1996: 123). Other typical signs of *khunyu* include the affected person grinding teeth, turning rigid, passing gas, or uncontrolled excretion. Some *asing'anga* consider these symptoms as first indications for the end of a seizure. Research data suggests that *khunyu* is frequently associated with other mental disorders, coming either at the same time or entailing one another (see below). With repeated seizures being unquestionably the most central distinctive symptom, even cases presenting a much more complex clinical picture are sometimes referred to as *khunyu*.[77]

In many cases of *khunyu*, the phases of the moon (*mwezi*)[78] are reported as having a significant influence on the occurrence of fits. According to this notion, a particular time of the month acts as a releasing mechanism triggering seizures in a person suffering from *khunyu*.[79] Many accounts on the connection between lunar phases and the occurrence of *khunyu* seizures do not provide a full contextual explanation, rather indicating that "maybe it happens whenever the moon appears". Further data relates *khunyu* to the times of growing or waning moon, arguing that fits occur "either when the moon is gone or when in its earliest stage", while other accounts agree that *khunyu* seizures are evoked "by the moon either coming out or coming in".

> "It is true, when the moon comes out [i.e. after new moon], they faint a lot – unlike when it is inside [i.e. at new moon] or it is coming in the middle [i.e. at full moon], then they have rest. During this time, parents are advised to take good care of their child because it can fall into anything [...]. I only know that they usually

---

77 As an example, an infant – previously diagnosed with hydrocephalus at a local health centre – receives traditional treatment (in the form of roots or *mitsitsi* prepared into *mankhwala akumwa* or 'medicine for drinking') which succeeds in stopping the cranium's growth. Even though all *asing'anga* involved acknowledge excess water within the child's cranium as having a crucial impact on the child's condition, however, the case is still determined as *khunyu* due to the characteristic corresponding fits.

78 On a more general level, moon and stars may serve as a means of divination in Southern Malaŵi. According to a Mang'anja account from Zomba District, a particular sight of the moon may announce the death of many people during the coming month. Likewise, an unusually bright star seen at night usually indicates either the death of a *mfumu* or another event of great importance. Surprisingly, the stars do not carry individual names – apart from a particularly bright celestial body close to the moon named *mkaziwamwezi* (i.e. 'the moon's wife'), thereby classifying the moon as male.

79 It has been mentioned earlier that "It is interesting to note the connection made between the phases of the moon and the apparition of an attack of epilepsy which is very similar to the belief found also in Europe or in other parts of the world" (Kalmanash 1968: 3). It is also represented in the performance of an aforementioned *nyau* mask, the *khunyu*-stricken character *Chiuli* (see *Chapter II.1.b*) whose dance is accompanied by the audience singing "When the moon moves this way, he falls, that way and he falls again".

fall most when it [i.e. the moon] is starting to come out" (Manueli Matundwe, a Sena *sing'anga*).

This prevalence timetable finds general approval among *khunyu* specialists. Thus, a Yao traditional birth attendant explains that

"[...] if the moon appears they [i.e. *khunyu* patients] do not stay well, and also whenever the moon goes towards darkness, they truly collapse frequently. Between these times they usually stay fine" (Joyce Chawa, a Yao *mzamba*).

Additional accounts also elaborate on the notion that the times of the month when fits occur have *quasi* diagnostic relevance by indicating the causation of the condition.[80] In this line of thought, a traditional healer points out that

"[...] if *khunyu* comes from the ancestors, you have seizures according to the moon" (Sapitwa Chagoma, a Lomwe *sing'anga*).

Even though general agreement exists on the correlation between the moon, *khunyu* manifestation, and its causative background, explanatory details may differ. Some accounts may thus state that *khunyu* caused by structural reasons is indicated due to the seizures occurring at full moon while others state that congenital *khunyu* results from prolonged and complicated delivery. The occurring seizures, consequently, resemble the struggle and near suffocation the child experienced during birth, and they always happen at the time of the month in which the child was born. According to a Yao *mfumu*, the time of the attacks may help to obtain further knowledge on the exact background of a case of hereditary *khunyu*. If inherited from the mother, he argues, the patient would suffer seizures early in the lunar phase – if it comes from the father's side, though, the fits would occur around the middle of the month.

The triggering effect of a certain time of the month is explained as an emotional reaction in the patients, being as if "one day the sun makes you sweat and another day it does not". At the same time, a connection is perceived to exist between the occurrence of *khunyu* and the female cycle. A Mang'anja farmer and *khunyu* patient thus reports that his seizures always happen when the moon is in the West – which is identified as the time when women usually have their monthly period.[81] Another Mang'anja farmer agrees, comparing the connection

---

[80] In addition to that, one Yao *sing'anga* explains that sometimes even conditions of *misala* (see *Chapter III.2.a*) may be related to the moon. In this case of structurally caused *misala*, the aggressive restlessness of the patient increases at the time of the month when his/her *misala* first emanated, being much calmer at other times.

[81] It is a frequently reported notion that women enter their monthly period (or, according to a typical expression, 'produce the taboos' or restrictions on sexual contact) at the same time – this usually being the end or the early days of every month. This is paralleled by information obtained by Kenson Malanga, who argues that, according to beliefs in Nsanje District, "The new

between his son's *khunyu* seizures and the lunar phases to the women's cycle of menstruation. A Ngoni craftsman also shares this sentiment, declaring that the deep relationship between *khunyu* and the moon is not only paralleled by the female cycle but also by rainfalls, which he sees as coming more abundantly when the moon cannot be seen.[82]

In contrast to all attempts to identify it with the biomedical definition of epilepsy, a number of cultural notions are connected to *khunyu* which distinguish it from Western concepts. Most importantly, a number of accounts stress that *khunyu* fits only occur at night time – and that such incidences are in direct correlation with the phases of the moon. Many accounts explicitly locate *khunyu* in the stomach, and thus, *khunyu* treatment usually requires imbibing very bitter medicine,

> "[...] to relax the abdominal muscles so that the sickness in the stomach goes, sometimes through urine" (Doris Petroyo, a Lomwe *sing'anga*).

More specifically, a *khunyu* condition is explained as being caused by too much saliva (*dovu*) gathering in the stomach and coming up to the heart (*mtima*). Due to this, the patient is said to experience breathing difficulties, and the saliva comes out through the mouth as foam (*thovu*).[83] A similar account relates *khunyu* to 'foam in the stomach' (*thovu m'mimba*) which rises up and blocks the throat from normal breathing. The ensuing seizures represent this choking fit, and frequent incidents of flatulence or defecation are attempts to free the stomach from the harmful foam, finally leading to amelioration.[84]

While it seems somewhat unclear whether or not *khunyu* can be defined in the same category of mental disorders such as *misala* or *kuzerezeka*, many accounts explicitly list *khunyu* among the most frequent disorders affecting the human mind (*matenda okhudza nzeru za munthu*). Nonetheless, the occurrence of *khunyu* is frequently connected to other complaints, indicating that the occurrence of congenital *khunyu* may be related to another health disorder in the mother – such as *likango*.[85] Likewise, *khunyu* is identified as a possible preliminary complaint leading to *kuzerezeka* as well as *misala*. *Khunyu* is also

---

moon is in great association with the menstruation periods of women" (Malanga 1971: No. 161).

82 Similar notions are reported by Kenson Malanga from Northern Malaŵi. A proverb from Karonga District thus indicates that "When there is a new moon it rains," and a saying from Chitipa District advises "Do not make long journeys just before the new moon appears; otherwise you get wet from rain" (Malanga 1971: No. 47, 99).

83 This is supported by a Lomwe *mfumu* stating that the foam showing at a patient's mouth comes from the stomach in order to clear up the breathing organs.

84 More sporadically, the blood (*magazi*) is mentioned as playing a part in *khunyu*. According to a Yao *mfumu*, human thinking is carried out by the fluctuation of blood in the brain. Abnormal secretions such as clotting blood can hinder this process, thus leading to *khunyu*.

85 For a more comprehensive depiction of *likango* see Morris 1996: 130-132.

mentioned as a possible side-effect of *mutu*. In spite of its otherwise fairly recognizable symptoms, *khunyu* is still carefully distinguished from other disorders which imply a temporary loss of consciousness or seizures. Thus, *chikasu* is mentioned as being sometimes mistaken for *khunyu* due to improper diagnostics, thereby leading to inappropriate therapeutic measures. On rare occasions, *khunyu* patients develop minor impairments in their everyday skills, such as a child that performs poorly in some areas of learning while meeting normal standards in others. It has been argued that a large majority of the patients diagnosed with epilepsy in Zomba Mental Hospital

> "[...] accused magic powers or witchcraft as being the cause of their disease. All of them, but one, had traditional medicine with not very much effect, but they were resigned to it" (Kalmanash 1968: 5).

In agreement with this assessment, a considerable number of *khunyu* cases are explained by the different forms of magic such as *ufiti*. This notion most frequently applies for severe and/or chronic cases for which no effective treatment can be found.[86] As mentioned earlier, the time of *khunyu* emergence may also provide some indication of its possible causation because

> "[...] the *khunyu* from *ufiti* happens when a person is already grown up" (Gordon Chitsulo, a Lomwe *sing'anga*).

In some cases, spirit interference also acts as a possible causative agent for *khunyu*, and the attacks of spirit agents – both *ziwanda* and other *mizimu* – can also cause victims to develop *khunyu*.[87] In the context of this study, though, the most significant number of *khunyu* cases is traced back to structural reasons (see *Chapter IV.3*) including notions of heredity or perinatal difficulties such as prolonged labour or premature delivery. Especially in case of *khunyu* occurring in children, it is emphasized that

> "[...] natural *khunyu* starts when a baby is still very young" (Gordon Chitsulo, a Lomwe *sing'anga*).

---

86 Some rare references also connect the occurrence of *khunyu* to the system of *kukhwima* (see *Chapter IV.1.c*). In this line of argument, the incidence of seizures shows a direct relationship to the personal interests of a malevolent person. Such cases are related and sometimes revealed due to the fact that *khunyu* "coming from persons gives you seizures every time that one wants to find some money, because sometimes he/she might fall only once per year, like every year in October".

87 Matthew Schoffeleers supports the occurrence of *njirinjiri* as a symptom of spirit possession (Schoffeleers 1968a: 166-7) (see *Chapter IV.2.d*). As a special case, a Lomwe *mfumu* describes his idea of *khunyu ya mizimu* as being caused by some spirits trying to take a victim to the spirit world – i.e. to die – whilst others struggled to keep him/her among the living. This conception of being spiritually dragged around in different directions was said to show in the patients' behaviour when struck by seizures.

2(f) Being Deformed, or Kulumala

It has been mentioned already that the distinction between mental and physical disorders is not always easy to draw within a Malaŵian context (see *Chapter I.1.b*) – a conundrum best illustrated by depicting the notion of *kulumala* itself. As a nosological category, the term *kulumala* refers to all kinds of disorders that manifest themselves in primarily physical terms, and it is the most commonly applied expression for a 'deformed body'. The Chicheŵa verb *kulumala* ('to be deformed, disabled' as well as 'deformity, disability') generally refers to physical disorders affecting the limbs of a person, and it takes alternative forms such as *wolumala,* meaning a 'cripple, lame person' (Paas 2003: 104, 113; Guerin 1985: 413). In a cross-cultural context, *kulumala* is the term that comes closest to the Western concept of disability. The term *kulumala* is regarded as neutral and non-derogatory, and it is accepted and advocated by Malaŵi-based organizations for persons with disabilities.

A large number of more or less synonymous expressions are used throughout the region to denote comparable disorders. Among these, the extremely popular Chicheŵa term *kupunduka* (also *kupundula*) appears to have a very broad meaning of impairment translating as 'to disable, cripple, maim, be deformed' (Paas 2003: 104; Zambezi Mission [eds.] 1986; Guerin 1985: 413; Scott 1965: 483). At the same time, the word *kupunduka* is described as being highly derogatory, denoting "somebody who cannot do anything, who is like a burden to the house". Its use is considered extremely offensive, therefore being discouraged from the side of organizations for persons with disabilities in Malaŵi. Further terms are connected to comparable obstacles in their application.[88] Most accounts agree that typical cases of *kulumala* are in-born and that they become apparent directly after birth. The main symptoms of *kulumala* include impairments concerning the limbs, i.e. legs and/or arms, of the patient.[89]

---

88 The Chicheŵa term *chilema* is used to attribute to a wide range of physical disorders, especially impairments of the lower limbs, and it has been specified that *chilema* refers to both "what is born with one or acquired" (Scott 1965: 61). Apart from the word *chilema* – translated as 'blemish, deformity, maiming' –, another linguistically related idiom is the verb *kulema,* meaning 'to be tired, heavy in various ways'. In addition, it can be found in compounds like *khala ndi chirema* ('deformed'), *kuchititsa chirema* or 'to disable', or *kuika chirema* meaning 'to cripple, maim' (Paas 2003: 104; Botne & Kulemeka 1995: 25; Zambezi Mission [eds.] 1986; Scott 1965: 61, 76, 233). Other equivalents for *kulumala* include the Chitumbuka terms *kupendala* or *kupendula* – meaning 'bent' – as well as the highly disrespectful Chicheŵa *kupuwala* or 'to be lame, disabled' (Paas 2004: 385).

89 For more unusual presentations of *kulumala*, a Yao traditional birth attendant gives account of her working experiences, saying that "there had been children who were born without the anus, the other one had the knees on the opposite side, the other one had a deformed leg, and another one did not have a neck" (Mercy Msawa, a Yao *mzamba*). Other accounts mention equally severe cases such as "children being born without their skin [*osupuka*]" – which is also

Thus, patients may be categorized as *wolumala* due to a 'somewhat unstable' leg, leaving them limping. Typical *wolumala* persons are depicted as depending on wheelchairs or crutches, and some accounts define this condition as denoting someone who "cannot do anything". At the same time, mild cases of *kulumala* may have less obvious presentations, as a traditional healer attests:

> "If one is not really careful with the examination one might think that the person is alright, while in true sense he/she is *wolumala.* We differentiate the way the patient walks – and how others walk. Then, we can tell that the person is *wolumala* because of *nyamakazi* which has actually attacked the hip or knee" (Doris Petroyo, a Lomwe *sing'anga*).

Even though categories such as *kulumala* are mainly defined by these physical symptoms, it is stressed that some mental symptoms are also connected to the condition. Among these, talking nonsensically or showing signs of confusion – which may resemble cases of *kuzungulira mutu* – are typical. Poor school performance may also be considered as a typical side-effect of children suffering from *kulumala*. But even more severe conditions – including those of a two year-old unable to sit or eat or a 15 year-old unable to care for her own body hygiene[90] – may be categorized as *kulumala*, illustrating that the physical limitations necessarily implied in this category represent neither the only nor necessarily the most prevalent problem connected to the given condition. Pointing out the differences and similarities between *kulumala* and *misala*, a Yao traditional healer explains that

> "A child cannot be born with *misala*, but with *kupuwala.* [...] When one part of the body is missing in the baby's head, then the baby becomes *wolumala.* This is what we call *kulumala*, not *misala*, no. Just think of those ones who salivate uncontrollably" (Linga Nasawa, a Yao *sing'anga*).

More detailed explanations on the background of *kulumala* refer to a model of blood potency as depicted earlier. Some accounts of *kulumala* therefore relate the apparent weakness of some part of the patient's body – e.g. a leg – to a lack of strength in the blood (*magazi ofooka*) or to blood drying up within the limbs, thus leaving them impaired. The health disorder *nyamakazi* may cause *kulumala* due to blocking the blood and leading to deformation, and infant *polyo* as well as prolonged *mutu waukulu* in a child can also lead to this condition. In addition,

---

considered as a form of *kulumala*. When asked about the different varieties of *kulumala* she has encountered, another *mzamba* mentions the birth of an albino (*napwere*), expressing her surprise to hear this child is successfully attending elementary school.

90 Thus, a Sena mother describes the condition of her 15 year-old daughter as being unable to wash herself or control her urine and stool. Due to some defective position of the daughter's foot, her condition is generally considered as *kulumala*.

kulumala may be a consequence of severe *misala*, and secondary disorders associated with *kulumala* include conditions of *matewe*.

Magical practices are a likely explanation for *kulumala*, and this usually follows the concepts of *ufiti*. In some instances, it can even be the effect of *kukhwima* rituals. Only few accounts relate *kulumala* to the interference of spirits – but especial cases of 'evil' *ziwanda* spirits causing *kulumala* are recorded nonetheless. Most frequently, though, these conditions are said to be caused by structural reasons, and among these, perinatal birth complications, accidents, and divine creation are mentioned (see *Chapter IV*).[91]

3. Discussing Culture, Medicine, and Categorization

It has been the purpose of the present chapter to provide the basic classifications which are crucial for the understanding of the cultural perception of mental disorder, representing the essential toolbox for any discourse on the matter as such. Technical as it may appear, the index of nosological categories provides a direct and more in-depth insight into the means given within the complex cultural framework of Southern Malaŵi – as expressed by language – which completes the more political, behavioural, ritual, or mythological factors contributing to the cultural construction of mental disorder.

As the most elementary finding, it has already been outlined that nosological classification is the result of a very wide public discourse operating on the basis of symptom patterns, and that specialized diagnosis – as depicted earlier on in this chapter – focus on determining the aetiological causation of a given mental disorder rather than its appropriate terminology. The nosology presented in the second half of this chapter thus represents a set of purely descriptive categories reflecting symptoms, and their analytic properties are very limited. The major mental disorder categories as presented here clearly indicate that most given categories may be traced back to various different modes of causation. This finding emphasizes the importance of emic models of aetiology which will accordingly be examined in the following chapter.

Disorder and Symbolic Temperature

It has been emphasized that some nosological categories in Southern Malaŵi draw a connection between the causation of sickness and traditional notions of symbolic temperature. The basic concept underlying this notion is an elementary

91 In Mzuzu District (Northern Region) it is said that "When a baby is born deformed, they believe it is God's wish – they do not think about diseases or malnutrition" (Malanga 1971: No. 74).

dichotomy between 'hot' and 'cold' dispositions which have a particular significance in the context of social – and, more especially, sexual – interaction. Contagion between the different symbolic temperatures is potentially dangerous, and traditional norms of behaviour (*miyambo*) therefore acquire particular importance as regulatory forces for its prevention. The respective *miyambo* provide general guidance on how to avoid harm when dealing with these symbolic conditions of 'heat' and 'cold' (Probst 1995: 10-11). As fire, blood, male semen and vaginal juices are associated with a potentially dangerous 'hot' condition, certain behavioural rules have to be observed in order not to endanger others – and particular concern refers to newborn children who are considered as 'cold' and especially vulnerable until this state is changed by ritual action.[92]

A number of situations are mentioned as causing *mdulo*. Most prominently, a man committing adultery during his wife's pregnancy can cause *mdulo* to his unborn child (Probst 1995: 9-10), while a pregnant woman having extramarital intercourse endangers her own as well as her child's well-being (Marwick 1965: 66-67). Likewise, a mother having intercourse during the first – restricted – months after delivery may cause *mdulo* in the infant child, while the contamination with dangerous 'hot' temperature may also be transmitted by means of salt (*mchere*) in food. A 'hot' wife – i.e. a woman during her menstrual period or after illegitimate sexual contact – adding salt to the family dinner would cause *mdulo* in her husband and children likewise (Morris 1996: 133-134).[93] The idea of sickness being caused by a breach of social norms is connected to the ancestral spirits (*mizimu*) who serve as guardians of the tradition. Apart from this, some other results of this chapter also deserve further accentuation in the present discussion. At first, some final remarks will address the definition of the term mental disorder as applied in this study. Secondly, it will emphasize the interconnection between the nosological categories as depicted above and the implicit stigmatization that goes along with their use. A third issue concerns the cultural notion of normality that can be deduced from the above presentations.

---

92 According to Maxwell Marwick, this is done during the Chewa ritual of *kutenga mwana* or 'taking the child' (see *Chapter II.1.b*). After their first marital intercourse that ends the sexually prohibited period after childbirth, the parents anoint the child with semen and vaginal juices and lift it over the fire, thus immunizing it against a certain degree of symbolic 'heat' (Marwick 1965: 66).

93 While extramarital intercourse always leads to degree of symbolic 'heat' that is considered dangerous to anyone when contacted, every form of sexual activity entails a 'hot' state. Therefore, a Lomwe *sing'anga* emphasizes that newborn children have to be protect from people who recently conducted sexual intercourse as long as they still are in the *chikuta* delivery house.

Mental Disorder Revised

In the presentation of the research objective for this study and its modifications during data collection, it has been outlined that local notions are widely incompatible with Western concepts of disability (see *Chapter I.1.a*). It is due to this realization that the superordinate concept mental disorder has been introduced and that some phenomena which conflicted with the Western cultural definitions – i.e. issues that qualify as mental illness or strictly physical impairments – had to be considered. The terminological survey as presented here should substantiate that emic concepts make no clear distinction between mental and other – i.e. physical – cases of disorder. Comparable findings have been presented from other areas of Africa. In case of Uganda, Susan Reynolds Whyte explains this absence of distinction due to the concept of competence:

> "In terms of social competence and consequences, the distinction between physical and mental impairments fades. The ability to identify and perform tasks requires an embodied mind. People fail to work because of weakness, laziness, lack of concentration, or lack of understanding that a task needs to be done, just as they may fail because of the sequelae of polio" (Whyte 1998b: 171-172).

The interconnection between physical and mental disorders – and the identification of seemingly physical conditions with mental consequences – can therefore be explained by functional factors. The lacking distinction between disability and mental illness in the cultural terminology of Southern Malaŵi is also not a unique phenomenon, but it reflects a cultural concept of health that regards all health disorders – at least on the conceptual level – as curable.[94] Therefore, the crucial distinction that separates temporary from permanent conditions within a biomedical discourse loses its ontological significance. The lack of a terminological distinction between mental illness and disability is legitimized by this notion of general curability that refers back to traditional medical culture. Within the more traditional discourse on medicine – and, more especially, on mental disorder –, traditional healers as well as their primarily rural customers frequently assess that, apart from the HIV/Aids pandemic, all health disorders may be healed by means of traditional medicine. This perspective is mirrored by numerous Christian churches which re-attribute the cultural notion of universal therapeutic feasibility to divine omnipotence. The representatives of organizations for persons with disabilities in Malaŵi, on the

---

94 Rather, this corresponds with Patrick Devlieger's assertion that "in central African countries, as often in the United States, people with mental problems are lumped together in one category. For example, no major distinction is made between mental retardation and mental illness. Instead, among the Shona people, for example, different terms describe different types of mental disability, depending on the individual's expressed behaviour" (Devlieger 1998: 60).

other hand, frequently narrate their difficult task of explaining the parents of a challenged child that its condition will never be normal in spite of diverse meetings with an occupational therapist. It is this same expectation of re-normalization that also constitutes a Malaŵian health seeker's most central frustration when accessing biomedical health services – and that encourages a trial-and-error approach to a pluralistic health system. In order to fully outline the relevance of this result, it will be addressed more comprehensively in the concluding chapter of this study.

Labelling and Stigmatization

It has been demonstrated that terms to classify mental disorder are, in general, applied rather freely in Southern Malaŵi on the basis of lay diagnosis and subsequent labelling. What is crucial about this generous use of mental disorder terminology is the fact that the majority of these terms have strongly pejorative connotations. Within an interview situation, patients – and their relatives – therefore frequently complain about the highly derogatory character of the expressions applied for their respective health conditions within their immediate social environment. The vocabulary available in common public discourse in itself bears a negative attitude, making it virtually impossible to address mental disorder in a non-judgmental way. This lack of appropriate linguistic tools is recognized and addressed in particular by representatives of organizations for persons with disabilities. Mussa Chiwaula, director of the Federation of Disability Organizations of Malaŵi (FEDOMA) therefore explicitly voices the need for a less derogatory disability language (Machado 2004: 4), and Steven Msowoya, the acting director of the Malaŵi Council of the Handicapped (MACOHA) likewise emphasizes the structural – i.e. linguistic – problems in addressing mental problems in a supportive way within the non-Anglophone rural communities of the country.[95] This terminological barrier is also recognized among biomedical health professionals who concede that

> "[…] most of these conditions, we learn them at school in English, but to translate or understand them in our own language is difficult. To find terms commonly used for this condition is also difficult unless maybe it's an institution just dealing with those mentally retarded patients, then maybe they can eventually find a common term" (Vivian Changata, a Mang'anja nurse).

---

95 In newspaper interviews, MACOHA representatives accordingly point out that "the language one uses to address people with disabilities and disability issues often has a direct bearing on the attitude of the user. Macoha officials further observed that the most important problem they faced was disability-friendly attitude of people at all levels, including the media" (Machado 2004: 4).

Many accounts assert lacking specificity in emic mental disorder terminology, and the parents of affected children frequently support the introduction of English terms into their home communities in order to circumnavigate the implicit stigmatization delivered by local language. This idealistic concern would leave the considerable non-Anglophone part of the population unable to participate, thus further aggravating the chasm between English and Malaŵian discourses. Thus, it may be assessed that the basic terminological understanding of a given mental disorder in Southern Malaŵi is very likely to encompass a first step towards social stigmatization. This observation emphasizes the importance of the terminological basis of cultural representation due to their impact on the social perception of the mentioned phenomenon. The terminological tools provided within a given cultural context must be understood as an expression of this same emic conception, creating a vicious circle of cultural predefinition and its re-enactment within a given society. It should, at the same time, be noted that Malaŵian nosological categorization is not an orthodox system of classification but rather provides an arsenal of categories applied on the basis of more or less collective representations concerning symptomatic patterns – e.g. the case of *misala* – as allocated by personal judgment. Therefore, Malaŵian systems of mental disorder classification grant remarkable freedom for personal agency, and the application of nosological terms suitable for a given case of mental disorder is always subject to an elaborated process of negotiation.

Cultural Limits of Normality

The present chapter also serves to give a deeper insight into Malaŵian concepts of health and disorder – which here, understandably, will have to focus on questions of mental health. The data presented throughout the previous sections has documented the high cultural importance of compliance to normative behaviour, making it a key criterion for the cultural conception of a normal mental condition. Therefore, every definition of 'mental' states refers back to an – explicit or implicit – idea of a culture specific notion of human normality. This respective notion of normal mental capacity becomes highly significant when investigating mental disorder in a given cultural context. Within a Western framework, the means of classification are various, making it possible to attest 'high' or 'low' mental functioning according to theoretical assessments such as IQ tests. In the given African context, these measures are neither available nor do they comply with prevailing cultural conceptions, and a Malaŵian professional working for a mental health organization thus discloses that

> "[…] there are a lot of mentally retarded patients in mild form, but they are just taken as failures in schools, somebody who is not doing very well. Maybe an assessment

> cannot be done to check if there is any mental retardation, it's just taken as 'This child is bad in class, he cannot do this' – not knowing that maybe it could be mental retardation. But some are just taken as being stupid, and among their friends, they can be mocked at" (Vivian Changata, a Mang'anja nurse).

Therefore, cultural processes distinguish 'normal' substandard performance in a given aspect of life – e.g. in school – from an allegedly pathological condition. The health-seeking behaviour exhibited in a given cultural context provides crucial evidence whether a condition is considered 'normal' – albeit maybe below the cultural average, such as a child being regarded as stupid due to poor performance at school – or pathological, thus requiring medical assistance and/or support. In the cultural context of Southern Malaŵi, this dichotomy is well developed when it comes to the concept of mental disorder. In order to better comprehend the cultural construction of mental disorder, it is highly relevant to distinguish 'normal' from pathological cases. In order to illustrate this issue, the Chicheŵa category of *kupusa* may be addressed. Translated as 'being foolish, being stupid' (Paas 2004: 384), *kupusa* is frequently applied in the description of mental disorder and in colloquial language likewise – with idioms such as *Iwe wopusa!* being equivalent to 'You fool!' Still, research accounts indicate that a condition of *kupusa* does not meet the requirements of mental disorders because it is explicitly agreed that *kupusa* is not curable – or rather, that the idea of applying therapy for such a condition would be ridiculous because 'It just happens that someone is dumb'. No specialized diagnosis is applied to define the aetiological background of this condition, no treatment is sought to remedy it. In a Malaŵian context, *kupusa* is, thus, a normal state. This fact gives an important insight into the cultural notions of normality and normal performance which shall be addressed further in the final chapter of this study.

Figure 2: The Yao *sing'anga* Vincent Chitete (left, with assistant) communicating with the spirits of his ancestors

IV.

Aetiological Categorization

> "I make divination, and then I know the origin of a certain *misala*, like this *misala* coming from God [*imachokera kwa Mulungu*]. But others come from magic [*kulodzedwa*], and yet others come by themselves" (Sapitwa Chagoma, a Lomwe *sing'anga*).

Previous chapters have argued that aetiology is a key category for the cultural conceptualization of mental disorder in Southern Malaŵi, and the present chapter means to substantiate this statement. It is, in this context, important to bear in mind the structural differences between biomedical and traditional pathology. While biomedical concepts are structured according to a direct and frequently *a priori* connection between a given disorder category (nosology) and a correlating causing factor (aetiology), traditional Malaŵian pathology does not necessarily make this one-to-one allocation between a particular aetiology and a health disorder category. Rather, every case of mental disorder is interpreted on the basis of a pluralistic catalogue of aetiologies, all of which are more or less suitable for the explanation of any kind of mental disorder. Due to the aetiologically unspecific character of local categories of sickness themselves, mental disorder may be explained by various widely different reasons, including notions of magic, or the direct influence of spiritual entities.

The way in which the pluralistic set of explanations for mental disorders is categorized is of some significance as this differentiation represents an interpretation of the cultural embodiment of the phenomenon itself. In Southern Malaŵi, a number of different reasons are associated with cases of mental disorder, and numerous studies in medical anthropology provide models of classification. Ezekiel Kalipeni differentiates four main categories of sickness causation in Malaŵi – these being *(a)* 'natural' causes (i.e. acts of God), *(b)* acts of other spirits (e.g. lineage spirits), *(c)* acts of sorcery and witchcraft, and *(d)* acts of persons other than sorcerers or witches – such as vengeance for sorcery, breach of taboo, and protective as well as anti-adultery magic (Kalipeni 1981: 110). Alternative systems of classification operate with comparable models.[1]

---

1 Similarly, Brian Morris differentiates *(a)* 'natural' reasons (including acts of God) from *(b)*

The present study applies a slightly modified model of classification, distinguishing only three main categories of mental disorder causation.[2] Here, the first distinctive complex refers to the variable forms of man-made magic manipulation – subdivided here into the forms of *ufiti*, *matsenga*, and the additional category of *kukhwima*. Secondly, concepts of spiritual intervention are acknowledged, recognizing different categories of spirit entities – such as *mizimu* and *ziwanda* – as well as the Supreme Being and its malevolent counterpart (i.e. Satan) as deliberately causing mental disorder. Thirdly, different notions of structural causation must be examined, falling into a number of categories as ranging from heredity to accidental causation and drug abuse.

1. Magic Manipulation

Magic represents one of the most prominent, classical areas of anthropological investigation. An exact definition of magic, at the same time, is obstructed not only by the term's wide colloquial application, but also by its high degree of abstraction from actual ethnographic fact. As a principle of social representation and action, 'magic' is hard to translate directly into cultural terms even though they might operate on the basis of comparable assumptions. Therefore, it should be noted that 'magic' will only serve as an analytic term here. On a general level, the term 'magic' should be understood as a concept also intrinsically related to ritual and traditional medicine. As Brian Morris points out,

> "The distinction often made by anthropologists between medicines and magic is not really applicable in the Malawian context, it hinders rather than helps understanding, for Asing'anga themselves do not make any such categorization, and there is no term in Chewa, which could be usefully translated as 'magic'" (Morris 1996: 49).

---

sicknesses associated with spirit entities, *(c)* magical reasons (such as *ufiti* and *matsenga*), and issues of *(d)* moral and/or ritual infringement (Morris 1996: 107-108). Karl Peltzer likewise distinguishes between 'natural' and 'supernatural' reasons (Peltzer 1987: 57). With respect to Zimbabwe, Deliane Burck tells 'natural' from cultural cases of disability, defining the former as those that "have a purely physical cause and that require only simple medical treatment [...] as well as those disabilities that are considered to be beyond treatment" whereas the latter denote that "apart from a physical defect, the condition reflects/reflected cultural or social problems in the family and/or the community and the interference of humans or spirits in the causation of the disability" (Burck 1989: 92).

2 In essence, the model applied here differs from others in its neglect of a 'breach of taboo' as a distinct category. The following account will present arguments justifying this interpretation of the aetiological discourse prevalent in Southern Malaŵi. The question of categorizing aetiological factors will receive some more consideration at the end of the present chapter.

Magic is not a concept that may be clearly demarcated from other fields of cultural reality such as religion, economy, or kinship – but it is a principal representation that permeates virtually all sections of social life. This thesis argues that the major semantic characteristic of magic is the fact that it allocates meaning according to criteria of analogy, e.g. on the basis of inherent similarity or association.[3] On this cognitive level, magic and scientific thought only differ insofar as the latter connects phenomena and their meaning in analytic terms, i.e. by investigating immanent properties through dissection. On a performative level, the application of magic generally assumes the form of ritual performance with frequently secretive character.

Especially in British anthropological tradition, 'magic' is usually defined by a pair of dichotomous subcategories: witchcraft and sorcery. While correspondents for both these terms have been identified in Malaŵian cultures, their use may again be somewhat misleading in itself (see below). In a more narrow sense, magic is hence used to subsume emic notions such as *ufiti* or *matsenga* – Chicheŵa concepts commonly translated as 'witchcraft' and 'sorcery', respectively – by thus stressing their structural similarities or in order to ensure comparability.

In ethnographic literature on Malaŵi, local concepts of magic are depicted according to this same dichotomous model, offering a broad distinction between two opposing concepts of magic under the Chicheŵa terms of *matsenga* and *ufiti*. These categories represent a clear-cut binary notion of magic, divided between the socially legitimate *matsenga* and the highly illegitimate *ufiti* (Soko 2002; Breugel 2001; Schoffeleers 1997; Peltzer 1987: 151-154; Wendroff 1985; Marwick 1965; ibid. 1952).[4] At the same time, Malaŵian experts in both *ufiti* and *matsenga* practices tend to deny the structural differences between the two, explaining that, on a conceptual level, "you have to know that *ufiti* is *matsenga*".[5]

---

3 This refers to the basic models as presented by James G. Frazer who identifies the central mechanism of magic as sympathy between cause and effect, following implicit laws of similarity and/or contact (Frazer 1922: 11-43).

4 The identification of the *ufiti* with witchcraft is widely accepted by bilingual Malaŵians and applied in the contexts of science, media, and everyday informal discourse alike. However, the concept pf witchcraft nonetheless bears considerable definition problems due to its deep roots in European and North American historical contexts. For the sake of clarity, this study favours the more precise emic category *ufiti* and avoids the term witchcraft on all occasions except in direct or indirect quote. The term sorcery will likewise be substituted by *matsenga* – in the hope of thus circumventing associative pitfalls caused by unclear and comparative terminology.

5 In addition, some accounts use alternative terms when referring to magic practices, thus further blurring the seemingly clear distinction between 'good' and 'evil' magic. As the most frequently used term, the near-neutral expression *kulodza* – translated as 'to do charm, to bewitch, to cast a spell, to kill magically' (Paas 2004: 232-233) – is applied to paraphrase an act of magic without instantly attributing it to either *ufiti* or *matsenga* categories.

1(a) Destructive Magic, or Ufiti

In present-day Malaŵi, notions of *ufiti* are intrinsically related to society and, more specifically, to notions of the causation of sickness. Studies in the 1960s already assessed that 55 percent of all cases of sickness – and, among these, usually the more critical ones – were socially attributed to *ufiti* (Marwick 1967: 105), and the own data strongly supports that *ufiti* explanations still form a major – if not the most prominent – causative category for mental disorder. In short, *ufiti* can be defined as the culturally illegitimate use of certain mythical powers, and persons practicing it – called *afiti* (sg. *mfiti*) – are both feared and severely prosecuted. The general characteristics of *ufiti* include the idea that the actions of *afiti* happen at night and in secrecy. *Afiti* are persons driven by unbridled hate and ruthless malice, living unrecognized within virtually every community. Moreover, it is a general rule that *ufiti* is only effective against persons of the own *chibale* (kin-group) while being ineffective against outsiders (Peltzer 1987: 151; Marwick 1965: 73), thus underlining the explicitly anti-social character of *ufiti*.[6] Within the network of extended families in Southern Malaŵi – and across ethnic boundaries –, it is commonly attested that "there is no kin group without its witch" (Schoffeleers 1997: 122).

When performing their anti-social deeds, *afiti* only partially operate in their material, physical shape. Usually, they emit their spirit – the *mzimu wa umunthu* – during night time while their bodies can be seen lying in bed, but the fact that their bodies are not involved in nocturnal activity does not protect them from potential harm if their evil deeds go wrong. Due to the implicit notion of *ufiti* being performed primarily by a spiritual agent, many of its practices are designed to manipulate the personality spirit (i.e. *mzimu wa umunthu*) of a chosen victim in order to cause harm to him or her. Although their spiritual shape is emphasized, *afiti* are notorious for transforming into horrendous-looking beasts with an extended nose, a long protruding snout full of carnassials, elongated ears, and sharp claws. Their enormous potbellies are seen as the emblematic storage room for their *ufiti* materials (*zizimba*) and indicate their craving for human flesh.

It is a widely shared notion that *afiti* use flat winnowing baskets (*malichero*, sg. *lichero*) as flying devices for their nocturnal ventures.[7] This form of *ufiti* only

---

6 Recent developments indicate that the idea of *ufiti* crossing kinship ties are becoming increasingly influential in Southern Malaŵi, thus shifting the phenomenon away from the more private sphere of the family towards a more overarching societal notion. For this update on recent developments, I am indebted to Joseph Chakanza (personal communication, 04/09/2008).

7 According to numerous accounts, these vehicles have to be refuelled with the blood (*magazi*) of a human victim. According to one Yao account, this notion of blood reflects an expression of the *mzimu wa umulungu* of the person – i.e. his or her life force.

provides the transport needed to perform the more abhorrent activities of the trade. Thus, *afiti* are known to attack human beings at night in order to harm and, in the most extreme of cases, kill them. Here, the weakest members of society are often regarded as preferred victims of these nocturnal attacks, and many deaths among children are ascribed to *ufiti* (Marwick 1965: 73-76). Applying *ufiti* generally requires the use of special materials (*zizimba*) which are conceptualized as objects of plant, animal and/or human origin – e.g. special parts of a (dead) human body. In many cases, it is assumed that *ufiti* murder is meant to provide the *mfiti* with the desired human body parts required for further magic activities. Some accounts state that *afiti* even lend each other human body parts, allowing fellow *afiti* to use extra pieces taken from their own victims as *zizimba*.[8] Here, *afiti* are said to be very particular in paying back these debts which have to be returned in congeneric fashion, so that

> "Some might have borrowed meat from a fellow *mfiti*, so now they want to return it. That is to say if someone borrowed the meat of a child, he/she has to give back that of a child as well. Yes, and if it is an elder person, he/she also has to give an elder person back, and to do otherwise would lead to quarrels" (Sapitwa Chagoma, a Lomwe *sing'anga*)

Even the actual parts of the corpse that are returned have to correspond exactly with those received before.[9] In addition to using corpses as raw material warehouses of *zizimba* materials, *afiti* are also characterized as eating human flesh. On many occasions, this devouring of human corpses is described as the decisive criterion for *ufiti*, and the first bite of human meat is seen as the ultimate initiation into the *afiti*'s anti-social network. *Afiti* are generally assumed to practice necrophagy by digging up corpses from their graves at night and devouring them in communal feasts, and they are constantly consumed with appetite for human flesh (Marwick 1965: 73-79).[10]

---

8 Here, it is explained that a corpse that has not been killed by means of *ufiti* is useless as *chizimba* due to its lack of power as identified in the blood – i.e. life force, *mzimu wa umulungu* – of the victim. But while a given *mfiti* can only kill members of the own *chibale*, he or she would have to kill many relatives all the time. As an alternative, *afiti* can share the body parts of a given corpse which are usable even for unrelated fellow *afiti* – provided the person was killed by *ufiti*.

9 The blood (*magazi*) of the dead person also constitutes a coveted commodity, and *afiti* allegedly use magic artefacts to raise the dead from their graves and remove their blood. As a former *mfiti* narrates, "We have an instrument [*chida*] with certain powers which we use to analyze. After calling out the name [i.e. of the dead person], he/she comes to the surface [i.e. from the grave]. Once we have done that, we take a hook to remove the blood from the body of that person. [...] We only remove want we want, like the heart and other parts like that" (Sapitwa Chagoma, a Lomwe *sing'anga*).

10 In illustration of this, Maxwell Marwick mentions that *afiti* receive a certain *mankhwala* from their *ufiti* masters which makes them insensitive against the stench of decaying human corpses. Moreover, they are said to protect themselves against rabies, which is seen as an immediate

Ufiti Background

In their actions, *afiti* are conceived to follow a number of clearly defined impetuses. Generally, jealousy and/or envy are considered as the first and foremost motivation for the use of *ufiti* against a fellow person, and personal greed as well as general hatred may further be added (Peltzer 1987: 151; Marwick 1965: 71, 82).[11] Also, *afiti* have the reputation of killing persons for the sake of using the corpse as either food or *zizimba*.

When the causation of mental disorder is concerned, the motivation of a potential *mfiti* is frequently subject to speculation. In case of a child being struck with mental disorder due to the alleged manipulations of *afiti*, this magic attack is likely to be interpreted as being directed against the family of the child rather than the infant itself. In this line of thought, a jealous *mfiti* uses magic so that the family has no benefit from the child due to its poor mental condition – so the parents of a child with a mental disorder are forced to spend considerable amounts of money and attention on its care in addition to minimizing its potential economic contributions. Accordingly, it is argued that *afiti* are more likely to target a first-born than any other child of a family, and that they may also cause mental disorder to a child in order to prevent it from inheriting family property.[12] In addition to this, some accounts mention *ufiti* being exercised out of personal ambition[13] while it is widely agreed that all *afiti* have to execute their powers on a regular basis in order to stay in practice. Moreover, *afiti* are considered to enjoy causing harm to fellow people, hence doing it for mere pleasure of it, and finally, *afiti* may also offer their services for money, thus creating the additional option that a hired *mfiti* may not have any personal interest in a given *ufiti* attack – save economic ones.

In a number of ways, *ufiti* training may lead to mental disorder in an infant apprentice, and most of these incidents have the character of a magic accident affecting the involuntary mfiti student. The most prominent of these notions

---

consequence of the eating of human flesh, by means of 'vaccinations' (Marwick 1965: 80) – i.e. *mipini* scarifications.

11 Accordingly, Johann van Breugel mentions a case of epilepsy which is diagnosed as resulting from *ufiti* used against a victim because of jealousy (Breugel 2001: 240).

12 It is argued that any *mfiti* trying to punish a family would target either the first-born child or all the children of the given family at once. In cases where the fourth or eighth-born are affected, in contrast, it is fairly unlikely that the incidence is related to *ufiti*. The exact position of the patient within the kin-group may therefore be a decisive criterion for the cultural identification of *ufiti* activities (see *Chapter IV.1.a*).

13 Currently, the common discourse on *ufiti* incorporates a number of ideas derived from modern-life situations. Thus, one *mfiti* from Zomba District is described as having killed numerous family members for the sole purpose of receiving promotion within the *ufiti* hierarchy. This represents the integration of a certain sense of Westernized business competition into traditional religious concepts.

implies that *afiti* take their apprentices for a ride in their flying devices at night as part of their *ufiti* education. These black 'aeroplanes' are created by magic means out of a winnowing basket (*lichero*), and can carry numerous persons anywhere at lightning speed. Many accounts agree that children may suffer from mental disorder due to falling out of these malichero during their nocturnal *ufiti* activities. According to a figurative expression, certain conditions of mental disorder – more specifically *kulumala* – are frequently associated with this idea, with the drop leaving bones twisted and broken and the person ultimately impaired. In some cases, this concept is surrounded by more detailed accounts – such as a Yao mother blaming an unknown *mfiti* for not taking good care when returning from a *lichero* ride. Usually, a *sing'anga* diagnosing a child's mental disorder as being related to a *lichero* crash draws a direct connection between the exact course of the accident and the condition of the child. Therefore, a child unable to use its left hand or leg would be assumed to have fallen on this side, and if the problem is perceived to be located in the head, it would be reckoned that the infant mfiti must have toppled headfirst.[14]

Yet one more reason for applying *ufiti* against another person is the *afiti*'s wish or need to pass their secret powers on to a potential successor. This kind of *ufiti* training requires an initial magic attack on that selected victim – usually an infant or even unborn child in the *mfiti*'s own kin-group. The foundation for the magical powers of *ufiti* is therefore generally laid out in early childhood. While *ufiti* is usually conceived as being handed down from parent to child or from grandparent to grandchild, even less closely related members of the same kinship group may act as either donors or recipients.[15]

The classical career of a *mfiti* therefore starts at infancy due to a night time attack by a ghostly creature, implanting certain substances – representing the 'germ' of *ufiti* – into the victim. This substance is usually conceived in the form of liquid which is instilled into the victims' mouth.[16] In the form of these *zizimba*

---

14 In some cases, these accidents are said to stem from successful anti-*ufiti* protection of one's property. Thus, a *lichero* crash could be caused by the *mfiti* trying to fly over magically protected territory – such as created by a strongly 'fortified' person or *wokhwima* (see *Chapter IV.1.c*).

15 While *ufiti*, as mentioned frequently already, is connected to kinship affiliation, the process of its transmission should be understood as a form of training rather than inheritance. Requiring an active act of contamination, this idea does not constitute a concept of inheritance in a quasi-genetic sense (see *Chapter IV.3.b*). Therefore, Malaŵian conditions clearly differ from Azande notions which acknowledge the unilineal inheritance of witchcraft by the following generation (see Evans-Pritchard 1963: 23).

16 Here, different substances are rumoured to form the liquid basis for this initial drink of *zizimba*. While one Yao account reckons that small children actually receive a soup made from human flesh, another Yao explains that the liquid substance is made with water that has been used in order to wash corpses. He also expresses his firm belief that nurses in government hospitals earn extra money by selling the water used in their mortuaries to paying *afiti*.

materials, the unwelcome gift of *ufiti* remains in the person's stomach as the manifestation of his or her secret powers. Once contaminated with *ufiti*, the magic potential is said to grow along with the child, lying dormant and unnoticed – even though an examination by an experienced *sing'anga* could reveal the hidden *ufiti*. Sooner or later, a *mfiti* – usually the donor – once again enters the victim's dreams in order to act as a teacher, providing instructions on the use of these hidden powers.[17] After this, the training proper begins, and the eating of human flesh as well as flying in a *lichero* mark the apprentice's final initiation into the secrets of *ufiti*.[18] As mentioned above, even an unborn child may become the target of *afiti* who want to pass their powers on to a new generation. Such an incident bears important strategic advantages for the *mfiti* because

> "There are also other children who are given *ufiti* while in their mother's stomach so they grow up with it. [...] The purpose is that it should not reveal anything. But some also want to hand it over to them if they are dying" (Sapitwa Chagoma, a Lomwe *sing'anga*).

While prenatal contamination therefore is a constant danger, the most immediate threat to a child occurs directly after birth. At this very young age, infants are considered as being so vulnerable to magic attacks that they require special protection from *afiti* who want to turn them into future apprentices.[19] Due to its mode of transmission, the stomach (*mimba*) has a close connection to *ufiti* as shared knowledge indicates that *afiti* store their dangerous – and revealing – *ufiti* materials (*zizimba*) in their bellies. Persons resisting the influence of a *mfiti* who tries to make them practice *ufiti* as well may be punished with sickness due to the *mfiti's* evil influence, and frequently, mental disorder would ensue.[20] Once a

---

17 Johann van Breugel mentions the notion that *ufiti* contamination in a child can be discerned by some outer signs. According to his account, "A child whose teeth on the upper jaw appear before those on the lower jaw is [...] held to be a future *mfiti*. In the past such children were drowned in a river. Even now mothers will try to hide the fact" (Breugel 2001: 223).

18 In some cases, children are said not to be susceptible to the involuntary gift of *ufiti* and therefore might regurgitate the *ufiti* material right after receiving it. In more unfortunate cases, the forced contamination with *ufiti* can lead to severe mental disorder in a child who, by personal disposition, is thus unable to accommodate it, meaning that "If a child is being taught the art of *ufiti* and it doesn't fit him/her, the child becomes *wozerezeka*. It sometimes looks like *misala*, but it is *kuzerezeka*, the *ufiti* is not befitting the child" (Doris Petroyo, a Lomwe *sing'anga*).

19 As a Mang'anja farmer elaborates, this fragile period lasts up to six months after birth – a time span corresponding with the parents' obligation to sexual abstinence (see *Chapter II.1.a*). All this time, the child sleeps with a light burning next to the bed, due to the notion that bright light keeps *afiti* off. A small kerosene lamp is said to suffice for that purpose.

20 Thus, a woman whose prolonged mental disorder has already been otherwise diagnosed as *misala* – and which is later identified as the possession by a *mfiti's* spirit – afterwards describes her situation as follows: "I have been seized by the spirit of my mother, who was a witch (*mfiti*) that ate people. Every night she comes to me asking for human flesh" (quoted from Schoffeleers 1997: 143).

child has been successfully accepted as an *ufiti* apprentice, its training continues in the form of nocturnal instructions and the participation in his or her master's activities.[21] Flying in a *lichero* basket is, as mentioned above, a typical part of *ufiti*, but a child's involvement in this also bears a particular kind of danger which is also relevant in the context of mental disorder causation.

Applying Ufiti

Among those applications of *ufiti* that are known to cause mental disorder in a given victim, the most commonly mentioned one is referred to as *nyundo* ('hammer') or, in Anglicized Chichewa, *hamala*. It is described as one of the most dangerous forms of *ufiti* which, on the receiving end, is experienced as a heavy blow on the head – and once stricken, a victim is not expected to survive for long.[22] With respect to its immediate effects,

> "One herbalist said it affected only the top of the head, that there was blood in the nose and mouth (tchuluka magazi, much blood) and that the inflicted person often dies" (Morris 1996: 120).

According to own research data, the destructive effect of *hamala* constitutes one of the most prominent forms of *ufiti* with respect to the causation of mental disorder.[23] Some experts feel free to share some of the technicalities underlying *hamala*, and according to a Lomwe specialist, the 'hammer' can be used for both causing mental disorder as well as killing a person because

> "If being hit just once, a person becomes *wozungulira mutu* because when you hit him/her, the blood goes down into the belly and clots there. If you hit him/her again, that person dies" (Sapitwa Chagoma, a Lomwe *sing'anga*).

Different persons give diverging accounts of the ingredients required for performing *hamala* magic. While a Lomwe *sing'anga* describes them as a match and the shard from a pot which had been used to store water for washing corpses,

---

21 As an excellent example of a typical *mfiti* career, Karl Peltzer quotes the story of a six year-old Chewa boy, confessing that "I was awake at night, our elder grandmother came and gave us medicine to drink and a piece of human flesh to eat. Then we started flying. From this point onwards we were able to practice witchcraft. For this training we had to pay one *tambala*" (quoted from Peltzer 1987: 164).

22 Brian Morris' gives one account of *nyundo* as denoting complaints such as a splitting, throbbing headache, accompanied by dimmed vision and caused by magic means (Morris 1996: 119-120). According to him, *afiti* may surround their victims' house at night and call them out so the victims "be hit with a hammer, and become ill with headache" (Morris 1996: 120).

23 When describing the causation of mental disorder – here with respect to conditions of *kuzungulira mutu* and *kuzerezeka* –, a Lomwe healer explains that "[...] some inherit it, others get it from *hamala*. They can hit a child while it is still in the stomach of its mother" (Sapitwa Chagoma, a Lomwe *sing'anga*).

a Mang'anja farmer states that the *chizimba* applied actually resembles a small hammer. The *mfiti* approaches the chosen victim in the translucent form of a *mzimu* and strikes him or her down with this likewise insubstantial hammer, thus causing the magical effect onto the victim.

For the most part, the cultural understanding of alleged *afiti* activities implies that they follow certain predefined formal patterns, constituting a vague catalogue of typical *ufiti* applications or 'spells' which, in part, are directly connected to the causation of mental disorder. As standardized applications of *ufiti*, their inner workings are associated with particular actions and typical ingredients in the form of *ufiti* materials (*zizimba*). These *ufiti* applications serve various purposes, including the magic theft of maize (*nfumba ya chimanga*)[24] as well as of property, disturbing social relationships, destroying crops or life-stock, killing unborn or newborn babies, causing infertility, impotence, and other kinds of health disorder as well as magic murder. As an example, an *ufiti* technique called *dzira* or 'egg' is mentioned in some accounts. Here, the actual egg of a chicken forms the central *chizimba*, and the magic effect of destroying a chosen victim's brain is symbolized by the crushing of the egg during the *ufiti* performance. With the egg white representing the brain and the yolk the human blood, this *dzira* form of *ufiti* is generally conceived as being applied in order to kill a person. In the causation of mental disorder, an *ufiti* application called *hamala* or 'hammer' represents a common feature as mentioned in numerous accounts. When meaning to cause mental disorder, some special *ufiti* applications are reportedly used in order to delay the delivery of a child. Described as 'locking the door to the womb', this technique causes children to be born with a severe mental disorders – such as *kulumala* – due to their belated birth.[25] Conversely, *ufiti* may also be used to cause abortion, and traditional birth attendants as well as *asing'anga* point out that a piece of the umbilical cord (*mchombo*), if stolen by a *mfiti*, could act as a *chizimba* for using *ufiti* against that same child.[26]

Due to their anti-social activities, *afiti* keep their true identity secret and, in order to maintain its secrecy, are said to cover up their destructive actions by making them appear unsuspicious. Thus, special forms of *ufiti* can be applied in

---

24 Hereby, another person's crop is magically transferred and replanted into the *mfiti's* own *munda* field. Similarly, the harvest can be removed from the victim's granary, to be found in the *mfiti's* possession afterwards (Marwick 1965: 70-73).

25 As a Lomwe *sing'anga* continues, the *zizimba* required for this technique include a piece of this particular pregnant woman's clothes, wrapped into a bundle.

26 Therefore, a Lomwe healer stresses the great responsibility of *azamba* midwives to prevent *afiti* from stealing the umbilical cord of a child from the *chikuta* delivery house. Here, the piece of *mchombo* acts as a focus that not only represents a symbolic 'entrance' to the victim's body, but that also connects the *mfiti* to the most fragile period of the victim's early life.

order to cause *mutu* in an infant victim – leaving the impression of a structural case which the preventive medicine (or *phula*) provided by the family failed to avert. Likewise, *afiti* are known to take advantage of persons' social misbehaviour and their violations of traditional rules of conduct (*miyambo*). A pregnant woman laughing about a person with a mental disorder and consequently delivering a child with the same problems may therefore be an actual victim of the hidden machinations of a *mfiti*. Taking the opportunity and concealing their evil deeds by attacking someone who violated a *mwambo*, *afiti* are reported to divert attention from their own actions. But while *ufiti* actions are considered responsible for a large part of all cases of mental disorder – and of unfortunate events in general –, the activity of these *afiti* also bears considerable dangers of them falling victim to mental disorder themselves. This effect can follow a number of lines, most of which will be addressed in the context of the different forms of protective magic prevalent in Malaŵi (see *Chapter IV.1.b* and *IV.1.c*). Other mechanisms are also culturally recognized, indicating that the person of the *mfiti* as such is indeed closely connected to phenomena of mental disorder – on both the giving and receiving end of it.[27]

Ufiti and Social Response

While large-scale campaigns against *ufiti* are well-documented in Malaŵian history (see *Chapter IV.4.a*), the fear of *ufiti* is an integral part in both rural and urban communities – constituting a threat to personal wellbeing, creating considerable social tensions, and endangering the integrity of the family unit itself.

In rural Zomba District, the Mang'anja subsistence farmer Gerard Mdindire and his wife Gracie experience the death of two members of the matrilateral kin-group within the uxorilocal compound, and both deaths are perceived as suspicious cases. Shortly after, Gracie gives birth to her first-born boy who soon displays symptoms of mental disorder. In the neighbouring village, Gerard's kin group blames his in-laws and repeatedly advises him to abandon his wife. He refuses, regarding these events as coincidence and putting his efforts into supporting family and child. Meanwhile the village community gets increasingly concerned about the incidents within this compound, and when notifying the group village headman, this grupu finally decides to have the matter investigated by a specialist in afiti hunting – a sing'anga wochotsa ufiti.

When the said specialist – a Lomwe from Mulanje District – arrives, he orders all the inhabitants of the respective compound to gather in the front yard. After some ritual

---

[27] Thus, *afiti* offending their personal familiar spirits or *ziwanda* (*Chapter IV.2.c*) may provoke a spiritual attack due to which they may get affected from mental disorder – more especially, from *misala*. Likewise, the loss of an *ufiti* snake (as depicted above) may cause mental disorder to the *mfiti* owner, and the process would be referred to as *kusavuka*.

preparations – which include the sacrificial offering of a chicken and ufa flour to the spirit of his dead sister who serves as the activating power of his magic ufiti-finding stick (mphambanya) – the mombole uses this said bamboo staff to find the responsible mfiti, knowing that the stick will point at every person present who is guilty of performing ufiti. He and his three assistants hold the mphambanya in a horizontal position, and as the prayers and libations to the sing'anga's late sister cease, the stick shows vehement movement. Ostensibly dragging the four men across the farm ground and zigzagging in between the potential culprits, the stick finally points out a number of alleged afiti, each of which fall to the ground helplessly as they are touched by the tip of the mphambanya. Out of a total of about 20 people living in the compound, the mombole's stick identifies four afiti, these being two elderly ladies between 50 and 60 years of age as well as two boys aged six and seven, respectively.[28] *The elder boy instantly admits receiving nocturnal instructions from the spirit of an unknown mfiti, haunting his dreams and teaching him the magical properties of plants and animal parts. Recently, he confesses, this night tutor instructed him to kill a person from the compound and, upon his refusal, forced him to cause mental disorder to the newborn boy instead. By his confession, he asks for protection from any further influence by this mfiti who might punish him for his betrayal.*

As everyone else denies the allegations and accordingly refuses to deliver their ufiti material (zizimba) stored otherwise – which would have proven their guilt –, the investigation continues. Using his magic staff to detect hiden zizimba, the mombole finally discovers secret ufiti material in the form of a black leather snake among the possessions of Gracie's mother. Upon closer analysis, it is affirmed that this namgogoda can only be used in order to magically steal property – hence indicating her innocence in the crimes currently under investigation. The six years-old boy is also found to have only limited ufiti knowledge and be incapable of the recent ufiti attacks. Among the belongings of the other lady, though, all kinds of zizimba are found – a hammer, a leather leopard, a black lichero, and the like –, many of which are regarded as crucial for ufiti murder and the causation of mental disorder. Due to this evidence, she is found guilty and, as she continues to claim her innocence, subjected to a special treatment in order to prevent her from causing any further harm. After receiving mankhwala akumwa that fails to cause her diarrhoea, the mombole produces some wooden and other ingredients, burns them, and rubs the ashes into mphini scarifications which he makes on specific places of the woman's body. Due to this 'vaccination', she is unable to exercise ufiti ever again under pain of death.[29]

---

28 The women are Gracie's mother and mother's elder sister. The former of the boys is a son of Gracie's elder sister, the other one a distantly related orphan who was taken up as a house-worker two years prior.

29 Therefore, "This medicine is for controlling or even breaking down the *ufiti* materials. If she ever flies again, she will die. And it happens!". This corresponds with an account reported by Karl Peltzer where a confessing *mfiti* receives medical treatment in the form of various *mankhwala* as prescribed by the *sing'anga* which are meant to prevent the *ufiti* tutor – here called the 'night mother' – from influencing the convict to perform further acts of *ufiti*. Additionally, *mankhwala*

At the end of the afiti-hunt, the mombole receives payment from the community for his services. The convicted afiti – especially the alleged principal culprit – face social ostracism in the community, but about six months after the event, that same woman explains that her situation in the village has almost gone back to normal. Neighbours, on the other hand, admit that a certain degree of social tension remains between the accused women and the community – and some villagers assert that the farmer who first brought the case to the agrupu's attention is living in danger of the afiti's vengeance.

In spite of the fact that *ufiti* allegations necessarily refer back to a relative (*mbale*) of the victim, many accounts confirm that *afiti* are known to hire out their services to private customers, making it conceivable that two non-interrelated families may engage in *ufiti* conflict via a member of the respective target *chibale*.[30] Rare as this notion may be, it represents an important concept of overcoming the otherwise strict kinship limitations of *ufiti* applicability, and it accentuates the possibility of neighbourhood quarrels and other social tensions being articulated in terms of alleged *ufiti* attacks.[31] The conception of *ufiti* therefore bears considerable room to articulate social stress not only within the confined sphere of kinship affinity, but also in the larger framework of the community.

Of all cases of mental disorder, a significant proportion is traced back to *ufiti* – and it even represents a common initial assumption within many communities. Due to this impressive level of cultural prevalence, *ufiti* permeates all sections of Malaŵian society. While being stereotypically associated with a highly traditional, rural setting, urban *ufiti* phenomena are also well-reported and, by modifying the original motifs into more modernist versions of much larger scale, may acquire significant political and social momentum. Neither status nor religious denomination nor level of education mark decisive distinctions in the cultural recognition of *ufiti*, and issues of gender have a very limited significance for association with *ufiti* practices.[32] Most Christian churches do not deny the

---

is applied to protect the boy's house from *afiti* who could either punish him for his unfaithfulness or seduce him into resuming his *ufiti* career (Peltzer 1987: 163-164).

30 It is assumed that addressing *afiti* with a request for magic services bears the danger of them punishing the potential client in order to stop him or her from revealing their secret identity. If agreement is reached, though, a person may cause harm to, e.g., non-related neighbours by finding a *mfiti* in this other kin group. The strong networks believed to exist among the *afiti* in a given geographical area are frequently mentioned to be helpful for identifying a suitable magic service provider.

31 Therefore, "in the villages when two families fight, [...] one family will say 'You will see' [*uona*]. So if the family says 'You will see' and something happens or even after a year or two a child is born having a disability, then they will still remember: he said 'You will see', and this is what he has done. So they will think that maybe somebody has been planning something bad to happen to the family" (Steven Msowoya, a Tumbuka disability organization representative).

32 It has been argued that the stereotypical Malaŵian *mfiti* is conceptualized as a woman from a weak economic background (Peltzer 1987: 151). In the 1960s, James Crawford suggested that

existence of *ufiti* but condemn its practices as satanic, confirming its ontological reality by incorporating it into their own cosmological system.[33] The different ethnic groups also display a fairly uniform notion of *ufiti*, and considering it a central albeit disagreeable part of their own cultural tradition.

In a contemporary context, *ufiti* is constantly in the focus of public discourse, and reports about recent *ufiti* activities or allegations are prominent in both national newspaper and radio broadcasting. At the time of this research, many media accounts reorted children being instructed as future *afiti* in urban centers such as Blantyre and Lilongwe.[34] The fact that – due to its strong ties to British Legal Codes – Malaŵian Law has no means to try cases of *ufiti* leaves all such instances under the jurisdiction of *bwalo* traditional courts which, in itself, leads to continuous legal problems (Brietzke 1974) (see *Chapter I.2.b*).[35] While traditional strategies of *ufiti* eradication are still severely prosecuted by law, many persons leave the court as innocent and return to their respective communities only to face a traditional court retrial which fully recognizes charges of *ufiti* on the basis of culturally defined evidence. At the same time, a person found guilty of *ufiti* homicide by the standards of the *bwalo* cannot be charged appropriately due to the fact that traditional courts do not have the authority to impose penalties exceeding a fine – which may therefore amount to the payment of some goats or a cow, or the loss of public office. Dissatisfaction with the sentences passed over alleged *afiti* by the *bwalo* can therefore lead to harsh social reaction, and narratives of occasional mob justice may be seen as an

---

the notion of the female *mfiti* is rooted in social considerations, stating that "if a Cewa man wishes to put an end to the marriage by accusing his wife of wizardry there is little to stop him" (Crawford 1967: 155). Similarly dated material, however, presents a slightly larger proportion of male Malaŵian *afiti* (Marwick 1967: 108). At present, some Yao from Chiradzulu District accordingly agree that men are much more likely to be associated with *ufiti*. Among the Tonga of neighbouring Zambia, as Elizabeth Colson, fathers are most frequently accused of witchcraft (Colson 2000: 333-358). It may therefore be concluded that, while some geographical and/or ethnic variations exist, there is no indicator for a general gender prevalence within *ufiti* accusations on a regional scale.

33 For more on the connection between *ufiti* and Satanism see *Chapter IV.2.c*.

34 Such cases are said to come to light sooner or later due to the fact that the respective schoolchildren become too tired to pay attention to their classes after spending their nights flying in *malichero* or desecrating graves.

35 Accordingly, paragraph 5 and 8 of the so-called Witchcraft Act in Malaŵian Law – issued in 1968 but being based on an act ratified in 1911 – states that "Any person who by his statements or actions represent himself to be a wizard or witch or as having or exercising the power of witchcraft shall be liable to a fine of £50 and to imprisonment for ten years. [...] The profession or calling of witchfinder or witchdoctor or of professional maker or mixer of poison is hereby declared to be an illegal calling and every person exercising or pretending to exercise such calling or profession shall be guilty of felony and shall be liable to imprisonment for life" (Government of Malaŵi 1968: 7: 02).

expression of the disruption between state jurisdiction and local concepts of justice.[36]

The present section has depicted *ufiti* as an antithesis to cultural notions of morality, social values, and human culture as such, putting the *mfiti* in direct opposition to the ethical concept of the person or *munthu* (see *Chapter III.1.a*). According to its mode of transmission, the phenomenon of *ufiti* itself meets some criteria of a health disorder – being received involuntarily by an innocent victim due to contamination. As prototypes of anti-social behaviour, the horrendous *afiti* are described as showing some signs of physical distortion, transforming into physically abnormal creatures in the course of their nocturnal activities – and thus losing all their human features. This is expressed, e.g., in Malaŵian folk art because

> "If you find those who make curios and ask if they have anything that portrays magic or witchcraft, there is a sense of abnormality. The carvings are not human figures, they are not portrayed in the way a human being is structured. They have a big stomach, they have a hunchback, a big mouth and so on. So anything that portrays evil is outside of what is expected in everyday live, and to some extent I think when somebody is disfigured people may tend to associate abnormality with evilness, there being something wrong" (Steven Msowoya, a Tumbuka disability organization representative).

The criterion of physical deviation accentuates a recognizable yet unspecific association between *afiti* and persons with mental disorders. The former have, moreover, already been described as the epitome of *mwambo* violation as such (see *Chapter II.1.a*). Some accounts, at the same time, mention persons with mental disorders as potential *afiti* who punish ill behaviour against them with relentless magic vengeance. The secret attacks of *afiti* are frequently assumed reasons for the occurrence of mental disorder, and *afiti* themselves also run the risk of contracting mental disorders due to their activities. This documents a close and multi-levelled correlation between *ufiti* and the occurrence of mental disorder in Southern Malaŵi.

1(b) Supportive Magic, or Matsenga

Forming the complementary counterpart to the evil manipulations of *ufiti*, the term *matsenga* is applied to denote those kinds of magic which are, in contrast to

---

36 Only recently, the need to re-introduce appropriate legislative measures for addressing *ufiti*-related cases has been addressed by the first National Conference on the Review of the Constitution held in Lilongwe in March 2006. Here, the representatives of the Traditional Authorities of the country expressed their concern that "the law must recognise witchcraft in Malawi and address the same accordingly" (Malawi Law Commission 2006: 39).

ufiti, not socially banned. This distinction, though, is far from monolithic – as it widely depends on the cultural perception of the given case and is thereby subject to interpretation. The use of *matsenga* is generally described as an open, non-secretive action which may therefore be practiced in bright daylight and which is regarded as visible, and it is predominately applied by local *asing'anga*.[37]

Learning *matsenga* is usually part of the spiritual instructions a *sing'anga* receives from a spirit taskmaster. Most of these practices are an important part of a future *sing'anga*'s responsibility, encompassing fields such as magic protection, support for professional success, or love magic. *Matsenga* is predominantly helpful and defensive in character – serving for protective, supportive, or even entertainment purposes. It represents a socially accepted art that is both publicly advertised and performed, it is seen as largely non-violent. In further contrast to *ufiti*, its effectiveness is independent from kinship ties, and its effects – if harmful – are said to come gradually (Peltzer 1987: 151). The use of *matsenga* in order to harm persons is limited to acts of retribution for inappropriate – e.g. criminal – behaviour (Peltzer 1987: 151).

The motivation for the use of *matsenga* is frequently identified as providing a service for a paying customer, and the clients hiring a *sing'anga* to perform *matsenga* on their behalf themselves aim for personal security, professional assistance, and the like. Moreover, the term *matsenga* is also applied for all sorts of magic trickery (Marwick 1965: 74), sometimes bearing some resemblance to Western ideas of stage magic or slight of hand and performed by *asing'anga* in order to attract customers in a village market setting. Their impressive acts of magic prowess are seen as an indicator of general expertise – while some *asing'anga* consider this popular form of canvassing as below the dignity of a truly competent spiritual expert. Such public acts of 'charlatanry' may include feats such as the demonstrative handling of – supposedly dangerous – animals[38] or the seemingly magical testing of blood group compatibility between persons.[39]

---

37 Accordingly, Maxwell Marwick characterizes the materials applied for *matsenga* practices as *mankhwala apoyera* or 'magic substances in the light' (Marwick 1965: 75). Karl Peltzer distinguishes the use of the term *matsenga* as denoting "traditionally witchcraft and positive magic and transitionally sorcery and positive magic" (Peltzer 1987: 151-152).

38 In one incidence on a rural market, a large crowd gathered around a *sing'anga* handling a long, bright green snake in the fashion of a snake-charmer. As many people in Southern Malaŵi tend to consider any green serpent as the dreaded green mamba (*Dendroaspis angusticeps*), the spectators shun away from its every move. Once surrounded by a large enough audience, the *sing'anga* removes the snake and calls volunteers into the flour-marked circle of his makeshift stand, promising to find out their names and health disorders without any additional information. In order to further fuel the public anticipation, he proclaims that he will turn a piece of black cloth on the floor into a chameleon.

39 Performed on random passers-by, this 'test' implies the use of pairs of small bamboo sticks

In addition to this actual trickery, many accounts also categorize other magic activities – including love magic, or practices that provide extra strength for a hard working person – as part of *matsenga* (Peltzer 1987: 150). Further forms of *matsenga* – such as making a person invisible or helping the client prevail in lawsuits or negotiations with the police – are also mentioned (Breugel 2001: 253-254). Such and similar *matsenga* activities, typically falling under the authority of local *asing'anga*, may even be listed on their service price lists.[40] For the sake of the current study, it may suffice to distinguish two broad categories of *matsenga* – firstly, as different forms of protective magic, and secondly, as various forms of magic trickery, persuasion, and illusionism which are frequently performed in a market setting – as entertainment, as a demonstration of magical power, or as life support.

In general, protective magic practices (*kutsilika*) are ritual actions performed by a *sing'anga*, and their efficiency refers to a closely defined piece of property such as a private house, a shop, a granary, or a maize field. The protection granted by *kutsilika* magic is not limited to the magic avoidance of unwelcome events – such as keeping a thief from stealing –, but many forms of *kutsilika* imply a magic punishment of alleged evildoers who trigger this magic effect. After the ritual performance – which may include burying certain activating substances (*zizimba*) on the site of the thus protected area[41] – it is assumed that every violation of this property activates a pre-specified effect, leading to a direct punishment of the culprit. As an example, it is stated that thieves stealing from somebody else's crops may encounter a huge snake scaring them away – while the serpent truly is nothing but a pencil-size piece of wood activated by *matsenga*. According to a Nyanja *sing'anga*, stealing protected goods can also cause limbs to become crippled while purloining pumpkins can cause the culprit

---

rubbed on two persons and laid out on a black plate which is then turned upside down. According to the *asing'anga* demonstrating this feat, the sticks either drop down or stay glued to the plate, depending on the harmony between the two persons. This trick – strongly encouraging associations with magnetism in a Western observer – draws a considerable crowd of spectators, supporting the advertisement of the *asing'anga*'s roadside shop.

40 The picture-framed price list of a Yao *sing'anga* from Salima District practicing in central Blantyre City therefore encompasses services such as *Zirengo, kuperekeratu K400.00* ('Bad luck, cash, 400 MwK'), *Kutsilika nyumba K500.00* ('Protecting the house, 500 MwK'), *Kutsilika thupi K290.00* ('Protecting the body, 290 MwK'), *Kutsilika sitolo K700.00* ('Protecting the store, 700 MwK'), *Anchito K900.00* ('For workers, 900 MwK'), *Mankhwala a bizinezi K400.00* ('Business medicine, 400 MwK'), or *Chikondi mubanja K300.00* ('Love in the family, 300 MwK') in addition to various applications of a more medical nature.

41 Thus, it is reported elsewhere that burying the bark of the poisonous *dangwe* tree (*Crossopteryx febrifuga*) below the door threshold leads to the immediate death of *afiti* upon entering the house. Hiding a certain medicine under the bed of an unfaithful wife can cause the mortal sickness *likango* in her lover, and various kinds of medicine can be used to protect the field, in some cases even infecting thieves with fatal health disorder (Marwick 1965: 70).

to develop a potbelly. Many spheres of society are intricately connected to notions of magic protection, playing an important part not only in Malaŵian everyday culture but also in the context of the causation of mental disorder. According to a local healer,

> "*Kuzerezeka* can be a punishment from people, depending on what people have done to their property. A person can indeed become *ozerezeka* [...] if a person stole somebody's property which was protected with charms" (Luka Dzaone, a Lomwe *sing'anga*).

Objects can be protected in different ways, and the actual magic effect depends on both the expertise of the acting *sing'anga* and the individual wishes of his or her client.[42] It should be noted that *kutsilika* can also be applied to secure individuals and/or their property from the influence of *afiti*. Therefore, strong *kutsilika* magic can help a person capture *ufiti* agents sent out to cause harm, and it can also prevent a *mfiti* from entering a house or flying over it at night. *Matsenga* can be applied to protect the corpses of deceased relatives from the necrophagous practices of *afiti*, thus turning graveyards and the graves themselves into subjects to protective magic.[43] Very strong forms of *kutsilika* are frequently identified with a notion known as *kukhwima* (see *Chapter IV.1.c*).

This section accentuates the decisive differences between *ufiti* and the notion of *matsenga* – not only in its technical conceptualization, but more especially in its social acceptance. The high degree of approval which *matsenga* practices receive within the cultural context of Southern Malaŵi is easily demonstrated by its complete lack of secrecy. *Matsenga* feats are not only offered publicly by practicing *asing'anga*, they are also displayed openly in a manner of stage magic, meant to both entertain and demonstrate the magic prowess of the *sing'anga* in question.[44]

1(c) The Ambivalent Art: Kukhwima

Studies on Malaŵian concepts of magic usually consent on a dualistic dichotomy between *ufiti* and *matsenga*. However, the results of the research presented here

---

42 According to a Yao *sing'anga*, maize fields are frequently protected in a way that would punish every thief trying to steal from it with *misala*. A Yao *shehe* agrees that a common reason for *misala* would be stealing *zinthu zotsilika* or 'protected things'. In addition, a Mang'anja *mfumu* explains that even a herd of cattle can be protected by *kutsilika* so that everybody stealing animals would be struck with mental disorder in the form of *misala*.

43 In this context, Maxwell Marwick mentions a 'graveyard magician' or *mabisalila* as a separate, specialized profession. These, he argues, are usually former *afiti* who have given up their anti-social ways in order to use their knowledge now for the benefit of society (Marwick 1965: 85).

44 This demonstrative display of protective magic is paralleled by John M. Janzen's accounts from the Kongo Central province of the Democratic Republic of the Congo (Janzen 1978: 160-161).

suggest that this exclusive distinction presents some major shortcomings and does not reflect the actual complexity of traditional concepts of magic. Rather, an additional kind of magic – located in the grey zone between the culturally sanctioned *matsenga* and the collectively banned *ufiti* – does exist, and its recognition is crucially important for the cultural construction of mental disorder in Southern Malaŵi. The independent magic category under scrutiny is distinctive from both *ufiti* and *matsenga* by its relatedness to economic and social success, by its implicit necessity of violating elementary cultural values in the ritual process, by its by-proxy functionality, and numerous other factors. In Chicheŵa, this complex of ideas is subsumed under the term *kukhwima*,[45] and persons under its powerful influence – i.e. *okhwima* (sg. *wokhwima*) – are distinct from the agents of *matsenga* and *ufiti* alike because

> "[...] *asing'anga* produce medicine, *afiti* harm people. *Okhwima* are neither, but they fortify themselves" (Issa Ndasimu, a Yao *sing'anga*).

Principle Notions of Kukhwima

Numerous accounts suggest that most people in Southern Malaŵi have at least basic knowledge about the concept of *kukhwima*. In most general terms, its principles are usually described like this:

> "If one wants to become rich he/she goes to a *sing'anga*. [...] When someone goes there, they reach an agreement on what the person wants, the *sing'anga* provides that and hands it over to the one seeking richness. [...] according to what someone wants, it may make another person *wolumala*, it can even make the latter *wozerezeka*. [He] can take this person's heart [*mtima*] and make it into a charm [*chithumwa*], and the way the victim behaves is the way the *chithumwa* brings in money" (Linga Nasawa, a Yao *sing'anga*).

In order to decipher the cultural meaning encoded in this statement, we have to acknowledge a number of basic notions surrounding the concept of *kukhwima*. Firstly, practices of *kukhwima* magic invariably and necessarily imply the idea of achieving a personal advantage at the cost of some form of compensation. In its core, this required sacrifice represents the violation of elementary cultural values, and its destructive character may be directed against another person as well as against the community and its cosmological order as a whole.[46] Additionally,

---

45 According to the consenting English rendition as given by bilingual Malaŵians, the verb *kukhwima* means 'to fortify' (Lwanda 2005: 265). Sometimes, the concept also appears in the applied grammatical form *kukhwimira*. A more extensive linguistic analysis of *kukhwima* creates a wide semantic field, including meanings such as 'to do charm, do witchcraft' or 'to be of age, be old' and 'to be ripe or mature' but also 'to be stiff, be stern' – or, most directly, 'to strengthen oneself with magic to be prosperous' (Paas 2004: 173).

46 This corresponds with an observation made by Alifeyo Chilivumbo who, with reference to

kukhwima is directly connected to kinship structures so that, while its beneficiary effects – i.e. richness, success, and the like – are clearly universal, the personal sacrifices required for its realization are inevitably directed against members of the own kin group (*chibale*), thus showing some structural similarities with the concept of the anti-social *ufiti*. Typically, *kukhwima* knowledge is in the possession of magic experts – i.e. of *asing'anga* and *afiti* likewise. At the same time, the benefit of *kukhwima* is not exclusively restricted to these experts themselves. Rather, it is a typical trait that specialists offer their *kukhwima* expertise to lay customers, acting as a paid service provider offering exact magic ritual prescriptions (*zizimba*) that have to be followed by the client at all cost. These instructions include acquiring certain materials as well as committing certain acts which, in any case, are of a highly anti-social character.[47] Thus, operating *kukhwima* usually consists of certain activities which have to be conducted by the client – and hopeful benefactor of the resulting effects – while the specialist gives the necessary instructions and contributes additional, more secret rituals which put the client's endeavours into a magic context. While *asing'anga* as well as *afiti* are among the typical holders of *kukhwima* expertise, it is also shared by persons such as village headmen, community elders, or other persons of elevated social status. The respective magic knowledge that is subsumed as *kukhwima* may be obtained from any of these specialists.

The motivation for the use of *kukhwima* is one of its most distinctive, even defining characteristics because it is exclusively applied to serve the immediate egocentric benefit of a given person. On a basic level, *kukhwima* may be used in order to achieve personal protection against threats such as theft, intrusion, physical harm, or magic attacks in the form of *ufiti*. The most frequently mentioned purpose for the use of *kukhwima* is the accumulation of material wealth, being part of a wider logical context of personal success, economic and otherwise. Therefore, intentions leading to *kukhwima* practices may also encompass purposes such as obtaining political power, reaching professional promotion, or achieving spiritual qualification.

Zomba District, states that "Richness in the rural men's cosmos is seen as a social disorder and is associated with kinsmen's death" (Chilivumbo 1976: 78). Such a human victim is usually referred to as *wokhwimiridwa*.

47 The general mechanisms underlying these magic practices have already been alluded to in previous publications even though they have not been investigated in more detail. With regard to Cheŵa concepts of medicine and magic, Maxwell Marwick thus states that "[...] especially potent forms [of medicine] require that the operator should commit incest with, or kill, a near relative" (Marwick 1965: 70). The use of specific forms of magic for the accumulation of wealth has previously been described as a typical trait of *ufiti*. Becoming rich could thus be achieved by killing one's own youngest child – or, alternatively, that of a sibling –, by magically destroying the own reproductive powers, or by having sexual intercourse with a brother or sister (Peltzer 1987: 146).

Protection and Fortification

In a number of ways, *kukhwima* magic can be performed in order to achieve a protective effect, and it goes beyond 'normal' *kutsilika* magic in the sense that it offers much stronger security that can even counteract *ufiti* or a violent assault. The most typical kind of *kukhwima* protection is applied in order to cast *ufiti* attacks back to its origin, causing the desired harmful effect back on the *mfiti*.[48] Furthermore, *kukhwima* protection can also cause mental disorder to malevolent *afiti* in other forms. A Lomwe *sing'anga* explains that over the years, the regular feasts of human flesh as required by a *mfiti* create an increasing danger of assaulting the corpse of a person who is well protected (*wokhwima*) against *ufiti*. Even after death, this protection causes *afiti* to contract mental disorders such as *kuzerezeka* upon desecrating the grave or touching the body because

> "What happens is that a *mfiti* is afraid of *okhwima*. The first thing is that you go to a *sing'anga* to scarify [*kutemera*] the body against dangerous things like these *afiti*. It can happen that this person dies a natural death, and if they [i.e. the *afiti*] want to eat at the graveyard or just approach that corpse, the result of that will be like that [i.e. becoming *wozerezeka*]" (Francis Muramu, a Lomwe *sing'anga*).

Moreover, *kukhwima* practices can also serve to guard a person or personal property. While ordinary *kutsilika* protection is applied for more general purposes, the stronger *kukhwima* magic is typically required to achieve effective protection from *ufiti*.[49] Accordingly, *okhwima* persons may protect their houses to the point that any *mfiti* flying across it comes crashing down. Even in many other respects, *kukhwima* defence can serve as a shield against *ufiti* attacks. But the protective functions of *kukhwima* are not limited to *ufiti* alone – even the magic protection of cattle or roadside shops is sometimes described as *kukhwima*, and in contrast to the protective effects of *kutsilika*, the *kukhwima* security usually leads to more severe magical repercussions against a potential thief.[50] In addition to that, some forms of *kukhwima* are said to create a physical

---

48 This backlash of evil intentions to the *mfiti* is sometimes called *kusavuka* (or 'not revealing'), and it is usually associated with symptoms of mental disorder typical for *kuzerezeka*. Usually, the term *kusavuka* is virtually synonymous not only with a mechanism of magic backlash due to *kukhwima* protection, but it also implies mental disorder as its effect.

49 According to quantitative data as provided by John Lwanda, considerable percentages of Malaŵian students – involved in primary, secondary, and as well in university education – consider *kukhwima* to represent effective *ufiti* protection (Lwanda 2005: 267). This notion is also recognizable in van Breugel's account according to which "The one who has such protective *mankhwala* [against *ufiti*] is a strong man *(munthu wokhwima)* with nothing to fear" (Breugel 2001: 222).

50 Therefore, one account indicates that a herd of thus protected livestock would turn into human warriors armed with *panga* machetes – and that the culprit would find himself in the exact same spot even after hours of trying to run away.

protection due to which the skin of the *wokhwima* becomes impenetrable, thus rendering the respective person invulnerable to knives and gunshots alike.[51]

The concept of *kukhwima* plays a crucial role in the context of the cultural perception of mental disorder and its causation in Southern Malaŵi. While magic protection constitutes one important part of *kukhwima*, another one aims at the acquisition of wealth and success. This second kind of *kukhwima* is closely related to magic death and the causation of mental disorder, both of which occur as removing an integral part of a given victim's personhood (see *Chapter III.1.a*). Technically, this particular kind of *kukhwima* is based on the notion of a magical theft of a victim's personality spirit (or *mzimu wa umunthu*) and its subsequent use for one's own personal benefit. The victim – who, as mentioned above, has to be a member of the same kin-group – may be killed in the process, with the *mzimu wa umulungu* leaving the body (*thupi*) to decompose and returning to the celestial realm. In other cases, the divinity spirit is unaffected by the *kukhwima* attack, stays united with the body and keeps it alive. In both cases, the removal of the victim's personality spirit – providing the central human cognitive functions – leads to a state of severe mental disorder in the person (Steinforth 2005).

The factual use of the stolen spirit of a person is of central interest here. Once a *wokhwima* takes control over the *mzimu wa umunthu* of a person from the same kinship group, he or she can use this *mzimu* in a number of ways to serve his or her personal purposes. Typically, the captured personality spirit is forced to work for the benefit of its *wokhwima* owner. Therefore, a businessman owning a maize-mill would use the personality spirit of a relative to safeguard high engine performance, leaving the invisible, immaterial *mzimu* to pull the driving belt on. If the *wokhwima* works as a freight carrier or a minibus entrepreneur, a captured spirit would be used to ensure good engine performance or high reliability of the vehicles, and a grocery shop owner could use the *mzimu* to act as an invisible marketing manager, impalpably pushing potential customers into the shop when they could have bought next door just as well.[52]

---

51 Allegedly bullet-proof persons can sometimes be found demonstrating their incredible power on rural or urban market places (Lwanda 2005: 266). Some accounts even concede that some forms of *kukhwima* can delay old age or prolong human life beyond its ordinary measure. Due to their strong protection from all sorts of harm, *okhwima* persons are therefore notorious to turn into evil *ziwanda* spirits after their deaths – very much comparable to the post-mortem transformation associated with *afiti* (see *Chapter IV.2.a*).

52 This crucial notion has already been addressed: "in 68 cases (44 adults and 24 children) out of the total of 451 it was alleged that someone had killed a person in order to put him in a maize-mill *(kuika mu chigayo)*. Sometimes there was a slight variant: in a shop *(kuika mu sitolo),* in a lorry *(kuika mu galimoto),* or simply to become rich *(anafuna kulemera)*. The belief that the owner of a maize-mill *(chigayo)* puts a person in the engine of the mill is explained, according to the popular version, in the following way. When a mill is running there is a sort of whining

Kukhwima and Authority

Asing'anga specialized in fighting ufiti – so-called asing'anga ochotsa ufiti – require specific knowledge as well as particular artefacts in order to conduct their professional work. Sapitwa Chagoma – a 23 year-old Lomwe mombole – explains that his own qualifications are related to the fact that, in his youth, he used to be a mfiti himself. Now that he is protected against further afiti attacks, he has dedicated his life to finding and fighting ufiti. The tool most essential for this task is his own mphambanya or ufiti-finding staff,[53] *and it was early in his using'anga career that his instructor told him how to make one:*

> "At that time, there were some instructions [*zizimba*] which he told me to follow so I would have a *mphambanya*. The *zizimba* included killing my own sister, the heart of a rabid dog, bones of a dog and also the tail of a hyena. [...] I killed her and put her into my craft [*muzantchito*], the *mphambanya*" (Sapitwa Chagoma, a Lomwe *sing'anga*).

In order to produce the desired mphambanya, the future mombole needs to kill a relative whose blood is used to oil the staff, and the deceased person's mzimu wa umunthu is transferred into the staff to become its activating agent (chizimba). The functioning of the mphambanya is based on the notion that – once activated – this spirit agent animates the wooden object to seek out persons contaminated with ufiti in its immediate vicinity. Bringing the artefact over from his house, Mr. Chagoma demonstrates its mode of operation.[54] *In order to activate the mphambanya, it is rinsed in a mortar with secret medical plants (mitengo) immersed in water. Then, a chicken is sacrificed by the sing'anga biting off its head and washing the staff with its blood. After that, the mphambanya is rubbed with ufa flour, and some ufa is poured into the staff through its three holes. Finally, the sing'anga starts singing, addressing the staff as 'achemwali anga' (my sister) while applying more ufa flour to its lower end.*

In order to operate the mphambanya, the participation of three voluntary assistants is required. All four persons hold on to the horizontally-aligned staff on pelvis level with one hand, the former bottom of the staff now indicating the front end held by the sing'anga

---

sound which suggests to simple folk that there is somebody inside the mill and in the past people who could not understand that a mill could work all by itself, believed that the owner of the mill had put a person inside it. When I asked the people whether they really believed this, they said »no«, not the person himself but his life-force *(mphamvu)*. The owner of the mill has captured the life-force of that person and turned it into a powerful *mankhwala*. [...] If someone talks about buying a *chigayo,* his own family will be on the alert and will stay away from him for fear that he might kill them or one of their children to use in a *chigayo*. People tell some extremely realistic stories about those who are supposed to be inside the *chigayo*" (Breugel 2001: 226).

53 The Chilomwe term *mphambanya* is equivalent with the Chicheŵa *namlondola* or 'divining stick' (Paas 2004: 313).

54 To an outsider, the *mphambanya* appears as a heavy bamboo stick of about 130 cm length and 7 cm diameter with natural holes on both ends plus an additional hole drilled into its side at mid-length. The top end is decorated with an animal tail – reportedly from a hyena –, and the surface of the staff is richly decorated with fine carvings resembling V-shape lines.

himself. As the staff suddenly jerks forward with force, one participant instantly loses grip of the mphambanya which now leads the remaining persons running across the compound's front yard for some minutes. Arbitrarily approaching present household members, the staff, still held by the sing'anga and his – at least in part – randomly appointed assistants, performs a series of shivering and revolving movements. The mzimu embedded in the staff, as the sing'anga explains later, is eagerly looking for a mfiti but cannot find one – due to this being a 'test run' meant for demonstration only. In order to appease her, the mombole finally sings another song, asking his sister to calm down again, and he also applies more ufa to the mphambanya's front end. The movement of the staff gradually slows down and finally ceases, and the sing'anga instructs his assistants to put the staff flat on the ground.

In addition to the mentioned acts of personal, ruthless ambition as represented in *kukhwima* it shall also be noted that knowledge – and personal use – of *kukhwima* practices are not only associated with *asing'anga* and *afiti*, but also with the elders and the powerful. *Kukhwima* is frequently described as representing the strength and authority of the elders as well as of traditional leaders such as village headmen, *agrupu*, or *mafumu*. As a Yao trader says,

> "A person who has no *kukhwima* protection is helpless like a baby [*ngati mwana*]" (David Kwela, a Yao businessman).

In a rural setting, most people tend to agree that many old persons know about some *kukhwima* rituals and that the initiation rituals performed for the installation of a new village headman – or, for that matter, a *grupu* or *mfumu* – will include him or her receiving some knowledge about applying *kukhwima*. In most cases, this expertise is said to focus on protection, providing a future office bearer with means for self-defence against potential *ufiti* assaults. Magic resilience to withstand and fight back all sorts of attacks is therefore considered a necessary disposition of a fully grown, mature person. In a more modern context, notions of *kukhwima* are frequently regarded as the secret behind the authority and power of political leaders, with magic 'fortification' facilitating their survival in the brutal competition of national politics and reaching their personal objectives. In many accounts, it is suspected that such politicians have acquired some considerable *kukhwima* expertise (Lwanda 2005: 22-23).[55]

---

55 Therefore, the former bodyguard of a Malaŵian politician points out the bitter need for *kukhwima* protection within national politics due to the unfortunate prevalence of *ufiti* throughout the country. For his own professional career, he explains, *kukhwima* protection was regarded a prerequisite. A local politician likewise recollects the last parliamentary elections during which – in order to secure his election as an MP for his constituency – he made contact with a local *sing'anga* who assured him that every constituent in the given polling station would end up making their mark behind his name on the ballot – if he followed the necessary instructions. Before the *sing'anga* presented his *zizimba* prescriptions, however, the local politician declined, being unable to raise the requested pay of 100 US$ – and also due to fear of

The use of *kukhwima* magic, however, is not limited to achieving political power and/or personal protection, but certain spiritual qualifications can also imply the idea that *kukhwima* support is required in order to obtain them. As exemplified above, a *sing'anga* wanting to create a certain magic artefact which empowers him to detect *afiti* is forced to follow certain *zizimba* instructions which clearly follow the pattern of *kukhwima* logic – and which include magic murder and the enslavement of a close relative's personality spirit. Numerous accounts indicate that the creation of an artefact that is crucial for the fight against anti-social forces itself strictly corresponds with the model of *kukhwima* magic – i.e. implying the breach of elementary social norms for the purpose of providing a secular object with its spiritual, socially validated properties.[56] Paradoxically, this suggests the conclusion that, according to cultural conceptions in Southern Malaŵi, social order has to be violated in order to be protected and perpetuated – or, in other words,

> "You have to use *ufiti* in order to fight *ufiti*" (Gerard Mdindire, a Mang'anja farmer).

Kukhwima Presctiptions

As has been pointed out already, an actual *kukhwima* expert is not necessarily the person benefiting from its magic effects. Rather, it is typical for *kukhwima* magic that a lay person addresses a renowned specialist for magic help in order to attain a defined personal goal – e.g. becoming rich. The specialist then provides the customer with the necessary magic prescriptions (*zizimba*) consisting of material components as well as ritual actions which have to be followed closely in order to achieve the desired effect. It is important to note that clients addressing a *kukhwima* expert do not know about the instructions they will receive for achieving their personal ambition, neither do they have the liberty to refuse adhering to these prescriptions once they have been specified (see below). At the

---

being forced to take magic action against his own kinsfolk.

56 It may be argued that this principle of banishing a spirit agent into an object in order to create a powerful tool applied in a culturally sanctioned context is not limited to the creation of the *ufiti*-finding staff. My research data strongly suggests that the general notion of the functioning of a *maula* device (see *Chapter II.2.a*) closely resembles that of the *mphambanya* or *ufiti*-finding stick. Thus, the *nsupa* may be interpreted as the container for an ancestral spirit (*mizimu wa makolo*) which then imparts its secret information onto its owner, a relative of the spirit agent. This corresponds with the high amount of care and appreciation a *sing'anga* displays when working with his/her *maula* as well as the frequent description of the fabrication of a *maula* is a dangerous, secretive, rare, and extremely important procedure. Elsewhere, John Lwanda hints at the former resident Hastings K. Banda's habit of carrying a *sing'anga*'s flywhisk (*litchowa*). Because "merely to carry this tail is usually sufficient to ensure protection from wizardry" (Sanderson 1955), the flywhisk was interpreted as a symbol for the president's eminent *kukhwima* protection (Lwanda 2008: 31).

same time, it has been mentioned that the instructions connected to *kukhwima* practices are explicitly anti-social in nature. As a Yao *mfumu* states,

> "When people want to become *okhwima*, they are told to kill their mother or their child. This is why you hear that a sudden death always comes from relatives [*achibale*] and not from just any person. If it was just anyone it would not be possible because they are not from one blood [*si magazi imodzi*]" (Usanene Kwela, a Yao *mfumu*).

This example illustrates again that *kukhwima* logic follows the *ufiti* model of being limited to the kin group – and that magic homicide is among the most typical actions that are connected to following *kukhwima* prescriptions.[57] Many other accounts, however, emphasize that *kukhwima* instructions may require the client to perform certain magic rituals to a child of the same kin-group (*chibale*) which cause that child to develop severe mental disorder – in the forms of *kuzungulira mutu*, *misala*, or *kuzerezeka*. Sometimes described as the alternative to killing a family member, the causation of mental disorder is part of the requirements that are given as *kukhwima* instructions – and therefore not negotiable.[58] In addition to causing mental disorder or sudden death to a given victim, the notion of incestuous sexual relationships is also very prominent in the context of *kukhwima* prescriptions. In most cases, it is concluded that a male client is instructed to have sexual intercourse with a close relative such as his mother or sister.

The notion of *kukhwima* is intrinsically related to the idea that declining to follow *kukhwima* instructions – as well as an involuntary failure in their observation – immediately triggers a magic backlash which is typically described as causing mental disorder in the respective client.

During a discussion with some members of a Christian charity organization, they recollect the case history of a former colleague recently affected by mental disorder. Lazarus Gwaza, an 18 year-old Mang'anja orphan from rural Zomba District, receives

---

57 These prescriptions may resemble *ufiti* applications such as *hamala* (see *Chapter IV.1.a*) – as expressed by a Lomwe healer stating that "Sometimes we tell a person to sleep with his mother or his sister, or that he should take a hammer [*hamala*] and hit a child like his own one, so that it will fall down" (Sapitwa Chagoma, a Lomwe *sing'anga*).

58 According to one *sing'anga*, "If one is born with a sickness such as *kuzungulira mutu*, it is a sickness coming from the relatives. If the parents of the child want to be *okhwima*, they go to a *sing'anga* to get the medicine so that they should use *kukhwimira* against their child for their business, and then, this child can have *kuzungulira mutu*. […] In the case of this *kukhwima*, some people may even manage to kill that child so they become rich. Things like that can even break up a family, like when the mother does not want them to kill her child so they become *okhwima*" (Manueli Matundwe, a Sena *sing'anga*). Likewise, it has been mentioned that clients may be asked to render their own reproductive organs useless as a sacrifice – but even here, no personal choice can be made.

support by the organization which pays for his driving school education so that he can take up a career as a professional driver. His course proceeds well, but as he receives a larger amount for his final exam, Lazarus fails to pass the test. It takes some negotiations before the organization agrees to cover his examination fees for a second and last attempt. Before taking this final chance to achieve his professional goal, Lazarus Gwaza tells a friend that he knows a way of making perfectly sure he will succeed this time. Contacting a renowned sing'anga in his area, he asks for magic support for his driving test. Payment is agreed, the sing'anga performs the initial rituals, and provides Lazarus with the necessary instructions (zizimba) which have to be followed at all cost. Only now he realizes that the procedures require activating agents of human nature, meaning that Lazarus Gwaza is supposed to kill a member of his own family in order to obtain the respective body parts. Unable to comply for the sake of a driving test, Lazarus refuses to adhere to the zizimba in spite of all the preparations made.

By the next day, Lazarus develops severe headaches (mutu) and feels compelled to stay at home. He starts talking incoherently and is heard praying to Satan, wishing death to his own family and neighbours, and involuntarily revealing his secret agreement with the local sing'anga. Medical treatment from a number of other asing'anga and later from a nearby hospital initially show some calming effect, but his condition always relapses and his state of mental confusion progresses. Prayer sessions – held by colleagues from the Christian charity organization in order to remove Satanic influences and re-establish divine protection – fail to take effect.[59] *As Lazarus Gwaza starts getting violent and the situation in the community becomes unbearable, the Christian organization provides money for transport and the patient is admitted to Zomba Mental Hospital. Being diagnosed with cerebral malaria, he is immediately admitted and remains in the institution indefinitely – while his former colleagues and his rural home community agree that the condition was caused by his failed attempts to secure his driving exams.*

Sometimes referred to by the term of *kuyaluka*, incidences of magic backlash usually manifest themselves in different forms of mental disorder.[60] It is crucial to note here that the breach of secret *kukhwima* instructions leads to mental damage on the side of the beneficiary, i.e. the lay client. Once a customer fails to keep the instructions received from the magic specialist, he or she is therefore subjected to a magic attack. As a Yao healer puts it,

> "[...] there is another cause of *misala* which comes because of traditional medicine, that the person wants to become rich and does not follow instructions given by the *sing'anga*. Then that person can go *misala*" (Vincent Chitete, a Yao *sing'anga*).

---

59 Some members of this Christian prayer group explain the lacking efficiency of their prayers by their discovery that, while they were praying over him every day, Lazarus' mother took him to other, non-Christian *sing'anga* at night, thus removing him again from the power and mercy of God that their prayers meant to invoke.

60 Thus, "Acquired *njirinjiri* while you are grown up can happen: the person wants to become *wokhwima* and he/she fails to follow the procedures" (Manueli Matundwe, a Sena *sing'anga*).

The most frequently mentioned situation causing this magic backlash effect on persons trying to follow *kukhwima* prescriptions is their inability to arrange the required incestuous relationship.[61] In the case of sudden mental disorder in a person formerly known to be either successful and/or very ambitious, emic explanations frequently relate to a failed attempt to conduct *kukhwima* magic.[62] The notion of failed *kukhwima* magic as a reason for mental disorder is a common concept throughout the ethnic groups of Southern Malaŵi, and a considerable number of people indicate personal knowledge of some reported cases from their respective communities. While these magic repercussions (*kuyaluka*) are reported to occur *quasi* universally – i.e. whenever *kukhwima* instructions are broken –, it is important to note that they are not conceived as inherent. Numerous accounts indicate, on the contrary, that this magic backlash is considered as an additional, deliberate machination and a form of counter insurance for the *kukhwima* expert. Accordingly,

> "Some people go mad [*kupenga*] when they want to become *okhwima*. In that case, it can happen that they are told to sleep with their mother or their sister. Therefore, if the mother or that sister refuses, the person might go *misala*. The reason is the medicine that they had drunk before" (Usanene Kwela, a Yao *mfumu*).[63]

A *sing'anga* or other expert is therefore assumed to include a certain form of *kuyaluka* magic into the preparatory steps of a *kukhwima* ritual – which may, as mentioned above, be administered in the form of a drink – without the knowledge of the customer. Specialists are said to do so as a magic precaution in order to prevent future accusations for incitement of anti-social magic. Due to this form of *kuyaluka*, though, their *kukhwima* customers would either fulfill their ostracized ritual instructions – thus sharing a joint guilt with the *sing'anga* – or be silenced by it, thus safeguarding they can never give away the specialist's identity.

---

61 It has been explained earlier that common notions of *kukhwima* rituals require the sexual contact between siblings or parent and child. The refusal of the respective relative – usually the sister or mother in the typical case of a male agent – to conduct incestuous intercourse therefore represents a typical scenario.

62 According to a Yao *mzamba*, "There was a certain person working as a clerk at the post office who had a Toyota Corolla car. When he went to the *sing'anga* he was told that if he slept with his own mother or his sister he would become rich. Unfortunately, this mother and sister did not agree with that, and so they refused. So this person went mental [*anapenga*]. […] He died with this *misala*" (Gift Makata, a Yao *mzamba*).

63 This formulation may be misleading as the Chicheŵa idiom *kumwera mankhwala* – "to drink medicine" – is applied not only for ingesting therapeutic liquids but for the internal use of medicine in a more general sense.

Prevalence of Kukhwima

In the light of the fact that the term does not find appropriate consideration in anthropological literature so far, the idea of *kukhwima* is reiterated by an impressively large number of accounts in the context of the causation of mental disorder in Southern Malaŵi.[64] Most accounts express the firm belief that persons use *kukhwima* to cause mental disorder to a family relative as a means to 'become rich' at the same time, and the idea that mental disorder may be caused by an individual not following *kukhwima* instructions is equally well-reported. In most of these accounts, the explanatory model of *kukhwima* is applied for particularly severe cases of mental disorder such as *kuzerezeka*, and especially in case of apparently in-born mental disorders, *kukhwima* is seen as the most likely reason. In rural as well as urban settings, the concept of *kukhwima* coins the understanding of mental disorder. Therefore, accounts frequently reiterate stories in which the economic success of nationally well-known businessmen and/or political figures is explained as being related to the mental disorder of a family member who are used as *kukhwima* sacrifice. In this line of argument, the relative success of one person and the mental peculiarity of one of that same person's relatives are interconnected to produce strong emic proof for the existence and importance of *kukhwima*.

When trying to locate *kukhwima* in distinction from the two main concepts of magic recognized in Malaŵi, their respective definitions have to be taken into consideration once again. As demonstrated above, older sources address notions of *kukhwima* as forms of *ufiti*, and these two categories do share some characteristics. *Kukhwima* resembles *ufiti* due to its strongly egoistic and anti-social nature that, among others, is expressed by its socially destructive limitation on the own kinship group. Its activities are designed entirely for the benefit of the individual and do not serve the common good of society. At the same time, *kukhwima* not only shares some characteristics with *ufiti*, but also with *matsenga* magic, considering its protective functions which are virtually indistinguishable from *kutsilika* – despite the fact that *kukhwima* is much more powerful because it requires a personal sacrifice. Moreover, *asing'anga* are usually the agents who provide the secret knowledge for the respective rituals, thus making it a service publicly available.

In contrast to these similarities, the idea of *kukhwima* also implies a number of notions which are distinct from other Malaŵian concepts of magic. As a central characteristic of *kukhwima* magic, the specialized knowledge about it is considered as shared property of some groups of persons, these usually being

[64] As John Lwanda demonstrates, between 55 and 67 percent of the Malaŵian university students interviewed replied to be aware of *kukhwima* practices (Lwanda 2005: 190).

asing'anga as well as *afiti* and other persons in socially elevated positions such as elders and traditional authorities. This condition must be regarded as a highly significant issue: while *afiti* may be detected against their will and *asing'anga* practice their art in public, the group of *kukhwima* specialists is much less easily defined. No cultural concept of proof exists for the use of *kukhwima* in the same way as for *ufiti*. In addition, the *kukhwima* expert may be distinct from the beneficiary applying it – making it even more difficult to trace the actual culprit and, likening *kukhwima* to a kind of *ufiti* by proxy. *Ufiti* and *using'anga* are both related to spiritual initiation whereas *kukhwima* can be practiced and learned independently. While *kukhwima* does not require the consumption of human flesh, it may still imply the use of body parts or the spirit of a blood relation (*mbale*). Its rituals are intrinsically related to the violation of fundamental cultural values – such as murder, incestuous sexual relations, or the theft of the human spirit –, but it does not bear the same social stigma of *ufiti* contamination. The fact that the concept of *kukhwima* is frequently associated with *ufiti* correlates with the observation that the term *ufiti* is not as clear-cut as would be comfortable. Some people in Southern Malaŵi tend to initially describe different concept of magic as *ufiti* – only to concede that this represents a very wide interpretation of *ufiti* as a phenomenological category upon closer inquiry. After all, the obvious conceptual differences between the two notions are fully recognized – including the fact that *kukhwima* is not connected to the consumption of human flesh, that its powers are not related to physical transformation, and that it does not correspond with a magically traceable and medically treatable contamination. So while it is a common concept to associate *kukhwima* with *ufiti* in a wider context, it is still considered distinctive – so that, in essence, it may be agreed that

> "*Kukhwima* is not the real *ufiti* [*ufiti weni-weni*], but it is part of *ufiti*" (Dennis Chemwali, a Lomwe merchant).[65]

In spite of the fact that *kukhwima* knowledge is usually acquired from *asing'anga*, the practices associated with it have a highly negative connotation due to the fact that they are only used for personal purposes such as protecting

65 From an emic perspective, this diffuse connection is explained as follows: "But there is *ufiti*, and it comes in two groups: there are some who have just used *kukhwima* on themselves but who do not eat humans, and then there are others who have gone further so that they do eat human meat. [...] Better are the others who protect themselves so that their place cannot be crossed by *afiti* as well as by thieves" (Usanene Kwela, a Yao *mfumu*). Other Yao accounts agree that *kukhwima* knowledge is only vaguely related to *ufiti* because, while some *afiti* may have expertise in this field, not all of them necessarily do. If the rituals for becoming rich were generally known to every *mfiti*, it is argued, they would all be very wealthy persons – which does not correspond with the generally non-status specific character of *ufiti* (see *Chapter IV.1.a*).

property or achieving power. *Kukhwima* is feared and considered as asocial – but is, at the same time, regarded as a prerequisite for any kind of personal authority, thus representing the harsh, dangerous side of elevated social positions. Engaging in these magical services is ostracized but not sanctioned.[66] It expresses a whole complex of cultural conditions such as a general suspicion towards personal ambition, an ambivalent perception of individual success and innovation.[67]

2. Spiritual Intervention

Apart from magic reasons – in which a human being acts as an initiator by ways of his or her personal secret powers –, spiritual causes also constitute a common model in the explanation of mental disorder in Southern Malaŵi. The manifold activities of spiritual agents provide a wide range of logic contexts which lead to the different variations of mental disorder as defined above. Regardless of religious denomination, the various entities of the spiritual realm are an integral part of cultural life, and they may be categorized on a number of hierarchical levels. While the importance of the Supreme Being has already been outlined, it is crucial to understand that this concept is, in the vast majority of cases, connected to some degree of syncretistic melange. As a core element of traditional religious thought, the belief in ancestral as well as independent spirits still permeates all the religious and ethnic factions of Malaŵian society, generating different kinds of religious syncretism.

The basic mechanism underlying the notion of spiritual intervention causing mental disorder assumes that of a spiritual agent – i.e. an immaterial, ethereal entity transcending the realm of the living – exercising its influence on a human person. This influence is always active and deliberate, but it may be permanent or temporary, complete as well as partial, and it can be conceived as either detrimental or beneficial. In the cultural context of Southern Malaŵi, the notion of mental disorder being caused by spirit agents may be equalized with phenomena of spirit possession or *kugwidwa mizimu* (see below). Spirit attacks affecting the mental health of a person are therefore related to the spirits' harmful presence within the human sufferer, thus causing states of confusion or,

66 Accordingly, a vast majority of Malaŵian students interviewed by John Lwanda declare that they would never think of using *kukhwima* – even though a large percentage believes in its efficiency (Lwanda 2005: 268).

67 This appraisal is shared by Johann van Breugel who expresses that "However, there surely exists a real preoccupation with the idea that a person who wants to become rich will stop at nothing and is ready even to kill in order to achieve his purpose" (Breugel 2001: 227).

in more severe cases, the loss of personal control over the body and its functions – all of which fall under the category of mental disorder.

Contextualizing Spirit Possession

Ethnic groups of Southern Malaŵi invariably attribute some cases of mental disorder to the influence of spirit agents. In a number of cases, the presentations of disorders caused by spirit influence comply with classical definitions of spirit possession.[68] This term corresponds fairly well with Chicheŵa notions where the phenomenon is usually referred to as *kugwidwa mizimu* – literally 'to be caught or trapped by *mizimu* spirits' or 'be possessed' (Paas 2004: 130; Chakanza 1998: 102). Spirit possession or *kugwidwa mizimu* may be loosely defined as an altered state of consciousness which, on an emic level, is experienced by the person as a loss of control over the body due to the dominance of a spirit agent.[69] The mental disorder caused by the control the spirit agent exercises over the affected person can be *(a)* latent as well as acute, *(b)* partial as well as total, and *(c)* temporary as well as perpetual conditions, and it can express itself in various degrees of deviant behaviour. According to Joseph Chakanza,

> "Spirit possession, then, is a cultural term which gives expression to the belief that a person who displays certain behaviour has been taken possession by an invisible being or power" (Chakanza 1998: 102).

In Malaŵi, cases of spirit possession are frequently referred to by names such as *majini*, *madzoka*, *vimbuza*, or *malombo*.[70] What requires clarification here is the question of how to classify these forms of spirit possession in analytic terms. In a local context, the above-mentioned categories are applied in a very broad way, alternatively depicting cultural phenomena such as *(a)* a mental health disorder category, *(b)* the spirit agent causing it, *(c)* its ritual remedy, or *(d)* the cult group performing it. While this clearly emphasizes the complex, pluralistic character of these categories as 'holistic' or total cultural phenomena, it also exemplifies the

---

68 An instructive survey of studies on spirit possession is provided by Janice Boddy (Boddy 1994: 407-434).

69 Therefore, "Spirit possession is always described as the spirit »entering the body« of a person. [...] The action of the spirit is expressed by the verb *–gwira* which has the general meaning of »to seize, catch, hold«. [...] From the viewpoint of the patient, possession in the strict sense is expressed by the verb *–gwa* (lit.: to fall). »When the patient 'falls' (*atagwa*), the spirit enters the body«" (Schoffeleers 1997: 116).

70 In Southern Malaŵi, many accounts consider these various spirit possession complexes as identical, defining their sole differences in terms of regional – i.e. ethnic – variations of an otherwise uniform concept. In these regional/ethnic terms, the *vimbuza*, e.g., is associated with the Ngoni and Tumbuka of the Northern Region while the *malombo* is allocated to the Cheŵa of the Central and Mang'anja and Sena of the Southern Region. The *majini* is connected to the Yao and Nyanja while *madzoka* is traced back to the Sena (Chakanza 1998: 102; Peltzer 1987: 165).

difficulties in distinguishing basic biomedical categories such as nosology, aetiology, therapy, and therapeutic organizations on the basis of local systems of classification. While some authors subsume the above terms as more or less distinct forms of 'spirit illness' – thus defining them as categories of nosological classification (Peltzer 1987) –, this interpretation may be somewhat misleading. Even though the manifest effects that spirit possession has on a given person follow culturally defined patterns, they do not seem to obtain the categorical acuteness of a nosological system. Rather,

> "The name of the 'disease' or 'affliction' is the same as the intruding spirit which is spoken of as either holding (*mizimu ikamugwira*, the spirit holds you) or as entering the 'head' of a person, and thus there is a close association between mental ailments and spirit illness" (Morris 1996: 120).

The symptoms attributed to a given form of spirit possession lack specificity and, crucially, their classical presentations are widely represented within the depictions of other mental disorder categories as well, thus only reiterating a basic, classical understanding of mental disorders under the condition of being caused by spirits. On the basis of own research results, however, none of the abovementioned spirit possession terms will be presented as a mental disorder category in its own right. Rather, most accounts agree that the respective terms – i.e. *majini*, *madzoka*, *vimbuza*, *malombo*, etc. – are associated with *kugwidwa mizimu* (or 'spirit possession') which, in turn, may lead to a condition of mental disorder that is usually addressed as *misala ya mizimu* – i.e. a spirit-induced case of *misala*.[71] A Yao person, e.g., may thus have an idea of the clinical picture indicated by someone 'having *majini*' (*ali ndi majini*) – but the pre-defined cultural knowledge connected to this condition derives from its acknowledged reason, i.e. spirit agents of the *majini* category.[72]

While recognizing the cultural complexity of concepts such as *majini*, *vimbuza*, *malombo* and *madzoka*, there is great necessity to classify these phenomena into clearer analytical categories. In doing so, *majini* will be regarded as a category of spirits while *vimbuza*, *malombo*, or *madzoka* will be understood primarily as therapeutic rituals.[73]

---

71 The motivations for a spirit agent to cause such a condition follow different mechanisms will be explained at greater length later (see *Chapter IV.2*).

72 Therefore, the category *majini* might imply a rough range of possible manifestations related to it, but it would not form a distinct picture generating a nosological category. Accordingly, statements such as "a person with *kuzungulira mutu* usually has *majini*" support this argument by disclosing *kuzungulira mutu* as a nosological and *majini* as its causative, aetiological category. Likewise, a traditional Muslim practitioner argues that "*Majini* can cause *misala*, invoking spirits which confuse the patient's mind" while a Yao group village headman defines *majini* as "whatever comes from the ancestors".

73 Field data – including linguistic evidence – suggests that, strictly speaking, the term *majini*

2(a) Categorization of Spirit Agents

For a general understanding of the different processes associated with the role of spiritual agents in the causation of mental disorder in Southern Malaŵi, it is essential to provide an overview of the different categories of entities that are relevant in this context. After all, the kind of spirit agent responsible for a given case of mental disorder makes a crucial difference to the perception and treatment of the incidence as such.[74] Within the scope of this study, the notion of spirits shall include not only the different kinds of entities associated with the deceased ancestors or with natural phenomena, but the Supreme Beings of the different ethnic groups and religious contexts – be they identified in Muslim, Christian, or more local terms – will also be incorporated in this category. The most generally applied term designating a spirit entity in Chicheŵa language is *mzimu*, and while its use appears unspecific at times, this category should be understood as a superordinate concept incorporating a number of implicit specifications of more or less clearly distinguishable kinds of *mizimu*. A very general – but not always consistent – distinction can be made between two dichotomous categories of spirits, differentiating those who are perceived as primarily helpful from those rather harmful by nature.

> "These ones are evil spirits [*mizimu yoipa*], and once they attack a person they make him/her stay *wozerezeka* or *womisala* and to walk around aimlessly. But there are other spirits which are good ones, and if they seize a person they want this person to live knowing about *mitengo* remedies" (Joyce Chaba, a Yao *mzamba*).

In itself, the category *mzimu* substantiates an immediate connection to the personal spirit (or *mzimu wa umunthu*) as an integral part of the human person (see *Chapter III.1.a*). It is, after all, this same spiritual force which, upon the physical death of a person, transforms into an ancestral spirit – or *mzimu wa makolo*. As intermediaries between the living and the Supreme Being, the *mizimu ya makolo* represent both messengers and the executive authority of divine will. Being affiliated to a specific cognatic kinship group (*chibale*), the ancestral spirits are the focus of rich ritual activity. Prayers (*mapemphero*), periodic sacrificial offerings (*nsembe*) and other acts of veneration endeavour to

---

denotes a category of spirits whose intrusion into a human person can lead to mental disorder. The term *malombo* is primarily applied with reference to a therapeutic ritual in the form of a drum and dance ceremony while *madzoka*, on the other hand, is explained as denoting either a dance ritual or a mental disorder. Likewise, *vimbuza* is used to refer to both a therapeutic ceremony and a sickness category.

74 Accordingly, "Sicknesses of the spirits [*matenda a mizimu*] are different – some are from *majini*, some are from an angel [*mngelo*]" (Mose Chingale, a Lomwe *sing'anga*).

perpetuate and/or re-establish good relationships with the ancestral spirits or gain their support when invoking divine intervention (see *Chapter II.1.b*). Places of ancestor worship are usually around the graveyard (*manda*),[75] and the *mizimu ya makolo* are known to contact their living descendants in dreams. If provoked, the wrath of the *mizimu ya makolo* can result in all kinds of misfortune including collective punishments with famine and drought as well as individual penalization with all kinds of health problems including mental disorders – although the *mizimu ya makolo* are not expected to cause lasting damage to a person's mental disposition. In part, the ancestral spirits are seen as delivering punishment to their offspring on their own accord while acting according to divine command in other cases – due to their mediating function.[76]

While Christian oriented *asing'anga* frequently reject the term *mizimu ya makolo* as a non-Christian category, they may receive comparable spiritual support from so-called prophetic spirits (or *mizimu ya mneneri*), fulfilling very similar functions. Therefore,

> "[…] these spirits of the ancestors might just lead you astray, but if you stay with your own spirit from God, you can get registered that you will be a doctor" (Mose Chingale, a Lomwe *sing'anga*).

Mizimu ya mneneri tend to represent Biblical figures such as apostles or saints, and they serve as divine inspiration facilitating *using'anga* work. When acting as familiar spirits of a *sing'anga*, the more traditionally defined *mizimu ya makolo* may also be referred to as *mizimu ya mbwebwe* (or 'spirits of divination') in their role of providing spiritual schooling and diagnostic/therapeutic inspiration for a given traditional healer.[77] In most accounts, the category of *mizimu yabwino* – i.e. 'good spirits' – is applied as a superordinate concept for all of the aforementioned *mizimu* who display a generally benevolent attitude towards the living.[78] Within the context of cosmopolitan religion in Southern Malaŵi,

---

75 The heavily forested groves around community graveyards constitute the symbolic borderland between the social domain and the wilderness dominated by the spirits. Cutting down trees or even pick up loose branches around the graves is frequently prohibited "because the spirits need some shelter".

76 In current Malaŵian discourse, these notions seem to blur easily in the face of the religious dogma that no *mzimu* could activity cause harm to a person unless approved by divine will. Thus, it is difficult to differentiate between the direct and active 'will of God' and the passive lack of divine protection – both leading to the same unwelcome results.

77 Understandably, the acceptance of this notion depends on the cosmological eye of the beholder. From a strictly Pentecostal point of view, these *mizimu ya mbwembwe* have therefore been identified as satanic servants which are regarded as by far worse than the *mizimu ya makolo*.

78 Especially with reference to the traditions of the *nyau* secret society, the *mizimu ya makolo* are also connected to the wilderness and the wild spirits (*zirombo*) inhabiting it (Morris 1995: 302). Therefore, they may be conceptualized in the shape of certain animals or even trees. In their identification with the *zirombo* and the bush land, the *mizimu ya makolo* are then considered as

however, the term *mzimu wabwino* is even incorporated as synonymous with the 'angels' or *malaika* and *angelo* in a Muslim or Christian framework, respectively, and in Christian scripture, the divine spirit is also referred to as *Mzimu Woyera* or Holy Spirit (Paas 1004: 311).

As the second main category of spirits, the *ziwanda* constitute a different notion of spirit altogether. Frequently described as a sub-category of *mzimu*, the personality spirits (*mizimu ya umunthu*) of particularly evil human beings – more especially of *afiti* – are said to turn into *ziwanda* after death, lingering on in order to bother the living.[79] According to Johann van Breugel,

> "*Ziwanda* are spirits of e.g. deceased witches or murderers who are refused entrance into the world of the spirits. They cannot be placated by offerings and the only defence against them is that of magic rites and medicines *(mankhwala)*. Those spirits are feared because they are unpredictable. When they are displeased they can send illnesses and other misfortunes" (Breugel 2001: 75).

The highly volatile and generally unforgiving nature of the *ziwanda* defines them as antagonistic to the *mizimu ya makolo*, and some sources even qualify their human origin. Therefore, *ziwanda* may also be conceived as independent spiritual entities – of equally malevolent and dangerous disposition – associated with the bush and wilderness.[80] As a common example, the 'mountain spirits' dwelling in the more remote ranges of the country are usually referred to as *ziwanda*, and they are frequently mentioned as causing health disorder to living persons.[81] Especially severe cases of mental disorder are likely to be attributed to *ziwanda* rather than *mizimu ya makolo* due to the formers' plainly destructive attitude towards the human body and mind.[82]

While *ziwanda* may thus alternatively be referred to as evil spirits (*mizimu yoipa*) within a local religious context, persons from both Muslim and Christian backgrounds frequently interpret the term as relating to demonic forces, or

---

the ultimate source of human fertility and vital energy (Morris 1998: 213-214).

79 More precisely, this fate awaits "witches *(mfiti),* murderers, those who rob people who are poor, and those who commit incest: they are excluded and will remain *ziwanda (mfiti, ochita chigololo, kuba, kupha, sadzalandilidwa)*" (Breugel 2001: 79). Accordingly, some accounts describe *ziwanda* as *mizimu ya ufiti* (Morris 2000: 250).

80 According to Matthew Schoffeleers, these "unrelated spirits are thought to be responsible for certain mental disorders in women and, more exceptionally, in men" (Schoffeleers 1968a: 442).

81 Many mountain ranges in Southern Malaŵi – including Zomba Plateau or Mount Mulanje – are reportedly inhabited by *ziwanda*, known to abduct careless travelers or drive them insane out of sheer malice because feeling offended by their intrusion. These spiritual representations of the dangerous wilderness may also originate from the above-mentioned notion of *ziwanda*.

82 Some dictionaries translate *chiwanda* as "a madness, supposed to come upon those who have murdered or slain in battle their fellow-men; they suppose that to disembowel the slain prevents this retributive madness" (Moxley 2001) or as "the madness or spirit which is supposed to come over a man when he has committed murder, or has slain anyone" (Zambezi Mission [eds.] 1972).

"*ziwanda* coming from Satan". Thus, some Malaŵian Pentecostal churches emphasize that mental disorder is mostly caused by attacks of demonic *ziwanda*.[83] In analogy with the relationship between God and His divine hosts, the evil spirits (*mizimu yoipa*) thus associated with the causation of misfortune are said to act on direct satanic orders.[84]

Linguistically derived from the Arabic term *jinnī*, the *majini* as represented in the Qur'ān imply a strong conceptual connection to Islam, the term *majini* is most commonly associated with the predominantly Muslim Yao. While the concept of *majini* spirits may be regarded as identical with the *mizimu ya makolo* or ancestral spirits in most instances, some accounts disagree with this equation. Two general lines of interpretation may therefore be distinguished. Among persons with a higher level of Qur'ān education, *majini* are depicted as clearly distinct from ancestral spirits, being conceived as a category of immortal spirits directly created by God which has been in existence ever since time immemorial.[85] As an original part of divine creation, *majini* may be of different dispositions.

> "In Islam, we have two different kinds of *majini* – the good ones and the bad ones. The good *majini* are associated with Satan [sic], and the bad *majini* are associated with witchcraft. The *majini* that are associated with Satan come about with many types of diseases" (Lazim Khananji, a Yao Muslim organization representative).

In contrast to this definition, the larger part of the accounts – representing the bulk of lay Muslim believers, but also non-Muslims with partial knowledge of the concept – generally tend to identify the *majini* with the ancestral spirits (*mizimu ya makolo*). In accordance with the latter, the *majini* are also said to avoid causing serious damage to the persons they possess. Rather, their attitude is to cause temporary mental disorder in a given victim as an act of spiritual reclamation (see *Chapter IV.2.d*) – i.e. in order to add weight to the demands on their living descendants.

This general outline of the different notions of spirit agents as recognized in Southern Malaŵi should not deceive the fact that additional categories exist.

---

83 In this context, the extreme and potentially dangerous condition of *misala* patients is described as being caused by a number of demons possessing a given person at the same time. In contrast to that, the more phlegmatic disposition of a *kuzerezeka* patient is explained by him or her being possessed by just one demon, indicating a less severe case.

84 A Catholic Priest thus explains: "I do not believe that there is witchcraft, but I know that there are evil spirits. [...] I think they are bad angels. I am sure that Satan is playing a role in many people's lives, and these are his messengers. Not that they are spirits of the deceased who have come back to trouble people, no" (Evans Cholo, a Lomwe Catholic Missionary).

85 More precisely, the Qur'ān describes the *jinn* as being created before mankind. In sūra 15: 26-27, it is stated that "Verily We created man of potter's clay of black mud altered, / And the jinn did We create aforetime of essential fire" (Pickthall 1930).

Many local terms specify spirit entities according to their affiliation to a given ritual – leading to notions of so-called *mizimu ya vimbuza* or *mizimu ya malombo* who are addressed in *vimbuza* or *malombo* dance rituals, respectively.[86] The exact identification of viable spirit categories, however, remains disputable. Overall, spirit entities can be conceptualized as 'good' or 'evil' in generalized terms – keeping in mind that the actions of a 'good' *mzimu wabwino* may, nonetheless, have harsh effects on an affected person. In many accounts, 'good' spirits act on behalf of the Supreme Being, and the following chapter will address this involvement in the causation of mental disorder.

2(b) Divine Retaliation

The religious makeup of Southern Malaŵi provides a number of different sets of cosmological hierarchy, all of which consist of religious entities attributed with greater and lesser power. Many accounts relate cases of mental disorder to the direct interaction with these powerful spiritual forces, and the central mechanism recognized in this context is that different spirit agents are assumed to cause mental disorder as a punishment for some form of moral transgression. As a basic principle, divine retaliation therefore presupposes some hidden justification and moral legitimacy of the condition caused. Cosmological structure as such is represented by the Supreme Being as well as by the spirit entities subordinate in the given spirit hierarchy, and it therefore manifests itself on different levels. Within a Christian framework, the Ten Commandments may be considered as cosmological norms of high authority, and local behavioural norms or *miyambo* constitute structurally comparable representations of cosmological order in a more traditional Malaŵian context. Transgressions against these sets of norms may be considered to result in direct punitive measures as taken by the respective spiritual powers.[87]

The question whether or not the Supreme Being – regardless of its incorporation in a mainly Muslim, Christian, or more traditionally defined context – may be inclined to impose direct punishment against a human trespasser with religious doctrine is a highly controversial issue and of particular

[86] As one example, a Sena *mfumu* explains that *madzoka* spirits can be described as *mizimu yongoponda* – or 'spirits who are just dancing'. Similarly, a Lomwe *sing'anga* explains that the *mizimu ya vimbuza* from the Northern Region and the *mizimu ya malombo* in the Nsanje District of Southern Malaŵi can equally be described as *mizimu ya ng'oma* or 'spirits of the drum', thereby defining their specific character only according to the therapeutic rituals needed as a cure against the disorder caused by them.

[87] Therefore, if the *mwambo* prohibiting the ridicule of persons with mental disorder is violated, "God wants to show them that laughing about those who are *opunduka* is not good so they stop that, and also that they should be a lesson to their friends" (Olive Pilimiti, a Nyanja *mzamba*).

interest to the overall result of this study. Linguistically, Chicheŵa expressions used in the context of divine punishment are frequently ambiguous, leaving it open to contextualization and interpretation whether they actually indicate divine retaliation or reasons of cosmological structure (see *Chapter IV.3*).[88] Numerous accounts severely reject the notion of divine punishment as a potential reason for mental disorder. Especially Christian-educated members of the Malaŵian population tend to dismiss any punitive concept of God, reasoning that

> "It is not true that God punishes people [*amamulanga*] in order to make them *misala* [*pomupengetsa*] or to make them *opunduka* because there are many people who are sinful, but even those who do not believe are still well. When things were like this that many of our friends on earth are *opunduka*, many people read the Bible but have no faith. Therefore *kupunduka* is not a punishment from God [*chilango chochokera kwa Mulungu*]" (Mose Chingale, a Lomwe *sing'anga*).

Due to the indiscriminate occurrence of mental disorder, structural explanations (see *Chapter IV.3*) are therefore favoured over divine ones. But in spite of the strong rejection which the notion of divine punishment receives in a more theological discourse, a broad majority of the accounts recognize the Supreme Being as an immediate and deliberate originator of mental disorder, agreeing with its punitive character.[89]

> "Why does God give a fine person the gift of being *wozerezeka*? You can be an alright person, but if you have messed it up with God somewhere, if you offend Him, He can give you *kuzerezeka* so that you repent. You have offended me, so I will give you *kuzerezeka* so you know the pain – because *kuzerezeka* does not just come to a person without any reason" (Doris Petroyo, a Lomwe *sing'anga*).

In spite of the fact that the *mizimu ya makolo* are commonly associated with the upkeep of traditional moral norms (*miyambo*), some accounts nonetheless indicate that divine intervention may also ensue if the culturally validated rights of a person with mental disorders are threatened.[90] Differing religious

---

88 Thus, expressions such as *chifuniro cha Mulungu* (meaning the 'wish/will of God') or *mphatso yochokera kwa Mulungu* (i.e. a 'gift coming from God') are commonly used to denote the divine causation of mental disorder. When clarifying the exact definition of *mphatso ya Mulungu*, it may, at the same time, yet be negotiable whether the condition is perceived as a punishment (*chilango*), as a person being punished (*kulangidwa*) by the Supreme Being – or not.

89 Some Christian groups concede that unfortunate incidences may be caused by a person's immoral behaviour because "[...] sometimes, you can get punished a bit in this world. Then, if you don't repent, you go for eternal punishment" (Andrew Chisadza, a Lomwe Pentecostal priest). According to Paul Kapapa, the Ngoni of Dedza District (Central Region) tend to regard persons with mental disorders (i.e. *wamisala*) as justly punished for their own or their ancestors' evil deeds against God (Kapapa 1977: 60).

90 As a Sena *mfumu* underlines, sexual abuse of a woman suffering from mental disorder could lead to the rapist developing that same kind of mental disorder as well – due to a direct punishment

orientations, however, imply modified codes of behavioural norms (*miyambo*) and distinct notions of moral transgression: a given action – e.g. the consumption of alcohol – may be considered inoffensive in one cosmological framework – e.g. a Catholic community – but be interpreted as a legitimate reason for divine retribution in most other Christian or Muslim contexts. In a Muslim framework, some accounts suggest that *ashehe* – obliged to excel in their meticulous adherence to religious behavioural norms – may be punished with mental disorder if disobeying their obligations to God.[91] Accordingly, the notion of divine punishment represents a common explanatory model for mental disorder which is neither limited to a given religious discourse nor a specific ethnic group, but which is supported by accounts from across the Southern Region.[92] On numerous instances, this concept overlaps with other notions of mental disorder causation, but its overall recognition is clearly suggested.

In addition to these cases of very direct divine penalization, some concepts of divine retaliation also imply more subtle ways of avenging human transgressions against cosmological order. A number of primarily Sena accounts thus allude to a model of indiscriminate divine punishment according to which a random person may be struck with mental disorder as a sheer demonstration of divine power.[93] At the same time, some accounts recognize the notion of the Supreme Being actively delaying or preventing the recovery of a person suffering from mental disorder. This condition is explained in didactic terms – as God wishing the respective person to learn a lesson from his or her respective health problem.[94]

---

from God.

91 In contrast to that, persons with a higher degree of Qur'ān education disclose that God could never be held responsible for punishing a person with health problems, but that punishment expects evildoers after death.

92 A Yao *shehe* from Zomba District and a Sena Christian *sing'anga* from Nsanje District thus agree that many cases of mental disorder are God's punishment for an offence committed by the family, and that newborn children are usually victims to this retribution. A Yao healer adds that such penalty also acts as a warning to the community not to ridicule God's creation. Accoording to another account, though, mental disorder usually affects "persons who like to laugh or maybe mock others. God can give *kupunduka* to them as well so they see what it is like. [...] God wants to show them that laughing about those who are *opunduka* is not good, so they better stop that – and also that they should be a lesson to their friends" (Olive Pilimiti, a Nyanja *mzamba*).

93 Explaining the birth of children with mental disorders, a *sing'anga* states that "On close examination it is not a special punishment [*chilango chapadera*] but it is just for other good people to take the lesson that God [*Mulungu*] exists in this world. [...] Their thoughts are so that they think that if this would befall me I would manage to be in the same problem that troubles this friend of mine" (Lexon Kondwani, a Sena *sing'anga*). Accordingly, "God Himself is supreme, and He creates whatever He wants so that we know that He is really there".

94 Moreover, divine retaliation is even conceived to exceed individual punishment in case of collective transgression. Therefore, a whole community violating divine law can invoke drought and famine as a conceivable means of communal retribution by the Supreme Being, and the birth

Different notions of the Supreme Being coexisting throughout Malaŵi seem to be relevant for the prevalence of punitive models of God. As a tendency, the concept of divine punishment is severely contested among Muslim specialists while the theology of the influential Pentecostal churches clearly argues in its favour. The Christian mainstream, on the other hand, also tends to reject this concept – but here, the notion of a direct and deliberate punishment by God is frequently substituted with the somewhat related idea of deprivation of divine protection.[95] The various discourses led at the same time argue on both sides – as well as in the 'grey zone' in between – of the conflicting concepts of active divine retribution versus imperturbable grace. However, the model of divine punishment causing mental disorder is referred to with some frequency, and the representatives of organizations for person with disabilities express their concern about the social stigmatization that goes along with this notion. Thus,

> "Where they say it's a curse, in some cases the family is stigmatized. So they don't want to help the family because everyone believes they must have done something wrong and that God is punishing them and they will not want to assist them. So you will have a mother or a father with a child with a disability who is not getting the support that they need to get because there is nobody who wants to assist them" (Steven Msowoya, a Tumbuka disability organization representative).[96]

In many instances, the abovementioned notion of neglect by the Supreme Being directly relates to the activities of 'evil', malevolent spiritual entities. Therefore, the actions of Satan (or Shayṭān) as well as the evil forces associated with him are also part of the wider discourse of divine retaliation. Reflecting the doctrine of divine omnipotence – meaning that "these things are happening because God permitted them to happen" –, the effects of demonic aggression are closely related to the notion of divine punishment.

---

of a child with mental disorders may therefore also be a warning directed at the village community as a whole.

95 A Lomwe priest explains this difficult distinction, saying that "God can leave people – go suffering! – for what they have done. Sometimes God wants people to pay the price. [...] all sufferings are just warning tones that a man should turn back to God" (Andrew Chisadza, a Lomwe Pentecostal priest). Therefore, a satanic attack may cause sickness – as a test of the strength of that person's faith.

96 Therefore, "you find other people hiding persons with disabilities in their houses – because to them, having a disabled child or relative is a curse from God – and you wouldn't really like to show it to the public or get the public to know. That's why for some of our programs we use volunteers who come from within the area of the village because those ones know better where to find the child or a person with a disability" (Peter Ngomwa, a Sena disability organization representative).

2(c) Demonic Aggression

In Southern Malaŵi, different spiritual forces are considered as 'evil' or, more specifically, as aggressively misanthropic. Their explicitly destructive actions – either more traditionally defined notions of *ziwanda* as well as the different shades of evil spirits surrounding the demonic forces as recognized by cosmopolitan religion – represent another main model for the causation of mental disorder. Being regarded as an expression of pure evil, aggressions of these agents are most frequently associated with the demonic forces connected to the ultimate evil in Muslim and Christian tradition – i.e. S͟hayṭān or Satan.

A number of accounts in Southern Malaŵi – particularly among the strongly Christian parts of the population – identify the devil as the causative factor for all human suffering, and particularly of mental disorder. On some occasions, the notion of a satanic attack leading to mental disorder is explicitly preferred to the idea of divine involvement because

> "[…] saying that this is a gift from God is just blaspheming the Lord! But we say it is just part of the devil's power. […] I do believe in that because God cannot give some harm to you, but it is just part of Satan's power. Therefore we do trust that through the name of Jesus, everything can work out well" (Gerard Mdindire, a Mang'anja farmer).[97]

In the Muslim discourse, there is wide agreement that, while the influence of S͟hayṭān is considerable, a personal attack against a person would be an unusual event; nonetheless, he represents the ruler of the evil powers seducing man to defy the laws of God. Some Pentecostal Churches associate the concept of satanic actions with *ufiti*, defining the latter as "part of the satanic deeds" while other indications at least concede to both systems being closely related. Accordingly, the two categories are conceived as potentially interconnected. The notion of satanic attack fills in the gaps created by the incompatibilities between religious tradition and Christian or – more rarely – Muslim dogma. In most cases, it replaces the otherwise common notion of divine punishment by introducing Satan as the evil, powerful counterpart to take over punitive responsibility from the Supreme Being.

> "Here you should just know why Satan also is a part of God because sometimes God permits evil things to happen. Most times God keeps his people protected, but if God sees the deeds of Satan he can turn to Satan so that he should do what

---

97 In accordance with this notion, a traditional birth attendant explains the threat of satanic influence to her everyday professional work, stating that "I usually know if there are some among us here who belong to Satan [*amusatana*]. Even if I cannot see this person I manage to be very accurate about this, and then I always send them [i.e. the pregnant women] away from here because I fear that this might cause me some misfortune" (Joyce Chawa, a Yao *mzamba*).

he wants. […] God creates man, therefore it is easy to punish him. But sometimes God punishes a person through Satan" (Sapitwa Chagoma, a Lomwe *sing'anga*).

During a discussion with Amanda Ndala, a Lomwe sing'anga, she shares the case history of a former patient suffering from misala. This patient, a young woman by the name of Duwa Sande, comes from a neighbouring rural community where she still lives. After successfully finishing her secondary school education in Chikwawa District, Duwa suddenly develops tormenting headaches, and she develops an almost irresistible urge to attack random persons and burn the houses of neighbours – which she voices in violent shouting fits. With this quasi textbook presentation of misala, the community apprehends the girl before she can cause serious havoc and send her to Chikwawa District Hospital. As staff there recognizes Duwa's obviously mental condition, they transfer her to Zomba Mental Hospital. She is admitted and, after a number of weeks, starts to recover. Being discharged after a total of three months, she is happy to return to her home community in Chikwawa District – but her condition relapses, and she is again admitted to Zomba Mental Hospital, now for a longer period.

Upon her return after almost a year, her relatives decide to consult Amanda Ndala in order to ensure that Duwa's condition does not worsen again. Maula diagnosis reveals that Duwa Sande is possessed by ziwanda spirits, and the sing'anga deduces that the woman is tormented exclusively for the sake of causing trouble in the community. The sing'anga contacts her ancestral spirits (mizimu) who prescribe appropriate medication to accompany an exorcism (mainly mankhwala a kusamba), and finally, the ziwanda are expelled. After the prescribed treatment, the patient recovers and reportedly has been fine ever since.

Below the level of immediate satanic activity, different categories of spirits are renowned for attacking persons out of pure malice and causing mental disorders as well as other health problems without any cultural legitimacy. In the majority of cases, this unlawful spiritual punishment is related to the overlapping categories of 'evil spirits' (*mizimu yoipa*) and/or *ziwanda*. The distinctive factor for such spiritual activities lies in their general motivation. *Ziwanda* spirits – in contrast to *mizimu ya makolo* – are conceptualized as focussing entirely on harming persons by delivering possibly lasting damage – which frequently comes in the form of mental disorder. Thus, a young child suffering from mental disorder may be defined as a victim of the *ziwanda* due to the assumption that it is too small to offend a spiritual agent.[98] As other spirit entities, the *ziwanda* are said to take possession (*kugwira mzimu*) of a human victim in the course of their attack, and their effects are seen to be more destructive than those of the ancestral spirits, and accordingly, more severe cases of mental disorder are attributed to *ziwanda* attacks. In a Muslim as well as a Christian discourse,

---

98 In analogy to Satan taking action against a person deprived of divine protection, it is also stated that the *mizimu ya makolo* can leave a human trespasser to be punished by the *ziwanda*.

different kinds of mental disorder may be explained by the presence of evil spirits – which are interpreted as *jinnī* belonging to the *'ifrīt* class or demons in the respective discourse. Therefore, numerous accounts describe mental disorder – especially states such as *misala* – in terms of demonic possession.

In the form of *ziwanda*, generally malevolent spirit entities are a fixed category in traditional cosmology. In the context of Islam and Christianity, the respective discourses provide additional spirit categories that are conceived as largely comparable with the traditional *mizimu yoipa*. The present section suggests that evil forces causing mental disorder to a person may be, on some level, connected to notions of the Supreme Being who permits evil influences to attack the human person. The various spirit agents in question here, at the same time, have an equally close conceptual connection to the actions of other spirits – such as the *mizimu ya makolo*.

2(d) Spiritual Reclamation

Not only in the cultural conception of mental disorder, but also in a much wider context of religious tradition in Southern Malaŵi, the concept of spiritual reclamation is of central importance. It encompasses the attacks of spirit entities for the sake of provoking a particular action or behavioural change on the side of the person. Therefore, while spiritual reclamation may still be considered a form of punishment imposed on a person, it already implies an embedded solution for this spiritual conflict: it represents a measure of reform, a deeply didactic act claiming the observation of behavioural guidelines – e.g. *miyambo* – in the form of a painful lesson. Accordingly, the concept of spiritual reclamation is *a priori* associated with a high degree of cultural legitimacy, and even though the *mizimu ya makolo* retain some of their human characteristics and thus still display some individual preferences, their superior status within cosmology usually justifies their demands.

> "For example, there are some people who become mentally disturbed because the *mizimu* want them to work in healing, and some are attacked by their *mizimu ya makolo* because they want them to change their behaviour, or else, to return to the church of their ancestors [*tchalichi kwa makolo ake*]" (Mose Chingale, a Lomwe *sing'anga*).

A large category of spirit attacks may be considered as didactically motivated, aiming to induce a behavioural change in a person due to causing mental disorder. All in all, this category is strongly in agreement to a concept which Victor W. Turner described as *rituals* or *cults of affliction* (Turner 1968: 1-24). As in Turner's Ndembu study, forgotten and/or neglected ancestor spirits express their discontent by causing disorders – including but not limited to reproductive and mental disorders (Turner 1975: 37). In our Malawian context, different mechanisms can be distinguished. The differentiation between immediate divine intervention and the activity of spirit agents – delivering punishment on behalf of and in agreement with the Supreme Being – is, in some cases, difficult. Therefore, it is not unusual to learn that

> "[...] the *mizimu* punish someone – but also God, who is the owner of this punishment. This is because the *mizimu* were created by God who is their proprietor" (Manueli Matundwe, a Sena *sing'anga*).[99]

As a general tendency, the violation of socially validated norms which are closely related to cultural tradition rather than to religious doctrine – including a particular exegesis of Qur'ān or Bible – are more likely to fall under the direct responsibility of the *mizimu ya makolo*. Their function as as preservers of tradition becomes apparent, referring back to the strong normative character of behavioural rules or *miyambo* (see *Chapter II.1.a*).[100] The *mizimu ya makolo* are the spiritual force responsible for punishing persons for their *mwambo* violations in order to maintain culturally validated forms of social behaviour. It is widely agreed that the ancestral spirits may retaliate upon a person for violating the cultural norms protecting the rights and dignity of a person with mental disorders.[101] In turn, *mzimu* punishment for culturally unacceptable behaviour is frequently handed out in the form of mental disorder.[102] Here, a direct connection between spirit activity and the concept of *mdulo* becomes apparent, and I will argue that *mdulo* contamination bears the characteristics of *mwambo* violation – indicating that the *mizimu ya makolo* can be identified as the actual agents causing the respective health disorder.[103] The wrath of the ancestral spirits,

---

99 This notion seems to be particularly prevalent among the Sena of Nsanje District. A Sena *mfumu* therefore declares that the *mizimu* belong to God who uses them as their executive power in order to punish person if necessary.

100 Previous studies have already suggested that, in Malaŵi, severe cases of mental disorder may be ascribed to the violation of cultural norms (Peltzer 1987: 58; Kapapa 1980: 207).

101 According to oral traditions from Chitipa District in Northern Malaŵi, laughing at a lame person is assumed to lead to bearing lame children oneself (Malanga 1971: No. 83). Some accounts, though, interpret this mechanism not on the basis of *mizimu* punishment, but in terms of magic powers on the side of the person with the respective disorder. According to this line of thinking, "children are also told not to stare for a long time, fearing that they [*opunduka* persons] could use *ufiti* against them so that they look the same" (Josephine Maboma, a Lomwe *mzamba*).

102 Therefore, a Yao husband quarrelling in the community during his wife's pregnancy may anger the ancestral spirits who may therefore harm his unborn child. According to a Mang'anja *mfumu*, failure to comply with sexual prohibitions surrounding birth and pregnancy is likewise avenged by mental disorder as caused by the ancestral spirits. Reports from the Northern Region of Malaŵi similarly indicate that a marriage between siblings or cousins is said to lead to the birth of crippled children due to the spirits' disapproval (Malanga 1971: No. 57).

103 Therefore, *mdulo* contamination is a common assumption if the development of a newborn child

however, is not always a matter that is settled by imposing a penalty on a given trespasser. Rather, a family failing to ritually resolve the reasons for their punishment and subsequently re-establish a positive relationship with the *mizimu* faces the threat of repeated spirit retaliation. The persistent stigma of 'bad luck' (*tsoka* or *chilengo*) due to a disrupted relation to the ancestor spirits can lead to the social stigmatization of a kinship group – and a general reluctance of intermarriage for fear of contracting an equally ill fate.

Retribution for Spirit Neglect

As another potential background for an attack by a *mzimu*, it is reported that persons can be punished by their deceased ancestors for not submitting to their personal needs – such as concerning their worship and the offering of sacrifices. While this constitutes a spirit punishment comparable to the cases mentioned above, it also represents a special case which justifies a distinction. Like the aforesaid *mwambo* guardianship, the concept of spirit neglect is based on the fact that the *mizimu ya makolo* require and deserve periodical donations of sacrifices (*nsembe*) and ritual attention. Unlike the former, spirit neglect always implies that a whole group of persons – i.e. the collective descendants of the deceased – fail to provide their late ancestor with the services he/she demands. Such offerings are selected according to the specific demands of a given *mzimu wa makolo*. In order to enforce that their personal expectations are met, ancestral spirits are known to attack a – frequently infant – member of the respective kin-group by causing mental disorder because the *mizimu*

> "[…] know that when a child is suffering, those having the biggest problems are the parents. Therefore they understand that by making them *opepera* they will receive a sacrifice. Sometimes the *mizimu* punish a person when they are asking for something but do not get it, so they just want that person to deliver" (Sapitwa Chagoma, a Lomwe *sing'anga*).

Ancestral spirits are reputed to use the vulnerable position of infants – and the importance of their wellbeing to the family – as leverage to support their claims.[104] In many such cases, the *mizimu*'s need for sacrificial libations is

---

does not proceed as normally expected – concluding that the husband committed adultery during pregnancy. In such a case, reconciliation with the *mizimu* is mentioned as the only way to save the child's life.

104 Therefore, "if you don't appease ancestral spirits then you are bound to get a mishap in one way or another. […] So people say if you don't do that, then the spirit of the dead person will be very unhappy […] and if you are unlucky, it is because of the ancestral spirit which is angry with you. That's what they believe. So it can be believed as well that there are disabilities in the community because the ancestral spirits are angry for one reason or another" (Peter Ngomwa, a Sena disability organization representative).

considered to motivate their actions, and in some accounts, they are even reported to first announce their concerns by appearing in their descendants' dreams – and only causing mental disorder in case of continued non-observance. Accordingly,

> "Most times when *mizimu* come to persons in their dreams they ask for food. So if people do not deliver that, they come and hit a person" (Sapitwa Chagoma, a Lomwe *sing'anga*).

The mechanism of spirit retribution for neglect also represents the classical model for mental disorders as related to *majini* – which is closely associated with the celebration of the Yao memorial ritual or *sadaka*. Accordingly, it is conceded that *majini* spirits may attack arbitrary members of their respective kin-group in order to show their demand for a *sadaka* ceremony – which has either been omitted entirely or did not meet the spirit agent's expectations. It is a central characteristic of *majini* activity that a human victim serves as the organ of a spirit agent – although it may still take considerable *using'anga* expertise to decipher the message hidden within the actions of the affected person. As the condition is intended to be temporary and resolvable in a peaceful and consensual way, the *majini* are not expected to inflict any serious damage to a victim's mental disposition, and due to the straightforward logic reason for such cases of mental disorder, the elementary therapeutic measures to cure such complaints are predefined as providing the desired services to the *mizimu*.

Penalizing Intrusion

While the majority of ancestral spirits – apart, to a limited extent, from their respective graveyards (*manda*) – have no personal sanctum that is perceived as their original domain, other spirit agents however do. It is distinctive for each of these powerful, so-called territorial spirits (see *Chapter IV.2.a*) to be associated with a certain geographic area that represents their residence and realm of power. Due to the close connection between these spirit agents and a given territory, persons trespassing through the area may therefore be obliged to observe specific behavioural rules (*miyambo*) in order to show their respect for the mighty spirit inhabiting the place. If these norms are disregarded, the penalty imposed on the person by a territorial spirit is frequently conceived in terms of mental disorder.[105] In addition, other spirit agents who are beyond human veneration

---

105 When approaching the secret shrine of Mbona in the hills of Nsanje District, visitors are required to follow numerous behavioural norms clustered around the worship of this important territorial spirit. Consequently, every uninvited passer-by desecrating the shrine premises would be attacked by *mizimu* guarding the place, and even invited guests have to make careful ritual preparations to appease Mbona – e.g. by wearing black clothes and rubber boots to pay homage

may also be ascribed to similar realms, thus making human intrusion dangerous and laden with ritual precautions. It is frequently reported that so-called 'mountain spirits' (i.e. *ziwanda*) haunting, e.g., the slopes of Mount Mulanje in Mulanje District expect travelers to obey particular codes of behaviour or face dire consequences.[106] Although the notion of spirit agents causing mental disorder as a reaction to the violation of their quintessential territory may arguably be regarded as a special form of *mwambo* guardianship, it still displays distinctive characteristics.

Spiritual Vocation

While some cases of more or less intentional spiritual punishment have been mentioned, the spiritual vocation for taking up the profession of a traditional healer (*sing'anga*) is a model that requires consideration. In itself, the concept of spiritual vocation represents an utterly constructive achievement of central cultural value – while its first manifestation, however, still comes in the form of mental disorder. In such a case, persons suffering from mental disorder are unable to recognize spiritual vocation as a reason, and even local diagnosis (e.g. *maula*) may not easily distinguish this special form of mental disorder from other possible reasons. The ideal career of a Malaŵian *sing'anga* begins with nocturnal visitations of an ancestor, entering the dreams of a future apprentice in order to impart the first *using'anga* lessons, and these night time encounters are referred to as *kulotetsedwa* or 'to be made to dream'. Before this consented teacher-student relationship is established, however, the *mzimu* usually expresses its plans for the successor elect by evoking different kinds of health disorder which, in many cases, take the form of mental disorder.[107]

---

to the spirit in its function as rainmaker. Otherwise his punishment is reported to manifest itself in *misala* or, less commonly, in *kuzerezeka* or *kulumala*. For in-depth research on the cult of Mbona in Southern Malaŵi see Schoffeleers 1979; ibid. 1966. Chingwe's Hole, a certain cave on the Western edge of Zomba plateau in Zomba District also has the reputation of being guarded by countless spirits. The supposedly bottomless pit is said to be haunted by both *mizimu ya makolo* and *ziwanda* spirits. Especially at night, the place is rescribed as a dangerous destination for careless visitors because its spirits are known to penalize inappropriate human behaviour by causing *misala* or *kuzungulira mutu*.

106 These spirits are said to show their favour by leaving plates of food – e.g. ripe fruit or *nsima* – by the side of the path for a chosen visitor to enjoy. Mentioning these gifts in front of other persons or sharing it with them, however, violates an implicit code of secrecy demanded by the spirits. Their reported retribution may inflict states of *misala* or *kuzungulira mutu*. The dangers thus associated with the higher reaches of Mount Mulanje are expressed by the name of its topmost summit – called *Sapitwa* or 'Don't go there.'

107 According to a Lomwe *sing'anga*, "I failed to eat, and my stomach was swollen as well. […] I had gone to hospital but it was not successful. I also went to this spirit doctor [*dokotala wa mizimu*]. When he examined me, he found out that it was the spirits who possessed me [*itandigwira*] and he gave me medicine so I got better" (Mose Chingale, a Lomwe *sing'anga*).

> "I was suffering from *misala*. [...] I went to a *sing'anga*. [...] I was given that one [medicine] for steaming the head, [...] one for drinking and another one for skin scarifications. [...] It took one week, but because the sickness came from the *mizimu*, the exact time cannot be spelled out. [...] when I was cured, the spirits came in and started telling me *mitengo* for medication. [...] But before the spirits come in, *misala* comes first. Then the spirits protected me, healed me, and started teaching me medicine" (Joseph Kamwendo, a Yao *sing'anga*).[108]

In many incidents, the state of mental disorder caused in an unknowing *using'anga* student is classified as *misala*, but less commonly, the condition may also manifest itself as *kuzungulira mutu* or *khunyu*. A person may be rendered *misala* for as long as it takes him – or his close kin – to understand the vocation the *mizimu* have chosen, and numerous accounts mention a person suffering for many years before the cause of their condition is correctly diagnosed and the spirits' demands can finally be met.[109] Once this is accomplished, the chosen apprentice receives *using'anga* training in the form of nocturnal, spiritual tuition, learning the diagnostic and therapeutic techniques of their trade in dreams (*kulotetsedwa*). This form of qualification represents the norm among *asing'anga* throughout Southern Malaŵi,[110] and a Sena healer reckons that

---

This initiation sickness may assume the classical form of symbolic death, as described by a Yao healer: "Most traditional healers start working as *asing'anga* through sickness. When he/she falls sick and dies, he/she meets the spirits [*mizimu*], and instead of being taken away [i.e. to the spirit realm], the *mizimu* send him/her back and teach him/her medicine, to go and heal people" (Linga Nasawa, a Yao *sing'anga*).

108 Similar accounts exist from throughout Southern Malaŵi. A Sena *sing'anga* narrates: "My father possessed me at the time after his death so that I was suffering for a long time. When this sickness troubled me, I had problems like *mbavi*, but I also had *kuzungulira mutu*. I tried very hard going to different *asing'anga*. It was much later when I heard that it is the spirit of my own father who was seizing me. They told me that I have to make a sacrifice [*kuthira nsembe*] to recover, and once I did that I got better" (Manueli Matundwe, a Sena *sing'anga*). A Christian healer recollects that, when suffering from *misala*, she experienced dream visitations by three Europeans (*azungu*) advising her to read the Bible and use its power for curing the sick. As soon as she complied with the demands of these *azungu* saints, her *misala* abated, and she acquired the qualifications of a *sing'anga a mizimu*.

109 Thus, a Lomwe *sing'anga* spiritually connected to Christian saints reminisces that "The *using'anga* came through sickness. I was sick from 1969 up to 1999. In 1991, the *mizimu* came out. Then, more *mizimu* came out including that of Saint Peter, so then I started working as a *sing'anga*. [...] This Saint Peter, through the word of God, comes in a dream while one is sleeping, and the *mzimu* comes and touches you and tells you that you should be doing this-and-this with these types of *mitengo*. From there you become sick because of that *mzimu*, and then you fall down and start speaking in different tongues. [...] I was suffering from headache [*mutu*]. When I have the headache, then the whole body gets a shock and starts shaking the way a dove does, shaking violently, and the *mzimu* comes and I start talking. [...] After Peter came Joshua, Theresa, and Luke, speaking in languages like Afrikaans, French, Chichewa, and Arabic" (Doris Petroyo, a Lomwe *sing'anga*).

110 More precisely, a *sing'anga* trained by the *mizimu* is regarded as far more powerful than a mere herbalist (a *sing'anga a mitengo* or *sing'anga a masamba*) who only learns from a human

> "Three quarters of the herbalists [*maherbalisti*] know their medicine through the spirits [*mizimu*]. They start being sick, then they start fainting. Later on they are told some medicines by the *mizimu*. With these medicines, when prescribed to a person without mistakes, the patient is cured. Thus most herbalists get their medicines through spirits. Even in parts like Zomba, Jali, or Govala, there are these types of herbalists, and they are mainly women" (Lexon Kondwani, a Sena *sing'anga*).

Throughout their career, *asing'anga* maintain a close relationship with their spiritual teacher, and it is not uncommon for them to work with more than one *mzimu* adviser at a time.[111] In the context of spiritual vocation, mental disorder therefore represents a prerequisite for the establishment of a close personal bond between a spirit master and its human student – and as the basis for the spiritual qualification and legitimacy of local healers in Southern Malaŵi. Essentially, the concept of spiritual reclamation as a reason for mental disorder is a very classical model. It encompasses the entire complex of spirit possession – which corresponds reasonably well with emic concepts of a *mzimu* capturing, holding, seizing, or attacking a person (*kugwidwa mizimu*). In the cases listed here, a person suffering from mental disorder is identified as guilty for his or her own condition in some way – this being, at best, ignorance of important culturally validated behavioural norms (*miyambo*) as imposed by a higher cosmological authority.

3. Structural Causation

In previous works of medical anthropology, one of the main categories of health disorder causation is usually described as 'natural' reasons – a term that, however, bears some problematic implications. In social anthropology, 'nature' is a notoriously difficult category to apply to any non-Western cultural context, and with immediate relevance for the framework of this study, Brian Morris accordingly argues that "there is no concept of 'nature' as such" (Morris 1996: 107) recognized in Malaŵi. A notion of 'natural' reasons hence proves hard to

teacher. Purely spirit-trained *asing'anga* (or *asing'anga a mizimu*) proudly disclose that they received no formal training whatsoever – apart from the spirits coming at night.

111 Typically, these different spirits develop their personal fields of medical expertise. Hence, "The first *mzimu* works for bigger problems. For example, when I'm asleep during the night, I dream of him telling me that the next day a patient will come with such-such problems and the sickness came because of this-this, from such-such a cause, and the medication you can use for that sickness is of this-this type. Then there is another *mzimu* which tells me about bad people. Say, there is a certain person [i.e. a *mfiti*] who is troubling another, so the *mzimu* tells me about the trouble-maker, that this evil person is doing this-this" (Vincent Chitete, a Yao *sing'anga*).

define – due to the fact that no Malaŵian concept exists and the Western concept of 'nature' does not play into it at all. In the framework of this study, the direct use of categories such as 'natural' or 'supernatural' will thus be avoided.[112]

As a substitute, this study offers the category of structural causation. This notion alludes to the dichotomy of structure and agency that has, among others, been addressed in the work of Pierre Bourdieu (Bourdieu 1977).[113] In a fairly liberal application of this model, structural causation of mental disorder shall be defined as a process that is ingrained in the structure of the human being and the cosmos, as an impersonal, *a priori* mechanism comparable to structural conditions such as 'man must die' or 'day follows night.' Structural reasons represent a part of cosmological order that does not require the active supervision of personalized spiritual forces but *quasi*-automatically connects certain causes with respective effects because 'this is the way things are.'[114] In spite of its deeply cosmological character, the structural causation of mental disorder may hence be distinguished from the decisive will of the Supreme Being due to the fact that the condition is caused *not* due to the situational decision of God *but* due to cause-and-effect mechanisms that are embedded in the divine composition of the material world as such. In short: structural causation can be attested if no embodied personal or spiritual actors but structural processes are discerned as responsible for the case of mental disorder in question.[115] Within the framework

---

112 This is further encouraged by the assessment of Mary Douglas who declares that "Even a small amount of reading in anthropology shows how very local and peculiar to our own civilization is the distinction between natural and supernatural" (Douglas 1985: 66).

113 As the core dichotomy of ontological sociology, this opposition has been introduced in reaction to deterministic models that define culture according to static, quasi self-evident structures. In contrast to this, agency represents freedom of choice and independent action, scope of interpretation, creative capacity, or modifying potential as found in persons shaping cultural reality. It should not be regarded as a strict analytic category, but as an interpretative tool that helps to distinguish different levels of cultural processes. The wider theoretical question on the relation between *general* and *particular* manifestations of culture refers back to the German physician-anthropologist Adolf Bastian (1826–1905 AD), introducing the distinction between 'elementary ideas' (*Elementargedanken*) and 'folk ideas' (*Völkergedanken*) as universal versus culture-specific expressions of human thought (Bastian 1881). His conception, moreover, was anteceded by the English philosopher John Locke (1632–1704 AD) and his notion of 'original' versus 'primary qualities' of man (Fiedermutz-Laun 1970: 77-88).

114 In Chicheŵa terms, this notion of structural causation is frequently described as 'things just happening' (*zimangochitika*) (see *Chapter IV.3*).

115 At the same time, this model of structural reasons therefore argues that all other categories qualify as agency-related – in terms of discernible embodied actors taking voluntary action. In this liberal application of the theoretic model and limited to the categorization of causative factors, agency cannot be identified as a force counteracting structure, but partially contributing to the maintainance of structure as such. In this line of thought, the cosmological order – including the human being, ancestral spirits, or cultural notions of magic – may be interpreted as structure while the actions of the person or spirit agents, magic and otherwise, indicate factors of agency.

of research, this concept admittedly represents the least prominent model of explanation. The notion of the structural causation of health disorders in general is more frequently referred to in cases of simple and easily cured ailments – such as headaches, colds, or sore throats – for which no medical specialist would be consulted, no specialized therapeutic steps taken, and no particular reason sought (Morris 1996: 106-107; Chilivumo 1976: 69-70).[116] With the idea of structural reasons representing the closest resemblance to biomedical models of aetiology – infection, accident, and the like –, local representations nonetheless feature specific and significantly different characteristics.

Competing cosmological systems in Southern Malaŵi share the assumption of a primordial, direct act of creation as performed by a Supreme Being, thus acknowledging an immediate connection between cosmological structure and divine will. The notion of cosmological structure being responsible for mental disorder is, at the same time, complex and difficult to define – as it represents, for a start, a terminological conundrum. Chicheŵa language provides different idioms to describe structural causation of mental disorder, with the term *chibadwa* indicating a birthmark, something natural, inborn, or hereditary, and *chilengedwe* meaning creation, environment, or nature (Paas 2004: 36; 49).[117] Other, frequently used expressions such as *chifuniro cha Mulungu* or *mphatso ya Mulungu* – i.e. the 'will of' or 'gift from God' – may equivocally denote concepts of punishment and creation at the same time.

At first sight, a distinction between two categories that are not clearly differentiated in emic terminology may appear artificial – and, in part, rightly so. Many accounts presumably referring to notions of structural causation cannot be positively distinguished from concepts of divine punishment. Nonetheless, the discrimination between the two models – i.e. of God as the divine punisher versus God whose creation just happens to bear certain hardships for mankind – is crucially relevant, being at the nucleus of the ongoing public discourse on mental disorder in Southern Malaŵi which negotiates biomedical notions against religious concepts as supported by local, Muslim, and Christian doctrine. The exact cultural identification of formula such as *chibadwidwe* or *mphatso ya Mulungu* is under constant discussion and subjected to processes of cultural change.[118] The explanatory model of mental disorder as part of a divine plan –

116 With regard to Northern Malaŵi 20 percent of health disorders have been attributed to such structural reasons (Wendroff 1985: 32-33). Maxwell Marwick asserts that a good 25 percent of the sicknesses examined during his own research were regarded as 'natural' cases (Marwick 1967: 105).

117 The strong cosmological implications of this term are indicated by it being derived from the word stem *–lenga*, meaning to create (Paas 2004: 223). The Supreme Being is also known under names such as *Namalenga* or *Mlengi*, referring to its function as Creator.

118 The notion of drug abuse leading to mental disorder is most common in this context while more

existing independently from and indiscriminate of the affected persons themselves – is therefore well-represented, most especially so among the Yao. Due to its partial consistence with biomedical models, this explanatory model is supported by some cosmopolitan religious organizations in Malaŵi who identify it as the quintessential logic underlying all other concepts of sickness. Here, Islam as well as the large mainstream Christian denominations – such as Catholic or Anglican churches – may be mentioned.[119]

3(a) Accidental Harm

Some cases of mental disorder are locally recognized as the result of purely accidental misfortune, and because this notion plays a central role in Western explanatory models – e.g. in contexts like genetic predisposition or virus infection –, it is important to recognize the specifically Malaŵian concept of such a category. As a basic definition, an accident represents an unfortunate, but more especially unintentional event. While human activity can certainly result in an accident which, in turn, may lead to a person suffering from mental disorder, it is crucial that accidental harm is an involuntary event that recognizes neither magic manipulation nor spiritual involvement. For local TBAs, complications during childbirth – such as prolonged labour – are frequently reported as indications of mental disorder perceived in a newborn child. Numerous accounts of parents with children suffering from mental disorder narrate that prolonged labour or lack of medical assistance during delivery marked the beginning of their child's condition, and nothing but an unfortunate situation is blamed for the outcome. Many parents describe the first realization of the child's health disorder as the newborn not crying (*sanalire*) after birth,[120] but premature delivery is also considered a common reason for infant mental disorders.[121] In addition,

---

sporadic accounts relate the harmful effects of *chamba* smoking to a wider, distinctly religious concept, identifying direct, voluntary punishment as the cause of the condition. Thus, a group of Yao *ashehe* and their pupils unanimously agree that smoking *chamba* is an offence which God punishes by causing *misala* to the wrongdoer. The Ngoni representative of a local Evangelical Church describes *chamba* smoking as a sin against God which will be avenged by mental disorder.

119 According to a Yao *shehe*, good and bad things likewise originate from God and have their justification in the world – including mental disorders. Moreover, all people are spiritually equal in the face of God, and the Qur'ān specifies three categories of people who have no sin before God – these being children before the age of 15 or their maturity initiation, sleeping persons, and the mentally challenged such as *omisala*.

120 A TBA explains that, after prolonged labour, a child "can be born with its head not working because it has been squeezed too much. It can be born with *misala* or even with *kuzungulira mutu*" (Josephine Maboma, a Lomwe *mzamba*).

121 In such a case, "A child that is born before the time has come can be born *wopunduka* or even confused in the head [*wosonekera m'mutu*] because it is born while its brain [*ubongo*] is not

> "Sometimes there is a child that is born, and it is in its sack, so if you want to remove that sack, it is possible that you hurt the child. Also, when a woman's child does not lie right and she is forced to deliver at the *azamba*'s place, she might hurt the child so maybe a leg can be broken" (Josephine Maboma, a Lomwe *mzamba*).

Children situated in a breach presentation at the time of delivery are addressed by a number of midwifery specialists who also point out the danger of expectant mothers not following their instructions during childbirth or not receiving qualified assistance in time.[122] The post-delivery care for the umbilical cord (*mchombo*) is often reported to be crucial for the child's mental health because

> "A mother can manage to neglect it [i.e. the child], but she can also fail to care well for the umbilicus [*mchombo*]. If the wound of a child stays open for a long time without healing off, the child can become confused [*kusokonekera*] in the brain" (Olive Pilimiti, a Nyanja *mzamba*).

Another form of perinatal birth defect makes a direct connection to the question of *chamba* abuse as discussed below (see *Chapter IV.3.c*), indicating that a pregnant woman smoking *chamba* or even drinking *mowa* may cause severe mental disorder to the unborn child. A child may suffer the same consequences due to its mother conducting hard physical labour during her pregnancy, and finally, bad hygienic conditions and carelessness on the side of the pregnant women are listed as further common reasons for infant mental disorders.

In different ways, sickness (*matenda*) is considered to be connected to the occurrence of mental disorder. Especially in case of a pregnant woman suffering severely, people in Southern Malaŵi assess a high risk for the mental condition of the coming offspring, and in a number of reported cases, the mothers of children with mental disorders explain that the problems of their children are related to their own poor health during pregnancy.[123] In a number of cases the sickness-related causation of mental disorder follows a more abstract concept of

---

mature yet, or even other parts of the body" (Josephine Maboma, a Lomwe *mzamba*). Certain *ufiti* practices have been mentioned which aim to delay delivery and thus cause mental disorder to the child (see *Chapter IV.1.a*).

122 Thus, "When staying at home [for the delivery] it happens that the mother of the child keeps her legs together, that the child has a big head [*mutu waukulu*]. If things stay like this, the brain of the child mixes with the blood so that the head of the child does not work" (Iselda Tchema, a Yao *mzamba*).

123 "A child can be born with *kuzerezeka*, and more especially this can happen according to a sickness that was in her [i.e. the mother's] body. These things can happen according to a sickness that can just come naturally [*mwa chilengedwe*] to the person. But it is not known if they come from the mother or not. But there is some evidence, so I can mention that the child can be born with *kuzerezeka* that does not come from *ufiti*. Just being born *wozerezeka*, that is possible, and it happens" (Gordon Chitsulo, a Lomwe *sing'anga*).

transmission. Therefore, sicknesses like *mabomo, chisonono,* or *chindoko* (see *Appendix 1*) in a man are reported to cause his children to have mental disorder – even after his own death.[124] Other references indicate that prolonged sickness is believed to cause some forms of mental disorder in a same person, the most frequently described concept being that long-lasting suffering may damage the brain – which, in turn, manifests itself in, e.g., *kuzungulira mutu*. Likewise, the continuous use of medicine – both biomedical and traditional – is described as a potential cause for mental disorder.[125] A fairly common explanation for mental disorder in newborn children refers to the idea of organic defect on the side of the parents. This defect, usually verablized as weakness or lacking strength (*kupanda mphamvu*), is described as based on structural factors which may lead to mental disorder on the side of the unfortunate offspring. Accordingly,

> "Others think that the man was not strong enough and that's why they gave birth to a disabled child. So they don't want to be associated with lazy men, and they feel that it's an embarrassment – like we have never had a disability in our clan, so how come that I have a disabled kid?" (Miriam Namanja, a Yao disability organization representative).

Most frequently, the idea of lacking strength (*mphamvu*) is directed to the father's semen (*mbewu*), although a lack of strength may also refer to the mother of a given child suffering from mental disorder.[126] As a variation of this concept, a child being born with mental disorders may indicate that a woman's ability to produce healthy offspring has been exhausted by too many children. In this case,

> "[...] let us say – a woman has given many births, then she can in the end give birth to a child with some limbs missing or can even bear someone who cannot speak, or a dumb person. All of this is because she has had too many births. A

---

124 A sickness like *likango* (see *Appendix 1*) is identified as connected to the occurrence *khunyu* because "For those born with it [i.e. *khunyu*], it usually starts at the time that this newly born child loses consciousness. After that it starts to show foam coming out of the mouth. This usually comes with the great *likango* [...]. So if I examine I usually find that she [i.e. the mother] has sores on the genitalia. In this case I cut them out and the child regains consciousness" (Joyce Chawa, a Yao *mzamba*).

125 Some rare accounts refer to a notion of contagion. Thus, "others think that disability is contagious, that it can be passed on from one person to another. [...] Normally when a disabled child sits or comes near you, you say »Don't come near me, you are going to give me your disability!«" (Miriam Namanja, a Yao disability organization representative).

126 A TBA explains that "I always tell them that this can happen if the uterus [*chipelekero*] is lacking strength or if the semen [*mbewu*] of the father is lacking strength" (Iselda Tchema, a Yao *mzamba*). Notably, a certain danger also lies in the attempt to overcome a state of lacking strength by traditional medicine because "Apart from the semen of the father, a child can be born with *kupunduka* of the leg or an arm, with bent legs or unable to see. These things can happen if the father can not impregnate [*ali osapeleka*] and has used some dark medicine [*makhwala achikuda*] so that he shall impregnate. So if that medicine which is given does not correlate with his/her body, the child is usually born *wopunduka*" (Iselda Tchema, a Yao *mzamba*).

child can even be born *wozerezeka*, with *khunyu* or with other problems" (Luka Dzaone, a Lomwe *sing'anga*).

Lacking strength can refer to various parts of the human body, but it typically is directly connected to reproductive organs and/or liquids such as a man's semen. This weakness is transmitted and manifests itself in the child, leading to typical states of mental disorder. Physical accidents (*ngozi*) are considered another possible reason for mental disorder, and due to the fact that mental disorders are largely associated with the human brain (*ubongo*), accidents affecting a person's head (*mutu*) are most prominent here. The notion underlying this concept implies that physical damage suffered to the brain subsequently leads to the loss of some of its functionality. In this way, traffic accidents are seen as possible reasons for *kuzerezeka*, *misala*, or *kuzungulira mutu*. While physical abuse of pregnant women does, in itself, certainly not qualify as an accidental event, cases of domestic violence may still be subsumed under this category. Violence against an expectant mother is mentioned as a likely reason for mental disorder on the side of the newborn, and more graphically, in the case of husbands beating their pregnant wives in the stomach, thus hurting the unborn child.[127]

The concept of structural reasons for mental disorder in Southern Malaŵi identifies a number of inherent logical connections which, conflicting with biomedical notions, emphasize cultural specificity. Even though an influence of biomedical discourse may, in part, be discernible in some of the explanatory models, the exact cultural conceptualization still shows significant differences with scientifically approved notions. As a further illustration of the conceptual differences between – and, at the same time, the common ground of – Malaŵian and Western common sense, a number of accounts also relate mental disorder – usually specified as *misala* – to a person thinking too much. Such pondering is described as particularly dangerous if focussing around personal problems such as poverty.[128]

"Thinking too much can make one become *wozerezeka*, because thinking on its own is a sickness. […] The central thing is that a person can have a problem come into his/her brain [*ubongo*] because, as I have already said, if a person thinks too much, then firstly that person can lose weight due to these thoughts, even if the person is not sick at all. The mere thinking in itself gives him/her a sickness which is to say that even if he/she eats, the body still becomes thin. It is central that if the

127 The actual conditions of mental disorder presented by the child are described as *kuzerezeka* or *kulumala*.

128 A Lomwe healer hence reckons that "*Kuzerezeka* from Western countries and *kuzerezeka* from here can be similar, but it can also be different. What really happens is that people think too much, and that can cause a person's head not to work properly" (Gordon Chitsulo, a Lomwe *sing'anga*).

thinking continues for a long time, he/she can think the wrong things [*zinthu zolakwika*] so maybe he/she will be *wozungulira mutu* because of these bad thoughts" (Luka Dzaone, a Lomwe *sing'anga*).

This peculiar concept is reported with some variation, and has already been mentioned in previous publications.[129] It illustrates the deduction that Malaŵian notions of structural causation of mental disorder do have some cultural autonomy and considerably exceed Western notions of 'natural' occurrence.

3(b) Heredity Transmission

While it seems tempting to consider Malaŵian notions of inheritance as mostly identical with biomedical models of genetics, the cultural specificitiy of local concepts still deserves attention. Hereditary mental disorder may be described as a somewhat inconsistent model usually expressed by Chicheŵa terms such as the aforementioned *chibadwa* – i.e. a 'hereditary' – or the verb *kuladza*, indicating heredity transmission.[130] First of all, Malaŵian notions of heredity as causing mental disorder show some striking similarities with Western concepts – connecting it to a transmission by blood (*magazi*), and constituting a corresponce with systems of descent. It is, at the same time, difficult to distinguish heredity transmission from the works of ancestor spirits – with the lines of transmission within a given kin group suggesting a close association of the one with the other.[131] Accordingly, most accounnts express a rather blurry understanding of the inheritance of mental disorder. Therefore,

"These children inherit [*kuyamwira*] it [i.e. *misala*] according to the clan [*mtundu*], so if there is a person who has six fingers, after some time another one

---

[129] Thus, exceptionally intelligent persons – being prone to excessive thinking – frequently develop mental disorder resembling *kuzerezeka*. At the same time, loneliness can also cause *misala* in a given person, being described as a consequence of unhappiness and brooding due to separation from the kin-group. According to data from Ntcheu District (Central Region), Kenson Malanga adds that "If you read many books you become mad" (Malanga 1971: No. 139). Further, Brian Morris remarks that, in Malaŵi, he "often heard it expressed that too much thinking causes headaches – a view also expressed in working class communities in Britain" (Morris 1996: 123-124).

[130] Additional expressions for heredity include *kutengera* – meaning 'to simulate, resemble' as well as 'inheritance, descent' (Paas 2004: 209, 422) and *kuyamwira* or 'to suck for something, to inherit' (Paas 2004: 500). The reappearance of specific health problems within a given family is likewise described by as *zobwerera*, or 'things coming back'.

[131] Thus, heredity is partially described as the ancestors disobeying divine law, or the evil spirits tormenting a deceased ancestor being passed on within the lineage – i.e. by blood transmission. Accordingly, these statements reveal this notion as part of a discourse of divine and/or satanic punishment (see *Chapter IV.2.b* and *IV.2.c*).

will also be born with six fingers. But sometimes the *mizimu* also have a part in this" (Sapitwa Chagoma, a Lomwe *sing'anga*).[132]

There is a difference between the mechanic recurrence of a certain mental condition within a given kinship context and the direct and deliberate manipulation of the *mizimu* ancestral spirits. This distinction is elaborated by a Nyanja TBA who, with respect to the occurrence of *khunyu*, explains that

> "Many times it starts when they have already grown and they do not sit anymore, that a child suffers from a fever. Others can start at the time when they are in public with their relatives, and many times people say that maybe this has come from people [i.e. by *ufiti*], or perhaps it is inherited from its parents [*zoladza kwa makolo ake*]. [...] Sometimes, the *mizimu* can seize a child [*kumugwira mwanayo*] and it starts to collapse – but that is not inheritance [*si kuladza*], no! I mean here that a child resembles one of its relatives [*amatengera mbale wake*] who also had *khunyu*" (Olive Pilimiti, a Nyanja *mzamba*).

Many accounts disclose that the repeated occurrence of a specific health disorder within a given family group (*chibale*) or clan (*mtundu*) is related to the spirit of an ancestor coming back – not in the form of spirit possession, but as involuntarily expressing itself in an infant descendant.[133] An ancestor who suffered from mental disorder inflicts the same problems on a child thereby resembling (*kutengera*) that deceased person.

> "They say this is not a disability, only her face looks like somebody who died some years ago. [...] they see a relationship between the person and the new-born baby, that the face resembles somebody who died years ago, and they don't accept that it is a disability unless after sensitization. In the village, it's a problem for them to differentiate between disability and heredity. Most of the times they say it is heredity, they say you know we had a grandfather or grandmother that looked like him or her" (Miriam Namanja, a Yao disability organization representative).[134]

The notion of inheritance in the causation of mental disorder in Southern Malaŵi is remarkably difficult to grasp. While its cultural recognition is undoubted, its precise conceptualization is hard – or, sometimes, impossible – to delineate from

132 A Yao TBA agrees that "some can be born with six fingers on their feet or hands. These things are possible, maybe there have been others like that in their clan [*mtundu*]" (Doreen Masamba, a Yao *mzamba*).

133 Accordingly, "What really happens is that the *mzimu* of a person who was *wozungulira mutu* comes back and stays with that child, with the purpose of making people remember him/her for a long time" (Sapitwa Chagoma, a Lomwe *sing'anga*).

134 Likewise, "there are some who are born with it [*kubadwa nazo*], but others resemble [*kutengera*] their old ancestors. If maybe there is one who has suffered, this child can resemble that. So this child just grows up with it [...]. It is not from the parents, but from the ancestors" (Vincent Chitete, a Yao *sing'anga*).

concepts or ancestor activity. Accounts referring a given case of mental disorder to inheritance usually indicate previous knowledge of previously occurring similar conditions within the same kin-group.

3(c) Drug Abuse

While drugs may appear as a rather specialized case within the discourse on the causation of mental disorder, the abuse of psychoactive substances actually represents one of the most prominent models of explanation. A considerable percentage of those cases of mental disorder admitted to Zomba Mental Hospital are associated with drug abuse. While some accounts advert to the dangers that substance abuse during pregnancy may inflicts on the unborn child,[135] the consequences of drug abuse are more typically expected to affect the person directly involved in it. Some accounts describe the internal processes in a pseudo-physiological fashion:

> "[...] another *misala* comes because of smoking *chamba* or drinking beer [*mowa*] excessively, which makes the brain boil" (Linga Nasawa, a Yao *sing'anga*).

Most accounts of drug abuse as causing mental disorder specify the substance in question as *chamba* – i.e. Indian hemp or *Cannabis sativa*. Numerous accounts list the abuse of *chamba* as one of the most common reasons for mental disorder, while quantitative surveys recently described 25% of the inmates in Zomba Mental Hospital as *chamba*-related cases (Williams, Kaponda & Levy 2002). Grown locally in many areas of the country, the use and abuse of *chamba* are typical associated with adolescent males, and it tends to be perceived as a rural phenomenon – most especially associated with young men working in the tourist destinations along the shores of Lake Malaŵi. Cultural stereotypes of a *chamba* smoker therefore correspond with the Rastafarian cliché (Nyirenda 2006), and especially older persons describe *chamba* abuse as a recent phenomenon. Accordingly,

> "Most of the young ones come to our clinics because of *chamba* abuse. What we get from the guardians or parents is that usually after these boys have abused drugs, *chamba*, they are seen behaving funny. They are said to use abusive language, being physically aggressive for no apparent reason, or stealing, causing all sorts of problems at or near their home. So when this comes to the extreme then the patient is brought to the clinics" (Vivian Changata, a Mang'anja nursing officer).

---

135 As a TBA explains, *kuzerezeka* may occur because "There are some parents who drink *mowa* or smoke *fodya* while they are expecting, which can also affect the newborn child" (Josephine Maboma, a Lomwe *mzamba*).

The cultural perception of *chamba* abuse has a high degree of moral implications, e.g. describing *chamba* smokers as lazy, unfit to be economically productive and contribute to the wellbeing of the community even before their condition develops into a full-grown state of mental disorder. Regular *chamba* usage is expected to result in *misala* or *kuzerezeka* while slight cases may be categorized as *kuzungulira mutu*.[136]

Moderate drinking of alcoholic beverages is frequently described as a difficult and challenging exercise bearing the constant danger of excessive drinking which may lead to subsequent mental disorder. Accordingly, statistical data from the mid-1980s classifies 15% of admissions in Zomba Mental Hospital as cases of alcohol addiction (Peltzer 1987: 218). Here, locally produced alcoholic products are more likely to be associated with mental disorder than Western-style drinks – e.g. the ubiquitous Carlsberg Lager. While alcohol is generally considered as potentially disruptive to the mental condition of the drinker, the locally distilled *kachasu* liquor is most prominent in the discourse of mental disorder causation. Nonetheless, the abuse of *mowa* – local maize beer – and *chibuku* – a milky brew made of sorghum, millet and maize – are also regarded as potential reasons for mental disorder if drunk in large quantities over an extended period of time.

Of all the notions relating the causation of mental disorder to structural factors, drug abuse is by far the most prevalent category. Even though it is largely considered a structural condition that the abuse of, e.g., *chamba* leads to *misala*, the complex as such is nonetheless surrounded by explicit social valuation which positions the phenomenon in the conceptual proximity of *mwambo* violation. *Chamba* smoking is described as a social vice which conflicts greatly with basic norms of productivity, responsibility, and behavioural control.

4. Therapeutic Solutions

The therapeutic means for the treatment of mental disorder are specific not only for the respective kind of mental disorder – i.e. for *misala* or *khunyu* – but also for the aetiological reason that has been determined. The fact that nosological

---

136 According to a Lomwe healer, "We can even tell that this type of *kuzerezeka* is a result from smoking *chamba*, that he/she over-smoked and damaged his/her own brain, and so the treatment is different" (Luka Dzaone, a Lomwe *sing'anga*). Some accounts explain the mechanism in close accordance with the concept of the person, describing that the poisonous *chamba* smoke enters the brain and drives out the person's *mzimu wa umunthu* – thus leaving the patient in a condition of spirit loss. Therapeutic approaches are therefore designed to coax the displaced *mzimu* back into the person.

categories resemble more a descriptive account of observed symptoms than analytic categories of sickness suggests that the aetiological causations identified as being responsible for a given case of mental disorder are, in fact, decisive for all ensuing therapeutic processes. It is, therefore, a frequently reported notion that mental disorder cannot be appropriately treated if its reasons have not been accurately diagnosed – thus making the acceptance of a given causation an ever greater factor in the health seeking behaviour concerning persons with mental disorder.

4(a) Breaking and Purging Magic

Meeting with Sapitwa Chagoma, a Lomwe anti-ufiti expert (sing'anga wochotsa ufiti), we take a walk around his community in rural Zomba District. Reaching the meagre compound of local subsistence farmers, he introduces me to the elderly Nyanja owners who live with their twelve year-old granddaughter, Liza, after her parents passed away the previous year. In obvious discomfort, the girl lingers on the house's khonde, leaving the impression of a scared child, and in her presence, the healer and the grandparents reiterate her case history.

Soon after her parents' death and her subsequent entering her grandparents' household, Liza developed complaints such as coughing and a swelling of the abdomen.Consulting a local health station, she received treatment of Amoxicillin (an antibiotic) and Panadol (the local Paracetamol brand) which failed to improve her condition. The grandparents subsequently consulted a local sing'anga, declaring that the girl hurt her chest falling out of her lichero flying device after visiting the graveyard with her ufiti teacher. The healer tries to cure her from her ufiti contamination by mankhwala akumwa, but the medicine fails to cause regurgitation and diarrhoea. Rather, Liza's stomach problems increase, and she finds herself unable to stand up due to excruciating pain. Finally she is taken to an expert in fighting ufiti – the mentioned Sapitwa Chagoma – who finally confirms the previous diagnosis. He elaborates that the girl's condition started with her going to collect her deceased brother's blood, flesh and heart from the graveyard. Her brother must have been well-protected against ufiti during his lifetime, as his corpse remained under strong kukhwima protection which lead to Liza's lichero accident. He administers more powerful mankhwala in order to rid the girl from her ufiti contamination, finally resulting in prolonged vomiting and diarrhoea. According to the sing'anga's experience, closer examination of her bodily expulsions would have revealed traces of ufiti material (zizimba) that had been stored in her bowels. Unfortunately, Doctor Chagoma did not get there in time to analyze stool and vomit, but it is agreed that – in spite of the abdominal problems she is still suffering from – the girl is cured and on her way to recovery.

When seeking therapy suitable for the treatment of mental disorder caused by the different forms of magic, traditional medicine is usually considered the one and only appropriate provider for efficient treatment.[137] For the treatment of all cases of mental disorder caused by magic, the identification of the responsible originator is elementary, and divinatory diagnostics (*maula*) are considered as a reliable technique for revealing the culprit and thus facilitating subsequent treatment. Once the evildoer has been located, the therapeutic process against the given mental disorder may begin – generally following the different models of traditional medicine (see *Chapter II.2.a*). An experienced *sing'anga* may also engage in counter-magic in order to break the *mfiti*'s detrimental influence on the victim – or to pressure the culprit to lift his or her magic from the patient by direct confrontation.[138] Many accounts of mental disorder due to *ufiti* imply the notion that the victim's condition is connected to a certain degree of contamination, and a particular therapeutic strategy is necessary in order to regain purity.

At numerous times in Malaŵian history, the fight against *ufiti* has attained the form of large-scale communal movements. Declaring *ufiti* the true cause of individual as well as collective suffering and responsible for epidemics, droughts, or floods, influential and charismatic *asing'anga* have taken great efforts to eradicate *ufiti* on a regional or inter-regional level, spearheading anti-*ufiti* movements of, in part, considerable size and distribution (Chakanza 1985: 227). Some of these movements – e.g. that of Kamwendo in 1930 AD, by Bwanali in 1947 AD, or by Nchimi Chikanga in the early 1960s AD – spread into neighbouring countries and attained remarkable political momentum (Soko 2002; Schoffeleers 1999: 408; Peltzer 1987: 156; Pöschl 1987: 135-136; Chakanza 1985: 228-232; Marwick 1975: 178-183).[139] Generally, these movements tend to follow messianistic ideas,[140] associating their leaders with supreme spiritual legitimacy. Specific is the use of mystic medicine to keep

---

[137] Both Pentecostal Churches and Islam in Southern Malaŵi tend to interpret all forms of magic as deeds of evil spirits. The identification of magic reasons in itself, therefore, refers to traditional religious notions and demands suitable therapy (see *Chapter IV.4.a*).

[138] Therefore, treatment against *misala ya ufiti* may include additional *mankhwala* which force the responsible *afiti* to expose themselves and confess their evil deeds.

[139] In 1934, Audrey Richards records the *bamucapi* movement among the Bemba in Eastern North Rhodesia (modern-day Zambia) which "recently swept from Nyasaland into Northern Rhodesia and later reached Southern Rhodesia and the Congo" (Richards 1975: 164). In Southern Tanzania, Roy Willis describes an anti-witchcraft movement called *kamcape* in 1943/1944 AD, tracing its origins to Nyasaland (Willis 1968: 190). The notion of an *ufiti* pandemic functions as a sign of general social and moral decline which questions the legitimacy of political authority. The explicitly political orientation of some anti-*ufiti* movements (Schoffeleers 1999), e.g. the Bwanali movement in 1947, led to violent governmental repercussions (Pöschl 1987: 136).

[140] Traditions about Kamwendo, founder of a 1930s movement, imply that he died and came back from the grave after two days to fight *ufiti* (Willis 1968: 189-190). Mpulumutsi, one of the successors of the famous healer Bwanali, similarly claims to have died from *ufiti* and been resurrected by his master (Marwick 1975: 180).

convicted *afiti* from further using their powers. In the tradition of the great Kamwendo movement, this liquid medicine is usually called *mchape* (literally 'cleanser'),[141] although the ingredients of the mixture itself apparently differ. The ingredients for this *mankhwala* are generally revealed to the charismatic leader due to spiritual vocation. As for its application,

> "People who were found to be witches had to drink a medicine by that name [*mchape*], which would kill them if and when they relapsed" (Schoffeleers 1999: 410).

The use of *mchape* in the treatment of *afiti* has been described as a mild variation of the *mwabvi* poison ordeal,[142] which was banned by the Nyasaland colonial government in 1911 AD.[143] According to Matthew Schoffeleers, though, *mchape* and *mwabvi* were already used as alternative treatments for ufiti in pre-colonial times (Schoffeleers 1999: 411). An elderly *mfumu*, however, remembers:

> "In the past, people in the group [*mtundu*] used to announce that a *mfiti* faces a medicine called *mwabvi*. When a person who had some *ufiti* drank that medicine, he/she died, but those who did not have any did not die, they just vomited. Those who died of this were not buried at the graveyard, but people managed to throw them into a cave or maybe into the forest" (Usanene Kwela, a Yao *mfumu*).

In spite of the somewhat inquisitorial approach of *mchape*, the procedure nonetheless aims to offer therapy and reintegration for suspected *afiti* into society (Vaughan 1983: 237).[144]

It has been explained before that *ufiti* is conceived as being intrinsically related to the presence of a material agent (*chizimba*) within the stomach of a person, and that his or her ability to apply magic is directly derived from that fact. Accordingly, the treatment for such a condition focuses on the patient receiving *mankhwala akumwa* which provoke severe vomiting and/or diarrhoea,

---

141 In 1954, another movement is mentioned, alternatively using the names of *kamcape* (i.e. 'small cleanser') or *wacauuta* (or 'people of Chauta [God]') thus emphasizing its religious character (Marwick 1965: 94).

142 In order to identify *afiti*, groups of suspects were forced to drink a certain poisonous potion, assuming that only innocent persons would regurgitate and survive (Marwick 1965: 87-88). Reportedly, the main ingredient if this potion was the bark of the *mwabvi* tree or *Erythrophleum suaveolens* (Morris 1996: 342-344). In 1903, *mwabvi* ordeals were apparently also conducted with fowl substitutes (Peltzer 1987: 154) while the use of a poison ordeal called *mwafi* is later reported among the Zambian Bemba (Richards 1975: 175).

143 According to the paragraph 2 of the Witchcraft Act first issued in 1911, "Trials by the ordeal of muabvi or other poison, fire, boiling water, or by any ordeal which is likely directly or indirectly to result in the death of or bodily injury to any person shall be and is hereby prohibited" (Government of Malaŵi 1968: 7: 02).

144 Somewhat unspecific, *mchape* may also be used "to protect people from all possible attacks by witches and sorcerers" (Marwick 1965: 94).

thus ridding the person of the internal *ufiti* contamination.[145] The general idea of *ufiti* as representing a form of contamination which has to be purged in order to achieve therapeutic success is very common.[146] In combination with this general medical approach, the different other forms of traditional medicine may appear, and skin scarifications (*mipini*) are one frequently applied form of it. In some cases, an additional *mphini* treatment is considered to reverse the physical effects of *ufiti* such as straightening an affected leg, etc. Also, washing with medicated water (*mankhwala akusamba*) might be part of the ritual, and it should be noted that while some therapeutic attitudes are typical for the treatment of mental disorder as caused by *ufiti*, symbolic elements are also a necessary part of the therapeutic ritual.[147]

The contamination with *ufiti* can be purified by means of traditional medicine, but at the same time, the motif of the *mfiti* who is 'cured' from its anti-social ways but who suffers a relapse is also very prominent.[148] In a more social sense, the transmission of *ufiti* also bears considerable danger as any person acquiring the reputation of practicing *ufiti* faces severe social consequences. In such a case, a preventive treatment applied to the culprit is supposed to make sure that this individual cannot resume its evil deeds. This form of therapy is usually described as including scarifications (*mipini*) made on the *mfiti* which are also applied on a patient after his/her *ufiti*-induced disorder has been treated – thus granting protection against future attacks (Pöschl 1987: 135-136). While the therapeutic approach of purging a patient in order to physically rid him or her from detrimental magic influence is specific for *ufiti*, the other techniques mentioned earlier may be widely applied for other magic-related mental disorders. A case of mental disorder due to protective *matsenga*, at the same

---

145 Accordingly, "When one drinks, he/she gets diarrhoea [*kutsegula m'mimba*] in order to get rid of all the bad things [*zonse zoipa*] there are inside the body. If it is a small child which might just have that diarrhoea, it might start walking when the sickness is gone because it was hindering it" (Mose Chingale, a Lomwe *sing'anga*).

146 One Lomwe healer describes her therapy for mental disorder due to *ufiti* as consisting of a boiled *mankhwala a kumwa* which takes effect so that "what is in the head and stomach comes out through vomiting".

147 Treatment of *ufiti*-related mental disorder may therefore be conducted "while the patient is seated on a hoe (*khasu*). When we finish making incisions with him/her on the hoe, we give him/her medicine to drink. Then, the patient will vomit everything out, or everything will come out as feces" (Henry Mwambo, a Yao *sing'anga*). In another instance, a mortar (*mtondo*) is mentioned for the patient to sit on.

148 As a former *mfiti* explains, "At first, I really was a *mfiti* myself, and it was my grandfather [...] who gave that to me. After some time my mother realized that I was a *mfiti*, so they drove it out of me. After that uncle of mine found out, he gave it back to me again. Then, I started to confess so my mother had it removed from me again, and I just found myself some medicine so I am fortified now. Right now, I stopped doing *ufiti*" (Sapitwa Chagoma, a Lomwe *sing'anga*). The notion of 'being fortified' (*ndikukhwima*) refers to the concept of *kukhwima* (see *Chapter IV.1.c*).

time, may sometimes require the cooperation of the *sing'anga* who created the protection in the first place and could therefore reverse it. Otherwise, the perspectives of successful treatment may be reduced. The same situation applies in the treatment of *kukhwima* practices – which requires the identification of the responsible expert in order to reverse the condition entirely.

In the cultural context of Southern Malaŵi, any magic action is conceived as surmountable by magic and/or traditional therapeutic means. Certain culturally acknowledged problems may aggravate the appropriate treatment of mental disorder caused by magic manipulations – including faulty aetiological allocation and/or identification of the originator, a situational inability to overcome a given charm, reluctance to tackle a given case (as identified in many cases of *kukhwima*) or, after all, the immediate final effect of the form of magic applied, e.g. *hamala* (see *Chapter IV.1.a*). On a general level, though, all such cases are regarded as curable by means of traditional medicine which has a reputation of particular expertise in issues of magic.

Different logic concepts connect the occurrence of mental disorder to practices of magic and that their medical treatment involves the full arsenal of traditional medicine – creating, at the same time, crucial connections to the social contextualization of the case – i.e. the identification and inclusion of a person responsible for the condition – as well as, in the case of *ufiti*, the material manifestation and location of the problem as a foreign substance in the person's system.

4(b) Restoring Cosmological Harmony

Even though therapeutic reactions to cases of mental disorder associated with spirit agents cover a wide area, they may be differentiated into two blanket categories – i.e. appeasement/accommodation and exorcism. As the bifurcation of different mechanisms as presented in the abovementioned section suggests, the perception of mental disorders varies greatly depending on the actual spiritual force that is recognized as being at the bottom of the aetiology.

Exorcising Malevolent Spirits

After a number of meetings with Vincent Chitete, a Yao sing'anga from Mangochi currently practicing in downtown Zomba, he mentions his expertise in treating mental disorders even over long distance. Describing the case of a relative in North America previously classified as mentally retarded, the sing'anga shrugs off the fact that the respective patient has been living with this condition for more than 30 years, offering to start long-distance treatment the following day. The objective of his treatment, he explains, would be to gain the support of his own mizimu ya makolo so that they, in turn, contact the patient's ancestors in the spiritual sphere and help them clear the obstacles limiting the patient's mental abilities.

Next day, Doctor Chitete and his young apprentice meet me off the busy market roads where he usually works and begins his preparations. Crouching between rock boulders, the sing'anga produces his materials out of a torn green travel bag and sets up his maula equipment – a nsupa gourd tightly wrapped with fabric with a small shard of mirror attached to one side. Burning splinters of some unspecified mitengo – which he keeps in plastic bags and white pill containers – he inhales the fumes evaporating from the fire, fanning the smoke towards his head with a flywhisk (litchowa). Finally, he addresses his mizimu ancestors in a lengthy prayer, accompanied by repeated eructation,[149] *and, after some minutes of silence, continues.*[150] *Finally, Vincent Chitete starts chanting:*

> "*Mizimu ya ku manda imavomera agogo* / spirits from the grave, answer, grandparents
> *ndivomereni ndivomereni agogo* / answer me, answer me, grandparents
> *izi ndi za malango agogo* / these [things] are from punishments, grandparents

149 Translation: "Thank you very much, Grace, thank you very much, Chatsalira Davio, you all. I am asking all you spirits, all of you. I'm able to do so because I'm immature and so I cannot know anything, but on this day I'm kneeling before you begging because what I am doing here is not for fun, it's a serious business and yet I'm only a child, I cannot know anything but through you spirits. You can help me with the problems we are facing now, you, Siliya, Tapiwa, you are the ones who can tackle this problem. But also I implore you, my granny Stella, granny Pastella, but also my sister Agnes and all the spirits of those who departed that you should all come together. I'm asking all these spirits of my ancestors before I do anything, the sacrifice which I'm offering now. I implore you, receive this sacrifice with two hands, but we don't know what we are going to do here, everything will come from you. I also beg all the four directions North, South, East and West from all dead people. Above all, your spirits are able to talk to any person anything from you. I know that a lot of people say that the dead are useless but a dead person is more important than a living person because we are able to see different kinds of things through your spirits. […] Please granny Siliya, granny Stella, granny Siyileni, my sister Agnes, my elder sister Tapiwa, I ask you because you are the ones who can do this job. And all those relatives who died – thank you very much. It's me, your grandson, begging you – to some I'm your son, to others your brother. I'm begging you all, grannies, sisters, brothers, fathers, you who are able to do anything" (Vincent Chitete, a Yao *sing'anga*).

150 Translation: "Thanks so much to all the spirits from the graveyard, the spirits from the grave can see and chat with people and right here where I am sitting, we have received several spirits but more spirits from the grave will come here to chat with us, and so all the spirits from all the four directions of the earth, thanks so much. But first you want your song which you usually sing when doing your work. Thank you very much, granny Pastella, I will sing your song. But I beg of you that when I sing the song your spirits should be happy and that the work which you are going to do should be done and receive my petition. What we are going to do here will not take place here but will take place far away. Please that person who is far away and whatever will happen here should go there before I sing your song. Please be around, my granny, thank you very much, since your other grandson is not here, I'm all alone, I will sing alone. He is gone where you sent him to do your work. I talked to him through the spirit and he told me that there are things to sort out there. Please, granny, look after him so that he does everything well just like everyone has been okay for us your children. Thank you very much" (Vincent Chitete, a Yao *sing'anga*).

izi ndi za ufiti agogo / these [things] are from *ufiti*, grandparents
izi ndi za matsenga agogo / these [things] are from *matsenga*, grandparents
koma zimapezeka zina za zilengo agogo / but others belong to misfortune, grandparents
ndivomerezeni agogo / agree with me, grandparents
chizimu chanu ine chidzandiuza agogo / your spirit will tell me, grandparents
chomwe ndingakupempha agogo / please, I only beg you, grandparents
ndivomereni agogo / answer me, grandparents
inu aSiliya, inu Kafereni gogo / you Siliya and you, grandparent Catherine"

Continuing with another short prayer,[151] *the sing'anga finally declares that his mizimu are ready to hear our request. Indicating the name of the person in question, he absorbs himself in a silent monologue for some minutes before suddenly proclaims the ritual concluded. Questioned about his ritual performance, he explains that his silent prayers were addressed to the spirit of the patient, and due to the distance between them, his own familiar mizimu – five different ones at the same time – facilitate the connection. After this, he can now diagnose the patient's mental disorder as caused by evil spirits (ziwanda) limiting his development. Moreover, the condition is said to relate to a particularly malevolent ancestor. By mediation of his mizimu ya makolo, these ziwanda could be expelled from the patient and protective ancestors (ziwanda zabwino, as he calls them) take care of the patient now.*

First signs of patient recovery, as Vincent Chitete continues, could be expected within a week's time, initiating a slow but ongoing process of positive development. He therefore suggests that, in one week, a telephone call to the patient's parents should indicate whether or not the treatment was successful – and determine the payment the sing'anga would receive. One week and a telephone call later – and without informing the North American relations from therapeutic endeavours taken meanwhile in Africa –, the respective faraway patient is described as having recently made noticeable progress in terms of personal independence and job responsibility; apparently, his laudable conduct had been commended at a number of occasions throughout the last week. By all available standards, this certainly qualifies as therapeutic success, and on our next meeting, the sing'anga receives his requested payment. On this occasion, the sing'anga discloses that he contacted his mizimu again in order to supervise therapeutic success. Being not completely satisfied with the progress, he promises to keep praying for an even quicker recovery – regretfully admitting, however, that a long and slow healing process should be expected.

[151] Translation: "Please all of you deceased, Tapiwa and all those who can know, the time I was with my grandparents who taught all these songs so that every person can get healed whether near or far away. But promise me that it will also work today. Please, grandparents, whatever I am going to do today, let it not fail because the person is far away, but when you take the name of the person for whatever cause of his/her sickness, whether through *ufiti* or inborn, let all sickness be healed through your help with the help of God and his/her ancestral spirits. Thank you very much, my grandparents. Thank you" (Vincent Chitete, a Yao *sing'anga*).

As compared to the punishment by the Supreme Being, the machinations of evil spirits are seen as a much more tangible issue. In a Christian frame of reference, though, the therapeutic approaches are virtually identical. Increasingly, faith healing practices – as provided by Pentecostal churches throughout the country – are also finding acceptance as a viable form of therapy for cases of mental disorder caused by *ziwanda*. Here, faith healing specialists are frequently attributed with special exorcism powers facilitating the therapy of mental disorder. With regard to *misala*, a Lomwe Pentecostal priest thus explains that a single word of authority may suffice to expel the demonic agent from a human victim, hence curing the condition. Even in the case of more traditional medicine, cosmological concepts form the overruling frame of reference. Most of these therapeutic techniques are complex rituals involving sacrifices for the helping *mizimu*, and especially in the case of spirit-induced mental disorder, the use of *mankhwala ofungatira* is highly recommended. By inhaling the healing smoke produced by it, the spirits would be driven out of the patient's head. This concept, as well as sacrificial offerings for helpful *mizimu*, is identical with ritual actions typical for the appeasement of benevolent spirits (see below).[152]

On various occasions, therapeutic rituals against spirit possession have a semi-public character and involve community participation – but exceptions to this rule can also be observed. Some accounts indicate that mental disorder related to dangerous spirits (*ziwanda*) should be treated at the victim's home or in a small hideout (*kanyumba komata*) in order to provide some privacy. Participation may be restricted to a few close family members, and the treatment as such focuses on the *sing'anga*'s own spirits (*mizimu ya makolo*) exorcising the destructive *ziwanda* from the patient.

Appeasing Benevolent Spirits

Drumming and dancing rituals for the treatment of spirit-induced mental disorder are addressed by various names in different areas and/or ethnic groups of Southern Malaŵi. Among the Sena, the term *madzoka* is the most commonly applied one, and it has been compared to the *vimbuza* among the Tumbuka, Cheŵa and Ngoni of the Northern Region.[153] As a therapeutic ritual for mental

[152] By means of ritual purification, one Sena ritual aims to prevent the recurrence of *mfutete* (see *Appendix 1*) in a given family. Whenever a child with this form of mental disorder is born, the stones of the hearth fire as well as the mats and clothes used by the mother are replaced while the woman is treated with *mankhwala ofungatira*. This treatment also applies for all people in the village who had sexual intercourse on the day this child was born – lest they also produce mentally disordered offspring.

[153] Other regional variations include *malombo* or *mashawe* (Morris 1996: 520; Peltzer 1987: 176). While some authors define *vimbuza* as a spirit illness (Morris 1996: 520; Hargreaves 1986: 27), a spirit affliction (Peltzer 1987: 165), or a "disease of possession" (Turner 1996: 71), other

disorder due to *mizimu* intervention, *madzoka* means to lure the spirit culprit into manifest possession in order to establish direct communication and discover its motivation. During public or semi-public dances, specialized *asing'anga* supervise the ritual proceedings and deduce further medication while patients (and ex-patients) engage in dancing. The ritual opportunity forn the spirit express itself through dance performance is explained to have an appeasing effect, and drumming and beer drinking facilitate its manifestation in the possessed victim. Some spirits are even known to take possession of a person with the sole purpose of receiving public recognition and ritual homage within dance rituals, broadly referred to as *mizimu yangoponda* or *mizimu ya ng'oma* – 'spirits which are just dancing' or 'spirits of the drum'. Further accompanying therapy usually involves different kinds of treatment, but a form of sacrifice (*nsembe*) donated to placate the angered spirits may be interpreted as the most central ritual action.

The concept of benevolent spirits (*mizimu ya makolo*) causing mental disorder by possessing a person is, in itself, strongly attached to Malaŵian religious thought. Accordingly, this category is not recognized in a Muslim or Christian framework which tends to dismiss spirit entities disturbing a person's mental integrity as evil – and dealing with them accordingly. As a general rule, appeasement of *mizimu yabwino* has a highly symbolic character, and medicine administered for the treatment of mental disorder due to *mizimu* is always part of a larger therapeutic ritual. On a traditional basis, the ritual appeasement of spirits possessing a person – and, therefore, his or her treatment – can be differentiated into a number of consecutive logical steps. The identification of the *mzimu* and its demands is the first prerequisite, and it may take the form of a drum and dance ritual such as *madzoka*. Secondly, the concerns of the spirit are targeted by holding a communal feast marked by sacrifices which is meant to appease the spirit, and thirdly, the spirit is extracted from the patient, making the healing proper. These steps, though, may or may not be performed in separate ritual contexts. If spirit possession is recognized as the reason for a given case of mental disorder, the first therapeutic – or, according to interpretation, additional diagnostic – processes typically involve public drum and dance rituals, sometimes accompanied with feasting and beer drinking. Once the spirit agent articulates itself in the form of manifest possession over the patient, its desires are investigated and may subsequently be satisfied – which leads to the *mzimu* relieving the patient. In addition to dance rituals, spirit sacrifices also constitute a central part of many therapeutic rituals addressing *mizimu* forces.[154] Therefore,

---

accounts mention the term as denoting both sickness and dance ritual (Soko 1988: 11; Kalipeni 1981: 111; Chilivumbo 1972: 4). Matthew Schoffeleers, moreover, emphasizes the cult structures of *vimbuza* (Schoffeleers 1979: 186).

154 Offerings of a goat or chicken mentioned as part of a *misala* therapy (Peltzer 1987: 181-182).

> "There are reasons like punishing a person for some evil deeds which he/she committed, so they [i.e. the *mizimu*] want them to acknowledge that they should offer a sacrifice [*nsembe*], such as a *sadaka*, for the *mizimu* to depart" (Sapitwa Chagoma, a Lomwe *sing'anga*).

Another classical technique for appeasing generally benevolent spirits is represented in the concept of *majini* – with the categorization as *majini* already indicating both aetiological background and therapeutic solution of the condition. Due to causing mental disorder in a person, the *majini* spirits – which here, as assessed earlier, represent a sub-category of *mizimu ya makolo* – are believed to express their personal demands which, most commonly, are connected to the Yao commemoration ritual or *sadaka*. According to Yao tradition, the bereaved are expected to organize this public rite in honour of their deceased relative, and if a *sadaka* is not performed appropriately – e.g. due to its considerable financial burden –, the respective *mzimu* takes measures to make its unease heard due to causing mental disorder to a random descendant. By identifying the responsible spirit as belonging to the *majini* category, a *sadaka* celebration is considered the predefined cure, acting as a sign of good will and a promise of closer adherence to the behavioural norms as demanded by the *majini* in the future.[155] Its therapeutic effects in such a case are regarded as easy and reliable. During the preparation and the conduction of the *sadaka*, the *majini* express their personal wishes through the possessed person, e.g. demanding a minimum number of invited guests or notifying their preferences in terms of the choice of food or drinks served.

As mentioned in the context of *madzoka*, other forms of treatment – in addition to dances and sacrificial offerings – may be associated with the appeasement of possessing spirits. Crucial to the therapeutic success, such medical actions are interwoven with cultural symbolism and, therefore, with cosmological meaning.[156] Frequently, the additional forms of traditional treatment indicate cultural notions of pathology – in the sense that a *mzimu* possessing a person is specified as entering his or her body either through the top of the head or via the back of the feet, and accordingly, treatment has to focus on these parts of the body in order to lure the spirit entities back out of it. A Lomwe

---

thus illustrate the importance of appeasement to the spiritual forces.

155 Therefore, the possession by a *majini* may indicate other kinds of moral transgression than an incorrect *sadaka* ceremony. In one case such, a *majini* protested against a descendant who had appropriated parts of the heritage this *majini* had left for his widow and orphans. Due to possessing the evildoer, the spirit made him publicly confess his turpitude. A communal *sadaka* was later celebrated in order to re-establish harmony between the living and the dead.

156 Some *mitengo* medications for mental disorder may therefore, e.g., be prepared by a *sing'anga* of the opposite sex to the patient – reflecting the gender of the spirit entity and the strong sexual connotations of mental disorders such as *misala* (Morris 1996: 122).

sing'anga explains that the strong, pungent smell of *mpungabwe* leaves, rubbed on the top of the patient's cranium, will cause the spirits to leave the possessed person.[157]

In addition to the mentioned therapeutic measures, many normative rules (*miyambo*) and ritual activities circle around the idea of preventing any offence against the ancestral spirits. Such rituals may include regular prayers and sacrifices in honour of the *mizimu* to perpetuate mutual agreement, but also relate to more precisely defined occasions.[158] A therapeutic ritual such as *madzoka* is typical for cases of mental disorder due to moral transgression, but the same ritual complex may apply in a case of spirit vocation, indicating that the ritual treatment of a person with a mental disorder may also resemble a first step towards initiation into the profession of a *sing'anga*.[159]

Achieving Divine Clemency

Expectedly, a case of mental disorder associated with the direct and deliberate will of the Supreme Being is considered exceptionally difficult to remedy. The overall curability of such cases of mental disorder is debated because

> "If you are punished by God, there can be no cure" (Issa Ndasimu, a Yao *sing'anga*).

Therefore, once divine punishment is accepted as the source of a given case of mental disorder, further therapeutic endeavours are frequently regarded as futile. The case may be considered unchangeable and the patient's condition accepted.[160] This situation, however, should not be misinterpreted as conceptual

---

157 This herb is identified as *Ocimum canum* (Morris 1996: 330), or Brazilian *Alfavaca*. Also referred to as *tchanzi*, *mpungabwe* is mentioned as an especially powerful treatment for *misala ya mizimu*. Alternative measures against troublesome *majini* include rubbing salt or paraffin onto the patient's head and heels, or extinguishing a brand of fire above it.

158 Accordingly, sacrificial offerings to the spirits may be applied to ensure their patronage for an unborn child, and post-natal appeasement is stressed for the sake of obtaining *mzimu* protection for a newborn child.

159 The concept of the mental-patient-turned-healer is a common feature in Southern Africa. John Janzen has subsumed this idea under the term *ngoma* (Janzen 1992), representing "a discourse on misfortune and healing connected with an institution which is, among other things, characterized by the fact that the healers who constitute and produce ngoma through their practices have become part of it through a transformation of someone who suffers into someone who heals" (Reis 2000: 1-2).

160 Notions of divine punishment may thus constrict integrative endeavours and maintain the *status quo* of persons with mental disorders because "instead of assisting children with disabilities to go to school some of them will not, because they will say this is what God has given us, and God wants things to be like they are. So these ones just have to grow up in the village, and all the time we will have to give them all what they need. They don't have to work because if you are making this particular person work it's like you are doing what God doesn't want, you are working against God" (Steven Msowoya, a Tumbuka disability organization representative).

incurability. Even the acknowledgment of a given case of mental disorder as unchangeable only reflects the therapeutic efficiency of the medical services available so far. A Yao TBA therefore states that

> "Myself, I agree that this [i.e. the birth of a *wopunduka* child] also happens to people who believe in God. Therefore, He punishes them because He wants to make them know their sins. Even if they go to the *sing'anga*, even if they go to hospital, persons like this one do not get healed, no, unless if they go to church and start praying. These things happen, even to children and grown-up persons themselves. […] It may be possible [to heal a *wopunduka* child by prayer] if the mother starts praying while the child is still small" (Iselda Tchema, a Yao *mzamba*).

The only exceptions that tend to be accepted as powerful enough to change a mental disorder originating from divine punishment are faith healing practices. In direct recognition of the divine source of the health problem, divine forgiveness is recognized as the logic solution for it. In present-day Malaŵi, many Christian communities – and, more especially, Pentecostal Churches – offer highly popular faith healing services which contribute considerably to the success of their evangelization efforts and raise patient expectations:

> "As for me, I am a Pentecostal believer and have taken her [i.e. her daughter] for prayers. […] But God hasn't touched her yet, maybe by and by God will touch her and then she will be healed – and then I will go on TV and radios to make announcements" (Miriam Namanja, a Yao disabled persons' organization representative).

Many relatives of persons with mental disorder who have, at some point, accepted the given case as divine punishment express their hope in a suitable religious group to bring divine grace to the punished. Reports about successful faith healing therapies being conducted for the otherwise hopeless are commonly narrated[161] – while repeatedly unsuccessful faith healing attempts are validated differently. While the discourse in Pentecostal Churches partially encourages patients to stay hopeful, it may also mark such cases by an assumed lack of faith.

Due to the specific motivations of the various categories of spirit agents in Southern Malaŵi, different therapeutic approaches are implemented in order to eliminate the problem and recreate spiritual order and equilibrium. After all, the identification of a spirit agent always implies an individual originator, and all cases therefore fall into two broad categories: while most notions recognize the patient's – or, likewise, a close relative's – actions as the original trigger that

---

161 Some accounts stress personal experience with cases of miraculous healing, e.g. within the Pentecostal Assemblies of God community, stressing the notion of true, faithful repentance as the key to therapeutic success.

caused the situation, some other concepts consider the affected person and their kinsfolk as innocent of the condition. Spiritual agents are not expected to act without cause, and it is only the most malevolent, incontrollable spirit entities that are known to attack human persons even though no social norm or behavioural precaution has been violated. Traditional treatment of spirit-induced mental disorder, accordingly, permeates social structure on various levels and can therefore be conceived as the social reproduction of health – in terms of a set of socially structured relationships (Basu 2002: 54; Janzen 1992: 154).

4(c) Fixing Accidental Damage

In Southern Malaŵi, the idea of providing a viable therapy for a condition of mental disorder that is associated with the very structure of the cosmos is very ambivalent, and the therapeutic expectations may depend primarily on the individual case and the symptoms displayed.

In some cases, structural conditions of mental disorder are considered as easily cured. One account describes a condition of *kulumala* as a faulty disposition of the blood vessels, with clotting blood blocking the veins and leading to numerous complaints. As a therapy, a *mphini* treatment is recommended to solve the blockage within the veins. As a second therapeutic step, the respective limb – e.g., a leg – would need to be straightened by mechanical means while special *mankhwala* are applied as additional support. Those cases of mental disorder considered comparably easy to treat include *khunyu*, and a large number of remedies for such conditions mention medicine for drinking (*mankhwala akumwa*) as the central therapeutic element.[162] Different recipes are described as highly efficient, leading to complete disappearance of all *khunyu* symptoms after just one therapy session. Preventive medicine – in the form of *zithumwa* (see *Chapter II.2.a*) – is also seen as being efficient especially in cases where a structural causation is assumed. The traditional *mankhwala a mutu* used to safeguard that the – 'natural' – process of the closing of a child's fontanel does not lead to mental disorder likewise supports the observation that traditional medicine is considered capable of treating some cases of mental disorder related to cosmological structure.[163]

---

162 Extensive studies on Cheŵa medical botany specify 30 different plants applied in the treatment of *khunyu* (Morris 1996: 511) while the report on a medical plants project gives the same number of recipies (Mwanyambo & Nihero 1998: Appendix 3). In many cases, numerous ingredients are required for a given *mankhwala*. In one reported recipe for *khunyu*, 18 different kinds of *mitengo* need to be soaked in water, producing beer-like foam. When drained, the water is given to the patient to drink 'one sip at a time'. The explicitly foaming quality of *khunyu* remedies is repeatedly stressed.

163 This *chithumwa* consists of a ring the size of a fingertip, made from the root of a millet stem

In many other cases, though, structural cases of mental disorder are described as notoriously difficult to treat. Encouraged by biomedical health officials, this attitude usually emphasizes the connection to the Supreme Being and religious concepts of divine will.[164] Mainstream Christian as well as Muslim approaches – which, as mentioned earlier, tend to favour structural explanations for all kinds of health disorders – may therefore reiterate the inevitability of the condition occurring while, at the same time, supporting the notion that divine intervention – rare and miraculous as it may be – could still provide immediate cure. This notion represents the theological key of Pentecostal health ministries which aim at mobilizing spiritual healing powers which are conceived as the ultimate therapeutic solution.

It has been argued already that the category of structural causation of mental disorder is far from homogeneous, and the present section should illustrate that the same applies also for its treatment. Certain conditions are considered to have remarkably reliable traditional remedies – e.g. *khunyu* – while other structural cases of mental disorder are conceptualized in closer connection to conditions of divine retribution.

5. *Discussing Cause and Effect in Mental Disorder*

Various results can be derived from the observations presented here. Most obviously, aetiological classification must be outlined as the single most decisive factor in the cultural construction of mental disorder – particularly including its social acceptance and therapeutic manufacture. The social situation of persons with mental disorders and their immediate kin in Southern Malaŵi is, at best, highly fragile. While my previous evidence presents social approaches by means of more ethnographic observations, the present analysis finally provides a wider emic basis. It is, after all, the result of cultural processes of aetiological categorization which allocates cultural meaning to the individual patient, and the

---

(*mapira*) and the menstruation cloth of a woman, usually the child's mother. This ring, sometimes called *phula* or 'security', put on a thread and tied around the child's neck, is considered a reliable prophylaxis for *mutu*. Applied no later than two weeks after birth, it takes effect after one week by the child's fontanel slowly closing. Other forms of *mankhwala a mutu* – sometimes called *likambako* – are likewise worn around the neck, but produced from beads. Alternatively, medicated water (a *mankhwala akusamba*) may be used to wash the child's head, which would work as reliably as the usual *phula*.

164 Therefore, "Another reason [for mental disorder] is that a person is born like that. God created him to be like that. [...] If it is God's will, what happens is that when they bring the patient to doctors like us, we just put some magical protection on his/her body, but the patient doesn't get cured because we cannot reverse God's will, it's very difficult" (Henry Mwambo, a Yao *sing'anga*).

mode of causation accepted in a given case indicates appropriate therapeutic steps and predefines the cultural expectations for its therapeutic success. In Malaŵi, nosological categorization is not at all vital for an understanding of the respective health disorder – it merely sums up symptomatic observations. The aetiological background is the critical factor, and its negotiation is part of a continuous social discourse. By and large, the explanatory models are almost exclusively connected to notions of personal responsibility due to which cultural labels are applied and the patients' chances for social participation, for inclusion and exclusion are negotiated. The social semantics of aetiological labelling are, however, not a monolithic system. The pluralistic character of the explanatory system emphasizes that any given case – i.e. any person – can be socially re-negotiated and re-evaluated according to a new aetiological classification. Here, factors of cultural change are crucial, and the increasing influence of certain – especially religious – frames of reference has already been insinuated.

Therapy and Constraint

The above depiction of therapeutic reactions to states of mental disorder should not belie the fact that not every action taken against affected persons may be regarded as therapeutic in this sense. In order to compliment the portrayal of the social response to mental disorder phenomena, it shall be noted here that numerous accounts mention the practice of restraining potentially violent persons. Most frequently mentioned is the tradition of tying affected persons to a wooden log which, sitting on their shoulders like a yoke, thus prevents them from attacking others or moving over longer distances.[165] This practice is well documented in the 1970s among the Cheŵa of the Central Region where

> "The »village idiot« is treated with respect. He is said to be »of the *mizimu*«. […] Certainly people have great patience with these mentally deficient, putting up with them and taking care not to treat them harshly. If they become dangerous, they will hamper their movements by fixing a big wooden log to their feet or on their shoulders. But they will not be allowed to go short of food as long as they stay in their village or in the vicinity where they are known. People put up with them and pay little attention when they cause trouble" (Breugel 2001: 85).

Recently, public discourse in Malaŵian national newspapers has addressed the continuity of such restrictive measures.[166] Obviously, the accounts relating to this

---

165 For photographical illustration of such a *gori* or constraining yoke, taken in 1950s Dedza District, see King & King 1997: 110.

166 For three years, as a newspaper article reports, a man from Lilongwe District was "[…] tied to a heavy log around his neck as a way of putting under him control because of his physical aggression towards other villagers, especially children. »We agreed as a village to put a log around [the patient]'s neck because that was the only way of protecting people and their property

custom typically address conditions of *misala* – in recognition of the generally aggressive and violent disposition associated with this form of mental disorder. The notion of publicly restraining persons with mental disorder in order to keep them from causing harm demonstrates that therapeutic measures are not necessarily the only actions taken in order to deal with a concrete condition, and not all cultural reactions to mental disorder are related to its causative background. Rather, some additional measures respond to disorder plainly on the basis of suppressing its symptoms, and socially ostracising and humiliating reactions – such as tying a person to a wooden log, a picture that, at least to the European beholder, is all too evocative of the proverbial pillory – may be applied indiscriminately of the general cultural validation of the condition.

Moreover, the public stigmatization and the consequent feeling of shame on the side of the respective kin-group may express itself in a very verbatim exclusion of persons with mental disorders – such as the confinement of the respective persons within their family homes. The representatives of local organizations for persons with disabilities consistently describe this as a common phenomenon in both rural and urban areas – successfully keeping even immediate neighbours ignorant of the existence of a person with a mental disorder living next door.[167]

> "I have come across such parents who have hidden their kids in the houses. […] They feed them and lock them because they don't want to be seen, they are ashamed. And one of them, someone tipped us so we went and discovered that girl who had severe physical disabilities. She had smaller limbs, both limbs. We talked to them and so on. This was a fourteen-year-old girl. […] So to them it was like I think we have something that we don't like and we don't want to be associated with it but we don't want to kill it. So we don't want people to know

---

from being harmed and destroyed« said [the village headman] [...]. He said what scared people was that [the patient] burnt four houses, pulling the walls down on himself, adding that he behaved like a wild animal by attacking adults and children. »We had no choice, but to put him under tight control and confine him to a place where he would not be in touch with other human beings« [...] [The patient's sister] said she had to take food to the bush where her brother had spent the last three years under inhuman conditions even during the rainy season" (Bottoman 2005).

167 While no firsthand evidence can be provided here, it is narrated as cultural fact and must therefore be seen as a common motif in the Malaŵian perception of the phenomenon. Accordingly, organizations for persons with disabilities sometimes employ community volunteers because of their better knowledge of actual family situations in their home communities. Based on her own research data from Botswana, however, Benedicte Ingstad questions the significance of hiding, neglect, or abuse, arguing that "what seemed like the most obvious case of a disabled person hidden away – a man locked up day and night in his hut – reveals a story of family love and concern when looked into more closely" (Ingstad 1995: 251). The general validity of this appraisal in the Malaŵian context is, as mentioned, difficult to assess.

that we have a kid like this" (Steven Msowoya, the Tumbuka representative of an organization for persons with disabilities).

Such practices illustrate the limitations of therapeutic activities while, at the same time, constituting an important contribution to the question of stigmatization. Accordingly, this complex will be addressed again in the final conclusion of this study.

Re-Interpreting Moral Transgression

Many studies on Malaŵian medical anthropology include categories of sickness causation related to breach of taboo or moral transgression (Peltzer 1987: 59-60) while the data presented here supports a modification of this model. Indisputably, moral transgression forms a central part of the cultural discourse of sickness causation. The concept underlying the notion of moral transgression is, in itself, apersonal: specific behavioural rules require observation and, if not maintained, some immanent factors lead to human affliction. As a classical example within the Malaŵian context, *miyambo* for the avoidance of *mdulo* may be of interest here. Implying a cultural concept of symbolic temperature, transgression of culturally defined behavioural norms may lead to sickness, mental disorder, or even death. Therefore, menstruating women, sexually active persons or hunters coming home from work – all of which are defined as symbolically 'hot' – have to avoid a newborn child, classified as symbolically 'cold,' or contaminate the infant with this dangerous, conflicting state of temperature. So far, this concept of *mdulo* has been interpreted as being based on a notion of an impersonal cause-and-effect relationship.

It has, at the same time, been rightfully pointed out that violations directed against the ancestors and their demands are also regarded as a potential origin of *mdulo* (Kalipeni 1981: 110; Marwick 1965: 66-67). Here, the conceptual connection between *mdulo* and spirit retribution becomes apparent, revealing spirit entities (*mizimu*) as the active agents causing sickness as a direct, deliberate, and strictly didactic punishment (Peltzer 1987: 59-61). This, in short, is the interpretation which has been applied within the context of this study. While acknowledging the mechanistic, non-personal character of *mdulo* causation, it has, equally convincingly, been emphasized that behavioural rules surrounding the avoidance of *mdulo* are associated with the ancestors, and that the spirits (*mizimu*) guard over their observance.[168] Taboos, as may be added on

---

[168] In other words: the conflict between 'hot' and 'cold' symbolic temperature and the cultural norms for their avoidance are a manifestation of the cosmological order, put in place by the Supreme Being and now protected by the *mizimu* who are responsible for their perpetuation. While the violation of these rules therefore leads to mechanical, inevitable punishment, the

a more general level, are therefore expressions of social order and ancestral power. *Mdulo* contamination is not absolute – it only represents an offence of certain culturally defined behavioural norms (*miyambo*) over which the ancestral spirits command in their function as guardians of the cultural values. In yet other terms: moral transgression is not a strictly structural concept – it is, rather, a principle that relies on the predictable use spirit entities make of their agency.

Dichotomies of Magic

It has been necessary to re-evaluate concepts of magic in Southern Malaŵi, argueing that a strict binary dichotomy of magic systems as postulated in many previously published accounts conflicts with the more complex notions indicated by current research findings – and severely impairs the understanding of magic's role within local notions of mental disorder. Agreeing with Brian Morris' assertion that, like the Cheŵa, most people in Southern Malaŵi "do not make a radical distinction between witchcraft and sorcery" (Morris 1996: 163), it may be argued that the differentiation between 'good' (*matsenga*) and 'evil' (*ufiti*) magic is only a contextual, idealized model which, on closer analysis, is outweighed by the existence of a far wider set of varying phenomena – subsumed here under the category *kukhwima* which exist in between the extremes as well as in the loopholes of cultural acceptance and prohibition. This discovery is highly relevant on several cultural levels, most importantly in providing the logical framework for one of the central models for the causation of mental disorder which could not be appropriately addressed and understood by the use of a binary model of magic.

It may be tempting but, supposedly, an over-interpretation to present the notion of *kukhwima* – in connection to *ufiti* and *matsenga* – in terms of a structuralist model, i.e. by defining both latter categories as opposing and contradictory elements and *kukhwima* as their mediation and resolution (Lévi-Strauss 1963: 224). It may, at the same time, be helpful to bear this model of polar duality in mind as it provides a logic perspective for the ambiguous character of the *kukhwima* concept. As the 'trickster' category of Malaŵian magic, *kukhwima* mediates between concepts of a greater good and an ultimate evil, representing the deeply human notions of utilitarianism, egotism, and asocial ambition. It is, however, not the intention of the present study to introduce *kukhwima* as a fixed third category of magic in addition to *ufiti* and *matsenga*. More in-depth research should be dedicated to this notion in order to clarify its character within the area of conflict between *ufiti* and *matsenga*. For

---

guardians overseeing over these traditions are spiritual forces which become personally active in passing punishment over to the human being.

now, it shall suffice to use the example of *kukhwima* in order to demonstrate that a straightforward, dualist model does not do justice to the much more sophisticated question of legitimate and illegitimate use of magic.

The introduction of the concept of *kukhwima* into the discussion on concepts of magic in Malaŵi is also relevant because it puts the phenomenon of mental disorder into the wider perspective of social system and hierarchy. Here, persons with mental disorders feature as the shadow image, the downside of social high achievers – and both polar conditions are regarded as causally interrelated, both detach the person from the cultural norm, and both therefore constitute some form of social deviation. *Kukhwima* magic provides the means for achieving personal success, and it is considered as inescapable that the accomplishments of the individual person presuppose the violation of cultural norm. While this procedure is socially frowned upon and regarded with awe, it is also accepted as a necessity – in perfect agreement with the common English idiom that you cannot make an omelette without breaking some eggs. This notion places the politically powerful and socially successful outside – or rather, beyond – the the reach of otherwise culturally binding values, and it may also help explain the problematic process of democratization in Malaŵi over the last two decades. The cultural reservations against *kukhwima* practices express themselves in the frequent inclusion of this notion into *ufiti* – even though the concept itself clearly falls short of a number of distinctive characteristics defining the actual *ufiti*, *ufiti weni-weni*. In consequence, *kukhwima* points to the cultural concept that personal power and authority are intrinsically linked with anti-social behaviour: cruelty appears as a prerequisite of power, and to obtain personal authority is to overcome local ideas of what is valued as morally good, desirable, and right.

Analogies of Cause and Effect

Numerous accounts presented in this and previous chapters have indicated that the cultural perception of mental disorder relates to a complex of symbolism. The structural patterns of this attribution between performative form and intended effect can, in essence, be described in terms of James Frazer's concept of sympathetic magic – operating according to an underlying law of similarity that is based on the assumption of imitative or contagious mechanisms (Frazer 1922: 11-43). *Ufiti* magic, therefore, implies a fairly basic assumption of an analogous connection between ritual action and magic effect – i.e. the magic procedures as including performance or utilized objects and the apparently senseless behaviour of a victim. A victim's condition of *kuthamanga misala* or 'running mad' is hence related to the *mfiti*'s ritual – by hanging the effective *zizimba* into a tree, the victim is forced to run around aimlessly just like the wind moves the dangling charms in the branches. The properties of the *zizimba* are likewise connected to the desired magical effect by a line of direct symbolic analogy.[169] Similarly, the understanding of *kukhwima* draws a very immediate analogous connection between the damage done and the advantages achieved by its magic use. Therefore, a case of *khunyu* caused by *kukhwima* would be interpreted in a way that links the occurrence of the victim's spasms to the beneficiaries' earning of money, as

> "Some people want to be *okhwimira* so that whenever this person falls down, they should have some money. […] That one [i.e. one form of *khunyu*] coming from persons gives you seizures every time that the other one wants to find some money, because sometimes he/she might fall only once per year, like every year in October" (Sapitwa Chagoma, a Lomwe *sing'anga*).

This concept is typical for the explanation of mental disorder symptoms. The periodic occurrence of complaints is seen as the time the responsible *wokhwima* benefits from the victim, explaining the otherwise inscrutable occurrence of mental complaints by an underlying pattern of voluntary causation.[170] This model applies for different manifestations of mental disorder, interpreted as indicating the evil-doer's personal intentions. Therefore, a *womisala*'s actions of walking aimlessly and bothering passers-by is analogous to the enslaved *mzimu wa umunthu* attracting customers for the business of a rich relative, and someone picking up garbage from the ground indicates the way his/her spirit is busy accumulating wealth for its *wokhwima* master.[171] The symbolic connection between magic ritual and the manifestation of mental disorder not only provides a framework for the conception of magic and its performative principles, but it also, in turn, allocates semantic logic to the symptoms of the individual patient. In doing this, it creates cultural meaning by embedding otherwise incomprehensible behaviour into a structure of magic cause and effect.

The same mechanism applies in the wide field of traditional normative rules (*miyambo*) which, in this line of argument, operate on the 'magic' basis of connecting cause and effect by analogical means – i.e. that moral transgression

---

169 Thus, a certain rare beetle is described as a vital *zizimba* needed to cause *khunyu*. Somewhat resembling a dung beetle, this insect is reported to feign death upon touch. When used in *ufiti*, the effect on the victim resembles the insect's characteristic of falling into a death-like condition. It is, however, a justified point of criticism to inquire *why* a given similarity between two particular entities is culturally identified as carrying magical potential.

170 "So, if their business is in groceries, whenever the child suffers from *kuzungulira mutu* is when the business goes well" (Manueli Matundwe, a Sena *sing'anga*). With reference to *kuzerezeka*, "A *mfiti* can damage a person's brain. What does a *mfiti* gain from that act? Money! Because when the patient becomes immobile, saliva coming out all the time, food coming out of the mouth, the same way money comes in" (Richard Nazombe, a Lomwe *sing'anga*).

171 So "another *misala* comes from persons if they want to use *kukhwima* for them. Like with a maize-mill, if someone is always just collecting garbage on the market, the same way these things speed up the business" (Francis Muramu, a Lomwe *sing'anga*).

leads to a punishment that reproduces its reason in the form of analogy or, more precisely, similarity. The principle of sympathy as depicted above is therefore applicable in various spheres of culture that surround the incidence of mental disorder in Southern Malaŵi.

Explanatory Pluralism

As a final and more general observation, any form of mental disorder can be attributed to a number of different causes, and it is due to the external – e.g. the social – framework as well as internal factors – e.g. the exact symptoms – that this allocation is conducted. Malaŵian aetiological models are marked by their pluralistic character. The cultural discourse always acknowledges more than one possible explanation, and which one of them is favoured in a given case is a matter of social negotiation, influenced by situational, contextual, and personal considerations. The pluralistic character of traditional aetiology easily allows different models of causations to be drawn on simultaneously with respect to one given case, each of which indicating not only dissimilar therapeutic procedures, but also representing conflicting cosmological systems. The different aetiological approaches of the competing health care providers in Southern Malaŵi therefore coexist in a wide, pluralistic medical landscape open to new concepts – as long as their therapeutic efforts are perceived as efficient.

Figure 3: The Lomwe *sing'anga* Sapitwa Chagoma preparing his *mphambanya* or *ufiti*-finding staff by 'washing' it with *ufa* (maize flour)

V.

Concluding Discussion

In any given cultural environment, health disorders necessarily constitute a challenge not only to the person they affect, but also to the community as a whole – and it would be an oversimplification to define this challenge as exclusively medical. Disorders that are perceived as primarily mental are certainly no exception, and in Malaŵi they clearly range amongst the health issues which pose the most immediate consequences to the affected persons. The medical problems as identifiable from a biomedical perspective are significantly aggravated by cultural conditions. And while biomedical services are supported by both national and international policies as the main agent to solve and overcome the plight of persons with mental disorders, their position within the medical landscape of Southern Malaŵi is still contended in different respects. Throughout the length of this thesis, the phenomenon of mental disorder has been presented within the complexity of its various, multi-layered spheres of cultural representation from a holistic perspective. The results are manifold.

Few publications address the topic of mental disorder and culture so far. With the main body of available data following a psychological, educational, or developmental focus – or presenting largely statistical information –, the need for qualitative anthropological accounts on cultural conceptions of disability and mental illness should be substantiated. A number of specific results have been deducted from the data presented in this thesis. Some of them have already been analysed in the context of their respective chapters while others will require further consideration in this conclusion. For the sake of lucidity, the main results of this thesis will be subsumed here.

It has been shown that *(1)* the application of the term disability is difficult – or rather, unsuitable – for Malaŵian cultural concepts.[1] The generic term mental disorder as used here may serve to express that various health disorders – from cases that would, in biomedical interpretation, qualify as mental retardation to

---

1 The term 'activity limitation' as supported by Mitch Loeb and Arne Eide, on the other hand, is analytically useful. It is, at the same time, not designed in order to represent emic, intentional notions, but it focuses on clearly functional criteria (Loeb & Eide [eds.] 2004).

mental illnesses, physical impairment, or epilepsy – are closely associated with mental limitations from an emic perspective. As a consequence, the absence of a distinction between 'temporary' and 'permanent' states of mental disorder indicates that *(2)* all cases of mental disorder are considered curable on a conceptual level and that failed therapeutic attempts only means that the appropriate medical specialist and/or health provider institution has not been identified yet – thus implicitly demanding for an extended search for treatment. Furthermore, the data shows that *(3)* cultural definitions of mental disorder as opposed to 'normal' mental performance and competence refer to the concept of the person. Mental disorder represents a deviation from the social norm, and on the basis of both functional and behavioural factors, the different Malaŵian cultures attribute mental disorder to persons who either *(a)* are unable or unwilling to perform certain essential tasks, or *(b)* show peculiar, non-normative behaviour that is considered deviant – both according to an emic perspective. Even forms of behaviour that simply counteract cultural values – e.g. lack of politeness or self-control – may be identified as indicators of mental disorder.

Moreover, it has been demonstrated that *(4)* mental disorder as a cultural phenomenon is part of a wide social context that tackles various spheres of social and cultural life. Mental disorder, therefore, does not represent an isolated or marginal phenomenon within Malaŵian societies, but it is of central cultural interest in numerous social situations – e.g. during pregnancy, in the context of personal success, or in moral instruction. It is therefore also notable that *(5)* a large codex of behavioural norms surround the occurrence and avoidance of mental disorder, thus emphasizing the cultural recognition of the phenomenon due to its representation in central cultural complexes such as ritual initiation, the rites of secret societies, or oral tradition. The principles underlying such taboos follow an implicit idea of analogy which also typically applies in the context of magic. In contrast to earlier assumptions, it has been further outlined that *(6)* the ancestral spirits are culturally recognized as the agents overseeing the observation of normative traditions and, potentially, causing mental disorder as a retribution for moral transgression or 'breach of taboo' in their role as the guardians of traditional values.

It has further been substantiated that *(7)* the classificatory process that is applied for mental disorder reflects a purely descriptive notion, focussing mainly on symptoms and syndromes. In itself, terminological categorization has a stigmatizing character which impairs social inclusion and – eventually – renders an unbiased and non-judgmental perception impossible. This linguistic fact presents an implicit problem to both organizational and personal efforts for reintegration and social acceptance – which are counteracted already by an initial labelling process. In this context, it is likewise crucial that *(8)* the causative factors that are identified for a given case of mental disorder predefine *(a)* the cosmological understanding of the phenomenon, but also *(b)* the social attitude and acceptance of the affected persons and their kin within the community, and *(c)* the therapeutic options favoured and expectations invested in them. It should further be noted that *(9)* the causative factors identified in such cases derive from a highly pluralistic complex of medicine and cosmology – and that the various cosmological contexts and their respective health services are to a very high degree regarded as mutually incompatible. While medical pluralism is by far no unexpected discovery in an African country, it is nonetheless both central and instructive that *(10)* cosmological pluralism, as a consequence of recent processes of cultural change, devaluates traditional norms aiming to protect the already vulnerable social position of persons with mental disorders. By scrutinizing formerly binding behavioural rules – which are associated not only with the social treatment but also with the causation of mental disorder –, cosmological pluralism works in disfavour of those in need of social support.

Within the process of attributing reasons to a given case of mental disorder, it is also notable that *(11)* magic concepts play a central role, and that the generally valid dichotomy between culturally valued and ostracized categories of magic may need some reconsideration – being transcended and expanded specifically in the context of mental disorder causation which is most closely associated with a set of magic notions that connects social positions of power, authority, or success with deeply anti-social magic action. In consequence, the different modes of explanation presented clearly indicate that *(12)* cultural ideas of the causation of mental disorder center around a principle of embodied responsibility – a notion that, according to the different modes of causation acknowledged within its pluralistic cosmological context, is highly likely to identify the affected persons and/or their immediate kin as 'scapegoats'.

1. Competing Conceptions

In order to complete the analysis on cosmological pluralism and its relevance in the context of mental disorder in Southern Malaŵi, some further considerations need to be added.

1(a) Perceiving Mental Disorder

In the introduction to his anthology on culture, classification, and intellectual disability, Richard Jenkins describes religion as one of the foremost cultural themes in the construction of incompetence (Jenkins 1998a: 19) – which is equally applicable for the construction of mental disorder in Southern Malaŵi. The present thesis has demonstrated that cosmological notions – and, more particularly, those of the person or the spiritual realm – are central to the cultural conceptualization of mental disorder. In essence, the person interprets and deals with mental disorder on the basis of four – more or less – distinct cosmological paradigms of loosely pre-defined notions. Here, *(a)* traditional cultural notions – which are also found as the underlying concepts of most other approaches – may be distinguished from religious dogmas in the context of *(b)* Islam and *(c)* Christianity as well as the rare occurrence of *(d)* biomedical approaches. In spite of significant support by governmental and international institutions, biomedical concepts can only claim limited success in establishing a wide-spread scientific alternative to the aforesaid ideas. The perception of mental disorder is determined by corresponding and/or conflicting cosmological representations – all of which are in a state of competition for dominance.

While biomedicine has for a long time been closely connected – if not, in the case of the early mission hospitals, positively identified – with the spiritual message of Christianity, the post-colonial differentiation of Christian churches has led to an increased spiritual conflict between biomedicine and Christianity. Western education plays a prominent part in the introduction of biomedical concepts, and it is due to the difficult situation of primary education facilities in rural areas that urban Malaŵians with at least elementary formal education find it considerably easier to relate to biomedical interpretations for mental disorder than their rural counterparts. While the accomplishments of biomedicine are widely acknowledged in specific areas of attested expertise, other parts of the population argue that biomedical therapy is useless against certain other kinds of disorders – i.e. especially those caused by magic and by spirit activity. The above presentation has already indicated that a majority of mental disorder cases are associated with such reasons. In spite of decade-long efforts of international aid organizations, national governments, and other agents, biomedical facilities are still difficult to access for a considerable part of the Malaŵian population. Infrastructural problems abide on a number of levels – even if the spatial distance between health seeker and biomedical health care provider may be covered with reasonable ease, the services may still be reduced due to situational unavailability of drugs, applications, specialized personnel, or the like. Accordingly, the overall recognition of biomedical services is, though highly supported and encouraged, still subject to varying opinions. This applies most particularly with respect to mental health services. The availability of biomedical care in terms of both disability and mental health has reached some level of coverage in the urban areas of the country and their immediate surroundings. For the majority of the population in the Southern Region, however, Western mental health and disability services are still extremely difficult to access on a regular basis.

A question developing over the course of the research focuses on the conceptual penetrability of alternative medical ideas and their degree of reciprocal acceptance and tolerance. It has been elaborated already that the relationship between biomedical, Muslim, Christian, and traditional health care facilities is mostly defined by mutual distrust and disrepute. Traditional cultural notions disagree with biomedicine on a number of instances, and they frequently challenge the efficiency of biomedical therapy for mental disorder. The scientific paradigm underlying biomedicine conflicts with the high relevance of cosmological explanations applied particularly in the context of mental disorder. Many Malaŵians therefore apply Western mental health facilities not as therapeutic institutions but as a means of social isolation – i.e. physically removing the problem by 'dumping' affected persons. Members of the community who are identified as a potential threat to their environment are confined to mental health institutions – such as Zomba Mental Hospital –, but when a former patient is discharged as healed, the local communities have severe problems in accepting therapeutic success due to the hospital's lack of spiritual authority. Thus, while biomedical institutions are forced to accept and respond to local interpretations of a deviant condition, the communities in turn find it hard to trust in Western practices and definitions of successful treatment of mental disorder. Not surprisingly, this problem of conflicting health philosophies is a bidirectional one. Biomedicine also gives no discernible recognition to the cultural specificity of mental disorder. Instead, Malaŵian forms of mental disorder are categorized into the broad, pre-defined biomedical nosologies with their respective aetiological backgrounds. Both of these not only have very limited relevance for the local health seeker, but they both conflict with elementary cultural assumptions on health and sickness, thus contradicting local cosmologies on a very basic conceptual level. Due to the difficulties in applying biomedical paradigms within a cultural context, the approach pursued in hospitals and health stations is increasingly questioned. Not fulfilling the metaphysical demands of patients and the wider communities alike, the trust in successful treatment is low. The frequent expectation of seeing therapeutic results in a short timeframe, moreover, also limits the validity of biomedicine as a feasible medical alternative.

While the different local medical services offer a variety of therapeutic options, the respective facilities are, at the same time, aggressively campaigning against each other. The health-seeking person is caught in the middle of these competing, almost mutually exclusive sets of ideas. In this position, local patients show a considerable degree of cosmological flexibility – a liberty to adopt conflicting concepts for explanation, depending on what serves best to meet their therapeutic demands. Therefore, it is due to the low efficiency of biomedical health facilities – as perceived within large parts of the population – in addressing issues of mental disorder that the Western scientific paradigm has so far proven difficult to implement in Malaŵi, leaving biomedicine as just another competitor in a heterogeneous and pluralistic medical field. While the non-judgmental approach of the biomedical paradigm is frequently attractive for affected persons and their kin – who try to operationalize Western concepts of explanation in their respective environments in order to remove blame –, they only have a limited degree of assertiveness as opposed to traditional explanations that target on 'making sense' of the condition in terms of cosmological concepts.

1(b) Producing Cultural Meaning

It has been elaborated at some length that diagnostic processes aim at establishing a larger semantic framework within which mental disorder is positioned. Understanding a given case of mental disorder is not so much defined as knowledge about its typical symptoms or underlying pathological states: it is, in fact, exclusively defined by the active and embodied forces identified as being involved. This fact underlies traditional diagnosis in a way that, as among the Nyole of Uganda,

> "The 'divinatory gaze' does not analyse dysfunctions within individuals, but sees them synthetically in relation to spirit and human agents" (Whyte 1998: 171).

The importance of other human – or formerly human – actors in the explanation of mental disorder demonstrates its highly relational character in Southern Malaŵi – i.e. conceptualizing the phenomenon as such not as an independent ontological fact but as reflecting a relationship between the affected person(s) and the wider social and/or cosmological framework. Patrick Devlieger thus convincingly argues that

> "[…] »relationship« is the core concept, for it is clear that in African thinking, the person with a disability is not the direct and primary focus of solutions. Points in the broader environment, such as the disabled person's family, ancestors, and God, are the focus" (Devlieger 1995: 104).

It is, therefore, the strong social embedding of the person that not only defines the requirements of personal competence, but a lack of competence is also traced back to causative factors situated within this same social sphere.

Constructing Responsibility

The difficulties in introducing biomedical notions of causation have already been outlined – and they apply not only in a Malaŵian setting but also in a wider African framework (Serpell, Mariga & Harvey 1993).[2] It has further been outlined that the reasons which are culturally identified and accepted as responsible for a condition of mental disorder are decisive for the social situation of persons suffering from such conditions. Here, a closer analysis has indicated that the nosological categories allocated to a given case of mental disorder are not distinctive for a given aetiology and that the reasons recognized for a given case of mental disorder are critical for the social recognition of the affected person as well as for subsequent treatment options. This multicausal – or, more precisely, polysemic (Sagner 2001: 186) – approach provides very few affirmative criteria relating one cases of mental disorder to one corresponding reason, thus emphasizing the central importance of social interpretation and ascription. These processes are highly contextual, incorporating social reality on a number of different levels (Ingstad 1995: 253-255). In the not uncommon situation that two *asing'anga*, a hospital doctor, and a local priest attribute four different reasons to the same particular case, the community as such is involved in a complex process of negotiation.

In Southern Malaŵi, some local ideas of causation show similarities to biomedical concepts – e.g. drug abuse, inheritance, or the notion of structural reasons –, but references to genuinely biomedical explanations for mental disorder are almost exclusively limited to the group of biomedical professionals. The local debate on mental disorder reveals a very general need for palpable explanations, and they are accepted best – if not only – by referring to the cosmological sphere. Here, the pluralistic field of mental disorder explanation provides various concepts – which can almost exclusively be reduced to a fundamental principle: the quest for a culprit. While both Muslim and cosmopolitan Christian communities encourage a charitable approach to mental disorder – thus interpreting the condition on a purely structural background and advocating for support for the affected persons –, the vast majority of

---

2 With reference to mental retardation, it is argued that "most laypeople in Africa in the 1980s still tend to attribute the condition to supernatural causes and view it with a mixture of anxiety and repugnance. Magical or religious explanations receive wider credence than biomedical, sociocultural, or psychoeducational perspectives. European missionaries, however, have played a pioneering role in many African countries in direct intervention on behalf of children with mental retardation and other types of developmental disability. Ideologically they have sought to counter indigenous explanations in terms of breach of taboo by the parents and punishment by spirits, advancing instead a Christian conception of the retarded child as a blessing, a special responsibility for society, and an opportunity for the beneficent expression of charity" (Serpell, Mariga & Harvey 1993: 3).

explanations for mental disorder can be distinguished as identifying persons with mental disorders (and their immediate kin) as either victims of unjustified attacks or as villains themselves. In a traditional context, notions of magic causation declare either the affected person (in case of *matsenga*) or someone within the kin-group (*ufiti*, *kukhwima*) responsible. In cases of spiritual intervention, the respective person with a mental disorder may either be an innocent victim (demonic aggression) or be – either personally or as a representative of a given kinship group – liable for upsetting the cosmological equilibrium. If structural reasons are identified, no immediate wilful causation is assumed – but the given case may nonetheless be attributed to the person's own misconduct (drug abuse), an issue within the kin-group (heredity), or a nondescript unfortunate event (accident). On the intersection between Christian representations and the traditional values that they incorporate, Pentecostal churches also have a tendency to explain mental disorder on the basis of notions which identify the affected person and/or their close kin as responsible (in the form of demonic aggression and/or divine retaliation).[3] Some Christian writers address this 'discourse of sin' in the context of human suffering as a misinterpretation of the scripture, insisting that Biblical accounts explicitly reject sin as a reason for disorder (Kabue 2004: 33).[4] In spite of this assessment, it is conceded that

> "Today, some Christian churches, especially in Africa, still preach that disabilities are a result of works of the devil. The presence of people with disabilities in such churches is viewed as a failure by the church to combat the devil. It is therefore seen as a challenge to the church that calls for constantly invoking Christ's power to heal, and when this does not happen the concerned person with disability is blamed for lack of faith" (Kabue 2004: 34).

Therefore, reasons for mental disorder can be distinguished as being *(a)* either caused by an active agent or by cosmological structure. This latter structural causation of mental disorder has been argued to be a comparably rare explanation, and the majority of cases are therefore related to the immediate agency of someone who is responsible for the condition. The damage thus done may be referred to an agent that is perceived as *(b)* either personal or spiritual (e.g. a *kukhwima* expert versus an angry *mzimu wa makolo*), and the causation of

3 In this line of thought, "The Bible says: all sickness originates from sin. [...] all sufferings are just warning tones that a man should turn back to God" (Andrew Chisadza, a Lomwe Pentecostal priest). The punitive character of the Supreme Being not only indicates an Old Testament concept of Christianity. Rather, it powerfully relates to local definitions of the Supreme Being as a bifacial and ambivalent entity (Devlieger 1995: 103).

4 The gospel according to John 9:1-3 reads: "And as [Jesus] passed by, he saw a man which was blind from [his] birth. And his disciples asked him, saying, Master, who did sin, this man, or his parents, that he was born blind? Jesus answered, Neither hath this man sinned, nor his parents: but that the works of God should be made manifest in him" (Cogliano 2004: 617).

such cases of mental disorder may further be conceived as being *(c)* either voluntary or involuntary (e.g. spirit retaliation versus accident), and *(d)* either socially legitimate or illegitimate (e.g. *matsenga* versus *ufiti*). In the vast majority of these cases, individual responsibility plays a crucial role in the perception of mental disorder – in the context of traditional culture as well as in (and overlapping with) the religious paradigms of Islam and Christianity. This concept of responsibility creates a rift not only within a given kin-group – due to mutual accusation and increased economic hardship – but also between the family unit and the community as such, who perceives incidences within that kinship group as a disturbance of cosmological and social harmony that needs to be straightened out by the latter to the satisfaction of the former.

The concept of *kukhwima* magic – as introduced and analysed in the previous chapter – represents a central notion that has a considerable impact on the public understanding of mental disorder. Due to it connecting the occurrence of mental disorder with the economic, political, or spiritual achievements of another person by magic means, it affects the cultural perception of personal authority and ambition as such. Frequent accounts mention that *kukhwima* magic – and, in many cases, the subsequent sacrifice of another person's mental health – as a principle in the Malaŵian perception of public life.

The importance of this notion for the local understanding of mental disorder should be obvious: it represents yet another connection between the violation of cultural norms and the causation of mental disorder. Here, a particular emphasis lies on the egoistic, asocial motivation – as well as on the fact that the practice of *kukhwima* is culturally outlawed while still constituting the ruling principle in the definition of cultural authority. It furthermore alludes to a cultural assumption due to which any remarkable achievement on the side of an individual person must be, on some level, detrimental for another – or, on a larger scale, that cultural values can only be upheld by being violated. It creates a picture in which the polar notions of 'good' and 'evil' – as represented in the categories of *matsenga* and *ufiti* magic – set the framework for 'normal' human activity and social practice: as benevolent yet ruthless, open yet hidden, enviable yet abhorrent, powerful yet immoral.

Terming Cultural Reality

In this study, a survey of local modes of classification has served as a terminological introduction and inventory of the wide cultural notions surrounding the phenomenon of mental disorder. The terminology available within a given society sets the tone for any kind of debate on a very basic level, and nosological categorization determines, to a considerable degree, how a given health disorder is situated within its cultural context. While this approach, to some degree, refers back to concepts of cognitive anthropology,[5] it simply serves to produce a reliable picture of the cultural representations of mental disorder, and it is applied here in combination with other approaches. On the basis of the categories presented, this thesis argues that the arsenal of terminological categories available to denote a given medical condition predefines its cultural perception – including symptomatic patterns, or possible negative connotations. This determinism is, however, far from stringent. Rather, to refer to a different set of theoretic terms again, it is a matter of personal agency how to deal with the structural lack of non-judgmental categories. Numerous accounts have, e.g., demonstrated that parents of children with mental disorder decline to label their child's condition as anything at all, or that the use of English – i.e. biomedical – terminology is preferred in order to circumvent implicit devaluation. This seemingly cursory difficulty is of great relevance for the efficacy of rehabilitation projects that operate from a biomedical perspective. While a frequently recommended solution in order to avoid implicit linguistic bias is the abovementioned use of English biomedical terminology, these terms come with the problem that they, along with their underlying concepts, are alien to the vast majority of the population of Southern Malaŵi – thus increasing instead of alleviating the communication gap between biomedical health care providers and the local patient. While the attempt is benevolent and follows a clearly humanitarian motivation, it cannot be expected to simplify the situation – nor is it likely to eradicate depreciative attitudes prevalent in the communities. In order to advance the local discussion of mental disorder, it is therefore essential to operate on the basis of terms that are both generally comprehensible and non-depreciative.

Emic nosology is therefore crucial for the understanding of the cultural dimensions of mental disorder – due to the fact that one of the most elementary problems is one of communicating the issue without implicit biases and connotations. In the context of mental disorder, the various local societies – and, more especially, their respective languages – categorize sickness according to symptom patterns. Culturally recognized symptoms define pathological behaviour and, therefore, social deviation. It is obvious that, in accordance with Richard Jenkins, a set of classificatory terms does not necessarily imply immanent consistency or coherence. Rather, the labelling process can be seen as "lumping together fundamentally un-alike individuals" (Jenkins 1998b: 222) on the basis of ostensibly formal criteria. The – admittedly incomplete – catalogue of nosological categories therefore provides a comprehensive outlook on the

---

5 As a short definition, "Cognitive anthropology investigates cultural knowledge, knowledge which is embedded in words, stories, and in artifacts, and which is learned from and shared with other humans" (D'Andrade 1995: xiv).

range of culturally recognized and differentiated forms of mental disorder and thereby, in its totality, presents a viable cultural definition for mental disorder in Southern Malaŵi as such. By addressing the key question of *Who is culturally deviant?*, terminological concepts in reverse give ample analytical evidence to derive a cultural definition of normality – which will be depicted at greater length below.

Victims and Villains

The principle of identifying personal – or spiritual – responsibility for any given case of mental disorder is quasi ubiquitous, but it is most closely associated with traditional medical procedures. The main criticism against traditional treatment of mental disorder is not referring to lacking effectiveness, but to the socially disruptive consequences of their diagnostic processes. A number of accounts indicate the rejection of traditional healing on the basis of the fact that in most cases, the *sing'anga*'s diagnosis would generate a culprit responsible for the condition. As these individuals usually belong to the immediate social environment of the patient, the assessment of the *sing'anga* frequently leads to considerable social tensions. As the father of a child with a mental disorder explains,

> "[…] people here have gone to visit *asing'anga*, but my mind was not upon that because *asing'anga* sometimes cause enmity. […] Because whenever an African doctor can come here, he cannot say that this is a mental illness, but he can say somebody is bewitching the kid. […] The *sing'anga* told me that the woman who was here [i.e. his WMeZ] has bewitched the kid. Therefore an enmity can become between me and […] that woman" (Gerard Mdindire, a Mang'anja farmer).

The causations recognized for the occurrence of mental disorder are not only crucial for psychological and social processes of identifying a scapegoat within or outside the immediate social environment. Rather, knowledge of the 'true' cause for mental disorder – as defined by common consent – also provides the decisive key for all following therapeutic procedures and the degree of social support and protection which patients and their families can expect to receive within their community. The inferior role of nosology in the cultural localization of mental disorder reflects this circumstance by allocating metaphysical meaning to a given phenomenon and immediately putting it into a social and cosmological perspective. The choice of treatment, therefore, is significant not only for the question of therapeutic success. Rather, the different cosmological notions applied attribute specific sets of meaning to a health condition which may make an important difference in the social conception of the affected persons and their close kin-group alike.

In its social context, the fact that the responsible being is usually located in the immediate proximity of the affected person – identifying either the patient him or herself, a close relative, or a deceased family member (an ancestral spirit or *mzimu*) as the culprit – has some negative effects on the living conditions of the respective families. Moreover, this idea of responsibility – in combination with its typical frame of reference – puts dealing with mental disorder under the competency of the respective kin-group who is expected to address and solve this affair internally. Intrusion into the jurisdiction of a kin group is conceived as inappropriate and illegitimate to an outsider unless the situation threatens the peace on the scale of the larger community.[6] It is beyond the range of community efforts to interfere with the private domain, thus making mental disorder somebody else's hardship to bear. More simplistically still, the attitude towards mental disorder frequently displayed in Southern Malaŵi may be described as being both *somebody else's fault* and *somebody else's business*. While the kinship groups of affected persons usually show preference for explanations that do not attach additional shame to them, considerable social pressure along kinship lines and from the community pushes for traditional forms of therapy that are most likely to place blame on a single person and thus free the other members of the kin-group from suspicion.

1(c) Cure and Curability

It has already been clarified that mental disorder categories are not central to the treatment applied. Even though nosological factors – as representing specific symptom patterns – are also reflected in the prescriptions of traditional therapy, the more general information refers to the sickness causation. In other words, while the nosology may resemble the fine adjustment of a given therapy, the aetiology represents its overall alignment, general direction, and logic intention. From an emic point of view, assuming the wrong aetiological factors necessarily leads to therapeutic failure while the different nosologies indicate individual implementations of therapy which may or may not be successful. The necessary clues for the reasons – and, therefore, the treatment – of mental disorder are obtained due to diagnostic procedures. At the same time, there seem to be no structural limit to therapeutic feasibility – thus leading to a more general

6 Within the context of this kinship dimension of mental disorder, the personal fate of the individual patient is secondary to the consequences that phenomenon has for the larger kinship group – thus revealing "a 'collective' orientation towards medicine" (Morris 1986: 374) in Southern Malaŵi. In his analysis of Songye concepts of disability, Patrick Devlieger likewise concludes that disability is defined as a family affair that is beyond the individual but, at the same time, below the cognizance of the community as a whole (Devlieger 1995: 100).

question of Malaŵian conceptions of curability. Notions of curability are subject to a wide cultural debate, and many accounts indicate that a notion of structurally universal curability is basically agreed. However, this does not necessarily represent a somewhat naïve expectation of instantaneous miracle cure – but a cultural notion that, even though it may take time and significant efforts, any form of mental disorder can be successfully treated. If a given case is not successfully treated in spite of repeated therapeutic attempts, the treatments received are understood as not appropriate for the specific condition and/or its origin – and therefore, the availability of alternative therapeutic services is central to the outcome of the overall treatment (see below).

In essence, the cultural concept of general curability bases on traditional notions of medicine and medical qualification. In a traditional context, ancestor spirits (*mizimu ya makolo*) are the quintessential providers of medical skills, and if the therapeutic measures taken by a traditional healer are regarded as unsuccessful, it is therefore concluded that a different *sing'anga* – operating with different spiritual advisors and therefore having different medical powers at his or her command – may receive the right therapeutic procedures to overcome the particular health problem. By transfer, this concept is also applied to non-traditional medical service providers.

Healing by Divine Authority

It is in this context that the increasing importance of Christian faith healing comes into play, and its growing acceptance as an alternative therapeutic option is stressed by its highly successful evangelization programmes. While the paradigms acknowledged by these – mainly Pentecostal – churches sharply reject all elements of traditional religion, many traditional structures are nonetheless reflected in their cosmology and rituals. An important difference between traditional religious beliefs and Christianity, however, refers to the amount of direct communication between the Supreme Being and the human person. Traditional religious notions generally assume a detached Supreme Being that is out of reach to human prayer and communication, and therefore subordinate spirit intermediaries – such as the *mizimu* – form the highest spiritual authority that can be accessed via specifically trained and elevated experts (*asing'anga*). Accordingly, even though their wisdom is limited due to their character as former human beings, the *mizimu ya makolo* still represent a superior source of information which, in the context of traditional medicine, is tantamount to medical knowledge. In contrast to that, Christian faith healing – and, to a limited degree, Christianized *using'anga* – claims to be in direct personal contact with the utmost cosmological power, perceived as a Supreme Being both omniscient and benevolent. This immediate access to divine sources of health and therapy surpasses the limitations of ordinary traditional healers and their ancestral guides by far. With this otherwise unimaginable connection to the ultimate cosmological powers, faith healing qualifies as a classic consequence for health disorders that, over a long period of health seeking, have proven to be beyond all spiritual forces that could be accessed.

This is the underlying argument that expresses itself in particular in the framework of the Pentecostal healing ministry. In the course of healing services, phenomena such as glossolalia demonstrate the direct presence of the Supreme Being within a given person, thus 'cutting out the middle men' that traditionally mediate between the human and the divine – i.e. the *sing'anga* and the ancestral spirit.[7] Other forms of faith healing likewise operate by emphasizing the superior character of the cosmological authorities that are applied. The direct therapeutic qualities attributed to Holy Scripture – i.e. the Qur'ān or the Bible – immediately derive from the assumption that supreme cosmological authority is connected to unlimited therapeutic possibilities. Healing power and religious – i.e. moral – authority are tantamount categories, and a reference to the cosmological sphere is therefore indispensable for successful therapy. It is exactly this cosmological quality of medical treatment that seriously aggravates the acceptance of biomedical health institutions. By comparison with traditional – as well as more recent – religious concepts, biomedical health procedures lack the moral quality and semantic depth that alternative services provide. Spiritual authority is considered as a decisive quality of therapeutic activity, and biomedical institutions find it difficult to translate their scientific concepts into local terms. It is therefore not unusual if denominational institutions of biomedicine – such as a Presbyterian or Catholic mission hospital – tend to have a better reputation than comparable governmental facilities who establish no connection between the therapeutic process and the cosmological realm.

In Search of the Cure

Due to the availability of cosmologically diverse health services and the frequent assertion that cure is never impossible, the health seeking process is only limited by the amount of time and effort the effected persons – patients and/or their relatives – can invest into it. In Southern Malaŵi, typical patterns of medical behaviour are likely to address *using'anga* as a primary treatment for mental disorder – which may, in part, be connected to its wide availability. Expectedly,

7 In a newspaper interview, the representatives of Evangelical and Pentecostal churches in Malaŵi therefore agree that "anybody who believes in Jesus can heal", arguing that "This issue can be looked at at three levels. At the first level, any Christian is given the power to heal. At another level, God may give the gift to specific individuals in the church and on the third level God may give the gift to apostles, those whom he has anointed to do the healing ministry" (Jimu 2005: 5).

this observation is more distinctive in rural areas, but traditional medicine is also in high demand in suburban and urban environments. Secondly, biomedicine is frequently sought in case of multiple unsuccessful attempts on traditional healing even though people frequently express their low expectations in visiting a hospital. Religious forms of healing tend to be considered if neither traditional nor biomedicine managed to reach the desired improvement – and especially in response to the little hope for recovery that is expressed by biomedical health specialists. This sequence, however, is situational. As mentioned earlier, some denominations strictly support religious forms of healing as the first and foremost – or even only – form of therapy while the Western-oriented urban population may exclusively address biomedical health services. The frequent character of mental disorder as being difficult to treat, however, encourages a pluralistic approach towards the various medical services available.

Especially in rural areas, *using'anga* medicine is crucial for basic health care and the primary destination for cases of mental disorder, but its reputation is being hollowed out by public and media portrayal which – in agreement with governmental policy – depicts biomedical health care as superior to any other treatment options. Faith healing – especially Christian phenomena which bear closer links to Western, thus ostensibly 'modern' notions – has an increasing standing in terms of its cultural acceptance and status. The *asing'anga*, however, may have long queues of patients waiting in front of their houses every day, but many interview participants initially deny any involvement with traditional medicine and claim government hospitals as the first and foremost source of treatment. For many Malaŵians, it takes considerable faith to admit their medical behaviour to a stranger – a clear result of Western-oriented media and education depicting traditional medicine as a backwards, old-fashioned tradition that conflicts with modern life, making it difficult for the individual to access it openly. This distrust is particularly distinctive in the context of the more religious forms of *using'anga* operating with ritual spirit possession – the traditionally most prestigious form of healing (Chakanza 1998: 101).

In all cases, the geographical range of the patients' health seeking behaviour is considerable. As emphasized before, a simple visit at the next government health center often requires long hours of traveling, and the distances covered in order to reach government hospitals or even specialized institutions for mental disorders are larger still. Moreover, it should be borne in mind that typically, these health seeking voyages imply not only the patient himself or herself, but also an extended therapy management group – the 'guardians,' typically a spouse, sibling and/or parent plus potential children, friends, and the like – who guide the patient and provide elementary care such as washing, cooking, and feeding. Therefore, the poor health condition of one person easily leads to a large part of the family being unable to maintain their respective economic activities. Such patterns of behaviour are also typical in case of traditional medical facilities: it is not uncommon for patients to cross national borders – e.g. into neighbouring Mozambique – in order to find a certain *sing'anga* known for particular professional expertise, and patients would also be accompanied by their close kin to provide for them for the duration of the treatment. Any thorough attempt to ameliorate a condition of mental disorder therefore bears a considerable economic threat to the immediate kin-group – a condition that does not help to encourage extended health seeking processes.

It is the heterogeneity and inconsistency of aetiological labelling that characterizes the social conditions of persons with mental disorder in Southern Malaŵi. For comprehensible reasons, most relatives of affected persons – as well as the people themselves – argue in favour of an explanation that discharges them from all responsibility while the wider community may apply other and diverse approaches for the same condition, reflecting not only their respective cosmological convictions, but also providing a platform for articulating social tensions.

What is questionable in this social context is the – e.g. interdenominational – recognition of therapeutic success. It may be assumed that, due to the cosmological heterogeneity of the region, it is far from self-evident that the allegedly successful cure of a given case of mental disorder will be accredited without scrutiny by adherents of competing cosmologies. It has been argued already that successfully treated patients from Zomba Mental Hospital – or, for that matter, any other biomedical health facility – frequently experience community exclusion because their home communities do not confirm their therapeutic success. A miraculous cure occurring due to Pentecostal healing services may not be accepted within a largely Muslim area – while, at the same time, this kind of health-and-cosmology-shopping behaviour is far from uncommon now and gaining social acceptance. The recognition of successful therapy is therefore subject to a process of social negotiation, happening on a strictly situational level. The cosmological transcendence especially of faith healing must be considered as insecure but a social option.[8] Due to the prevalent concept that explains cases of mental disorder as being quintessentially caused by culturally inappropriate actions committed within the patient's extended kin-

8 Therefore, persons strictly rejecting local medicine from the perspective of Muslim or Christian orthodoxy may still be convinced of its efficiency – in spite of its alleged moral damnability. In addition, there is a tendency within the lay population to identify the Supreme Being as one and the same so that cure provided by a competing religious organization might still be accepted as authentic. Evidently, the name applied for the Supreme Being is *Mulungu* in the Chicheŵa translations of both Qur'ān and Bible, and both Muslim and Christian spirit entities – e.g. angels (*angelo*) – are conceived in analogy to the traditional notion of ancestral spirits.

group, the notion of structural curability does not enhance the chances for social inclusion of an affected person. Rather, curability as a factor is secondary to the fact itself and does not lead to increased efforts for inclusion or reintegration.

Essentially, the social integration of a person with mental disorder thus depends on the question whether or not the condition is conceived to be successfully cured. As in the case of future *asing'anga* cured from their initiatory spirit complaint, reintegration may commence after the identification of the cause and its remedy – and it may even result in acquiring an elevated social status. Here, the relational character of mental disorder concepts – as mentioned above – is important. Traditional as well as religious forms of therapy focus on re-establishing social cohesion due to restoring cosmological harmony. It is, therefore, not so much the person but the group – or, more precisely, the person within its social and cosmological network – that is the center of therapeutic measures. In case of mental disorder, not a person's living conditions, but social relationships are at stake; therefore, the affected person is not so much the center of communal interest of action, but the quest for its semantics, reasons, and ritual amelioration. Its metaphysical dimension, the *reason why* cosmological order is thus disrupted is by far more crucial than the condition of the patient as such (Sagner 2001: 197; Devlieger 1995: 104). The meaningfulness of mental disorder is a central trait, and knowledge of its aetiological background opens the path to its especially ritual therapy. Treatment does not necessarily strive to technically cure the condition – even though such an outcome is always considered structurally possible and desired –, but to restore cosmological harmony. The order thus re-established also redefines a person with mental disorder as a whole human being – even if the symptoms may remain (Connors & Donnellan 1993: 275).

2. Competence and Stigmatization

At last, it is time to come back to the central theoretical question that aims to localize the social perception of persons with mental disorders in Southern Malaŵi in between the polar notions of stigma and competence. The previous chapters have provided ample material for this issue which shall finally be evaluated.

2(a) Normality and Normativity

In the context of this study, it has been a central task to provide a thorough picture of the symptoms that are associated with the different states of mental disorder. In doing so, these symptoms can be pieced together to develop an overall picture of the central criteria that define mental disorder in its cultural context. This, in turn, may give important insight into its necessary counterpart – i.e. that of a normal mental condition – due to which a cultural concept of normality becomes tangible. After all, the exposure to the different constitutes the identity of the normal (Sagner 2001: 199) which makes social deviance a definitive category for the ideal of normality.

The Normal and the Deviant

On the basis of the circumstantial descriptions of what constitutes a mentally abnormal and pathological condition (see *Chapter III*), it is possible to deduce a general notion of normality – in the sense of normal mental behaviour and capacity – as a kind of inverted imprint. While the sets of symptoms that are given for specific categories of mental disorder may have a comparably unspecific character – i.e. distinguishing permanent (e.g. *misala*, *kuzerezeka*) from recurrent states (*khunyu*, *kuzungulira mutu*), violent (*misala*) from lethargic (*kuzerezeka*) behaviour, or infant (*mutu*, *kulumala*) from typically adult (*misala*) occurrence –, they may still be analysed for their principal content.

In any given framework, local notions of normality refer to a number of factors which indicate environmental expectations – and it may therefore be emphasized once more that competence is entirely based on cultural allocations, and that the requirements to be socially categorized as competently normal reflect central cultural values (Devlieger 1998: 65). In Southern Malaŵi, the most central factors defining normal competence may be summarized as follows: as primarily functional qualities, criteria such as *(1)* economic productivity or *(2)* procreativity are of crucial importance, and they are conceived as a necessary part of cultural definitions of normality and the most central difficulties associated with mental disorder. Furthermore, social qualities such as *(3)* the ability for social interaction and association within the community and *(4)* the observation of basic cultural norms are described as crucial to constituting a 'normal' person.

Undisputedly, economic productivity is an important criterion of normality – with the inability to perform and manage the daily work and therefore contribute to the kin-group's livelihood being a basic human necessity in rural areas. A condition of limited productivity is perceived as both abnormal and dangerous for the survival of the family. This criterion of economic autonomy includes the cognitive as well as activity-related prerequisites because "The ability to identify and perform tasks requires an embodied mind" (Whyte 1998: 171-172). Therefore, technical knowledge – about how to exercise household or farming tasks, organize the necessary activities autonomously, and deal with the yield, tools, etc. in a responsible way – are interconnected with the physical fitness and readiness to execute them. The high social importance of procreation – i.e. the ability to find a spouse, produce and conceive offspring – is a frequently mentioned part of local notions of normality and competence.[9] For many persons with mental disorders and their immediate kin the small chances of starting a family constitutes the main concern connected to the condition as such. While the nuclear family thus constitutes the core cell of social integration into community life, it is frequently reported that families break down as a consequence of the occurrence of mental disorder within it.

Subsequently, the appropriate functioning within these social networks is also considered a vital part of normal mental competence. The will and ability to socialize and associate with the wider community represents an important part of social existence and therefore defines normal behaviour and competence. It has been shown that normal competence among children and adults alike is to a high degree defined in terms of social interaction while social isolation, on the other hand, is seen as an indicator of mental disorder – which applies to voluntary as well as involuntary acts of exclusion, to loners and outcasts alike.[10] In a wider sense, it should be noted that communication limitations – such as deafness or muteness, but also less severe conditions – may also prevent a person from being recognized as fully competent. Compliance with basic culturally defined codes of normative behaviour is also important in the emic definition of normality. Many persons therefore agree that 'doing abnormal things' – i.e. the violation of fundamental social conventions such as public nudity – is a culturally validated indicator of mental disorder, and even the behaviour of young children can be subjected to critical analysis and, subsequently, be labelled as mental disorder.[11] Malaŵian value hierarchies allot great normative importance to qualities such as a reasonable temper, meekness and polite behaviour, and a significant lack of these capacities – being overly agitated, easily aroused, or disrespectful – is also easily perceived as indicating a condition of mental disorder.

---

9 Even if occurring independently from cases of mental disorder, lacking fertility – i.e. impotence in men as well as barrenness in women – must therefore be understood as a prominent reason for social ostracism and the loss of full personal normality.

10 Accordingly, Duff MacDonald mentions that persons choosing to seclude themselves from the community would be considered 'mad' by their immediate kin (MacDonald 1882: 144).

11 Shamefulness and modesty (*manyazi*), e.g., represent high cultural values especially for young women and girls. At a certain age, a child is expected to internalize these behavioural norms and not expose him or herself in public. Accordingly, the careless and slightly revealing sitting position of a six year-old girl may be conceived neither as a social deficit nor as a deliberate display of nonconformist provocation against the normative rule – but as an indication of a pathological condition of mental disorder.

Normality Reconsidered

Essentially, the criteria thus established as defining the cornerstones of cultural conceptions of normality are relational in nature, thus allocating competence not on the basis of individual skills but of interpersonal interaction – a picture that is paralleled by accounts from other African societies. With regard to Zimbabwe, Patrick Devlieger states that competence is defined in relation "to family and gender roles and the ability to communicate as a condition for assuming such roles" (Devlieger 1998: 73), and in a similar line of argument, Susan Reynolds Whyte asserts that, among the Nyole of Uganda,

> "Ultimately, the social incompetence of mentally disabled persons lies in their inability to extend and strengthen their families through social activities and relationships. Those who are unmarried are unlikely to find a spouse, so they cannot contribute to family growth through relations of affinity and procreation" (Whyte 1998: 171).

This entirely relational notion of the normal human mind, though mentioned with great sophistication before, is an important conclusion that merits emphasis (Jenkins 1998b: 227)[12] – as is its dependence from a local socio-cultural context. It is the very character of these culturally defined classifications that they reflect a local life-world – thus making it necessary to assess that certain conditions which, in a Western context, are categorized in terms of mental health may not qualify as such in Southern Malaŵi, and vice versa. While learning aptitude – communicated in a local context as a child's inability to learn what other children at the same age do – is described as a child being lazy or 'lacking intelligence' (*opanda nzeru*), this situation is emphatically explained as a normal i.e. non-pathological condition. In such a case, no causation is identified and no therapy sought, and some accounts compare the condition to one person being born taller or the other one shorter.[13] It is in the life situation and the specific hierarchization of cultural relevance that the benchmarks of competence are defined. In European and North American society, individualistic values such as independence, personal success, or self-reliance outweigh more 'socio-centric', group-oriented values like interdependence or sociability (Klotz 2003: 18) which

---

12 According to him, "As G.H. Mead suggested long ago, *mind* exists in the social spaces, in the mutuality of interaction, between embodied individuals [...]. It is in interactional processes of social construction that mind, selfhood and society emerge" (Jenkins 1998b: 227).

13 Therefore, "[...] the concept of mental retardation only has a social validity in rural African subsistence economies when the degree of retardation is sufficiently severe to become conspicuous against a background of loosely defined biological sequences. Individual differences in developmental rate are easily tolerated in African societies where multi-age groups are the norm both in play and in work settings and where socially distributed cognitive work is a highly valued pattern of social activity" (Serpell, Mariga & Harvey 1993: 5).

can be recognized in the data presented here. These divergent notions of competence and, ultimately, personhood have an immediate impact on the cultural construction of incompetence, deviance, and disability.

> "[...] the problem is not the person with disabilities, the problem is the way that normalcy is constructed to create the 'problem' of the disabled person" (Davis 1997: 9).

Field data suggests that, in Southern Malaŵi, a normal mental condition is defined by sets of competencies that are considered essential. They include functional and social skills which reflect very basic, elementary standards of competence and which relate back to a rural, agrarian tradition. Even in an urban context, similar notions apply – although the exact functional (e.g. less focus on agrarian chores due to more professional flexibility) as well as the social (i.e. less behavioural regulations due to a higher degree of social heterogeneity) requirements may be conceptualized slightly differently. All in all, the cultural determination of normality is an obvious fact, and in a research situation, the degree of deviance displayed by a European researcher himself – however hard he may try to 'blend in' to his host culture – should never be underestimated. It is therefore not surprising if some Malaŵians express that, strictly speaking, all *azungu* could be considered as having some kind of mental disorder – as expressed by their constant deviation from the behavioural norm.[14]

It must, however, be taken into consideration that the criteria subsumed as a normal mental disposition in this article show striking similarities with the concept of the person (*munthu*) as addressed earlier on in this study. Both concepts emphasize productivity as well as social responsibilities – specifically including the adherence to behavioural norms. While a general identity of these two concepts shall not be contended, it is nonetheless important to consider the interrelation between personhood and a non-pathological or 'normal' mental disposition in the multi-layered framework of Southern Malaŵian cultures.

2(b) Attaching the Stigma

Some anthropological studies have pointed out that conditions such as mental disorder – or even twin births – tend to be interpreted as radically different from

---

[14] In a humorous way, Steven Lane picks up this issue as a central theme of his 1995 booklet *The Wild Azungu*, returning a questionable favour done by Walter A. Elmslie who, in 1901 AD, gave a sensational and antagonizing account of his life *Among the Wild Ngoni* in Northern Malaŵi (Elmslie 1970). Documenting the culturally incomprehensible behaviour of the 'wild *azungu*' or Europeans, Steven Lane makes a somewhat moralistic statement against the secularism of post-modern society (Lane 1995).

the cultural norm, and the affected persons' difference would *necessarily* be regarded as a bad omen, a sign of evil, impurity, or another symbol of severely negative character leading to direct and immediate ostracism and exclusion from society (Schlosser 1952: 226-227). In essence, this notion is in line with the concept of stigma as formulated by Erving Goffman and addressed in the introductory chapter of this thesis. In this section, its relevance within the framework of culture shall be examined.

Limits of Social Interaction

Conditions of mental disorder occurring in Malaŵi bear considerable risks for the social situation of the affected persons and their immediate kin alike. While, on an economical level, the "effort of care and compensation" (Whyte 1998: 173) is already a significant challenge for the generally impoverished rural family, social pressures of stigmatization aggravate the problem significantly and question the readiness of the community to associate with a given person or kinship group. In case of potentially violent states of *misala*, the affected persons may easily be considered as disturbers of the communal peace – which constitutes a frequent reason for communal intervention and subsequent expulsion or admission to specialized institutes such as Zomba Mental Hospital.

All in all, stigma is attached according to two basic notions. On the one hand, it has been stated that the perception of a given case of mental disorder reflects its aetiological categorization, and that the different degrees of in- and exclusion are also related to a specific causation. A person whose mental disorder is ascribed to ancestral spirits may hence experience considerable negligence within the community, being regarded as justly punished for his or her own wrongdoings. In case of causation by *ufiti* – the worst of all categories that is connected to considerable social fear –, the kin-group of the victim is under scrutiny and may be avoided not only because of the stigma attached to its deviant member, but also because of the unspeakable deeds that another person in this kin-group obviously performs during the night. Even if some empathy exists within the community for an innocent *ufiti* victim that is left mentally disordered, the hatred and abhorrence against the person responsible already marks a considerable social stigma. The same applies, to a lesser extent, to cases of *kukhwima* magic which also stigmatizes an entire kin-group due to the assumption of their anti-social actions. After all, these aetiological frameworks are seen as an indicator of severely disrupted relationships – within the community, the large kinship group, and the cosmological sphere at large (Devlieger 1998: 58).

On the other hand, a person may also be stigmatized on a very immediate, quasi non-analytical level. Considerable stigma is connected to the actual behaviour of persons with mental disorders, and their constant violation of cultural norms represents a manifestation of their lacking normality. Here, the criteria of normality as depicted above provide a general outline – in the sense that unprovoked violence, lack of self-control, or rude behaviour in public, e.g., are heavily stigmatized. More basic concepts of normality relate to the regulation of bodily functions: uncontrolled salivating is described as a classical and heavily stigmatized indicator of mental disorder – and direct, ill-founded contact with dirt or litter is equally likely to provoke stigmatization. This inability of persons with mental disorders to conform to cultural standards of behaviour not only leads to collective stigmatization but also to a feeling of shame on the side of the respective kinship group – which may result in even more stigmatizing measures. Certain forms of treatment for persons with mental disorder in Southern Malaŵi – such as the restraint of affected persons by means of ropes and wooden weights as well as their actual confinement – have already been exemplified. Such practices may be considered as stigmatizing on the one hand. On the other, however, they represent a reaction to – and escape from – social stigmatization by active exclusion which underlines the considerable social pressure that is connected to conditions of mental disorder as such. As another result, some parents of children with a mental disorder distance themselves from them, expressing their unwillingness to put up with their affected child or describing the respective person as utterly useless to both family and community. These reactions, however, are related to the severity of the given case and degree of stigmatization that is connected to its particular representation.

Integration Improbable

Social exclusion and stigmatization are a well-documented fact in Southern Malaŵi. The parents of children with mental disorders usually provide some non-ambiguous accounts of stigmatization within their respective communities. On the side of these family members, the frequent feelings of shame and embarrassment exacerbate the living conditions of persons with mental disorders. Discouraging any public association with their mentally disordered kin, the social experience of shame further aggravates the affected persons' social participation, and it keeps their relatives from making additional health service options available to the patients – thus refusing access to, e.g., rehabilitation or other programs. The stigma connected to conditions of mental disorder also constitutes a severe challenge to the reintegration of persons who, by biomedical standards, are considered as successfully cured.

> "Usually they come there, saying this patient should go to Zomba Mental Hospital, we don't want him anymore in the community. So usually this hospital

is like the dumping place for the patients who are giving problems at their homes. They really don't like them. There is a stigma on this condition, and it makes it difficult for the guardians to accept the patients back into the community" (Vivian Changata, a Mang'anja nursing officer).

Even if discharged as successfully cured, persons returning from Zomba Mental Hospital to their local communities are stigmatized – which applies most specifically for ex-patients who had been associated with violent behaviour. Therefore, children are advised to avoid the respective persons as possibly dangerous, thus leading to a situation where social stress becomes a central concern for persons with mental disorders that even outweighs the more obvious challenges of their respective conditions.[15]

2(c) Attributing Competence

It may, at the same time, be incorrect to portray Malaŵian conceptions of mental disorder solely on the basis of stigmatization. Issues such as the direct connection between mental disorder and the initiation of traditional healers, on the contrary, illustrate that mental disorder may indeed be the result of a culturally highly valued process of spiritual vocation. The accounts of oral and ritual traditions have indicated how cultural representations provide a framework for the recognition of personal competence. People with mental disorder are encouraged to develop personal competence in spite of potential social resistance, and some references are made to the unexpected potentials that affected persons may possess.

Therefore, we can assess that deviation from the cultural norm does, in terms of mental performance, not necessarily lead to stigmatization and social exclusion. Rather, the degree of competence that is granted to the person is subject to negotiation, and due to an underlying concept of structurally universal curability (see above), its character is – at least as a matter of principle – situational. Society recognizes considerable degrees of gradation which give room for personal difference without instantly inflicting stigma on the respective person, and in some – especially slight – cases, people in Malaŵi are less likely to be labelled and stigmatized as pathological than they would in a Western context.[16] The specific definition of normality that is modelled according to

---

[15] Therefore, it has been agreed that the "need for emotional support surpassed economic support when asking for what type of assistance [...] was needed in daily life" (Eide 2004: 50).

[16] Robert Serpell and others thus rightly assume that "Using the Western conceptualization of mental retardation then, we would expect that mild degrees of mental retardation would not be a subject of parental anxiety or of stigma for the child in the traditional rural African setting, whereas moderate or severe degrees of mental retardation would be sufficiently conspicuous to

cultural requirements thus prevents people from stigmatizing labels – i.e. Western concepts such as 'learning disability' or 'autism' – by acknowledging their general competence.

In Southern Malaŵi, the competence approach is essentially part of the classificatory process as such. It is due to their acknowledged competences that people are *not* categorized as having a mental disorder – or that they are de-stigmatized as successfully cured. Moreover, not all states of mental disorder are culturally associated with complete incompetence; states of *khunyu* or *kuzungulira mutu* are seen as occurring temporarily, and some cases of *kulumala* may be connected to a large extent of competence – while states of *misala, kuzerezeka* or *mutu* are, in contrast, frequently explained as people who 'cannot do anything at all,' who are 'completely useless' or 'just a cabbage.' In continuous conditions of mental disorder, the competence that is granted to an affected person is defined by his or her ability to meet the criteria of normal personhood – a process that provides a yardstick for the severity of a given case.

In a historical context, local culture used to provide protective measures operating in favour of the patient in the form of behavioural rules of a directly imperative nature (*miyambo*). Due to processes of cultural change and the devaluation of traditional instructions, these protective measures no longer fully apply; they are questioned, their validity vitiated, their social protective qualities are endangered. As a classical representation of initiatory teaching, local rules of behaviour are no longer regarded as a sacrosanct institution within a pluralistic society – but even scrutinized by experimental means.

Religious agencies try to substitute this loss of moral obligation by bringing in values of compassion and charity. But due to several reasons – including the enormous economic pressure prevalent in Malaŵi, the limited influence and partially contradictory exegesis of Christian churches –, the message of compassion does not make up for the loss of community support experienced by persons with mental disorders. The charitable efforts, nonetheless, are appreciated, and religious organizations are frequently mentioned as a motor of change for the cultural perception of mental disorder. Due to the growing influence of the religious communities, it is argued that Muslim and Christian notions of charity are slowly gaining social momentum, thus helping to improve the situation of persons with mental disorders. This is supported by a biomedical professional who expresses her conviction that

> "I think the church is also helping to improve in a special way because in the church they talk of loving one another. So because somebody would have a

---

require some kind of special social judgment to take place" (Serpell, Mariga & Harvey 1993: 10).

> mentally retarded patient or a leper, they would be afraid of putting them away and then they will always think of bad things, but when they go to church, they would hear the preacher preaching love for one another, even when somebody has got a problem. That makes people not to think of bad things on somebody with a mental problem" (Vivian Changata, a Mang'anja nursing specialist).

Muslim and Christian values are therefore described as a positive impact on the social acceptance of persons with mental disorders.[17] This hopeful perspective, however, is contrasted by the appraisal of representatives of organizations for persons with disabilities who challenge the functional value of religious notions of charity in dealing with mental disorder. According to this argument, a charitable approach to mental disorder is perceived as mere alms-giving – thus creating more dependencies, counteracting the concept of empowerment, and contradicting central developmental goals. The protective measures as introduced by religious agents are seen as missing the point – due to not focussing on the competence of the affected persons but on caring for them in spite of their assumed incompetence. Once again, the recognition of competence depends on the cosmological frames of reference that are applied in any given case.

In Southern Malaŵi, it is considered culturally appropriate and respectful behaviour to ignore and avoid persons with mental disorder and to be oblivious of their actions, acting as if they were invisible. While being definitely distinct from public abuse, this tradition of ignorance manifests a form of social exclusion that, nonetheless, counteracts social integration. As a very general discovery, two different streams of argument are discernible in the cultural perception of mental disorder. While inclusive, social-protective elements are clearly prominent in the context of oral and ritual tradition, social stigmatization plays an equally powerful part. While some accounts from other regions of Malaŵi show positive attitudes and associations with persons with mental disorders,[18] infant deviance is generally perceived as a pathological state in the Southern Region that is connected to stigmatizing assumptions. All in all, the majority of affected persons – and/or their immediate kin – represented in this study state that they experience considerable social ostracism in their own communities, being avoided, openly despised, and ridiculed. Fewer accounts describe their social environment as indifferent to the condition or even helpful.

---

17 Therefore, "Women nowadays are able to understand and appreciate what the Lord has given to them due to that they understand the gospels. It was hard to understand in the past because there were few churches. And again they are not so disappointed anymore when they remember that the government will intervene and help the child in its education and other needs" (Mercy Msawa, a Yao *mzamba*).

18 In parts of the Tonga area in Nkhata Bay District (Northern Region), the birth of a child with a visible physical disorder is reported as a welcome sign for future prosperity.

This demonstrates that, while stigmatization is a central mechanism in the cultural debate on mental disorder, inclusion and mutual support are nonetheless existent. Organizations for persons with disabilities introduce themes such as 'Disability is not Inability' (*kulumala si kulephera*). Clearly, this motto reflects the programmatic mission of proclaiming and supporting the competence of persons with mental disorder – as well as its recognition within the communities. Its social implementation is determined by the pluralism of competing cosmologies and their specific medical and social agendas.

2(d) Persons and Non-Persons

In numerous ways, this thesis addresses the question whether or not a person with a mental disorder in Southern Malaŵi acquires full personhood according to emic criteria. It has, in general, been agreed that cultural definitions of *umunthu* make an explicit effort for inclusiveness and accommodate all human beings regardless of their individual capabilities. It has also been pointed out, however, that the general inclusion of persons with mental disorders under the category *munthu* does not comply with its actual definition (see *Chapter III.1.a*). Moreover, an earlier section in this chapter has demonstrated that significant similarities connect the concept of the person (*munthu*) with that of a normal mental condition. This leaves the argument in a dilemma, as etic data analysis suggests a deduction which emic classification emphatically denies – i.e. the notion that people with mental disorder are perceived as non-persons. However, while the cultural concept as expressed on numerous accounts shall not be challenged, the diverse factors which compromise the personhood of those suffering from mental disorder must still be addressed.

Dangers of Depersonalization

One of the most instructive results developed in this study refers to Malaŵian concepts of magic. As a concept distinct from the formerly documented kinds of magic manipulation, *kukhwima* is a notion that has particularly close connections to mental disorder. In essence, a substantial part of *kukhwima* practices consist in the magic theft of the human spirit of personhood, also called *mzimu wa umunthu*. Not only according to this common term, the functions of this human entity are intrinsically related to personhood as such: it represents human reasoning, decision-making, self-control, and – as a future ancestor spirit – social involvement. The loss of this substantial part of the person constitutes a severe condition of mental disorder that is identified as a lack of all mental coordinative and cognitive skills.

Further inquiries in the personhood of *kukhwima* victims – and persons with mental disorders as a whole –, however, are generally countered with the explanation that the sacrifice of a person's *mzimu wa umunthu* must be considered as a temporary condition. A powerful *sing'anga* who succeeds in discovering the culprit may reunite body and personality spirit at once – and even if the condition is never remedied, the respective *mzimu wa umunthu* will be released to act as an ancestral spirit (*mzimu wa makolo*) after the death of its *wokhwima* master. In such a case, the *umunthu* of a person suffering from mental disorder is safeguarded due to the fact that the missing faculty of personhood is connected and therefore still represents a part of the human being – even if it may be separated from the body over an indefinite period of time. What could be attested, though, is that the temporary loss of a spirit of personhood (*mzimu wa umunthu*) leads to a condition of temporary de-socialization (Platenkamp 1998: 61-62). As the quintessential link between the person and the social sphere – including the cosmological realm as well as the immediate social environment –, the loss of a spirit of personhood deprives a person of its social embeddedness, thus leaving merely embodied life force. While this body-lacking-personhood is embedded in a given kinship group by blood (*magazi*) and physical representation, its vertical links with the larger social sphere stay attached to the missing *mzimu wa umunthu*, thus creating a "non-social condition of 'life'" (Platenkamp 1998: 62).

This situation is altered even further, however, if the connection between the body (*thupi*) and the spirit of personhood has never been ritually established. An earlier chapter has referred to the differences in funeral rituals as held for stillborn children (*nsenye*) which, in short, receive a minimal ritual care which may be interpreted as reflecting a notion of incomplete personhood. Moreover, additional material presented in the conclusion of that same chapter (*Chapter II.3*) has indicated that infanticide as a reaction to apparent deviation is a fixed motif among different ethnic groups in Southern Malaŵi. The notion of killing a newborn child due to its apparently deviant condition, however, enforces the question whether they may be conceptualized as incomplete human persons. In combination with the previous account that describes a – quasi admittedly incomplete – *kukhwima* victim as complete person, the actual core of the question of personhood becomes apparent. It is, in fact, the ritual introduction into society that constitutes personhood – and maintains it even in the unfortunate case of losing one's governing mental faculty. Thus, the results here support and substantiate an observation among the Cheŵa, expressing that

> "Small children who die before their parents have performed a special ritual called *kutenga mwana* (to take the child), by which a child is incorporated into the family, are not considered to be real human beings. Their spirits will not be

> received into the world of *mizimu*, because they lack something essential. On the contrary a child who is »taken« will be received into the spirit world, however young it is. The spirit of a child who has not been »taken« has to await rebirth in another child who its own mother or her close relative conceives. In the meantime it is considered a *chiwanda*" (Breugel 2001: 83).

Umunthu or personhood, therefore, is an idealistic category that is attached to the human being in a ritual context and is independent from actual performance. Even if a person with a mental disorder is conceived as lacking integral parts of full personhood, this temporary condition is of no consequence for his or her status as *munthu* – which also implies the embeddedness into the cosmological order in terms of constituting a future ancestral spirit (*mzimu wa makolo*).

Life in the Creases

In his remarkable 1987 study on disability in the United States, Robert Murphy compares the social position of persons with disabilities with the liminal status of the initiate during ritual initiation, existing 'betwixt and between' the cultural spheres and removed from society (Murphy 2001: 131). Unlike a typical *rite de passage* would suggest, however, their liminality is a permanent condition of living on the threshold of society and personhood (Murphy 2001: 45; Willett & Deegan 2001: 137-138; Murphy et al. 1988; Gennep 1960). According to Robert Murphy,

> "The long-term physically impaired are neither sick nor well, neither dead nor alive, neither out of society nor wholly in it. They are human beings but their bodies are warped or malfunctioning, leaving their full humanity in doubt. They are not ill, for illness is transitional to either death or recovery. [...] The sick person lives in a state of social suspension until he or she gets better. The disabled spend a lifetime in a similar suspended state. They are neither fish nor fowl; they exist in partial isolation from society as undefined, ambiguous people" (Murphy 2001: 131).

In 1999, Patrick Devlieger offers a slightly different perspective by conceptualizing disability in neither universalistic nor strictly relativistic terms. He argues that disability should be considered as an interstitial category, thus situating persons with disabilities "in between the structural categories that define cultures" (Devlieger 1999: 299) – rather than outside (Goffman 1967) or at their liminal ends (Murphy et al. 1988). Seeing this interstitial position as a positive, powerful and innovative challenge to cultural structures, Devlieger locates persons with disabilities not at the margin of society but within its creases (Devlieger 1999: 299). This approach seems well applicable in a Malaŵian context where it has already been argued that the phenomenon cannot be regarded as marginal due to its high representation within various spheres of social life. While questions of disability – or, to maintain this study's terminology, of mental disorder – are reflected and therefore included in many parts of the cultural sphere, the respected persons exist in between emic categories. They are neither outside nor on the edge of cultural concepts of personhood (*umunthu*), but they constitute full persons which, nonetheless, may be incapable of achieving the idealistic concepts that – theoretically – constitute personhood. Due to their situational inability to exercise their structurally affirmed and normatively granted competencies, persons with mental disorders are, in other words, fully in and completely out of society at the same time.

With respect to mental competence, and also in a wider scale, Southern Malaŵian culture has a notably egalitarian quality that attaches a stigma to both over-achievement and underperformance. Both of these extremes are, in one way or the other, related to notions of mental disorder. Elevated social positions of status – as expressing itself in economic success, political or spiritual authority – is associated with anti-social acts causing mental disorder in an innocent victim, while cognitive curiosity as manifested in deep thinking or reading are signs of mental disorder in itself. Low mental performance, though, is attributed to either the acts of others – be it human or spirit agents – or of the victim him or herself which, likewise, result in mental disorder. While the scope of normality offers some space for individual interpretation and agency, it strongly opposes the concept of individual difference according to strict cultural criteria that define conformity as a central value. In a way, social pressure therefore has it that

> "[...] the average then becomes paradoxically a kind of ideal, a position devoutly to be wished" (Davis 1997: 12).

The rehabilitation of incompetence in the form of mental disorder cannot be achieved by technical means of medicine. Rather, as Patrick Devlieger points out, it is the restoration of relational embeddedness that must be recognized as a key – and, indeed, a therapeutic – factor to any re-integrative ambitions (Devlieger 1998: 58). In case of mental disorder in Southern Malaŵi, traditional medical practices are indispensable in order to

> "[...] restore »relational embeddedness«, as the social domain of relationships are perceived as being in need of restoration rather than the individual self. (This is in stark contrast to the Western bio-medical model that emphasis [sic] individual physiology and rehabilitation as the causes and cures for disability.) Even an individual's social and personal competencies are not divorced from the social context within which they exist. Competency is always perceived as the way in which an individual creatively deals with their particular situation" (Klotz 2003: 19).

3. Conclusions and Recommendations

The present thesis has corroborated that mental disorder, as a cultural phenomenon, plays a prominent role in various spheres of Malaŵian culture. Its recognition within present-day needs for both human rights and health security, but also its representation in central medical and spiritual spheres challenges the Muslim and Christian world-view as well as the more traditional notions transcending the aforementioned two. In the general cultural framework of Southern Malaŵi, mental disorder is part of a highly complex and, at the same time, multi-layered debate that ranges between severe social ostracism and inclusive protectionism. Sources of ritual action and oral literature clearly emphasize the high cultural value of support for the deviant while, implicitly, indicating the great need for formal measures of social integration. This lays out the basic features of the cultural construction of mental disorder, leading over to a more sophisticated understanding of how mental disorder can be culturally defined and distinguished.

Local people tend to have divided opinions about recent changes in the situation of persons with mental disorders, but it is frequently agreed that these processes are highly relevant. On a very basic level, it is argued that the relevance of the phenomenon as such has increased enormously within the last decades. Due to the significant population growth and continuing problems of providing adequate medical services for the ever-growing society, the total numbers of persons with mental disorders are described as having multiplied – along with their everyday occurrence. Therefore it is argued that the wider recognition of mental disorder must be regarded as a fairly recent phenomenon. Some accounts also give credit to the increased availability of governmental health facilities that help to avoid – or deal with – cases of mental disorder. At the same time, some people lament the cultural reality that the existence and – however limited – availability of specialized institutions for persons with mental disorders encourages the communities to dispose of persons they might otherwise have learned to include. The improved availability of special education facilities, however, is seen as a positive development as it offers persons with mental disorders – usually *kulumala* – chances to develop vocational skills and overcome their activity limitations.

Even though this appraisal strikes a hopeful note, it must be noted that these developments are embedded in a complex network of counteractive processes. The different providers of medical services play a crucial role in ongoing process of cultural change and in the social positioning of persons with mental disorders. Their conflicting interpretations leave the affected persons and society as a whole without culturally binding conceptions, and more extreme perceptions of the phenomenon are introduced. The data presented throughout this study has demonstrated that, as a fundamental and, indeed, integral Malaŵian social structure, behavioural norms (*miyambo*) are a traditional tool that regulates social life in general – and that is particularly relevant for the cultural construction of and social interaction with mental disorder. Previous analysis (see *Chapter II.3*) has indicated the disruptive processes of cultural change as questioning the validity of these normative 'taboos' and falsifying their analogous mechanisms without introducing new standards of conduct to take over their social functions. With regard to the traditional *miyambo*, it is agreed that

> "A taboo system upholds a cultural system and a culture is a pattern of values and norms, social life is impossible without such a pattern" (Douglas 1985: 68).

Due to the dynamics of cultural change presently on the way, these socially protective measures lose their general recognition and cultural validity – consequently leading to a loss of social support for persons with mental disorders. This process is, to some degree, caused by competing cosmological concepts that fail to maintain a cohesive framework of moral values, and factors such as economic and population pressure only add to the social disruption. Changing local concepts of cosmology and, as its element, of medicine play an important role in all spheres of human life, and the cultural perception of mental disorder is likewise affected. The competition between rivalling cosmologies has been in effect for some decades already – at least since the effective introduction of cosmopolitan religion and scientific biomedicine by the mid 19th century AD. It is only recently, however, that the pluralism of worldviews and explanations fully hits the Malaŵian mainstream in its rural environment, and the current success of Pentecostal churches – due to their particular emphasis on providing faith healing and their firm belief in its ultimate therapeutic power – can serve as an indicator of the timeliness of this development. For persons with mental disorder, recent processes of cultural change tip the fragile balance between protection and exclusion – with detrimental effects on the affected persons.

The various paradigms that address mental disorder in Southern Malaŵi show the complexity of its cultural contextualization. A lack of interaction and cooperativeness between the general agents of health care creates a kind of pluralism that, in its core, is but a plurality of mutually exclusive notions which does not help the average health seeker. Dialogue is urgently needed in order to establish medical standards and provide guidelines for more coordinated, patient-compatible health care services. From the perspective of this study, traditional and biomedical services are the main agents in this context – as representing the institutions most favoured by patient engagement and governmental as well as international support, respectively. In the form of traditional healers' associations, local *asing'anga* have already established a forum that has been known to encourage cooperation with government agencies. It is certainly conceded that the philosophical gaps between Western notions of science and traditional *using'anga* may, at times, be hard to bridge, but further efforts are essential in order to produce a consistent medical environment that suits patient needs. This requires the introduction of shared standards on the side of both traditional and biomedicine – in the sense of general agreements about *which* health care provider should primarily offer *which* particular services for *which* given condition under *which* circumstances. In essence, this suggestion results in a more general inclusion of traditional medicine into national health care – an undertaking that has already been tested in the inclusion of traditional birth attendants (*azamba*) and also, in part, with traditional healers (Msonthi 1983a). Future inclusive efforts should negotiate on eye level which contributions can or cannot be provided by either biomedical or traditional health care providers, and which parts of medical expertise and social responsibility can be shared. As a prerequisite, further research has to be conducted in order to assess the respective fields of expertise of the different health care services. This task, admittedly, is a challenge – as it should provide results that are scientifically acceptable due to research methods that are culturally appropriate.

Field research has substantiated that the use of indigenous categorizations is indispensable in order to see a bigger picture and face ontological realities on the terminological ground of the culture in question. Therefore, the mere introduction of a new English language code is unlikely to prevail in addressing the cultural issues of mental disorder. Here, the idea of culture-bound syndromes offers a much more applicable approach towards a cultural understanding of non-Western concepts of mental health problems. After all, the present thesis strongly suggests that the implementation of European – thus likewise culture-specific – notions of disability and/or mental illness into an African context has only very limited avail. Structural demarcations between disability and health disorders such as chronic illness are not an ontological necessity, and non-Western cultures may recognize conditions as disabling which, from a biomedical point of view, do not relate to the category of disability at all (Helander 1995: 73-93; Whyte & Ingstad 1995: 5-7). As a contribution illuminating the cultural complexity and specificity of the various troubles of the human mind in Southern Malaŵi, this thesis means to encourage further research – not only in order to further complete the insight into the medical culture of the country itself, but with respect to a greater comprehension of issues of mental health as a whole.

Figure 4: Judith Chilunga, a Mang'anja subsistence farmer, waiting outside a rural health center with her son and other parents with children living with a disability

Appendices

Appendices

1. Glossary

Most of the below mentioned terms stem from Chicheŵa language – which, along with English, is the national language of Malaŵi and the first language for the Cheŵa, Nyanja, Mang'anja, and Ngoni ethnic groups. In all cases, an abbreviation in brackets indicates the origin of word as belonging to a certain language, these being:

ar = Arabic	sn = Chisena
ch = Chicheŵa	sw = Kiswahili
en = English	tu = Chitumbuka
gr = Greek	ya = Chiyao
lm = Chilomwe	

The following translations are according to explanations given within the research situation. Wherever possible, I have verified my rendering of the terms due to the use of a number of dictionaries listed below (see *Appendix 3.b*).

ashehe aduni [ya] – s̲hayk̲h̲ and former *sing'anga*
bambo (pl. *abambo*) [ch] – father, Sir
banja (pl. *ma-*) [ch] – nuclear family
bishopo (pl. *ma-*) [ch] – (from *bishop* [en]) a bishop
boliboli [sn] – category for persons with visual problems, especially in cases connected to complete loss of the eyes;[1] refering to empty eye sockets, the term has very derogatory connotations
boma [ch] – district
bongololo [sn] – category for a condition causing severe weight loss and a deteriorating overall condition; partially identified with *litsiro*
bwalo [ch] – traditional court
chakufwa [tu] – extremely derogatory category for forms of mental disorder, denoting "somebody or something which is already dead, or a useless being"
chamba [ch] – Indian hemp (*Cannabis sativa*)
Chauta – (lit. "Big Bow") the Supreme Being, the Creator
chepa nzeru, ku- [ch] – mental disorder category; see *kuzerezeka*
Cheŵa (pl. *Acheŵa*) [ch] – ethnic group in the Central Region

[1] In biomedical terms, this concept is interpreted as a consequence of so-called river blindness (*onchocerciasis*).

chibale [ch] – kinship group
chidzimba [sn] – condition leading to infant mental disorder; connected to a newborn child defecating while its umbilical cord (*mchombo*) is being cut[2]
chifufu [ch] – mental disorder category; see *khunyu*
chihinduhindu [ch] – mental disorder category; see *khunyu*
chikasu [ch] – (lit. "yellow") condition causing infant mental disorder; may imply seizures similar to *khunyu* and/or symptoms such as belly pain, very yellow urine, swelling of the stomach, or loss of appetite, yellow spots in mouth and on hands; vomiting through the nose after breastfeeding may be a first sign of infant *chikasu*[3]
chikuta [ch] – delivery house
chilango (pl. *zilango*) [ch] – punishment
chilema [ch] – mental disorder category; see *kulumala*
chilengo (pl. *zilengo*) [ch] – misfortune
chilowero [ya] – delivery house
chimanga [ch] – maize (*Zea mays*)
chinamwali [ch] – initiation ritual
chindoko [ch] – potentially fatal condition transmitted by sexual contact; if a woman's husband dies of *chindoko*, her children conceived in a future marriage will be affected by mental disorder[4]
chitayo [ch] – category translated as abortion or still birth; male condition caused by men having intercourse with a woman shortly after her aborting or within the restricted months after her delivering a child; symptoms include pains in the lower abdomen, or skin turning black around the navel; death strikes the male patient within 24 hours after contact (Paas 2004: 71)
chitenge [ch] – cloth
chithumwa (pl. *zithumwa*) [ch] – amulet or charm
chitsiru [ch] – category denoting "folly, madness; a fool, a senseless person, an idiot; an addled egg; one who leaves his wife and marries another" (Moxley 2001); not applied for pathological forms of mental disorder, may be compared to *kupusa*
chiwanda (pl. *ziwanda*) [ch] – category of evil spirits
chiwewe [ch] – mental disorder category defined as "madness, of the dog, but also applied to man" (Moxley 2001); explained as being caused by dog bite; symptoms resemble *misala*[5]
chiwongo [ch] – patrilineal clan membership, or name of reference
chizimba (pl. *zizimba*) [ch] – activating agent or instruction for magic and/or medicine
chizonono [ch] – condition mentioned as cause for mental disorder; sexually transmitted,

---

2 The resulting condition called *chibayo* is a condition that, in biomedical terms, is interpreted as pneumonia (Paas 2004: 36).

3 In biomedical terms, this concept is generally interpreted as yellow fever (with *chikasu* meaning 'yellow'), and some informants apply this term (*yelo fiva*) synonymously.

4 In biomedical terms, this concept is usually interpreted as syphilis (Paas 2004: 53).

5 From a biomedical perspective, this concept is generally interpreted as rabies (*hydrophobia*) (Paas 2004: 77).

is related to the causation of *kulumala* in the same way as *chindoko*[6]

dovu [ch] – saliva

dwala, ku- [ch] – (lit. "to suffer" or "be with child") imprecise category sometimes applied for mental disorder (Paas 2004: 99)

dziko [ch] – country, nation

funtha, ku- [tu] – mental disorder category; see *misala*

gogo (pl. *agogo*) [ch] – grandparent

gona, ku- [ch] – category translated as 'to sleep', figuratively used as being foolish or nonsensical; applied for a child showing poor performance as compared to age-mates, e.g. at school, or boys showing feminine behaviour; reportedly caused by malnutrition, e.g. lack of mother's milk; comparable to *kupusa* (Paas 2004: 123)

grupu (pl. *agrupu*) [ch] – (from *group* [en]) group village headman

gule wamkulu [ch] – (lit. "big dance") dance ritual of the *nyau*

gwira mzimu, ku- [ch] – to possess a person

gwiridwa mzimu, ku- [ch] – to be possessed by a spirit

hamala [ch] – (from *hammer* [en]) form of *ufiti*; also *nyundo*

–ipa [ch] – bad, evil

jini (pl. *majini*) [ya] – see *majini*

Kafula (pl. *Akafula*) – mythical ethnic group

kafumbata [ya] – condition leading to mental disorder; passes from affected mother to newborn child, requires instant treatment to save the child's life; even if successful, the child may later suffer from mental disorder[7]

kanyera [ch] – condition expressing itself in symptoms such as belly pain or severe weight loss; may lead to mental disorder or death after prolonged suffering (Drake 1976: 203)[8]

kape [ch] – colloquial expression denoting a person behaving inadequately; term is highly derogatory and figurative (Paas 2004: 152)

–kazi [ch] – female

khalidwe (pl. *makalidwe*) [ch] – behaviour, moral character, demeanour of a person

khate [ch] – condition manifesting itself as skin rash; prolonged suffering leads to loss of body parts or death; reportedly infectious, patients are ostracised; considered incurable once fully developed[9]

kholo (pl. *makolo*) [ch] – ancestor

khungu [ch] – category applied for visual impairment; has slightly negative connotation (Paas 2003: 43)

khunyu [ch] – mental disorder category (see *Chapter III.2.e*).

---

6 In biomedical terms, this concept is interpreted as gonorrhoea (Paas 2004: 55) or diarrhoea.

7 In biomedical terms, this concept is interpreted as tetanus.

8 Some accounts identify *kanyera* with HIV/Aids (Wolf 2003) while others equate this concept with bilharzia (*schistosomiasis*), leukemia, kidney infection, liver defect, or haemorrhoids (Paas 2004: 152).

9 In biomedical terms, this concept is usually identified as leprosy (Paas 2004: 164; Drake 1976: 203).

khwima, ku- [ch] – a kind of magic (see *Chapter IV.1.c*)
–kulu [ch] – big
kumudwa, ku- [ch] – condition of severe sadness, depicted as rare phenomenon;[10] not considered pathological but normal, sane reaction to specific hardships in life – e.g. death of a close relative
Kwacha – Malaŵian currency (MwK)
libale [lm] – female health condition affecting the genitalia; if an affected woman gives birth, respective children are in danger of dying or developing mental disorder[11]
lichero (pl. *malichero*) [ch] – winnowing basket
likango [ch] – condition causing mental disorder in a child if found in a pregnant woman due to premature or delayed delivery; symptoms include genital warts, sores, or swellings on the anus; also pain in the lower abdomen, very yellow urine, swelling of the stomach, loss of appetite, and itching skin; affected women are unable to produce milk normally but keep lactating; their children show symptoms like fever, body sores, failing to cry after delivery, or loss of consciousness; described as curable by expert *asing'anga* only
lilime (pl. *malilime*) [ch] – tongue
litchowa (pl. *matchowa*) [ch] – flywhisk
litsiro [ch] – category literally translated as 'dirt' or 'filth' (Paas 2004: 232); described as causing severe weight loss, leaving a patient "unable to do anything" in a state of mental disorder
liwombo [ch] – anterior fontanel (*Fonticulus anterior*)
lobola [ch] – bride price
lodza, ku- [ch] – to 'bewitch,' enchant, jinx
lodzedwa, ku- [ch] – to be 'bewitched'
Lomwe – ethnic group in the Southern Region
lumala, ku- [ch] – mental disorder category (see *Chapter III.2.f*).
mabomu [ch] – condition related to various stomach complaints; severe cases may have fatal outcome; transmission by sexual contact and by heredity; can result in mental disorders, related to the causation of *kulumala* in the same way as *chindoko* (see above); if a woman whose first husband has died of *mabomu* takes a new husband, her future children may suffer from *kulumala*[12]
madzoka [sn] – category sometimes listed as mental disorder; in this study, it is regarded as a form of therapy (see *Chapter IV.2*)
magazi [ch] – blood
majini [ya] – (from *djinn* [ar]) category of spirits; sometimes listed as mental disorder; in this study, it is regarded as a category of spirit agents (see *Chapter IV.2*)
makolo (sg. *kholo*) [ch] – see *kholo*

---

10 A Lomwe catholic priest identifies *kukumudwa* as depression, expressing his opinion that extended family systems prevent a high prevalence of depression as found in European or North American societies.

11 In biomedical terms, this concept is frequently identified as candidiasis.

12 In biomedical terms, this concept is interpreted as gonorrhoea (Paas 2004: 240) or diarrhoea.

malā'ika [ar] – angel in a Muslim context
malilime [ch] – (lit. "tongues") speaking in tongues, glossolalia
maliro [ch] – corpse, funeral
malombo [ch] – category of spirits
malungo aakulu [ch] – (lit. "big fever") category denoting a possible cause for mental disorder[13]
manda (pl. –) [ch] – graveyard
mankhwala [ch] – medicine
mapasa (sg. *phasa*) [ch] – category denoting persons born as twins; past accounts describe the birth of twins as highly abnormal, indicating misfortune for the respective family; reportedly, both children would have killed after birth;[14] presently, the birth of *mapasa* is accepted as a normal condition; occurrence is sometimes explained as hereditary, assuming that it reoccurs in a given kin-group (Paas 2004: 373)[15]
matalasimu (sg. *talasimu*) [sw] – (from *ṭilasm*, pl. *ṭalāsim* [ar] and τέλεσμα [gr]) Qur'ān verse used as medicine
matenda [ch] – sickness
matewe [ch] – category defined as a bone defect; bones of an affected child are reported as weak and bending easily, frequently causing mental disorders; occurrence is rescibed as congenital[16]
matsenga [ch] – magic or 'sorcery'
maula (sg. *ula*) [ch] – divination through objects
mayi (pl. *amayi*) [ch] – mother, Madam
mbale (pl. *abale*) [ch] – member of the same kinship group
mboma [ya] – category denoting a child born with both male and female genitals; condition is described as rare and connected to mental disorder
Mbona – territorial spirit with cult centre in Nsanje District
mbumba [ch] – matrilineage
mbusa (pl. *abusa*) [ch] – pastor or minister
mbwambwa, ku- [sn] – mental disorder category described as similar to *kuzerezeka* and *misala*; defined as an effect of prolonged illness on the side of a child's parents, occurs congenitally
mchape [ch] – medical substance used by anti-*ufiti* movements
mchere [ch] – salt
mchombo [ch] – umbilical cord, navel
mdulo [ch] – prominent category in Malaŵian medical anthropology; reflects idea of a breach of behavioural norms (*miyambo*) resulting in dangerous and potentially fatal

13 In biomedical terms, this concept is identified as cerebral malaria.
14 A mother of twin daughters mentions a Ngoni tradition according to which a sole surviving twin infant would be given the fruit of the *mvunguti* tree (i.e. the sausage tree, *Kigelia africana*) in order not to feel lonely.
15 A Lomwe mother specifies that her own twin children had been preceded by her own mother and her mother's mother both having twin siblings.
16 In biomedical terms, this concept is translated as rickets or *osteomalacia* (Paas 2004: 256).

health disorder in a third person (see *Chapter II.1.a*);[17] based on a notion of symbolic temperature which causes contamination and may be defined as a "mysterious disease, said to be caused by the transgression of a taboo on sexual intercourse" (Paas 2004: 264);[18] frequently depicted models relate the condition to a menstruating woman putting salt into the relish, thus endangering the lives of husband and/or children eating of it; symptoms include general weakness comparable with *kuzerezeka*, affected persons' hair becomes thin and springy while the whole body – especially feet and belly – swell up; other symptoms include loss of appetite, stunted growth, coughing, chest pains, oedema and diarrhoea while patients vomit blood in the final stage; common first assumption in case of delayed development in infants, frequently associated with terminal outcome; different forms of traditional treatment are reported, but only experienced *asing'anga* are seen fit to cure; transmission can be prevented by means of prophylactic medicine given to children (Morris 1996: 132; Probst 1995: 11; Chilivumbo 1976: 77; Drake 1976: 205)[19]

mfayi [sn] – mental disorder category; see *khunyu*

mfiti (pl. *afiti*) [ch] – practitioner of antisocial magic, a "witch" or "wizard"

mfumu (pl. *mafumu*) [ch] – chief or headman

mfumu yaikulu [ch] – (lit. "great chief") group village headman or *grupu*

mfutete [sn] – mental disorder category leaving affected children unable to sit, walk, eat, or talk; sometimes described as a child being born feet first, so that the legs stay weak and poorly developed; complex notions exist concerning treatment and prevention

mimba (pl. –) [ch] – belly or abdomen

misala [ch] – mental disorder category (see *Chapter III.2.a*)

mizimu (sg. *mzimu*) [ch] – see *mzimu*

mkulu (pl. *akulu*) [ch] – elder or notable person

mlevi (pl. *alevi*) [ch] – (from *levite* [en]) local leader of a Zionist church

mngelo (pl. *angelo*) [ch] – (from *angel* [en]) angel, benevolent spirit within Christian or Muslim context

mombole [lw] – *sing'anga* specialized in *afiti* hunting

moyo (pl. *miyoyo*) [ch] – life force, health, well-being

mphambanya [lw] – magic staff for detecting *afiti*

mphini (pl. *mipini*) [ch] – skin scarifications applied as treatment

mpostoli (pl. *apostoli*) [ch] – (from *apostle* [en]) leader of a Pentecostal church

mtengo (pl. *mitengo*) [ch] – tree, medicine made from woody plant

---

17 It is suggested that *mdulo* is originally identical with *tsempho* according to Chewa tradition, even though some sources conceive them as different conditions in other areas (Morris 1996: 132-135).

18 It may be debated whether *mdulo*, as usually suggested (Morris 1998: 235; Chilivumbo 1976: 77), represents a nosological category proper, or whether it encompasses an aetiological process which is associated with typical symptom manifestations. For the scope of this study, *mdulo* will be considered as a disease category which may lead to secondary mental disorders.

19 In biomedical terms, manifestations of *mdulo* have been interpreted as either pulmonary tuberculosis or kwashiorkor (Morris 1996: 134).

mtima (pl. *mitima*) [ch] – heart
mtundu (pl. *mitundu*) [ch] – clan, abstract relationship category
mudzi (pl. *midzi*) [ch] – village
Mulungu – Supreme Being; see *Chauta*
–muna [ch] – male
munthu (pl. *anthu*) [ch] – person, human being
mutu (pl. *mitu*) [ch] – head, headache; also mental disorder category (see *Chapter III.2.d*)
mutu waukulu [ch] – (lit. "big head") condition that may lead to mental disorder; is described as 'severe or splitting headache', symptoms including reddened eyes, nocturnal screaming fits, or confusion, nosebleed, dizziness, and panic attacks; may develop into *misala* in the long run; occurrence described as hereditary – i.e. a child contracting it from the mother by breastfeeding – or as caused by evil spirits (*ziwanda*)[20]
muzu (pl. *mizu*) [ch] – root, or medicine produced thereof
mwabvi [ch] – poison ordeal formerly used to detect *afiti*
mwalimu (pl. *waalimu*) [sw] – (from *mo'ālim* [ar], *mwalimu* [sw]) Muslim scholar
mwambi (pl. *miyambi*) [ch] – proverb
mwambo (pl. *miyambo*) [ch] – normative instruction, tradition, custom
mwanamphepo [ch] – (lit. "child of the wind") prominent category in the medical anthropology of Malaŵi; symptoms described as muscle cramps in the stomach of a woman; dark spots or blisters on the skin, slowly developing into sores; stomach pain and swellings, yellow urine, or loss of appetite; leads to increased sexual desire, is transmitted by sexual intercourse; severe female cases – *mwanamphepo waukulu* or 'big child of the wind' – may be related to menstrual and reproductive problems;[21] sometimes infected woman are said to deliver twins (*mapasa*) or children suffering from *kulumala* (Morris 1996: 113-114)[22]
mzamba (pl. *azamba*) [ch] – traditional birth attendant, midwife
mzimu (pl. *mizimu*) [ch] – category of spirits, usually identical with *mzimu wa makolo*
mzimu wa makolo [ch] – category of lineage spirits
mzimu wa umulungu [ch] – spirit of divinity, a component of the person
mzimu wa umunthu [ch] – spirit of humanity, a component of the person
mzimu woipa [ch] – category of evil spirits
Mzimu Woyera [ch] – Holy Spirit in Christian context
mzungu (pl. *azungu*) [ch] – European, Westernized Malaŵian, or albino;[23] described as

---

[20] In biomedical terms, *mutu waukulu* has been interpreted as cerebral malaria.

[21] Brian Morris mentions a number of other symptoms, all of which show the common denominator of being related to the stomach. Swellings and sores are the most typical manifestations (Morris 1996: 112-113).

[22] In biomedical terms, Steven Paas interprets *mwanamphepo* as influenza while Karl Peltzer describes it as a merely psychosocial complaint (Paas 2004: 308; Peltzer 1987: 88).

[23] The term *mzungu* for a light-skinned foreigner is also used in Kiswahili and other East-African Bantu languages. Steven Paas offers the literal translation of *mzungu* as a "wonder maker" (Paas 2004: 312).

synonymous with *napwere* (see below), but mostly used for 'Whites'; mythic evidence suggests a connection between its creation and divine punishment (Braathen 2005: 48-49)[24]

namkungwi [ch] – female initiation specialist

namlondola [ch] – magic staff applied to detect *afiti*

nantongwe [ch] – therapeutic ritual

Napolo – territorial spirit around Zomba Plateau

napwere [ch] – category applied for persons with light skin pigmentation, is considered derogatory; birth of *napwere* children connected to social stigmatization of the family;[25] affected persons are said to show poor performance in school and work, implying mental limitations; causation is described as hereditary (Braathen 2005: 49)[26]

ndiche [ya] – category refering to persons with a physical challenge – more especially of the lower extremities; applied for persons using tricycles

ndondoli [ch] – mental disorder category denoting a condition described as identical with *kuzerezeka* (see *Chapter III.2.b*)

ngaliba [ya] – male initiation specialist among the Yao

Ngoni (pl. *Angoni*) – ethnic group in Malaŵi

ngozi (pl. –) [ch] – accident

njirinjiri [ch] – mental disorder category; see *khunyu*

nkhawa [ch] – condition translated as 'anxiety' or 'worry' (Paas 2004: 329); not considered mental disorder in itself, prevalence is reportedly low; may be caused by thinking too much – especially about personal problems; may constitute preliminary phase of *misala* in prolonged cases

Nkhonde – ethnic group in the Northern Region

nkhoswe (pl. *ankhoswe*) [ch] – guardian of a matrilineage

nsembe [ch] – ritual sacrifice to the ancestor spirits

Nsenga – ethnic group in the Southern Region

nsenye [ch] – stillborn child

nsima [ch] – thick porridge prepared from maize meal (*ufa*)

nsupa (pl. –) [ch] – gourd, calabash or medical horn

ntchofu [ch] – condition associated with stomach-aches; pregnant women being affected

---

24 In their record of a Cheŵa myth on the origin of albinism, Matthew Schoffeleers and Adrian Roscoe mention "albinos, who are called »Azungu«, that is whitemen" (Schoffeleers & Roscoe 1985: 109-111), thereby identifying albinism with being non-African or European. In this myth, the affected persons are depicted as being punished by the Supreme Being as a result of their parents' violation of cultural values (*miyambo*). In biomedical terms, the word *mzungu* is generally interpreted as a person with hypomelanosis (albinism) (Paas 2003: 18).

25 It may be narrated hence that "a certain woman gave birth to *napwere* twice, and she killed both babies and pretended that she had given birth to dead children. She did not want to live with a *napwere* child. [...] She was afraid to be laughed at."

26 In biomedical terms, a *napwere* is generally interpreted as a person with hypomelanosis (albinism) (Paas 2003: 18).

may lead to a newborn child with mental disorders[27]

nthenda (pl. *matenda*) [ch] – see *matenda*

nyamakazi [ch] – condition primarily affecting the limbs or joints; intense pain reportedly results from blockages keeping the blood from supplying some body parts; may lead to mental disorder[28]

Nyanja (pl. *Anyanja*) – ethnic group in the Southern Region

nyau [ch] – male secret mask society; see *gule wamkulu*

nyaulikobiri [ch] – category referring to a person with light complexion[29]

nyentchera, ku- [ch] – mental disorder category translated as "being retarded, or having a stunned growth" (Paas 2004: 343); used by some organizations for persons with disabilities as mental retardation; symptoms described as general weakness

nyundo [ch] – (lit. "hammer") see *hamala*

nzeru [ch] – intelligence or wisdom

pendala, ku– [tu] – mental disorder category; see *kulumala*

pendula, ku- [tu] – mental disorder category; see *kulumala*

penga (misala), ku- [ch] – mental disorder category; see *misala*

pepera, ku- [ch] – mental disorder category; see *kuzerezeka*

pepetulidwa, ku- [ch] – mental disorder category described as mild confusion, careless or foolhardy behaviour; presentations include persons considering themselves invulnerable to attacks – especially by *ufiti* – or failing to respond to dangerous situations; condition may be caused by *ufiti*

phuma [ch] – condition expressing themselves in coughing and breathing difficulties; pregnant women being affected are considered to be extremely dangerous for the life of the child[30]

polyo [ch] – condition associated with deformed limbs; described as possible side-effect of *kuzungulira mutu*[31]

punduka, ku- [ch] – mental disorder category; see *kulumala*

pusa, ku- [ch] – condition of reduced cognitive competence, translated as 'to be foolish, be a fool'; also applies for slow learners or persons with slow reaction; though sometimes mentioned in context of mental disorder and even equalized with *kuzerezeka* or *misala*, its defining condition of 'just being stupid' is described as a normal disposition (Paas 2003: 187; Botne & Kulemeka 1995: 39; Zambezi Mission [eds.] 1986)

puwala, ku- [ch] – mental disorder category; see *kulumala*

sadaka [ya] – (from *ṣadaḳa* [ar], "gift, almsgiving") post-mortuary ritual among the Yao

Sena – ethnic group in the Southern Region

---

27 In biomedical terms, *ntchofu* has been interpreted as colic, or enlargement of the scrotum (Paas 2004: 336). In other cases, it is equated with cerebral malaria.

28 In biomedical terms, this concept is interpreted as rheumatism (Paas 2004: 341).

29 In biomedical terms, this concept is interpreted as hypomelanosis (albinism) (Paas 2003: 18).

30 In biomedical terms, this concept is usually interpreted as asthma (Paas 2004: 376).

31 Due to its name and obvious derivation from the English *polio*, this concept is usually identified with the biomedical category poliomyelitis.

shayṭān [ar] – devil in a Muslim context
shehe (pl. *ashehe*) [ya] – (from shaykh [ar]) Muslim religious leader
Shona – ethnic group in Eastern and Central Zimbabwe
sing'anga (pl. *asing'anga*) [ch] – traditional healer
sokonekera mutu, ku- [ch] – mental disorder category; see *kuzungulira mutu*
supuka, ku- [ch] – extremely dangerous condition in newborn children described as them being born without skin; traced back to an infectious sickness in the parents, more especially the expectant mother
Tambala – Malaŵian currency subunit (100 Tambala = 1 Kwacha)
thovu [ch] – foam
thupi (pl. *matupi*) [ch] – body
tibi [ch] – (from eng. "TB") condition associated with severe coughing, loss of body weight, and chest pain; may have fatal outcome, also identified as potential reason for *misala*[32]
Tonga – ethnic group in the Northern Region
tsamba (pl. *masamba*) [ch] – plant leaf, or medicine produced thereof
tsempho [ch] – complex notion of health disorders caused by social misconduct; "disease believed to occur to the ones who eat the relish that was salted by a woman who has just given birth" (Paas 2004: 440); usually considered identical with *mdulo* (see above) (Morris 1996: 132-135)[33]
tsilika, ku- [ch] – to protect by magic means
tsoka (pl. –) [ch] – misfortune, bad luck
Tumbuka – ethnic group in the Northern Region
tumidwa, ku- [lm] – condition in children conceived in marital intercourse during sexually prohibited periods; depicted as identical with *kunyentchera* and potential reason for *kuzerezeka*
ubongo (pl. –) [ch] – brain
ufa [ch] – maize flour
ufiti [ch] – anti-social magic, "witchcraft"
ufumu [ch] – chieftainship
ula (pl. *maula*) [ch] – see *maula*
umunthu [ch] – personhood
using'anga [ch] – traditional healing
uzamba [ch] – midwifery, gynaecology
vimbuza [tu] – category sometimes listed as a form of mental disorder; in this study, it is regarded as a specific form of therapy (see *Chapter IV.2*)
yaluka, ku- [tu] – category of mental disorder translated as 'to be mad, insane' (Paas 204: 499); appears as depiction of certain forms of *misala* implying a mechanism of magic backlash; addressed in the context of aetiology (see *Chapter IV.1*)
Yao (pl. *Ayao*) – ethnic group in the Southern Region

---

32 Due to its name, this condition is usually identified as tuberculosis in biomedical terms.

33 In biomedical terms, this concept has been interpreted as malnutrition (kwashiorkor) or tuberculosis (Paas 2004: 440).

zerezeka, ku- [ch] – mental disorder category (see *Chapter III.2.b*)
zungulira mutu, ku- [ch] – mental disorder category (see *Chapter III.2.c*)

2. Abbreviations

A number of abbreviations are mentioned or used in the course of this study. For the sake of easy reference, the following list summarizes all the short forms applied in the text.

CA .... Consensus Analysis
CHAM .... Christian Health Association of Malaŵi
DAAD .... Deutscher Akademischer Austauschdienst (a.k.a. German Academic Exchange Service)
DOR .... Disabled Persons' Organization Representative
FEDOMA .... Federation of Disability Organizations in Malaŵi
ICF .... International Classification of Functioning, Disability and Health (WHO 2001b)
ICIDH .... International Classification of Impairments, Disabilities and Handicaps (WHO 1980)
MACOHA .... Malaŵi Council for the Handicapped
MAP .... Malaŵi against Physical Disabilities (formerly known as Malaŵi against Polio)
MwK .... Malaŵian Kwacha, the Malaŵian currency (MwK); exchange rate: 190 MwK ≈ 1 EUR (March 2009)
NSO .... National Statistical Office of the Republic of Malaŵi
PODCAM .... Parents' Organization of Disabled Children Malaŵi
PWD .... Person with Disabilities
ROR .... Religious Organization Representative
SAFOD .... Southern Africa Federation of the Disabled
ST/A .... Senior Traditional Authority
SubT/A .... Sub-Traditional Authority
T/A .... Traditional Authority
TBA .... Traditional Birth Attendant
TH .... Traditional Healer
WHO .... World Health Organization
WMP .... Western-Trained Medical Professional
WWU .... Westfälische Wilhelms-University of Münster

3. Bibliography

3(a) Scholarly Articles and Monographs

Ackerknecht, Erwin H.
1971 *Medicine and Ethnology: Selected Essays*. Bern: Huber.

Ager, Alastair & Wendy Ager
1989 *An Investigation of the Needs of Mentally Retarded Individuals within Malawi: Implications for the Provision of Community-Based Rehabilitation*. (Unpublished Manuscript) Zomba.

Alpers, Edward A.
2000 Towards a History of the Expansion of Islam in East Africa: The Matrilineal Peoples of the Southern Interior. In: David S. Bone (ed.), *Malawi's Muslims*, pp. 27-63. Blantyre: CLAIM.
1975 *Ivory and Slaves: Changing Patterns of International Trade in East Central Africa to the Later Nineteenth Century*. London: Heinemann.
1972 The Yao in Malawi: The Importance of Local Research. In: Bridglal Pachai (ed.), *The Early History of Malawi*, pp. 168-178. London: Longman.

Amanze, James N.
2002 *African Traditional Religion in Malawi: The Case of the Bimbi Cult*. Zomba: Kachere Series.

Anderson, Allan H.
2002 The Newer Pentecostal and Charismatic Churches: The Shape of Future Christianity in Africa? In: *Pneuma* 24 (2): 167-184.

Barnes, Colin, Geof Mercer & Tom Shakespeare
1999 *Exploring Disability: A Sociological Introduction*. Cambridge: Polity Press.

Barnes, Colin & Geof Mercer (eds.)
1996 *Exploring the Divide: Illness and Disability*. Leeds: Disability Press.

Barnes, Colin, Mike Oliver & Len Barton (eds.)
2002 *Disability Studies Today*. Cambridge: Polity Press.

Barton, Len (ed.)
1996 *Disability and Society: Emerging Issues and Insights*. London: Longman.

Bastian, Adolf
1881 *Der Völkergedanke im Aufbau einer Wissenschaft vom Menschen und seine Begründung auf ethnologische Sammlungen*. Berlin: Dümmler.

Basu, Helene
2002 Afro-indische Besessenheitskulte im interkulturellen Vergleich (*Sidi-goma* in Indien; *zâr* in Ostafrika; *candomblé* in Brasilien). In: *Zeitschrift für Ethnologie* 127 (1): 41-55.

Benedict, Ruth
1934 Anthropology and the Abnormal. In: *The Journal of General Psychiatry* 10: 59-80.

Birch de Aguilar, Laurel
1996 *Inscribing the Mask: Interpretation of Nyau Mask and Ritual Performance among the Chewa of Central Malawi.* Fribourg: University Press.

Boddy, Janice
1994 Spirit Posession Revisited: Beyond Instrumentality. In: *Annual Reviews in Anthropology* 21: 407-434.

Bone, David S.
2000a An Outline History of Islam in Malawi. In: David S. Bone (ed.), *Malawi's Muslims*, pp. 13-26. Blantyre: CLAIM.
2000b The Development of Islam in Malawi and the Response of the Christian Churches c. 1860-1986. In: David S. Bone (ed.), *Malawi's Muslims*, pp. 113-152. Blantyre: CLAIM.
2000c Islam in Malawi: an Annotated Bibliography. In: David S. Bone (ed.), *Malawi's Muslims*, pp. 196-216. Blantyre: CLAIM.
1987 The Muslim Minority in Malaŵi and Western Education. In: *Religion in Malawi* 1: 28-32.
1982 Islam in Malawi. In: *Journal of Religion in Africa* XIII, 2: 126-138.

Bone, David S. (ed.)
2000 *Malawi's Muslims: A Historical Perspective.* Blantyre: CLAIM.

Bonongwe, Francis J.M.
2005 Initiation Rites for Boys in Lomwe Society: A Dying Cultural Practice? In: Joseph C. Chakanza (ed.), *Research in African Traditional Religion*, pp. 5-22. Zomba: Kachere Series.

Booth, Joseph
1998 [1897] *Africa for the African.* Zomba: Kachere Series.

Bosworth, Clifford E.
2000 Ṭilsam. In: Peri J. Bearman et al. (eds.), *The Encyclopedia of Islam. New Edition: Volume X*, pp. 500-502. Leiden: Brill.

Bourdieu, Pierre
1977 [1972] *An Outline of the Theory of Practice.* London: Cambridge University Press.

Braathen, Stine H.
2005 *Albinism in Malawi: A Qualitative Study on Attitudes and Beliefs.* (Unpublished Master Thesis) Oslo.

Braathen, Stine H. & Benedicte Ingstad
2006 Albinism in Malawi: Knowledge and Beliefs from an African Setting. In: *Disability & Society* 21 (6): 599-611.

Breugel, Johann W.M. van
2001 *Chewa Traditional Religion.* Blantyre: CLAIM.

Brietzke, Paul
1974 Murder and Manslaughter in Malawi's Traditional Courts. In: *Journal of African Law* 13 (1): 37-56.
Bruwer, Johannes P.
1955 Unkhoswe: The System of Guardianship in Cewa Matrilineal Society. In: *African Studies (Johannesburg)* 14: 113-122.
Burck, Deliane J.
1989 *Kuoma Rupandi (The Parts Are Dry): Ideas and Practices Concerning Disability and Rehabilitation in a Shona Ward.* Leiden: Africa Studiecentrum.
Carr, John E. & Peter P. Vitaliano
1985 The Theoretical Implications of Converging Research on Depression and the Culture-Bound Syndromes. In: Arthur Kleinman & Byron J. Good (eds.), *Culture and Depression*, pp. 244-266. Berkeley: University of California Press.
Chakanza, Joseph C.
2000a *Wisdom of the People: 2000 Chinyanja Proverbs.* Blantyre: CLAIM.
2000b Traditional Healers in Malawi. In: *The Lamp* 21: 20-22.
1998 Health and Healing: New Developments in Spirit Mediumship in Malawi. In: Klaus Fiedler, Paul Gundani & Hilary Mijoga (eds.), *Theology Cooked in an African Pot*, pp. 101-105. Limbe: Assemblies of God Press.
1987 Some Chewa Concepts of God. In: *Religion in Malawi* 1: 4-8.
1985 Provisional Annotated Chronological List of Witch-Finding Movements in Malawi, 1850-1980. In: *Journal of Religion in Africa* XV: 227-243.
1979 *A General Survey of Independent Churches in Malawi.* Aberdeen: University of Aberdeen Press.
Chakanza, Joseph C. (ed.)
2005 *Research in African Traditional Religion: Initiation Rites for Boys in Lomwe Society and other Essays.* Zomba: Kachere Series.
2004 *African Ancestors' Religion: Chipembedzo cha Makolo Achikuda.* Zomba: Kachere Series.
Chakanza, Joseph C. & Kenneth R. Ross (eds.)
1998 *Religion in Malawi: An Annotated Bibliography.* Blantyre: CLAIM.
Chavunduka, Gordon L.
1978 *Traditional Healers and the Shona Patient.* Gwelo: Mambo Press.
Chigona, Gerard
2002 *uMunthu Theology: Path of Integral Human Liberation Rooted in Jesus of Nazareth.* Balaka: Montford Media.
Chilivumbo, Alifeyo B.
1976 Social Basis of Illness: A Search for Therapeutic Meaning. In: Francis X. Grollig & Harold B. Haley (eds.), *Medical Anthropology*, pp. 67-79. Den Haag: Mouton Publishers.

1972 Vimbuza or Mashawe: A Mystic Therapy. In: *Journal of the African Music Society* 5 (2): 6-9.

Chimombo, Steve
2003a Folkstories and Disabilities. In: *WASI* 15 (1): 9-11.
2003b Proverbs of Disability. In: *WASI* 15 (1): 17-19.
1988 *Malawian Oral Literature: The Aesthetics of Indigenous Art.* Zomba: Centre for Social Research.

Connors, Jeanne L. & Anne M. Donnellan
1993 Citizenship and Culture: The Role of Disabled People in Navajo Society. In: *Disability, Handicap and Society* 8 (3): 265-280.

Crawford, James R.
1967 *Witchcraft and Sorcery in Rhodesia.* London: Oxford University Press.

D'Andrade, Roy
1995 *The Development of Cognitive Anthropology.* New York: Cambridge University Press.

Daneel, Marthinus L.
1998 John Maranke. In: Gerald H. Anderson (ed.), *Biographical Dictionary of Christian Missions*, pp. 431. Grand Rapids: Eerdmans Publishing.

Davis, Lennard J.
1997 Constructing Normalcy: The Bell Curve, the Novel, and the invention of the Disabled Body in the Nineteenth Century. In: Lennard J. Davis (ed.), *The Disability Studies Reader*, pp. 9-28. London: Routledge.

Davis, Lennard J. (ed.)
1997 *The Disability Studies Reader.* London: Routledge.

DeGabriele, Joseph
1999 When Pills Don't Work: African Illnesses, Misfortune and Mdulo. In: *Religion in Malawi* 9: 9-23.

Devlieger, Patrick J.
2000 The Logic of Killing Disabled Children: Infanticide, Songye Cosmology, and the Colonizer. In: Jane Hubert (ed.), *Madness, Disability and Social Exclusion*, pp. 159-67. London: Routledge.
1999 Developing Local Concepts of Disability: Cultural Theory and Research Prospects. In: Brigitte Holzer, Arthur Vreede & Gabriele Weigt (eds.), *Disability in Different Cultures*, pp. 297-302. Bielefeld: Transcript.
1998 (In)Competence in America in Comparative Perspective. In: Richard Jenkins (ed.), *Questions of Competence*, pp. 54-74. Cambridge: Cambridge University Press.
1995 Why Disabled? The Cultural Understanding of Physical Disability in an African Society. In: Benedicte Ingstad & Susan R. Whyte (eds.), *Disability and Culture*, pp. 94-106. Berkeley: University of California Press.

Dietrich, Albert
2004 al-Būnī. In: Peri J. Bearman et al. (eds.), *The Encyclopedia of Islam. New Edition: Volume XII*, pp. 156-157. Leiden: Brill.

Dijk, Rijk van, Ria Reis & Marja Spierenburg (eds.)
2000 *The Quest of Fruition through Ngoma: The Political Aspects of Healing in Southern Africa.* Oxford: James Currey.

Dorpmüller, Sabine
2005 *Religiöse Magie im "Buch der probaten Mittel".* München: Harrassowitz.

Douglas, Mary
1985 [1979] Taboo. In: Arthur C. Lehmann & James E. Myers (eds.), *Magic, Witchcraft and Religion,* pp. 64-68. Mountain View: Mayfield Publishing.
1970 [1966] *Purity and Danger: An Analysis of Concepts of Pollution and Taboo.* Harmondsworth: Penguin.

Drake, Anne M.
1976 *Illness, Ritual, and Social Relations among the Chewa of Central Africa.* Durham: Duke University.

Dreezens-Fuhrke, Joyce
1996 *Behinderung als Zeichen: Soziokultureller Umgang mit Behinderung in einer javanischen Gesellschaft zwischen Tradition und Gegenwart.* Münster: Lit.

Edgerton, Robert B.
1993 *The Cloak of Competence: Revised and Updated.* Berkeley: University of California Press.
1977 A Traditional African Psychiatrist. In: David Landy (ed.), *Culture, Disease, and Healing*, pp. 438-445. New York: Macmillan.
1970 Mental Retardation in Non-Western Societies: Toward a Cross-Cultural Perspective on Incompetence. In: H. Carl Haywood (ed.), *Social-Cultural Aspects of Mental Retardation*, pp. 523-559. New York: Appleton-Century Crofts.
1967 *The Cloak of Competence: Stigma in the Lives of the Mentally Retarded.* Berkeley: University of California Press.

Eide, Arne H.
2004 Discussion. In: Mitch E. Loeb & Arne H. Eide (eds.), *Living Conditions among People with Activity Limitations in Malawi*, pp. 147-155. Trondheim: Sintef.

Eide, Arne H. & Mitch E. Loeb
2004a Concepts. In: Mitch E. Loeb & Arne H. Eide (eds.), *Living Conditions among People with Activity Limitations in Malawi*, pp. 37-45. Trondheim: Sintef.
2004b Living Conditions among People with Activity Limitations in Low Income Countries. In: Mitch E. Loeb & Arne H. Eide (eds.), *Living Conditions among People with Activity Limitations in Malawi*, pp. 46-

63. Trondheim: Sintef.

Elmslie, Walter A.
1970 [1901] *Among the Wild Ngoni: Being Some Chapters in the History of the Livingstonia Mission in British Central Africa.* London: Cass & Co.

Englund, Harri
1996 Between God and Kamuzu: the Transition to Multiparty Politics in Central Malawi. In: Richard Webner & Terence O. Ranger (eds.), *Postcolonial Identities in Africa*, pp. 107-135. London: ZED.

Evans-Pritchard, Edward E.
1976 [1937] *Witchcraft, Oracles and Magic among the Azande.* Oxford: Oxford University Press.

Fiedermutz-Laun, Annemarie
1970 *Der kulturhistorische Gedanke bei Adolf Bastian: Systematisierung und Darstellung der Theorie und Methode mit dem Versuch einer Bewertung des kulturhistorischen Gehaltes auf dieser Grundlage.* Wiesbaden: Franz Steiner Verlag.

Fiedermutz-Laun, Annemarie, Franz Pera, Elmar T. Peuker & Florian Diederich (eds.)
2002 *Zur Akzeptanz von Magie, Religion und Wissenschaft: Ein medizinethnologisches Symposium der Institute für Ethnologie und Anatomie, Westfälische Wilhelms-Universität Münster.* Münster: Lit.

Fiedler, Klaus
1999 Charismatic and Pentecostal Movements in Malawi in Cultural Perspective. In: *Religion in Malawi* 9: 27-38.

Fiedler, Rachel N.
2005 *Coming of Age: A Christianized Initiation among the Women in Southern Malawi.* Zomba: Kachere Series.

Foucault, Michel
1989 [1961] *Madness and Civilization: A History of Insanity in the Age of Reason.* London: Routledge.

Frazer, James G.
1922 [1914] *The Golden Bough: A Study in Magic and Religion.* London: Macmillan.

Gamitto, António C.P.
1960 *King Kazembe and the Marave, Cheva, Bisa, Bemba, Lunda, and Other Peoples of Southern Africa: Being the Diary of the Portuguese Expedition to that Potentate in the Years 1831 and 1832.* Lisbon: Estudos de Ciências Políticas e Sociais.

Gennep, Arnold van
1960 [1909] *The Rites of Passage.* London: Routledge & Kegan Paul.

Goffman, Erving
1967 *Stigma: Über Techniken der Bewältigung beschädigter Identität.* Frankfurt a.M.: Suhrkamp.

Government of Malaŵi
2006 *National Policy on Equalisation of Opportunities for Persons with*

Disabilities. Zomba: Government Printer.
1995 *Constitution of the Republic of Malaŵi*. Zomba: Government Printer.
1971 *Handicapped Persons Act*. Zomba: Government Printer.
1968 *Laws of Malawi*. Zomba: Government Printer.

Great Britain
1983 *Mental Health Act 1983*. London: Her Majesty's Stationery Office.

Greenberg, Joseph H.
1963 *The Languages of Africa*. Bloomington: Indiana University.

Gregory, Chris A. & Jon C. Altman
1989 *Observing the Economy*. London: Routledge.

Greifeld, Katarina
1995 Einführung in die Medizinethnologie. In: Beatrix Pfleiderer, Katarina Greifeld & Wolfgang Bichmann (eds.), *Ritual und Heilung*, pp. 12-31. Berlin: Reimer Verlag.

Gwaltney, John L.
1970 *The Thrice Shy: Cultural Accommodation to Blindness and Other Disasters in a Mexican Community*. New York: Columbia University Press.

Hahn, Robert A.
1995 *Sickness and Healing: Anthropological Perspective*. New Haven: Yale University Press.

Hanks, Jane R. & Lucien M. Hanks Jr.
1948 The Physically Handicapped in Certain Non-Occidental Societies. In: *Journal of Social Issues* 4 (4), 11-20.

Hargreaves, Bruce J.
1986 Plant Induced 'Spirit Possession' in Malawi. In: *Society of Malawi Journal* 39 (1): 26-35.

Heintze, Beatrix
1970 *Besessenheitsphänomene im Mittleren Bantu-Gebiet*. Wiesbaden: Steiner Verlag.

Heintze, Beatrix (ed.)
1973 *The History of the Chewa (Mbiri ya aChewa) by Samuel Josia Ntara*. Wiesbaden: Steiner Verlag.

Hinderling, Paul
1981 Ist der »Medizinmann« ein Divinator, Exorzist, Heilkundiger, Hexer, Kräuterarzt, Kultführer, Orakelsteller, Schamane, Seher, Wahrsager, Zauberer? In: *Curare* 4: 115-127.

Hofmeyr, Agnes L.
2000 [1910] Islam in Nyasaland. In: David S. Bone (ed.), *Malawi's Muslims*, pp. 165-172. Blantyre: CLAIM.

Holzer, Brigitte, Arthur Vreede & Gabriele Weigt (eds.)
1999 *Disability in Different Cultures: Reflections on Local Concepts*. Bielefeld: Transcript.

Hubert, Jane (ed.)
2000 *Madness, Disability, and Social Exclusion: The Archaeology and Anthropology of "Difference"*. London: Routledge.

ILO (International Labour Organisation)
1983 *Vocational Rehabilitation and Employment (Disabled Persons) Convention No. 159*. Internet Publication, URL: http://www.ilo.org/ilolex/cgi-lex/convde.pl?C159

Ingstad, Benedicte
1995 Mpho ya Modimo – A Gift from God: Perspectives and "Attitudes" toward Disabled Persons. In: Benedicte Ingstad & Susan R. Whyte (eds.), *Disability and Culture*, pp. 246-263. Berkeley: University of California Press.

Ingstad, Benedicte & Susan R. Whyte (eds.)
2007 *Disability in Local and Global Worlds*. Berkeley: University of California Press.
1995 *Disability and Culture*. Berkeley: University of California Press.

Izzi Dien, Mawil Y.
1997 Sukūt. In: Clifford E. Bosworth et al. (eds.), *The Encyclopedia of Islam. New Edition: Volume IX*, p. 806. Leiden: Brill.

Janzen, John M.
1992 *Ngoma: Discourses of Healing in Central and Southern Africa*. Berkeley: University of California Press.
1978 *The Quest for Therapy – Medical Pluralism in Lower Zaire*. Berkeley: University of California Press.

Jenkins, Richard
1998a Culture, Classification and (In)Competence. In: Richard Jenkins (ed.), *Questions of Competence*, pp. 1-24. Cambridge: Cambridge University Press.
1998b Towards a Social Model of (In)Competence. In: Richard Jenkins (ed.), *Questions of Competence*, pp. 222-229. Cambridge: Cambridge University Press.

Jenkins, Richard (ed.)
1998 *Questions of Competence: Culture, Classification and Intellectual Disability*. Cambridge: Cambridge University Press.

Jonker, Cor
2000 The Politics of Therapeutic N'goma: The Zionist Churches in Urban Zambia. In: Rijk van Dijk, Ria Reis & Marja Spierenburg (eds.), *The Quest of Fruition Through Ngoma*, pp.117-132. Oxford: Currey.

Jules-Rosette, Bennetta
1975 *African Apostles: Ritual and Conversion in the Church of John Maranke*. Ithaca: Cornell University Press.

Kabue, Samuel
2004 Living with Disability. In: Arne Fritzson & Samuel Kabue, *Interpreting Disability*, pp. 24-48. Geneva: WCC Publications.

Kalipeni, Ezekiel
1981 Traditional African Healing of Mental Illness as Compared with Western Psychiatry (Clinical Psychology). In: *Journal of Social Science* 8: 109-125.
Kalmanash, J.
1968 *Some Considerations on the Problem of Epilepsy in Malaŵi.* (Paper presented at the XVIe Réunion Europeenne d'Information Electroencephalographique) Marseilles.
Kambalametore, Sylvia, Sally Hartley & Richard Lansdown
2000 An Exploration of the Malawian Perspective on Children's Everyday Skills: Implications for Assessment. In: *Disability and Rehabilitation* 22 (17): 802-807.
Kapapa, Paul
1980 The Role of the Traditional Healer in Malawi and Zambia. In: *Curare* 3: 205-208.
1977 Krank und gesund – eine Zuweisung durch die Gruppe? Studie an zwei Bantugruppen in Malawi. In: Ekkehard Schröder (ed.), *Faktoren des Gesundwerdens in Gruppen und Ethnien*, pp. 59-64. Wiesbaden: Steiner Verlag.
Kaspin, Deborah
1996 A Chewa Cosmology of the Body. In: *American Ethnologist* 23 (3): 561-578.
1993 Chewa Visions and Revisions of Power: Transformation of the Nyau Dance in Central Malawi. In: Jean Comaroff & John Comaroff (eds.), *Modernity and Its Malcontents*, pp. 34-57. Chicago: University of Chicago Press.
Kathuria, Ravinder & Robert Serpell
1998 Standardization of the Panga Muthu Test: A Nonverbal Cognitive Test Developed in Zambia. In: *Journal of Negro Education* 67 (3): 228-241.
Kiev, Ari
1972 *Transcultural Psychiatry.* New York: Free Press.
1964 The Study of Folk Psychiatry. In: Ari Kiev (ed.), *Magic, Faith and Healing*, pp. 3-35. New York: Free Press.
King, Michael & Elspeth King
1997 *The Story of Medicine and Disease in Malawi: The 130 Years since Livingstone.* Blantyre: Montford Press.
Kleinman, Arthur
1980 *Patients and Healers in the Context of Culture: An Exploration of the Borderland between Anthropology, Medicine, and Psychiatry.* Berkeley: University of California Press.
1977 Depression, Somatization and the 'New Cross-Cultural Psychiatry'. In: *Social Science and Medicine* 11: 3–10.

Kleinman, Arthur & Byron J. Good (eds.)
1985 *Culture and Depression: Studies in the Anthropology and Cross-Cultural Psychiatry of Affect and Disorder.* Berkeley: University of California Press.

Klotz, Jani
2003 *The Culture Concept: Anthropology, Disability Studies and Intellectual Disability.* (Paper presented to the Disability Studies and Research Institute Symposium) Sydney.

Kok, Bregje de
2004 *Christianity and African Traditional Religion: Two Realities of a Different Kind.* Zomba: Kachere Series.

Koty, John
1934 *Die Behandlung der Alten und Kranken bei den Naturvölkern.* Stuttgart: Hirschfeld.

Kubik, Gerhard
1987 *Nyau: Maskenbünde im südlichen Malawi.* Wien: Verlag der Österreichischen Akademie der Wissenschaften.

Lane, Steward S.
1995 *Among the Wild Azungu.* Blantyre: Montfort Press.

Lévi-Strauss, Claude
1963 [1958] *Structural Anthropology.* New York: Basic Books.

Lienau, Cay
1981 *Malawi: Geographie eines unterentwickelten Landes.* Darmstadt: Wissenschaftliche Buchgesellschaft.

Linden, Ian
1979 Chisumphi Theology in the Religion of Central Malawi. In: Matthew J. Schoffeleers (ed.), *Guardians of the Land: Essays on Central African Territorial Cults*, pp. 187-208. Gwelo: Mambo Press.
1975 Chewa Initiation Rites and Nyau Societies: The Use of Political Institutions in Local Politics at Mua. In: Terence O. Ranger & John Weller (eds.), *Themes in the Christian History of Central Africa.* Berkeley: University of California Press.

Lindgren, N.E. & Matthew J. Schoffeleers
1985 *Rock Art and Nyau Symbolism in Malawi.* Limbe: Department of Antiques.

Loeb, Mitch E.
2004a Results. In: Mitch E. Loeb & Arne H. Eide (eds.), *Living Conditions among People with Activity Limitations in Malawi*, pp. 77-145. Trondheim: Sintef.
2004b Conclusions. In: Mitch E. Loeb & Arne H. Eide (eds.), *Living Conditions among People with Activity Limitations in Malawi*, pp. 157-159. Trondheim: Sintef.

Loeb, Mitch E. & Arne H. Eide
2004 Summary. In: Mitch E. Loeb & Arne H. Eide (eds.), *Living Conditions*

among People with Activity Limitations in Malawi, pp. 11-21. Trondheim: Sintef.

Loeb, Mitch E. & Arne H. Eide (eds.)
2004 *Living Conditions among People with Activity Limitations in Malawi: A National Representative Study*. Trondheim: Sintef.

Longue, Molly
2003 *From Chinamwali to Chilangizo: The Christianization of Pre-Christian Chewa Initiation Rites in the Baptist Convention of Malawi.* (Unpublished Master Thesis) Pietermaritzburg.

Lory, Pierre
1997 Shādhiliyya. In: Clifford E. Bosworth et al. (eds.), *The Encyclopedia of Islam. New Edition: Volume IX*, pp. 172-175. Leiden: Brill.

Lux, Thomas
2003 Krankheit und ihre kulturellen Dimensionen. Ein ideengeschichtlicher Abriss. In: Thomas Lux (ed.), *Kulturelle Dimensionen der Medizin,* pp. 145-176. Berlin: Reimer.

Lwanda, John L.C.
2008 *Colour, Class and Culture: a Preliminary Communication into the Creation of Doctors in Malawi.* Glasgow: Dudu Nsomba Publications.
2005 *Politics, Culture and Medicine in Malawi.* Zomba: Kachere Series.
1993 *Kamuzu Banda of Malawi: a Study in Promise, Power and Paralysis – Malawi under Dr Banda (1961 to 1993).* Glasgow: Dudu Nsomba Publications.

Macdonald, Duff
1882 *Africana or the Heart of Heathen Africa.* London: Simpkin Marshall & Co.

Machleidt, Wielant & Karl Peltzer
1991 Die Chilopa-Zeremonie: Ein Opferritual für mental (geistig) Kranke Patienten in einem traditionellen Heilungszentrum in Malawi. In: *Psychiatria Danubina* 3 (1-2): 205-227.

Mahomed, Imuran S.
2000 The Development of Tariqas in Malawi: Qadriyah, Shadhiliyah and Sukuti. In: *Religion in Malawi* 10: 19-24.

Malanga, Kenson P.
1971 *Some Malawi Beliefs and Medicinal Plants.* Zomba: Soche Hill College.

Malawi Human Rights Commission
2006 *Cultural Practices and Their Impact on the Enjoyment of Human Rights, Particularly the Rights of Women and Children in Malawi.* Lilongwe: MHRC.

Malawi Law Commission
2006 *Summary of the Proceedings of the First National Conference on the Review of the Constitution.* Lilongwe: Malawi Law Commission.

Margoliouth, David S.
1978 Kādariyya. In: Clifford E. Bosworth et al. (eds.), *The Encyclopedia of Islam. New Edition: Volume IV*, pp. 380-383. Leiden: Brill.

Marwick, Maxwell G.
1975 [1950] The Bwanali-Mpulumutsi Anti-Witchcraft Movement. In: Maxwell G. Marwick (ed.), *Witchcraft and Sorcery*, pp. 178-183. Harmondsworth: Penguin.
1967 The Sociology of Sorcery in a Central African Tribe. In: John Middleton (ed.), *Magic, Witchcraft, and Curing*, pp. 101-126. Garden City: Natural History Press.
1965 *Sorcery in Its Social Setting: A Study of the North Rhodesian Chewa.* Manchester: Manchester University Press.
1952 The Social Context of Chewa Witch Beliefs. In: *Africa* 22: 120-135.

Matiki, Alfred J.
2000 Problems of Islamic Education in Malawi. In: David S. Bone (ed.), *Malawi's Muslims*, pp. 153-163. Blantyre: CLAIM.

Mitchell, J. Clyde
1956 *The Yao Village: A Study in the Social Structure of a Nyasaland Tribe.* Manchester: Manchester University Press.

Morris, Brian
2000 *Animals and Ancestors: An Ethnography.* London: Berg.
1996 *Chewa Medical Botany: A Study of Herbalism in Southern Malawi.* Hamburg: Lit.
1994 *Anthropology of the Self: The Individual in Cultural Perspective.* London: Pluto Press.
1991 *Western Conceptions of the Individual.* New York: Berg.
1989 Medicines and Herbalism in Malawi. In: *Society of Malawi Journal* 42 (1): 34-54.
1987 *Anthropological Studies of Religion: An Introductory Text.* Cambridge: Cambridge University Press.
1986 Herbalism and Divination in Southern Malawi. In: *Social Science and Medicine* 23 (4): 367-377.
1985 Chewa Conceptions of Disease: Symptoms and Aetiologies. In: *Society of Malawi Journal* 38: 14-38.

Mphande, David K.
2006 *Tonga Proverbs for Teaching and Preaching.* Zomba: Kachere Series.
2003 *Tonga Proverbs from Malawi.* Internet Publication, URL: http://www.afriprov.org/ebooks/tongaproverbs.htm
1996 The Use of Malawian Proverbs in Moral Instruction. In: *Religion in Malawi* 6: 9-14.

Msonthi, Jerome D.
1983a Traditional Medicine Research in Malawi. In: *Journal of Social Science* 10: 120-131.
1983b Traditional Birth Attendants in Malawi: Their Role in Primary Health

Care and Development. In: *Society of Malawi Journal* 36 (1): 40-44.

1983c The Herbalists Association of Malawi as a Profession. In: *Society of Malawi Journal* 37 (2): 45-53.

Mühlmann, Wilhelm E.

1938 *Methodik der Völkerkunde.* Stuttgart: Ferdinand Enke Verlag.

Mumba, McDonald

2006 An Outcry for Malawi's Domestic Violence Act. In: *Mfulu* March 2006: 5.

Munthali, Alister, Sidon Konyani & Mitch E. Loeb

2004 Context. In: Mitch E. Loeb & Arne H. Eide (eds.), *Living Conditions among People with Activity Limitations in Malawi*, pp. 27-36. Trondheim: Sintef.

Murphy, Robert F.

2001 [1987] *The Body Silent: The Different World of the Disabled.* New York: W.W. Norton.

Murphy, Robert F., Jessica Scheer, Yolanda Murphy & Robert Mack

1988 Physical Disability and Social Liminality: A Study in the Rituals of Adversity. In: *Social Science and Medicine* 26 (2): 235-242.

Muyebe, Stanislaus & Alexander Muyebe

1999 *The Religious Factor within the Body of Political Symbolism in Malawi, 1964-1999: a Bibliographical Essay.* Parkland: Universal Publishers.

Mvula, Enoch

1990 The Performance of Gule Wamkulu. In: Isidore Okpewho (ed.), *The Oral Performance in Africa*, pp. 80-97. Ibadan: Spectrum.

Mwanyambo, Montford L. & Dickson A. Nihero

1998 *Medicinal Plants and Biodiversity (Malaŵi) Project: Final Technical Report.* Zomba: National Herbarium and Botanical Gardens of Malaŵi.

Neubert, Dieter & Günther Cloerkes

2001 [1987] *Behinderung und Behinderte in verschiedenen Kulturen: Eine vergleichende Analyse ethnologischer Studien.* Heidelberg: Winter.

Nicolaisen, Ida

1995 Persons and Nonpersons: Disability and Personhood among the Punan Bah of Central Borneo. In: Benedicte Ingstad & Susan R. Whyte (eds.), *Disability and Culture*, pp. 38-55. Berkeley: University of California Press.

NSO (National Statistical Office Malaŵi)

2005a *Integrated Household Survey 2004-2005.* Zomba: NSO.

2005b *Statistical Yearbook 2005.* Zomba: NSO.

1998 *Malawi Population and Housing Census 1998, Report of Final Census Results.* Zomba: NSO.

1987 *Survey of Handicapped Persons, Malaŵi 1983.* Zomba: Government Printers.

NSO & ORC Macro
2005 *Malawi Demographic and Health Survey 2004*. Calverton: NSO & ORC Macro.
2001 *Malawi Demographic and Health Survey 2000*. Zomba & Calveton: NSO & ORC Macro.

Ntara, Samuel J.
1973 [1944] *The History of the Chewa (Mbiri ya aChewa)*. In: Beatrix Heintze (ed.), *The History of the Chewa (Mbiri ya aChewa) by Samuel Josia Ntara*, pp. xix-160. Wiesbaden: Steiner Verlag.

Nyirenda, Clement M.
2006 *Rastafarianism in Malawi – a Front for Chamba Smokers or a Faith Community: The Case of Blantyre, Zomba and Lilongwe Rastas*. Zomba: Kachere Series.

Oliver, Mike
1996 A Sociology of Disability or a Disablist Sociology? In: Len Barton (ed.), *Disability and Society*, pp. 18-42. London: Longman.

Olivier de Sardan, Jean-Pierre
1994 Possession, affliction et folie: Les ruses de la thérapeutisation. In: *L'Homme* 131 (3): 7-27.

Pachai, Bridglal
1972 Ngoni Politics and Diplomacy in Malawi: 1848-1904. In: Bridglal Pachai (ed.), *The Early History of Malawi*, pp. 179-214. London: Longman.

Panjwani, Ibrahim A.G.
2000 [1979] Muslims in Malawi. In: David S. Bone (ed.), *Malawi's Muslims*, pp. 181-195. Blantyre: CLAIM.

Peltzer, Karl
1987 *Some Contributions of Traditional Healing Practices towards Psychosocial Health Care in Malawi*. Eschborn: Fachbuchhandlung für Psychologie.
1983 *Traditional Care and Treatment of Mentally Sick In-Patients in Three Different Healing Centers in Malawi*. Zomba: Chancellor College.

Peltzer, Karl & Sophie Kasonde-Ng'andu
1989 The Role of Traditional Healers towards Children's Mental Handicap and Development Disabilities in Lusaka. In: Robert Serpell, Dabie Nabuzoka &. F.E. Afolabi Lesi (eds.), *Early Intervention, Developmental Disability and Mental Handicap in Africa*. Lusaka: University of Zambia.

Phiri, Desmond D.
2004 *History of Malawi: From Earliest Times to the Year 1915*. Blantyre: CLAIM.
2000 *History of the Tumbuka People*. Blantyre: Dzuka Publishing.
1999 *Let Us Die For Africa: An African Perspective on the Life and Death of John Chilembwe of Nyasaland*. Blantyre: Central Africana.

1982 *From Nguni to Ngoni: A History of the Ngoni Exodus from Zululand and Swaziland to Malawi, Tanzania and Zambia.* Limbe: Popular Publications.

1976 *John Chilembwe.* Lilongwe: Longman.

Platenkamp, Josephus D.M.

1998 Health as a Social Condition. In: *Folk* 40: 57-70.

Pöschl, Rupert

1987 Basis-Heilung durch den traditionellen Heilkundigen? In: Berthold Bös & Angelika Wörthmüller (eds.), *Krank heilen*, pp. 129-150. Saarbrücken: Breitenbach.

Probst, Peter

1999 Mchape '95, or, the Sudden Fame of Billy Goodson Chisupe: Healing, Social Memory and the Enigma of the Public Sphere in Post-Banda Malawi. In: *Africa* (Edinburgh) 69 (1): 108-138.

1995 *Dancing AIDS: Moral Discourses and Ritual Authority in Central Malawi.* Berlin: Das Arabische Buch.

Richards, Audrey I.

1975 [1935] A Modern Movement of Witch-Finders. In: Maxwell G. Marwick (ed.), *Witchcraft and Sorcery*, pp. 164-177. Harmondsworth: Penguin.

Rotberg, Robert I.

2005 John Chilembwe: Brief Life of an Anticolonial Rebel. In: *Harvard Magazine* 107 (4): 36-37.

Sagner, Andreas

2001 Behinderung und Kultur. In: *Zeitschrift für Ethnologie* 126: 175-207.

SAHIMS (Southern Africa Humanitarian Information Network)

2002 *Human-Development ATLAS, Chart and Map Library: Malawi District Boundaries.* Internet Publication, URL: http://www.sahims.net/gis/Sahims_Gis_Data/malawi%20districts.bmp

Sanderson, G. Meredith

1955 The Use of Tail-Switches in Magic. In: *The Nyasaland Journal* VIII (1): 30-56.

Schlosser, Katesa

1952 Körperliche Anomalien als Ursache sozialer Ausstoßung bei Naturvölkern. In: *Zeitschrift für Morphologie und Anthropologie* 44 (1/2): 220-236.

Schoffeleers, J. Matthew

1999 The AIDS Pandemic, the Prophet Billy Chisupe, and the Democratization Process in Malawi. In: *Journal of Religion in Africa* 29: 406-441.

1997 *Religion and the Dramatisation of Life: Spirit Beliefs and Rituals in Southern and Central Malawi.* Blantyre: CLAIM.

1992 *River of Blood: The Genesis of a Martyr Cult in Southern Malawi, c. A.D. 1600.* Madison: University of Wisconsin Press.

1991 Twins and Unilateral Figures in Central and Southern Africa:

Symmetry and Asymmetry in the Symbolization of the Sacred. In: *Journal of Religion in Africa* XXI (4): 345-372.

1979 The Chisumphi and Mbona Cults in Malawi: A Comparative History. In: J. Matthew Schoffeleers (ed.), *Guardians of the Land*, pp. 147-186. Gwelo: Mambo Press.

1968a *Symbolic and Social Aspects of Spirit Worship among the Mang'anja.* (Unpublished PhD Thesis) Oxford.

1968b *Social Functional Aspects of Spirit Possession in the Lower Shire Valley of Malawi.* (Paper presented at the University Social Sciences Council Conference, Dec. 30, 1968 to Jan. 3, 1969) Kampala.

1966 *M'bona the Guardian Spirit of the Mang'anja.* (Unpublished Master Thesis) Oxford.

Schoffeleers, J. Matthew & Adrian A. Roscoe

1985 *Land of Fire: Oral Literature from Malawi.* Limbe: Popular Publications.

Schoffeleers, J. Matthew (ed.)

1979 *Guardians of the Land: Essays on Central African Territorial Cults.* Gwelo: Mambo Press.

Serpell, Robert

1993 *The Significance of Schooling: Life Journeys in an African Society.* Cambridge: Cambridge University Press.

Serpell, Robert, Lilian Mariga & Karyn Harvey

1993 Mental Retardation in African Countries: Conceptualization, Services, and Research. In: *International Review of Research in Mental Retardation* 19: 1-39.

Shakespeare, Tom

1994 Cultural Representation of Disabled People: Dustbins for Disavowal? In: *Disability and Society* 9(3): 283-299.

Shepperson, George & Thomas Price

2000 [1958] *Independent African: John Chilembwe and the Origins, Settings and Significance of the Nyasaland Native Rising of 1915.* Blantyre: CLAIM.

Simons, Ronald C. & Charles C. Hughes (eds.)

1985 *The Culture-Bound Syndromes: Folk Illnesses of Psychiatric and Anthropological Interest.* Dordrecht: D. Reidel Publishing Co.

Soka, L. Daniel

1999 [1953] *Mbiri ya Alomwe.* Blantyre: Dzuka Publishing.

Soko, Boston J.

2002 *Nchimi Chikanga: The Battle against Witchcraft in Malawi.* Zomba: Kachere Series.

1991 The Vimbuza Phenomenon: Dialogue with the Spirits. In: *Religion in Malawi* 3: 28-33.

1988 The Vimbuza Possession Cult: The Onset of the Disease. In: *Religion in Malawi* 2: 11-15.

1987 An Introduction to the Vimbuza Phenomenon. In: *Religion in Malawi* 1: 9-13.

Sommerfeld, Johannes
1987 Zwischen Koexistenz und Konkurrenz: Zum ungleichen Verhältnis von Schulmedizin und traditionellen Heilsystemen in der Gesundheitsversorgung. In: Berthold Bös & Angelika Wörthmüller (eds.), *Krank heilen*, pp. 75-89. Saarbrücken: Breitenbach.

Steinforth, Arne S.
2005 *Enslaving the Spirit: On Magic and Mental Disorder in Southern Malaŵi.* Zomba: Chancellor College.
2001 *Itanani Sing'anga – Call the Doctor! Untersuchungen zum Wandel traditioneller medizinischer Konzepte in Malawi.* (Unpublished Master Thesis) Münster.

Stiker, Henri-Jacques
1997 [1982] *A History of Disability.* Ann Arbor: University of Michigan Press.

Strohbehn, Ulf
2005 *Pentecostalism in Malawi: A History of the Apostolic Faith Mission 1931-1994.* Zomba: Kachere Series.
2000 *Physical Healing and Exorcism in Malawian Pentecostal Churches.* (Unpublished Master Module) Zomba.

Szasz, Thomas S.
1976 [1970] *Die Fabrikation des Wahnsinns.* Frankfurt a.M.: Fischer.
1961 *The Myth of Mental Illness: Foundations of a Theory of Personal Conduct.* New York: Dell.

Thorold, Alan P.H.
2000 The Yao Tariqa and the Sukuti Movement. In: David S. Bone (ed.), *Malawi's Muslims*, pp. 13-26. Blantyre: CLAIM.

Tilisho, Lucas
2003 *The Abiding Influence of African Traditional Religion in Christian Living: A Survey of Balaka Parish Area.* (Unpublished Master Thesis) Zomba.

Turner, Victor W.
1989 Symbols in African Rituals. In: Arthur C. Lehmann & James E. Myers (eds.), *Magic, Witchcraft and Religion,* pp. 55-63. Mountain View: Mayfield Publishing.
1975 *Revelation and Divination in Ndembu Ritual.* Ithaca: Cornell University Press.
1968 *The Drums of Affliction: a Study of Religious Processes among the Ndembu of Zambia.* Oxford: Clarendon Press.

Üstün, T. Bedirhan, Somnath Chatterji, Jerome E. Bickenbach, Robert T. Trotter II & Shakhar Saxena
2001 Disability and Cultural Adaption: The ICIDH-2 Cross-Cultural Applicability Research Study. In: Bedirhan T. Üstün et al. (eds.), *Disability and Culture*, pp. 3-19. Seattle: Hogrefe & Huber Publishers.

UN (United Nations)
2006 *Draft Convention on the Rights of Persons with Disabilities.* Internet Publication, URL: http://www.un.org/esa/socdev/enable/rights/ahc8adart.htm
1993 *Standard Rules on the Equalization of Opportunities for Persons with Disabilities.* Internet Publication, URL: http://www.un.org/esa/socdev/enable/dissre00.htm
1983 *World Program of Action concerning Disabled Persons.* New York: United Nations.
1948 *Universal Declaration of Human Rights.* Internet Publication, URL: http://www.un.org/Overview/rights.html

UNDP (United Nations Development Programme)
2005 *Human Development Report 2005: International Cooperation at a Crossroads*. New York: UNDP.

Vail, H. Leroy & Landeg White
1989 Tribalism in the Political History of Malawi. In: H. Leroy Vail (ed.), *The Creation of Tribalism in Southern Africa*, pp. 151-192. London: Currey.

Vajda, László
1964 Traditionelle Konzeption und Realität in der Ethnologie. In: Eike Haberland, Meinhard Schuster & Helmut Straube (eds.), *Festschrift für Ad. E. Jensen*, pp. 759-790. München: Klaus Renner Verlag.

Vaughan, Megan
1983 Idioms of Madness: Zomba Lunatic Asylum in the Colonial Period. In: *Journal of Southern African Studies* 9: 218-238.
1982 *Models of Madness: Zomba Lunatic Asylum in the Colonial Period.* Zomba: Chancellor College.

Welling, Menno
2000 Integrating Narratives of the Past: Challenges of Interdisciplinary Research and the Case of the Maravi States of East-Central Africa, c. 1500-1859 AD. In: *Religion in Malawi* 10: 29-35.

Wendroff, Arnold P.
1985 *'Trouble-Shooters and Trouble-Makers': Witch-Finding and Traditional Malawian Medicine.* New York: City University Press.

Werner, Alice
1968 [1933] *Myths and Legends of the Bantu*. London: Frank Cass.
1964 African Mythology. In: Louis H. Gray & Canon J.A. MacCulloch (eds.), *The Mythology of All Races in Thirteen Volumes. Volume VII.* New York: Cooper Square Publishers.

White Fathers
2007 *Large Detailed gif Map of Malawi.* Internet Publication, URL: http://www.thewhitefathers.org.uk/362mlmap.gif

WHO
2006a *World Health Statistics*. Geneva: WHO.

2006b *World Health Report 2006: Working Together For Health.* Geneva: WHO.

2001a *International Classification of Functioning, Disability and Health (ICIDH-2): Final Draft.* Geneva: WHO.

2001b *International Classification of Functioning, Disability and Health (ICF).* Geneva: WHO.

2001c *World Health Report 2001: Mental Health – New Understanding, New Hope.* Geneva: WHO.

1980 *International Classification of Impairment, Disabilities, and Handicaps (ICIDH).* Geneva: WHO.

Whyte, Susan R.

1998a *Questioning Misfortune: The Pragmatics of Morality in Eastern Uganda.* Cambridge: Cambridge University Press.

1998b Slow Cookers and Madmen: Competence of Heart and Head in Rural Uganda. In: Richard Jenkins (ed.), *Questions of Competence*, pp. 153-175. Cambridge: Cambridge University Press.

1995a Constructing Epilepsy: Images and Contexts in East Africa. In: Benedicte Ingstad & Susan R. Whyte (eds.), *Disability and Culture*, pp. 226-245. Berkeley: University of California Press.

1995b Disability between Discourse and Experience. In: Benedicte Ingstad & Susan R. Whyte (eds.), *Disability and Culture*, pp. 267-291. Berkeley: University of California Press.

1991 Family Experiences with Mental Health Problems in Tanzania. In: *The National Mental Health Programme in the United Republic of Tanzania. Acta Psychiatrica Scandinavica* 364 (83): 77-111.

1990 Problems in Cross-Cultural Research on Disability. In: Frank J. Bruun & Benedicte Ingstad (eds.), *Disability in a Cross-Cultural Perspective*, pp. 197-208. Oslo: University of Oslo Press.

1986 The Cultural Construction of Epilepsy in East Africa. In: Raben Rosenberg, Fini Schulsinger & Erik Strömgren (eds.), *Psychiatry and Its Related Disciplines*, pp. 161-168. Copenhagen: World Psychiatric Association.

1981 Men, Women and Misfortune in Bunyole. In: *Man* 16 (3): 350.

Whyte, Susan R. & Benedicte Ingstad

1995 Disability and Culture: An Overview. In: Benedicte Ingstad & Susan R. Whyte (eds.), *Disability and Culture*, pp. 3-32. Berkeley: University of California Press.

Whyte, Susan R., Sjaak van der Geest & Anita Hardon

2003 *Social Lives of Medicines.* Cambridge: Cambridge University Press.

Willett, Jeffrey & Mary J. Deegan

2001 Liminality and Disability: Rites of Passage and Community in Hypermodern Society. In: *Disability Studies Quarterly* 21 (3): 137-152.

Williams, Chyvette T., Chrissie P. Kaponda & Judith A. Levy
2002 *Smoking Chamba: Marijuana as an Emerging Risk Factor for HIV/AIDS in Malawi.* (Paper presented at the 14th International AIDS Conference, International AIDS Society) Barcelona.
Williamson, Jessie
1955 *Useful Plants of Nyasaland.* Zomba: Government Printer.
Willis, Roy G.
1968 The Kamcape Movement. In: Maxwell Marwick (ed.), *Witchcraft and Sorcery*, pp. 184-198. Harmondsworth: Penguin.
Witte, Marleen de
2005 The Spectacular and the Spirits: Charismatic and Neo-Traditionalists on Ghanaian Television. In: *Material Religion* 1 (3): 314-335.
Wolf, Angelika
2004 Aids and the Discourse on Morality in Malawi. In: *Religion in Malawi* 11: 44-48.
2003 Aids und Kanyera in Malawi: lokale Rezeption eines globalen Phänomens. In: Angelika Wolf & Viola Hörbst (eds.), *Medizin und Globalisierung*, pp. 203-229. Münster: Lit.
2000 *AIDS in Malawi: Lokale Diskurse eines globalen Phänomens.* (Unpublished Master Thesis) Berlin.
1996 Essensmetaphern im Kontext von AIDS und Hexerei in Malawi. In: Angelika Wolf & Michael Stürzer (eds.), *Die gesellschaftliche Konstruktion von Befindlichkeit*, pp. 23-36. Berlin: Verlag für Wissenschaft und Bildung.
Yap, Pow M.
1969 The Culture-Bound Reactive Syndromes. In: William Caudill & Tsung-Yi Lin (eds.), *Mental Health Research in Asia and the Pacific*, pp. 33-53. Honolulu: East-West Center Press.
1965 Koro: A Culture-Bound Depersonalization Syndrome. In: *British Journal of Psychiatry* 3: 45-50.
Young, T. Cullen
1950 Kinship among the Chewa of Rhodesia and Nyasaland. In: *African Studies* 9: 29-31.

3(b) Works of Reference

Anderson, Gerald H. (ed.)
1998 *Biographical Dictionary of Christian Missions.* Grand Rapids: Eerdmans Publishing.
Bearman, Peri J., Thierry Bianquis, Clifford E. Bosworth, Emeri J. van Donzel & Wolfhart P. Heinrichs (eds.)
2004 *The Encyclopedia of Islam. New Edition: Volume XII.* Leiden: Brill.
2000 *The Encyclopedia of Islam. New Edition: Volume X.* Leiden: Brill.

Bentley, Mayrene & Andrew Kulemeka
2001 *Chichewa.* München: Lincom.
Bosworth, Clifford E., Emeri J. van Donzel & Charles Pellat (eds.)
1978 *The Encyclopedia of Islam. New Edition: Volume IV.* Leiden: Brill.
Bosworth, Clifford E., Emeri J. van Donzel, Wolfhart P. Heinrichs & Gérard Lecomte (eds.)
1997 *The Encyclopedia of Islam. New Edition: Volume IX.* Leiden: Brill.
Botne, Robert & Andrew T. Kulemeka
1995 *A Learner's Chichewa and English Dictionary.* Köln: Köppe.
Cogliano, Dan
2004 *The King James Version of the Holy Bible.* Internet Publication, URL: www.davince.com/bible
Crosby, Cynthia A.
1980 *Historical Dictionary of Malawi.* Metuchen/London: Scarecrow Press.
Guerin, J.
1985 *A Concise English – Chicheŵa Dictionary.* Blantyre: Privately Printed.
Johnson, Frederick
2003 [1939] *A Standard Swahili – English Dictionary.* Nairobi: Oxford University Press.
Mangoche, Mbeer V.B.
1995 *Chichewa Guide for Tourists.* Blantyre: Dzuka Publishing.
Massana, Joseph M.
2005 [2000] *Chichewa – English Dictionary.* Lilongwe: Likuni Press.
Moxley, Jeri
2001 *Chewa.Mtenje2001.* Internet Publication, URL: http://bantu.berkeley.du/CBOLDFTP/CBOLD_Data/Chewa.Mtenje2001
Paas, Steven
2005 *English – Chicheŵa/Chinyanja Dictionary.* (Third Edition, Revised and Enlarged) Zomba: Kachere Series.
2004 *Chichewa/Chinyanja – English Dictionary.* Zomba: Kachere Series.
2003 *English – Chicheŵa/Chinyanja Dictionary.* Zomba: Kachere Series.
Pickthall, Marmaduke W.
1930 *The Meaning of the Glorious Koran: An Explanatory Translation.* London: Alfred A. Knopf.
Pschyrembel, Willibald (ed.)
1994 *Klinisches Wörterbuch.* Berlin: de Gruyter.
Salaun, Noel
1987 [1969] *Chicheŵa Intensive Course.* Lilongwe: Likuni Press.
Sanderson, G. Meredith
1954 *A Dictionary of the Yao Language.* Zomba: Government Printer.
Scott, David C.
1892 *A Cyclopædic Dictionary of the Mang'anja Language Spoken in*

British Central Africa. Edinburgh: Church of Scotland.
Scott, David C. & Alexander Hetherwick
1951 [1929] *Dictionary of the Nyanja Language: Being the Encyclopædic Dictionary of the Mang'anja Language.* London: Lutterworth Press.
Thomson, Thomas D.
1955 *A Practical Approach to Chinyanja.* Zomba: Government Printer.
Turner, Wiliam Y.
1996 [1952] *Tumbuka/Tonga – English and English – Tumbuka/Tonga Dictionary.* Blantyre: Central Africana.
Zambezi Mission (ed.)
1986 *Student's English – Chichewa Dictionary.* Blantyre: CLAIM.

3(c) Newspaper Articles

Bottoman, Lucas
2005 Lilongwe Man Yoked for Three Years. In: *The Nation Online* December 15 (2005). Internet Publication, URL: http://www.nationmalawi.com
Jimu, Jacob
2005 Healing Ministries: Why Do Pentecostals Dominate? In: *The Weekend Nation* February 19-20 (2005): 5.
Kasunda, Anthony
2005 Defilement of Mentally Retarded Girl Shocks Govt. In: *The Daily Times* March 1 (2005): 3.
Ligomeka, Brian
2003 Health Malawi – Quest for Cheap AIDS Treatment Fuels Fake Drugs Boom. In: *Inter Press Service* July 23 (2003). Internet Publication, URL: http://www.aegis.com/news/ips/2003/IP030724.html
Lusinje, Ellen
2004 Aids Drug Test Causes Stir. In: *The Nation Online* August 12 (2004). Internet Publication, URL: http://www.salan.org/news_views/news_detail.asp?art_Id=715.
Machado, Francis
2005 Chambe Sales Plummet. In: *The Daily Times* February 7 (2005): 2.
2004 'Use Gentler Language When Talking Disability'. In: *The Daily Times* December 2 (2004): 4.
Mponda, Felix
2004 In Malawi, Aids 'Cures' Multiply Amid Growing Despair. In: *Agence France Presse* November 29 (2004). Internet Publication, URL: http://www.aegis.com/NEWS/AFP/2004/AF0411D1.html
Muwamba, Emmanuel
2006 Disabled People Regarded as Cure for Aids – Minister. In: *The Nation Online* August 5 (2006). Internet Publication, URL:

http://www.nationmalawi.com

Ntonya, George
2005 Killing Bucks on TB Drugs: Peddlers' Days are numbered. In: *The Nation* March 15 (2005): 13.

Somanje, Caroline
2005 Kumbuyo Earned K1m in Three Days. In: *Malawi News* April 9-15 (2005): 2.

4. Interview Indices

Interview Index in Alphabetical Order

The names of informants used within the context of this study have been changed in the majority of cases. This was done in order to honor the wish for anonymity on part of the informants. Those persons thus listed under synonyms are indicated by asterisk (*). Those names that remained unchanged represent those informants that were approached in their function as an official representative of a relevant organization.[34]

Achawe*, Peter: Forestry Worker (Yao – m). Interview conducted in Chawe (Zomba D.), 27/03/05 (CA14)

Adaba*, Bernette: Subsistence Farmer (Mang'anja – f). Interview conducted in Makwapolo (Zomba D.), 27/07/04 (PWD13)

Almnes, Thorild: Program Adviser at the Ministry Responsible for People with Disabilities (Mzungu – f). Interview conducted in Blantyre City (Blantyre D.), 15/07/04 (DOR10)

Asiri*, Madokotala: Three Traditional Healers (Nyanja, Lomwe, Lomwe – all m). Interview conducted in Jali (Zomba D.), 31/03/04 (TH02-04)

Atatu*, Ashehe: Three Traditional Islamic Leaders (all Yao – all m). Interview conducted in Songani (Zomba D.), 30/11/04 (ROR07-09)

Banda, Rachel: Managing Director of an Orphan Care Organization (Tumbuka/Chewa – f). Interview conducted in Nandolo (Zomba D.), 16/02/04; in Nandolo (Zomba D.), 28/04/04; in Nandolo (Zomba D.), 30/06/04 (CA01)

Boucher, Claude A.: Catholic Missionary (Mzungu – m). Interview conducted in Mtakataka (Dedza D.), 20/07/04 (ROR01)

Chagoma*, Sapitwa: Traditional Healer (Lomwe – m). Interview conducted in Pahuwa (Zomba D.), 14/01/05 (TH22)

Chamangwana, Immaculate: Executive Director at a Psychiatric Institution (Yao – f). Interview conducted in Kalimbuka (Zomba D.), 20/02/04 (WMP01)

Changata*, Vivian: Community Nurse (Mang'anja – f). Interview conducted in Kalimbuka (Zomba D.), 14/05/04 (WMP03)

Chawa*, Joyce: Traditional Birth Attendant (Yao – f). Interview conducted in Kazembe (Zomba D.), 19/11/04 (TBA04)

Chemwali*, Dennis: Small Scale Businessman (Lomwe – m). Interview conducted in Makwinja (Zomba D.), 18/01/05; in Makwinja (Zomba D.), 11/03/05 (CA08)

Chemwali*, Patricia: Officer at a Youth Organization (Yao – f). Interview conducted in Makwinja (Zomba D.), 19/11/04; in Pahuwa (Zomba D.), 14/01/05 (CA03)

Chikosi*, Kafele: Traditional Healer (Lomwe – m). Interview conducted in Mindano (Zomba D.), 14/04/04; in Mindano (Zomba D.), 02/03/05 (TH13)

[34] As my primary sources, I have filed and organized the interviews listed here as personal archive material for further future use. The synonyms given for the interview partners do not follow a given taxonomy and may, in part, appear atypical; they reflect, however, some personal information given by the interview partner.

Chilunga*, Judith: Subsistence Farmer (Mang'anja – f). Interview conducted in Makwapolo (Zomba D.), 27/07/04 (PWD07)

Chimanga*, Gladys: Subsistence Farmer (Yao – f). Interview conducted in Makwapolo (Zomba D.), 27/07/04 (PWD06)

Chimbayo*, Chuma: Village Headman (Sena – f). Interview conducted in Ngabu (Chikwawa D.), 07/12/04 (T/A08)

Chimombo, Steve: Freelance Writer (Yao – m). Interview conducted in Oldnaisi (Zomba D.), 24/02/04 (CA09)

Chingale*, Mose: Traditional Healer (Lomwe – m). Interview conducted in Mpalume (Zomba D.), 18/11/04 (TH17)

Chirika*, Miriam: Subsistence Farmer (Mang'anja – f). Interview conducted in Makwapolo (Zomba D.), 27/07/04 (PWD12)

Chisadza*, Andrew: Pentecostal Church Pastor (Lomwe – m). Interview conducted in Kazembe (Zomba D.), 24/02/05 (ROR16)

Chitenye*, Elina: Subsistence Farmer (Sena – f). Interview conducted in Chapilira (Nsanje D.), 08/12/04 (PWD21)

Chitete*, Vincent: Traditional Healer (Yao – m). Interview conducted in Kazembe (Zomba D.), 14/07/04; in Mulunguzi (Zomba D.), 16/07/04; in Kazembe (Zomba D.), 23/07/04 (TH15)

Chitsulo*, Gordon: Traditional Healer (Lomwe – m). Interview conducted in Mayaka (Zomba D.), 06/04/04 (TH03)

Chiwaula, Mussa: Executive Director of an Organization for Persons with Disabilities (Shona – m). Interview conducted in Maselema (Blantyre D.), 26/02/04 (DOR01, PWD19)

Cholo*, Evans: Catholic Missionary (Lomwe – m). Interview conducted in Chikwawa Boma (Chikwawa D.), 09/12/04 (ROR12)

Dzaone*, Luka: Traditional Healer (Lomwe – m). Interview conducted in Thondwe (Zomba D.), 14/04/04 (TH11)

Dzinkambani*, Leonard: Group Village Headman (Mang'anja – m). Interview conducted in Marka (Nsanje D.), 07/12/04 (T/A07)

Fiedler, Klaus: Baptist Priest (Mzungu – m). Interview conducted in Nandolo (Zomba D.), 13/02/04 (ROR02)

Gada*, Austin: Traditional Healer (Yao – m). Interview conducted in Chabulika (Zomba D.), 24/02/05 (TH23)

Ganizani*, Elise: Subsistence Farmer (Mang'anja – f). Interview conducted in Makwapolo (Zomba D.), 27/07/04 (PWD05)

Genamu, Francis: Physiotherapist (Lomwe/Shona – m). Interview conducted in Kalimbuka (Zomba D.), 30/03/04 (DOR04)

Juma*, Asale: Subsistence Farmer (Ngoni – f). Interview conducted in Mtambo (Zomba D.), 23/02/05 (PWD22)

Jumbe*, Filisi: Subsistence Farmer (Nyanja – f). Interview conducted in Khanda (Zomba D.), 12/04/05 (PWD27)

Kafwafwa*, Lawrence: Village Headman (Mang'anja – m). Interview conducted in Malemia (Chikwawa D.), 09/12/04 (T/A11)

Kaliati*, Wopaka: Traditional Healer (Lomwe – m). Interview conducted in Kazembe (Zomba D.), 03/03/04 (TH01)

Kaliwo*, Joseph: Traditional Authority (Mang'anja – m). Interview conducted in Marka (Nsanje D.), 07/12/04 (T/A06)

Kamwendo*, Joseph: Traditional Healer (Yao – m). Interview conducted in Songani (Zomba D.), 05/04/04 (TH07)

Kerac, Marko: Hospital Pediatrician (Mzungu – m). Interview conducted in Chichiri (Blantyre D.), 07/04/04 (WMP02)

Khananji, Lazim: Islamic Training Center Coordinator (Yao – m). Interview conducted in Mbenderana (Chikwawa D.), 09/12/04 (ROR11)

Kholowa, Janet: Revenue Authority Officer (Chewa – f). Interview conducted in Mulunguzi (Zomba D.), 13/01/05 (CA07)

Kondwani*, Lexon: Traditional Healer and Village Headman (Sena – m). Interview conducted in Chiwarika (Chiradzulu D.), 16/04/04 (T/A02, TH14)

Kulanga, Ben: Apostolic Pastor (Nyanja/Lomwe – m). Interview conducted in Ndirande (Blantyre D.), 16/11/04 (ROR04)

Kwaporo*, Ajabu: Subsistence Farmer (Yao – f). Interview conducted in Makwapolo (Zomba D.), 27/07/04 (PWD14)

Kwayera*, Harry: Medical Assistant (Mang'anja – m). Interview conducted at Makwapolo (Zomba D.), 27/707/04 (WMP05)

Kwela*, David: Small Scale Businessman (Yao – m). Interview conducted in Chikwawa Boma (Chikwawa D.), 08/12/04; in Mtambo (Zomba D.), 23/02/05; in Nkanda (Zomba D.), 02/03/05 (CA06)

Kwela*, Matthew: Retired Police Officer (Yao – m). Interview conducted in Nkanda (Zomba D.), 02/03/05 (CA13)

Kwela*, Steven: Small Scale Businessman (Yao – m). Interview conducted in Namirongo (Zomba D.), 29/11/04 (CA04)

Kwela*, Usanene: Group Village Headman Councilor (Yao – m). Interview conducted in Folomaylesi (Zomba D.), 03/03/05 (T/A12)

Lemu*, Omali: Traditional Authority (Yao – m). Interview conducted in Kawinga (Machinga D.), 03/12/04 (T/A05)

Lijenda*, Jostina: Office Secretary (Lomwe/Ngoni – f). Interview conducted in Nandolo (Zomba D.), 01/03/05 (CA10)

Maboma*, Josephine: Traditional Birth Attendant (Lomwe – f). Interview conducted in Chapola (Zomba D.), 19/11/04 (TBA05)

Madzi*, Oliver: Nursing Officer (Lomwe – m). Interview conducted in Mtukudzu (Nsanje D.), 07/12/04 (WMP06)

Makata*, Gift: Traditional Birth Attendant (Yao – f). Interview conducted in Makumbanjira (Zomba D.), 10/01/05 (TBA07)

Masamba*, Doreen: Traditional Birth Attendant (Yao – f). Interview conducted in Mpalume (Zomba D.), 18/11/04 (TBA02)

Maseko*, Samson: Welder (Ngoni – m). Interview conducted in Mulunguzi (Zomba D.), 01/03/05 (CA12)

Matundwe*, Manueli: Traditional Healer (Sena – m). Interview conducted in Mtukudzu

(Nsanje D.), 07/12/04 (TH19)

Mbewe*, Isobel: Subsistence Farmer (Nyanja – f). Interview conducted in Khanda (Zomba D.), 12/04/05 (PWD24)

Mdindire*, Gerard: Subsistence Farmer (Mang'anja/Yao – m). Interview conducted in Nkagula (Zomba D.), 11/05/04; in Nkagula (Zomba D.), 26/07/04; in Nkagula (Zomba D.), 26/11/04; in Nkagula (Zomba D.), 06/01/05; in Nkagula (Zomba D.), 24/01/05; in Kazembe (Zomba D.), 07/02/05 (PWD01)

Mgulu*, Lizi: Spokeswoman of a Group Village Headwoman (Yao – f). Interview conducted in Ndaje (Machinga D.), 30/11/04 (T/A04)

Mkandawire*, Godfrey: School Teacher (Tumbuka/Yao – m). Interview conducted in Nkagula (Zomba D.), 12/004/05 (CA16)

Mlowa*, Fanny: Subsistence Farmer (Yao – f). Interview conducted in Makwapolo (Zomba D.), 27/07/04 (PWD03)

Mphadwe*, Isaac: Group Village Headman (Mang'anja – m). Interview conducted in Malemia (Chikwawa D.), 09/12/04 (T/A10)

Mpila*, Jenny: Subsistence Farmer (Mang'anja – f). Interview conducted in Makwapolo (Zomba D.), 27/07/04 (PWD09)

Msawa*, Mercy: Traditional Birth Attendant (Yao – f). Interview conducted in Walala (Chiradzulu D.), 17/11/04 (TBA01)

Msowoya, Steven: Executive Director of an Organization for Persons with Disabilities (Tumbuka – m). Interview conducted in Limbe (Blantyre D.), 09/03/04 (DOR02)

Munthali, Aleister: Medical Anthropologist (Yao – m). Interview conducted in Nandolo (Zomba D.), 03/05/04 (DOR08)

Muramu*, Francis: Traditional Healer (Lomwe – m). Interview conducted in Mayaka (Zomba D.), 06/04/04 (TH08)

Mverani*, George: Group Village Headman (Yao – m). Interview conducted in Namirongo (Zomba D.), 29/11/04 (T/A03)

Mwale, Miriam: Pentecostal Church Administrator (Nyanja – f). Interview conducted in Ndola (Zomba D.), 23/02/05; in Ndola (Zomba D.), 24/02/05 (ROR15)

Mwambo*, Henry: Traditional Healer (Yao – m). Interview conducted in Mayaka (Zomba D.), 06/04/04 (TH09)

Mwandama*, Thandizeni: Subsistence Farmer (Nyanja – f). Interview conducted in Khanda (Zomba D.), 12/04/05 (PWD25)

Mwimiko*, Annie: Traditional Healer (Lomwe – f). Interview conducted in Kadjawo (Chikwawa D.), 10/12/04 (TH21)

Myachikadza*, Steven: Health Surveillance Assistant (Sena – m). Interview conducted in Mtukudzu (Nsanje D.), 07/12/04 (WMP07)

Naliwa*, Abu: Executive Director of a Muslim Youth Organization (Yao – m). Interview conducted in Kalimbuka (Zomba D.), 01/12/04 (ROR10)

Namanja, Miriam: Chairperson of an Organization for Persons with Disabilities (Yao – f). Interview conducted in Chichiri (Blantyre D.), 15/07/04 (DOR09, PWD18)

Nankwenda*, Maliya: Subsistence Farmer (Nyanja – f). Interview conducted in Khanda (Zomba D.), 12/04/05 (PWD26)

Nasawa*, Linga: Traditional Healer (Yao – m). Interview conducted in Lambulira

(Zomba D.), 05/04/04 (TH06)

Nazombe*, Richard: Traditional Healer (Lomwe – m). Interview conducted in Thondwe (Zomba D.), 14/04/04 (TH10)

Ndagula*, Mary: Subsistence Farmer (Mang'anja – f). Interview conducted in Makwapolo (Zomba D.), 27/07/04 (PWD02)

Ndala*, Amanda: Traditional Healer (Lomwe – f). Interview conducted in Mbenderana (Chikwawa D.), 08/12/04; in Mbenderana (Chikwawa D.), 09/12/04 (TH20)

Ndano*, Fatima: Subsistence Farmer (Yao – f). Interview conducted in Makwapolo (Zomba D.), 27/07/04 (PWD08)

Ndasimu*, Issa: Traditional Healer (Yao – m). Interview conducted in Nkanda (Zomba D.), 01/12/04 (TH18)

Ndirani*, Janet: Occupational Therapist (Yao – f). Interview conducted in Ndirande (Blantyre D.), 01/04/04 (DOR06)

Nganga*, James: Subsistence Farmer (Mang'anja – m). Interview conducted in Makwapolo (Zomba D.), 28/07/04 (PWD17)

Ngawinga*, Musa: Traditional Islamic Leader (Yao – m). Interview conducted in Ndaje (Machinga D.), 30/11/04 (ROR06)

Ngomwa, Peter: Executive Manager of a Training Center for Persons with Disabilities (Sena – m). Interview conducted in Magomero (Zomba D.), 11/03/04 (DOR03)

Ngota*, Samuel: Office Assistant (Tumbuka – m). Interview conducted in Nandolo (Zomba D.), 01/03/05 (CA11)

Nguludi*, Christopher: Catholic Missionary (Sena – m). Interview conducted in Chikwawa Boma (Chikwawa D.), 09/12/04 (ROR13)

Ngwira*, Kingsley: Environmental Scientist (Tumbuka – m). Interview conducted in Oldnaisi (Zomba D.), 02/04/05 (CA15)

Njole*, Fulata: Subsistence Farmer (Mang'anja – f). Interview conducted in Makwapolo (Zomba D.), 27/07/04 (PWD15)

Nkanda*, Salifu: Traditional Islamic Practitioner (Yao – m). Interview conducted in Namirongo (Zomba D.), 29/11/04 (ROR05)

Nkosi*, John: Office Accountant (Ngoni – m). Interview conducted in Nandolo (Zomba D.), 29/06/04 (CA02)

Nkulu*, Tiyende: Subsistence Farmer (Mang'anja – f). Interview conducted in Makwapolo (Zomba D.), 27/07/04 (PWD11)

Noloma*, Saladi: Traditional Healer (Yao – m). Interview conducted in Blantyre City (Blantyre D.), 29/07/04 (TH16)

Nsanjika*, Chimwala: Subsistence Farmer (Ngoni – f). Interview conducted in Mtambo (Zomba D.), 24/02/05 (PWD23)

Nsomba*, Arthur: Subsistence Farmer (Mang'anja – m). Interview conducted in Makwapolo (Zomba D.), 27/07/04 (PWD04)

Nthawi*, Esther: Subsistence Farmer (Mang'anja – f). Interview conducted in Makwapolo (Zomba D.), 27/07/04 (PWD10)

Nyemba*, Edward: Special Education Teacher (Ngoni – m). Interview conducted in Ndirande (Blantyre D.), 12/05/04 (DOR07)

Nyolo*, Afike: Subsistence Farmer (Sena – f). Interview conducted in Chapilira (Nsanje

D.), 08/12/04 (PWD20)
Petroyo*, Doris: Traditional Healer (Lomwe – f). Interview conducted in Lambulira (Zomba D.), 14/04/04 (TH12)
Phiri, MacEvans: Clinical Psychiatrist (Tonga – m). Interview conducted in Kalimbuka (Zomba D.), 14/05/04 (WMP04)
Pilimiti*, Olive: Traditional Birth Attendant (Nyanja – f). Interview conducted in Chibisa (Zomba D.), 10/01/05 (TBA06)
Plackett, Rachel: Volunteer at the Ministry Responsible for People with Disabilities (Mzungu – f). Interview conducted in Blantyre City (Blantyre D.), 01/04/04 (DOR05)
Pungwe*, Charles: Subsistence Farmer (Lomwe – m). Interview conducted in Mpumbe (Machinga D.), 03/12/04 (CA05)
Strohbehn, Ulf: Apostolic Priest (Mzungu – m). Interview conducted in Ndirande (Blantyre D.), 17/05/04; in Ndirande (Blantyre D.), 16/11/04 (ROR03)
Tambala*, Mwai: Group Village Headman (Yao – m). Interview conducted in Jali (Zomba D.), 30/03/04 (T/A01)
Tchema*, Iselda: Traditional Birth Attendant (Yao – f). Interview conducted in Thomu (Chiradzulu D.), 18/11/04 (TBA03)
Tembo*, Tsiku: Group Village Headman (Sena – m). Interview conducted in Ngabu (Chikwawa D.), 07/12/04 (T/A09)
Tumani*, Edith: Student (Mang'anja – f). Interview conducted in Makwapolo (Zomba D.), 28/07/04 (PWD16)
van Gent*, Els: Psychiatric Nursing Student (Mzungu – f). Interview conducted in Mulunguzi (Zomba D.), 16/12/04 (WMP08)
Walala*, Siyani: Traditional Healer (Sena – m). Interview conducted in Mbulumbuzi (Chiradzulu D.), 02/04/04 (TH05)
Zuzunda*, Fedson: Evangelical Pastor (Ngoni – m). Interview conducted in Chikwawa Boma (Chikwawa D.), 10/12/04 (ROR14)

Interviewee Group Key

CA .... Consensus Analysis – including all not otherwise specified informants.
DOR .... Disability Organization Representative – including all professionals working for governmental as well as non-governmental organizations with a specific focus on persons living with disabilities.
PWD......... Person with Mental Disorders – including the affected persons themselves, their closest relatives, their responsible guardians and spokespersons.
ROR .... Religious Organization Representative – including *abusa* priests, pastors, lay preachers, bishops, *ashehe* shaykhs, and traditional religious authorities.
T/A .... Traditional Authority – including *nyakwawa* village headmen, *agrupu* group village headmen, sub traditional authorities, *mafumu* traditional authorities, senior traditional authorities, as well as their respective representatives.
TBA .... Traditional Birth Attendant – including trained as well as untrained *azamba*

midwives.

TH............ Traditional Healer – including *asing'anga.*

WMP........ Western-Trained Medical Professional – including all kinds of Western-trained medical personnel such as medical doctors, psychiatrists, midwives, and nursing staff.

5. Tables

Table 1: Ethnic Composition of Malaŵi

Ethnic Group	*Percentage*
Cheŵa[35]	33%
Lomwe	17%
Ngoni	12%
Nkhonde	1%
Sena	4%
Tonga	2%
Tumbuka	10%
Yao	13%
Others	7%
Total	*99%*

(NSO & Macro 2005: 26)

Table 2: Health Care System

Institution	*Total No.*	*Government*	*CHAM*	*Total Beds*
Hospitals	82	41	41	10,250
Primary Health Care Centers	331	246	85	2,970
Dispensaries, Maternity Clinics	87	69	18	290
Mental Health Institutions	2	1	1	153

(NSO 2005b: Table 3.1)

35 Including Mang'anja and Nyanja.

Table 3: Disability Rates and Ratios

Disability Rates	*1983*	*2004*
National	2.9%	4.2%
– in Northern Region	3.3%	n/a
Mzuzu District	1.3%	2.3%
– in Central Region	3.2%	n/a
Lilongwe District	1.5%	1.4%
– in Southern Region	2.9%	n/a[36]
Blantyre District	1.2%	2.7%
Zomba District	2.1%	6.4%

(Loeb 2004a: 82; NSO 1987: ii, 12)

Table 4: Disability Character and Occurrence

Disability Cases	*1983*	*2004*
– seeing impairment	21%	23.0%
– hearing impairment	13%	15.7%
– communication impairment	n/a	3.2%
– physical disabilities	18%	43.1%
– mental illness or retardation	9%	n/a
– intellectual, emotional, or learning disorders	n/a	11.5 %
– epilepsy	19%	n/a
– old age	n/a	0.6%
– asthma	5%	n/a
– other disabilities	16%	2.7%[37]
Disability Onset	*1983*	*2004*
– congenital	15%	23%
– between 0 and 4 years of age	31%	25.6%
– between 5 and 49 years of age	45%	38.7%
– after 50 years of age	9%	12.7%

(Loeb 2004a: 108-109; Loeb & Eide 2004: 16; NSO 1987: ii, 5-6)

---

[36] For better intra-regional comparison, the numbers from other districts within the immediate research area are given as follows: Balaka (6.0), Chikwawa (3.1), Chiradzulu (4.0), Machinga (4.0), Mangochi (6.2), Mulanje (3.2), Nsanje (5.5), Phalombe (4.4), and Thyolo (2.8) (Loeb & Eide [eds.] 2004: 174-179).

[37] These other forms of disabilities indicated by the respondents are specified as "goiter, bent back, itching, immature waist, deformed face" (Loeb 2004a: 107).

Table 5: Interview Index According to Group Prevalence[38]

Interviewee Group	*No.*	*Percentage*
CA	22	16.06%
DOR	10	7.3%
PWD	32	23.36%
ROR	18	13.14%
T/A	12	8.76%
TBA	7	5.11%
TH	28	20.44%
WMP	8	5.84%
Total	*137*	*100.01%*

Table 6: Interview Index According to Religious Affiliation

Denomination	*No.*	*Percentage*
Christian (not specified)	32	27.35%
Evangelical	10	8.55%
Muslim	18	15.38%
None	2	1.71%
Not stated	19	16.24%
Pentecostal	13	11.11%
Presbyterian	10	8.55%
Roman Catholic	13	11.11%
Total	*117*	*99.99%*

Table 7: Interview Index According to Gender Prevalence

Gender	*No.*	*Percentage*
Female	46	39.32%
Male	71	60.68%
Total	*117*	*100%*

---

38 See also Appendix 4. Both the number of interviews conducted with a single informant as well as the number of participants within a given interview is taken into account. Two interviews – one with two THs and a consecutive one-on-one interview with one of them – would therefore be counted as three interviews in the TH column.

Table 8: Interview Index According to Ethnic Affiliation

Ethnic Group	*No.*	*Percentage*
Chewa	1	0.85%
Lomwe	21	17.95%
Mang'anja	19	16.24%
Mzungu[39]	7	5.98%
Ngoni	6	5.13%
Nyanja	8	6.84%
Shona	2	1.71%
Sena	9	7.69%
Tonga	1	0.85%
Tumbuka	5	4.27%
Yao	38	32.48%
Total	*117*	*99.99%*

39 The Chicheŵa term *mzungu* is generally applied to refer to all European or North American persons indiscriminately and does therefore, strictly speaking, not denote a ethnic affiliation – arguing from an emic *mzungu* perspective.

6. Index